Employment, Growth and Development

NEW DIRECTIONS IN MODERN ECONOMICS

Series Editor: Malcolm C. Sawyer, *Professor of Economics, University of Leeds, UK*

New Directions in Modern Economics presents a challenge to orthodox economic thinking. It focuses on new ideas emanating from radical traditions including post-Keynesian, Kaleckian, neo-Ricardian and Marxian. The books in the series do not adhere rigidly to any single school of thought but attempt to present a positive alternative to the conventional wisdom.

For a full list of Edward Elgar published titles, including the titles in this series, visit our website at www.e-elgar.com.

Employment, Growth and Development

A Post-Keynesian Approach

Edited by

Claude Gnos

Associate Professor, Université de Bourgogne, Dijon, France

Louis-Philippe Rochon

Associate Professor and Director, International Economic Policy Institute, Laurentian University, Sudbury, Canada and Co-editor, Review of Keynesian Economics

Domenica Tropeano

Associate Professor, Faculty of Economics, University of Macerata, Italy

NEW DIRECTIONS IN MODERN ECONOMICS

Edward Elgar
Cheltenham, UK • Northampton, MA, USA

Published by
Edward Elgar Publishing Limited
The Lypiatts
15 Lansdown Road
Cheltenham
Glos GL50 2JA
UK

Edward Elgar Publishing, Inc.
William Pratt House
9 Dewey Court
Northampton
Massachusetts 01060
USA

A catalogue record for this book
is available from the British Library

Library of Congress Control Number: 2009941136

FSC www.fsc.org
MIX
Paper from responsible sources
FSC® C018575

ISBN 978 1 84844 068 5

Typeset by Servis Filmsetting Ltd, Stockport, Cheshire
Printed and bound by MPG Books Group, UK

Contents

Contributors

Mohamed Aslam is a senior lecturer with the Department of Economics, Faculty of Economics and Administration, University of Malaya, Kuala Lumpur. He holds two PhDs. The first is from the University of Malaya and the other from the Hiroshima City University, Japan. His main areas of research are international trade policy, regional economic integration, international macroeconomics and post-Keynesian economics. He has written articles on various subjects relating to the Malaysian economy, macroeconomics and regional economic integration, and has advised the Malaysian government on a few development projects. He is on the editorial board of the *Research Journal of Asia Pacific*, *Pakistan and Journal of Southeast Asia Studies*, Malaysia.

Riccardo Bellofiore is Professor of Political Economy, 'Hyman P. Minsky' Department of Economics, University of Bergamo, Italy and Research Associate in the History and Methodology of Economics Group at the Faculty of Economics and Econometrics, University of Amsterdam, The Netherlands. He teaches monetary economics, history of economic thought, and theories of knowledge in Bergamo, and history of economic thought in the Political Economy PhD program in Pavia. His current research interests include the economics of globalization, the development and crisis of contemporary capitalism, endogenous theories of money, Marxian value and crisis theory, and economic philosophy.

Mehdi Ben Guirat is an interdisciplinary PhD candidate in Economics at the University of Missouri at Kansas City and a research associate at the International Economic Policy Institute, Laurentian University, Ontario, Canada. He is currently researching different economic relations between regional trading blocs, especially between the European Union and African countries. His dissertation topic and some of his recent publications relate to how to break economic dependence in developing countries.

Fernando J. Cardim de Carvalho is Full Professor of Economics at the Institute of Economics at the Federal University of Rio de Janeiro, Brazil. He obtained his PhD in Economics from Rutgers University (USA) in 1986. A former chairman of the National Association of Graduate Schools of Economics of Brazil, he has done consulting work for, among others, the National Development Bank of Brazil, CEPAL, G24 and NGOs such as Ibase (Brazil), Action Aid USA, and WEED World Economy, Ecology and Development (Germany). He is the author or co-author of five books, including *Mr Keynes and the Post Keynesians* (Edward Elgar, 1992), has published in journals such as the *Journal of Post Keynesian Economics*, *Cambridge Journal of Economics* and *Banca Nazionale del Lavoro Quarterly Review*, and has contributed over 40 chapters to book collections.

Taha Chaiechi completed her PhD in Economics in 2009 at the University of Newcastle, Australia, during which she developed substantial expertise in econometric techniques, specifically shock-response modelling. She joined James Cook University in 2009. With her background in applied economics, econometrics and modelling, She has considerable skill at systematically modelling dynamic relationships between economic, environmental, and/or social variables. She became a university finalist in the 'My research in 3 minutes' competition in the Early Career Researcher (ECR) category, winning Discipline and Faculty rounds. She has twice received the 'Inclusive Practice Acknowledgement Award, IPAA' from James Cook University in 2010 and 2011.

Mickaël Clévenot obtained his doctoral degree in economics in 2006. He is a member of LEG – Laboratoire d'Économie et de Gestion de l'Université de Bourgogne, Dijon, France. He is a lecturer in economics at the University of Burgundy. His principal area of research deals with the impact of financial liberalization and the financalization of the French economy. He also works on the financial liberalization of emerging markets and the financial integration of the EMU. His analytic framework is shared between French regulation theory and post-Keynesian models, more specifically the stock–flow consistent approach. This analytical framework allows him to represent the struggles between the different economic agents and their consequences on several financialized growth regimes.

Eugenia Correa is Professor in Economics, Finance and Development at the Mexico National University. She has a PhD degree from the Mexico National University and is a member of the Mexican Science Academy and of the National Research System. She received the Economics Research Award from the Mexico National University. Her research interests are in areas of macroeconomic financial policy, financial systems and feminist economics. She is author and editor of more than 25 books, and also more than 100 contributions for journals and books.

Claude Gnos is Associate Professor of Economics at the University of Burgundy and Director of the Center for Monetary and Financial Studies in Dijon, France. He is the author of *L'Euro* (Management et Société, 1998) and *Les grands auteurs en économie* (Management et Société, 2000), and co-editor of *Post Keynesian Principles of Economic Policy* (Edward Elgar, 2006, with Louis-Philippe Rochon) and *The Keynesian Multiplier* (Routledge). He has also published a number of articles on monetary economics, circuit theory and the history of economic thought, which have appeared in books and refereed journals (*Journal of Post Keynesian Economics*, *Review of Political Economy*, *International Journal of Political Economy*, *Economie Appliquée*, *Revue d'Economie Politique*, *Economies et Sociétés*).

Yann Guy is a PhD student at LADYSS (Laboratoires Dynamiques Sociales et recomposition des espaces) at the Université Paris Diderot – Paris 7. His thesis focuses on financial macroeconomics, and in particular on the study of the impact of market finance, in contrast with bank finance, on firms' investment behaviour in Western countries and especially in France. The empirical work consists in undertaking a comparison between the phenomena observed at the microeconomic level from consolidated group accounts and at the macroeconomic level from national account data.

Joseph Halevi studied at the University of Rome. He teaches in the Department of Political Economy at the University of Sydney and regularly at the Université de Nice at the CEMAFI and at the Université de Grenoble Pierre Mendes France. He has published with *Economie Appliquée*, *Banca Nazionale del Lavoro Quarterly Review*, *Monthly Review*, and has written chapters in a number of co-edited books both by himself and with other colleagues.

Dany Lang is Associate Professor (maître de conferences) at Université Paris 13. He is the coordinator of the task group 'Post-Keynesian analyses and modelling' of the Center of Economics of Paris North (National Center for Scientific Research). His research interest are on growth, unemployment, inflation, labour economics, as well as on related epistemological issues. He has published various papers in several journals, such as the *Journal of Post-Keynesian Economics*, the *Review of Political Economy* and the *International Review of Applied Economics*. He currently teaches macroeconomics, labour economics and modelling, at both undergraduate and graduate level. He lectures at Paris 13, but also at the Université de Haute Alsace in Mulhouse and the University of Paris 1 Panthéon-Sorbonne. Previously, he taught and led research at the Université d'Aix-Marseille 2 (where he received his doctorate), at Sciences Po Toulouse and at the National University of Ireland, Galway.

Noemi Levy Orlik received her PhD in Economics from the Universidad Nacional Autónoma de México (UNAM), Mexico City, in 1999. She is Professor in the Economic Department at UNAM. Her areas of research are monetary economics, with particular attention to development issues of Latin American countries, with specific emphasis on finance and financial institutions in developing countries. She is presently coordinating the research project 'Financialisation and Economic Growth', financed by DGAPA-UNAM. She belongs to the Mexican System of National Research (SNI-CONACYT). She has published two books and edited seven, coordinated journals issues and written multiple papers that have been published as book chapters and paper-journals.

Julio López took his BA in Economics at the Universidad de Chile, and his PhD at the University of Warsaw, Poland. He is currently Full Professor of Economics at the Universidad Nacional Autónoma de México, and has been Visiting Professor at the Universidad Autónoma de Barcelona and the Ecole des Hautes Etudes en Sciences Sociales. He was until recently the editor of *Investigación Económica*, the scientific journal of the Faculty of Economics of the Universidad Nacional Autónoma de México. He is the author of three books and the editor of another two. He has published in the *Journal of Post Keynesian Economics*, the *International Review of Applied Economics*, the *Review of Political Economy*, *Banca Nazionale del Lavoro Quarterly Review*, *Economie Appliquée*, the *Brazilian Journal of Political Economy*, *Trimestre Económico*, *Metroeconomica*, *Revista de Economia Contemporanea*, *International Journal of Political Economy*, and *Investigación Económica*, among others.

Wesley C. Marshall graduated from the College of William and Mary, USA with a BA in Political Science. He received his PhD in Latin American Studies at the Universidad Nacional Autónoma de México, with a dissertation entitled 'The role of state-owned commercial banks in the trajectory of the banking systems of Mexico, Argentina and Uruguay (1988–2007)'. Wesley C. Marshall has several articles and chapters of books published in various countries, and has participated in a number of national and international conferences

Etelberto Ortiz Cruz is Distinguished Professor at Universidad Autónoma Metropolitana, México. He recently published a book on structural change policies in Mexico, which advances an assessment on the policies established during the last 25 years. There he emphasizes the leading role of monetary policy and the adverse consequences for development and stability. He also has published a number of articles on inflation targeting in small open economies.

Corinne Pastoret is Associate Professor at Laurentian University, Sudbury, Canada. She holds a doctorate from the University of Dijon on the role of banks in post-Keynesian monetary theory. Her research also deals with employment guarantee policy in developing countries, with an emphasis on Argentina. She is currently studying the issue of financing economic growth in Latin American and Maghreb countries and is interested in resource-based development policies in Canada.

Louis-Philippe Rochon is Associate Professor of Economics at Laurentian University, Canada, and Director of the International Economic Policy Institute. He has authored over 90 journal and book articles, and has written or edited numerous books, including *Credit, Money and Production* (Edward Elgar, 2005), *Modern Theories of Money: The Nature and Role of Money in Capitalist Economies* (Edward Elgar, 2003, co-edited with Sergio Rossi), *Monetary and Exchange Rate Systems: A Global View of Financial Crises* (Edward Elgar, 2006, co-edited with Sergio Rossi), and *Credit, Money and Macroeconomic Policy* (Edward Elgar, 2011, with Claude Gnos). His papers have appeared, among other places, in *Review of Political Economy*, *International Journal of Political Economy*, *Metroeconomica*, *Journal of Economic Issues*, *Economie Appliquée*, and the *Journal of Post Keynesian Economics*. His research is on macroeconomic and monetary theory and policy, and post-Keynesian economics.

Mark Setterfield is Professor of Economics in the Department of Economics at Trinity College, Hartford, Connecticut and Associate Member of the Cambridge Centre for Economic and Public Policy at Cambridge University, UK. His main research interests are macrodynamics (with a particular focus on the development and application of concepts of path dependence) and post-Keynesian economics. He is the author or editor of several books on macroeconomics, and has published in journals including the *Cambridge Journal of Economics*, *Journal of Post Keynesian Economics*, *European Economic Review*, *Review of Political Economy*, *Journal of Economic Issues* and *The Manchester School*.

Engelbert Stockhammer is Professor at Kingston University, London, UK. His research areas are macroeconomics, applied econometrics, European integration, financialization and heterodox economics. Recently his research has focused on the demand effects of changes in functional income distribution, economic policy in Europe and the macroeconomic effects of financialization. He has published many articles in journals, including the *Cambridge Journal of Economics*, *Journal of Post Keynesian Economics*, *Structural Change and Economic Dynamics*, *Review of Radical Political Economics* and *Journal of Economic Issues*. He has published a book on *The Rise of Unemployment in Europe* (Edward Elgar 2004) and co-edited *A Modern Guide to Keynesian Macroconomics and Economic Policies* (Edward Elgar, 2011).

Domenica Tropeano is Associate Professor of Economics at the faculty of Economics of the University of Macerata (Italy). She has an MA from the University of Warwick and a doctorate from the European University Institute. She has studied and published in the field of history of economic thought, history of macroeconomics and is currently working on the issue of macroeconomic policies and globalization.

Vincent Vernay is a PhD student at the University of Burgundy, Dijon, France. He is a member of the Center for Monetary and Financial Studies in Dijon. He took part in several colloquiums these last years and is a member of the Association for the Development of Keynesian Studies (ADEK in French) and the French Association of Political Economy (FAPE). His main interests are in employment, macroeconomics, monetary theory and history of economic thought.

Introduction: post-Keynesian economic policy – a post-crisis view

Claude Gnos, Louis-Philippe Rochon and Domenica Tropeano

Whether the worldwide crisis is over is a question that is not easy to answer. After all, economic performances have differed considerably from one country to another, and while banks, where the crisis originated, are now doing much better, the lingering macroeconomic effects are still being felt. Nowhere is this more evident than in the USA, where there is increasing talk of a second recession, and within Europe, where some countries, such as Greece, Ireland, Portugal and Italy, are approaching a catastrophic end, exacerbated no doubt by the strict austerity measures now being contemplated by the European Parliament.

And while it has already been almost four years since the crisis began, the prospects for sustained growth seem far away, leading some now to be openly discussing the industrialized world's own 'lost decade'. Indeed, it is surely legitimate to ask: where will growth come from? On the consumption side, consumers do not seem to be in any hurry to spend; rather, they seem unable to spend. With historic levels of debt, consumers will more probably be busy reducing those debt levels than consuming. Indeed, in most countries, growth in nominal wages has been flat, resulting in decreasing wage shares. In addition, income distribution has become even more skewed, with the top 1 per cent of income earners increasing dramatically their share of total income and total wealth. In the end, consumers are being squeezed and are unlikely able to contribute much to the growth process.

Investment is stagnant in many countries, and governments generally are now adopting austerity measures in an effort to eliminate deficits and reduce debt/GDP ratios. In other words, with $(C + I + G)$ growth probably minimal, the prospects for growth will rely on exports. This means an increasing number of industrialized countries vying for markets abroad, such as developing countries like China, India and Brazil. But will this be sufficient to sustain worldwide growth?

On the financial side, banks everywhere seem to be doing better (passing the so-called stress test); even European banks and markets appear to be doing better, although they are only cautiously optimistic. And yet lending has not resumed sufficiently to sustain the growth process. In an endogenous money framework, growth arises from aggregate demand, and is sustained through new bank loans to the private sector, allowing them to hire labour, pay wages and begin production.

Moreover, while inflation remains low in many countries, in contrast unemployment remains stubbornly high. Many economists and policy advisers are urging a second round of fiscal expenditure in order to prevent a further decline in economic activity. However, one thing is certain: signs keep changing from one quarter to another. The crisis was surely no ordinary crisis; it was a crisis of capitalism. And this 'great crisis' certainly has led to some new thinking about economic policy. Governments and central banks around the world adopted a panoply of innovative and rather unorthodox policies.

STRUCTURE OF THE BOOK

In the first part of the book the chapters deal with issues related to employment policies, economic growth and development, while the second part is dedicated to development and growth issues in open-economy developing countries.

In Part I some major issues of capitalism are analysed from different perspectives. For example, the first chapter discusses economic policy choices to be made in an environment where the solution to the realization problem is damaging to the workers. Two other chapters deal with the different forms of financial capitalism in European countries, such as France and Italy. Another chapter discusses the relation between employment and neoliberal policies in the labour market. The attempts to give a meaning to some familiar concepts such as the concept of the labour market itself as the NAIRU (non-accelerating inflation rate of unemployment) are also enlightening from a heterodox perspective.

In Part II the same problems are discussed from the point of view of a small open developing economy, whose growth is constrained by several factors relating to its type of foreign exchange rate regime, its type of approach regarding movements of capital and the way in which monetary policies are realized. In these chapters, contrary to pure theoretical standard models, the real policy issues faced by some countries are presented as well as the consequences of these decisions. In this context alternative recommendations based on Keynesian ideas are made, in contrast with the Washington Consensus view.

Riccardo Bellofiore and Joseph Halevi outline in their chapter the conditions of contemporary capitalism and present suggestions as to how economic policy should work to modify these conditions. Having given an answer to the problem in respect of the realization of profits, the authors go on to give advice for a leftist economic policy. Capitalism is based on scared workers, terrorized savers and indebted consumers. Furthermore, capitalism has been able to create precarious part-time employment by boosting military spending and debt-financed consumption. Even if there is a sort of Keynesianism now, the current asset-based Keynesianism is predicated on the ability of monetary authorities to support and even to produce financial bubbles. Thus a redefinition of the composition of spending is necessary in order to change its created employment. Bellofiore and Halevi argue that monetary and fiscal policies alone will not work in the present form of capitalism. Due to this, a radical redefinition of the content and composition of governmental spending is needed. The authors argue that to modify income distribution in real terms, it is necessary to generate an active demand policy with the structure of investment. As a result, Bellofiore and Halevi warn that no such policy can be implemented without introducing the segmentation of capital markets and further controls over capital flows.

The chapter by Mehdi Ben Guirat and Corinne Pastoret deals with the economic development pattern of the Maghreb countries. They discuss data based on the composition of GDP and on the economic specialization of these countries, stating that their development is limited by their dependence on foreign imports and by the exclusive production of a few export goods. Ben Guirat and Pastoret conclude that a closer integration into the Mediterranean area might favour a different type of development.

Mickaël Clévenot and Yann Guy develop the idea that the passage from the 'Fordist regime' to a finance-dominated regime may not be easy for countries like France, which do not have the necessary institutional complementarities. The authors use to this end a set of equations describing the balance sheets of different institutional components of the French economy and build a model resembling the one put forward by Lavoie and Godley. The authors argue that the Fordist crisis, which started in the late 1960s, gave rise to significant economic, institutional and political modifications. During the crisis all institutions were affected: state interventions, competition, international regime, the monetary system and wage relations. The authors build a closed-economy model that focuses on the monetary system and wage relations; they then examine the effects of some changes, such as a rise in wages and in dividends. Their conclusion is that from an economic viewpoint, France has indeed entered into a financialization regime but institutions have not kept pace with the new economic development. This explains the low rate of accumulation of the French economy. Thus firms profit from financial dynamics as shareholders rather than as capitalists. The institutions have to adapt to the new regime as a sustained accumulation pattern must follow.

Domenica Tropeano investigates whether the current decline of the Italian economy can be traced back to financialization. In principle, financialization is not so important for an economy in which many firms are not quoted on the stock exchange and in which shareholders' interests should not matter. The author argues that financialization may have deep effects in such an environment by changing the perceived financial norm and the target return on capital. The author draws on a model by Lavoie (1995a), extending it to an open economy. She uses this model to look at the effects of an appreciation, thus replicating the appreciation of the euro in recent years and its possible effects on the Italian economy. The results of such an appreciation would be a fall in the rate of growth and accumulation, and in the realized rate of profit. This picture, however, does not fit well with some stylized facts. In Italy, the rate of growth and capital accumulation have slowed down while the rate of profit and profit share have clearly increased. The increase concerns average profit share and average profit rate, while indeed the profit rate is declining in the manufacturing sectors but rising in the services sector. At this point a different interpretation is presented, which is no longer based on the financialization hypothesis but rather on the increase in the degree of monopoly power in the Italian industrial sectors, given the increase in mark-up. This process would have been favoured by the privatization process of previously public enterprises. The author shows what might have happened by using a model by Dutt (1995) with two sectors. In this model, in the long run the accumulation of capital is still governed by aggregated utilization and profitability, but the allocation of capital among sectors and their growth depends on the profit rate differential. The profit rate differential might have shifted resources to the service sectors, which would have been favoured by the privatization process. In this case, financialization would be a consequence of the increase in monopolistic competition, which in turn could be responsible for the decline.

In their chapter, Dany Lang and Mark Setterfield show the many weaknesses that the empirical literature on NAIRU still presents. As already stated, the NAIRU includes a pre-Keynesian vision of the economy in which money is neutral and aggregate demand is irrelevant at least in the long run. Now Lang and Setterfield start looking at the methods used in empirical literature to estimate a value for the NAIRU. The first attempts in this direction start from a Phillips curve equation that should be homogeneous of grade one for lagged or expected inflation. A more recent strand of literature focuses instead on measuring the trend rate of unemployment from time series data. In the plain version this involves calculating a moving average of the unemployment data and labels it NAIRU. The second, more sophisticated, strand employs filters to extract a trend rate of unemployment from an unemployment time series generated by a statistical model. This method is used by Ball and Mankiw. Its main drawback is that they assume homogeneity of grade one to exist while not testing for it. Their results are therefore questionable. As the authors put it, 'the designation of trend unemployment as a unique and stable supply-determined equilibrium rate of unemployment consistent with stable inflation is nothing more than that – a designation'. The NAIRU then passes from a testable hypothesis to an article of faith. Research on NAIRU not relying on testable hypotheses and being just measurement without theory is defined as degenerative.

Engelbert Stockhammer's chapter aims to establish a link between the economic policies carried out in Europe and their different national employment situations. After changes to an increasingly flexible labour market, according to the neoliberal ideology an increase in employment should have been warranted. But these changes notwithstanding, Stockhammer argues that unemployment is still as high in Europe. Furthermore, he examines the effects of monetary and fiscal policy as the fall in the wage share on unemployment. Stockhammer argues that monetary policy should not be considered as truly relevant to that issue, while restrictive fiscal policy due to the implementation of the Stability and Growth pact carries a major responsibility. The decline in the wage share, which may be a consequence of deregulated labour markets and financialization, might have contributed to the fall in aggregate demand and thus in demand for labour as well.

In Chapter 7 Vincent Vernay first criticizes the neoclassical microeconomic foundation of the labour market, in particular the idea that labour is a commodity and is exchanged on the market for money. He argues that labour is a flow and exists economically only in respect of the utility form in which it is embodied. It logically follows that it cannot be exchanged on a market. Vernay asserts that the formation of wages is not a relative exchange but an absolute exchange. Wage earners receive the entire output they gave rise to in money form (the physical output being deposited in firms). Along the same lines, the payment of wage earners cannot be defined as a purchase of labour since money only exists in society as it is attached to the real objects produced. Money has no purchasing power unless associated with physical output, so it cannot be used to buy anything. The author concludes that the formation of wages is by no means the result of a market process.

In Part II Mohamed Alsam discusses the determinants of exchange rate regime/(policy) choice for developing countries. The author argues that the choice must be based on the characteristics of each individual country rather than on abstract theoretical prescriptions. As to the experience of Asian countries, he reminds us that before the financial crisis of 1997–98 those countries were recipients of capital inflows to a great extent. This has led to an appreciation of the currency and to an expansion of internal credit supply given the inability of central banks to properly sterilize the inflows. This inability in turn was due to the lack of a wide enough pool of state bonds (deficits were small) in which open-market operations could be conducted. Therefore, to avoid the bad consequences of inflows, developing countries should use some form of capital control.

Julio López and Fernando J. Cardim de Carvalho argue that a short-run macroeconomic policy with the aim of increasing growth in countries with an unemployed labour force and idle production capacity along Keynesian/Kaleckian lines is possible. The basis of such a policy should be the increase in aggregate demand, the direction of credit supply towards selected sectors and the improvement of the competitiveness of domestic products. This requires, however, a careful management of the exchange rate, which allows a moderate devaluation to increase competitiveness. The losses to real wages and to firms for the increase in the cost of servicing debt and importing intermediate products should be compensated by taxes on the sectors that enjoyed high profits before the devaluation took place. For example, the depreciation may involve a dual or multiple exchange rate system. In other cases, the depreciation might be accompanied by subsidies to domestic production, provided that firms pass on lower costs to prices, and measures are taken to ensure that subsidies are indeed passed on to consumers. Alternatively they argue that a country could lower the value added tax rate for basic consumption goods, or make money transfers to lower-income groups. Another important point is that the authorities should be able to regulate capital movements and, as a consequence, restrictions to the full capital mobility should be enforced if necessary.

The chapter by Taha Chaiechi deals with the economic development of Hong Kong from a post-Keynesian point of view. The author takes a standard post-Keynesian macroeconomic model inspired by Stockhammer's work to test some propositions/assumptions. In particular the author analyses the dynamic relationship between financial development, accumulation (of what?), income distribution and employment in a way that considers simultaneous interaction (within a systems approach). Chaiechi deconstructs the response of Hong Kong's economy to the shocks based on financial development indicators. The macroeconomic model seems to improve as the financial sector is included. The empirical results of the SVAR (structural vector auto regression) and the impulse response function suggest that there is a short-run, a long-run, and mostly positive relationship between financial development and economic growth indicators in Hong Kong.

The main thesis of the chapter by Eugenia Correa is that debt inflows/increase to developing countries are the consequence of bank-led monetary expansion while borrowers must settle the debt with surplus and wealth transfers. The author argues also that there is an inherent tendency to overindebtedness in developing countries. This is caused by a greater increase in the cost of credit for corporations, governments and other local entities than the growth of income that must be used to service this debt. Correa argues, furthermore, that monetary and financial liberalization were not a suitable means to increase resources for local investment, but rather mechanisms to achieve the export of local and foreign investors' surpluses. Moreover, Correa analyses the potential effects of the economic policies based on the Washington Consensus. The author strongly advocates the view that the Washington Consensus policies have dismantled the endogenous growth capacity of Latin American economies. Financial liberalization and the region's capital outflows have restricted growth and have undermined profits of domestic companies, depending mainly on the domestic market. The model proposes a new financial structure able to rebuild the relationship between banks, firms and the government. In order to disrupt the causal chain leading to increased inflows, increased indebtedness and increased outflows, the author thinks that it is essential that money is not managed by private conglomerates. Deposit banks must be regulated by new social institutions so that money expansion is directed towards employment and growth.

In her chapter, Noemi Levy Orlik argues that the rate of interest is a distributional variable as a result of social conflicts among the ruling sectors of the society (entrepreneurs, *rentiers* or financiers and workers). In order to reach such a conclusion the author first reviews the history of thought debate on the nature of the interest rate and thereafter the current discussion within both the new classical macroeconomics and the post-Keynesian field. As to the latter, the author concludes that there is a wide agreement that the rate of interest is determined by the central bank. Furthermore, the rate of interest does not affect investment, but the distribution of income. The author then uses the different positions in the theoretical literature to establish whether they may be applied to a developing economy such as Mexico. For Mexico the author finds that a lower monetary rate of interest does not induce higher investment spending or higher credit volumes. Also monetary interest movements do not cause over(under)indebtness. She argues further that the Mexican central bank reaction function is non-neutral and it favours financial capital (*rentiers* or financiers). The external dependence of the Mexican economy requires an overvalued exchange rate. Thus the exchange rate needs to be overvalued for external capital flows to finance current account disequilibria and finance external inputs for economic growth to take place. As a result, in the case of devaluation, the central bank raises the interest rate to compensate foreign portfolio investors for the losses incurred and thus worsens the condition of wage earners.

Wesley C. Marshall argues that financial liberalization and its related reforms have failed to generate their (publicly stated) objectives. They have succeeded instead in achieving a hidden objective, namely the expansion of American and European multinational corporations (MNCs) that has undermined the fulfilment of explicit objectives. As a matter of fact, a large part of foreign direct investments has taken the form of mergers and acquisitions, most of them directed towards publicly owned companies in Mexico, Brazil and Argentina. In these three countries the rates of gross capital formation/growth/creation have fallen instead of increasing; in contrast, profit remittances have greatly increased. In Mexico, profits earned by the banks after privatization and foreign ownership through the interest rate spread as a proportion of total performing loans have exhibited a constant increase, growing from 18.63 per cent in 2002 to 28.26 per cent in 2006. Foreign banks operating in an oligopolistic market keep interest rate spreads and commissions at higher levels than those of their home countries. The author concludes that without substantial changes in their domestic economic policies, the dominance of foreign capital in local economic structures will lead to stagnation and balance of payments disequilibrium.

Etelberto Ortiz argues that the current inflation-targeting regime in the context of a small open economy requires the central bank to act as a 'tyrannical auctioneer' that sets a vector of prices enclosing the exchange rate, the interest rate and the wage rate. The central bank is able to act as the 'tyrannical auctioneer' as it recognizes that there are disequilibria associated with its choice of price vector related to a growing disequilibrium in the balance of payments and in the financial condition between commercial banks and firms. The author considers that hindering the more important source of adjustment for economies facing long-run or structural inflationary pressures such as its productivity growth is one of the major failings of the central bank as a tyrannical auctioneer. This is caused by the impossibility of firms to introduce technological, organizational and financial innovations to respond to disequilibria. Finally, Ortiz Cruz argues that this failing destroys the virtuous circle of productivity and accumulation.

PART I

Labor, employment policies and distribution

1. Deconstructing labor: a Marxian–Kaleckian perspective on what is 'new' in contemporary capitalism and economic policies*

Riccardo Bellofiore and Joseph Halevi

1. INTRODUCTION

The neoliberal turn of the early 1980s established a powerful stagnationist tendency, but from the mid-1990s onwards, political countertendencies were activated that solved, albeit temporarily, the problem of an insufficient effective demand, at the same time weakening and fragmenting labor.[1] These political processes and mechanisms – the epicenter of which is in the USA – gave way to a new kind of interventionist economic policies.

To be sure, the active intervention of the state has never really disappeared, not even in the years of UK Prime Minister Thatcher and US President Reagan. Whoever thinks that neoliberalism is a return to *laisser faire* – the actual historical existence of the latter being, as Keynes was well aware, rather dubious – is mistaking ideology for facts. Yet we think there is something 'new' in contemporary capitalism and in its economic policies that requires a new understanding.

2. HOW THE NEW CAPITALISM REALIZED MONEY PROFITS FOR A WHILE. . .

The stagnationist tendency took hold in the 1980s and in the early 1990s. The deregulation of capital movements, the restrictive monetary policies, the attack on welfare provisions, and the aggressive competition of global players in manufacturing and service sectors have all been at the root of the low and unstable levels of investment and of the violent compression of the share of wages, and often of real wages, hence of workers' consumption. The novelty of the 1990s manifests itself in two phases. The first phase belongs to the golden years of the new economy, especially after June 1995 when the long-term decline of the US dollar was halted and reversed by the deliberate policy of the Federal Reserve – sustained by the Bundesbank – to stave off the collapse of Japan. The renewed strength of the US dollar and the Federal Reserve's monetary policy favored the Wall Street boom in stock prices that led to an expansion of consumption, and of investment, particularly in the technology sectors tightly linked to financial services. The whole process depended in an essential manner upon the private sector going into deficit, with expenditure higher than disposable income. Thus, in the second part of the Clinton presidency, when the state budget deficit was turned into a surplus, private debt replaced a shrinking public debt. Rising household indebtedness was, in turn, guaranteed *vis-à-vis* financial institutions by that very rapid expansion of financial wealth.

The collapse of the 'irrational exuberance' bubble determined the end of the most naive delusions about the new economy, but it did not produce a vertical fall of the US and – by implication – of the world economy. The crisis in the US economy was short-circuited by a quick and massive injection of liquidity and by lowering the interest rate to practically zero, as well as in the resumption of a deficit-orientated fiscal policy leading – contrary to the Clinton years – to a renewed rise in the public debt. In short, the crisis was avoided by the creation of endogenous money and by relying again on war Keynesianism.

Yet we cannot stop here and conclude that the latter is the sole form of Keynesianism compatible with, and acceptable to, contemporary capitalism. We cannot conclude that for two reasons. First because – as we have already hinted – the new economy, no matter how paradoxically, relied on an efficacious form of Keynesianism through the financial lever via the command over money exercised by the Federal Reserve. Second, low interest rates and military spending were not enough to kick-start the US economy, and that of the world.

We come now to the second phase of our narrative about the novelty and changes of the 1990s. Large injections of liquidity and military spending guaranteed a floor to the fall of economic activity. However, the factors that have enabled the upswing in the cycle of the world economy are related to two other circumstances that are far from being purely contingent. The first circumstance is the USA's relations with Asia, first and foremost with China and India (Halevi 1999; Halevi and Lucarelli 2002; Halevi and Kriesler 2006). The second is given by banks' willingness to finance consumption entailing households' rising debt. A key element in banks' behaviour has been the financing of the 'real-estate' bubble, which was on the verge of a sharp deflation in 2006, giving way to the subprime crisis of 2007.

The subprime crisis can be seen as a bubble on a real tendency based on the stagnation of real wage earnings that was bypassed by the kind of 'financial' paradoxical Keynesianism that relied on the speculative bubbles on assets as we hinted above, and to which we shall shortly return.

Technically, as reported by the excellent *Financial Times* on 17 August 2007, the crisis surfaced in February when Nova Star and New Century, respectively the largest and second-largest US lenders, declared losses due to customers defaulting on their mortgage payments. Through the risk distribution mechanism embodied in derivatives, conceived as a way to both avoid and gain from risk, lenders' losses traveled quickly through the financial blood vessels, hitting the hedge fund branch of the Swiss multinational group UBS. Given that the entire derivatives system is based on raising money by using debt collateral in a manner unrelated to incomes, the subprime problems rapidly affected credit markets, making the crisis into a credit and not just a liquidity one.

The crisis in the subprime markets was loudly announced and yet it became inevitable because prudential behavior had been eliminated by the fact that capitalists' financial rents had become the main objective of accumulation. Indebtedness, initially by business corporations and now overwhelmingly by households, lies at the root of the contemporary financial system in a way that is different from the debt creation in a context of the expansion of real incomes and the effective demand it engenders. Corporate debt was the product of the stagnation of the 1970s, and household debt is essentially the outcome of stagnant real wages. The economic trick, initially applied in the USA and later spreading to Europe, has been the systemic transformation of debt into a source of future financial gains – a fully institutionalized Ponzi situation abetted by governments and monetary authorities.

The subprime crisis can therefore be seen as the prosecution of the mechanism of new capitalism and its corresponding economic policy. When the 2000–2001 crisis was overcome in mid-2003, and the rise in interest rate after 2004 risked halting the revival of economic growth based on the housing bubble, this latter was kept alive thanks to the subprime borrowers. All this notwithstanding, the house of cards collapsed when real-estate prices started to decline – a modified version of the 'financial instability hypothesis' leading to a 'Minsky moment'.[2]

At the international level, Asia has been covering the USA's twin deficits for years. Schematically we may capture the essence of the contemporary situation as follows. Net world demand is predominantly generated by Anglo-Saxon capitalism and it is supplied through a productive cycle largely based on delocalized production processes. The key variable in the positive dynamics of demand is private indebtedness, which in the USA has grown exponentially. On the whole, net savings of the private sector, even of households, are now negative. Banks, busy as they are in sustaining consumption, provide firms indirectly – but not less efficiently – with both liquidity and market outlets for their production, so that finance to households' consumption is in fact finance to firms' production and guarantees an adequate effective demand. Asia is also the new world manufacturing engine, and it exploits a huge 'industrial reserve army' of labor, while deindustrialization and the new service economy at home – that is, in the mature countries – inescapably gives rise to generalized precariousness in job and working conditions.

If today there is some kind of Keynesianism, it is of this kind, and it is quite consistent with a growing 'casualization' of the labor force, so that the ensuing 'full employment' is intrinsically precarious and unstable. It is a 'financial' form of Keynesianism: it is an asset-based Keynesianism, a 'privatized' Keynesianism, crucially dependent on the ability of the banking system to support or even produce bubbles. It was initially, in the heyday of the new economy, centered mainly on the stock exchange bubble, later on the real-estate bubble – both pushing up, through a wealth effect, consumption through indebtedness. All this is temporarily allowing to 'close' the monetary circuit from the effective demand side. It is neither a new stable regime for the extraction of surplus value, nor is it a stagnationist regime.

Workers are sucked into the vortex of this infernal whirlpool activated by such 'financial' Keynesianism not only as workers (squeezed by restructuring at home and competitive pressure from outside), but also as savers and as consumers. They are involved in the financial markets, in different degrees depending upon the institutional set-up of the countries concerned, as investors of their own monetary savings (these are being now mobilized without any impediment and national controls following the dismantling of the national pension systems and the concomitant rise of institutional investors), and as debtors towards the banking system (because of consumption and mortgage loans to households). Such is the general economic tendency everywhere, supported and driven by the active 'new' economic policies. In a vicious circle of expanded reproduction, it produces an accelerated 'deconstruction' of labor as well as a radical redesign of the modalities regarding the extraction of value and of surplus value.

The axis of this new model – which, it must be stressed, assigns to the USA the primacy of expansive monetary and fiscal policies, that is, exactly the opposite of the European Central Bank + Maastricht parameters +

Dublin's Stability Pact model – can be then portrayed as follows: low wages, precarious jobs, budget deficits, high indebtedness, plus absorption of wage earners in the financial circuits *qua* investors[3] and debtors. The problem of effective demand, that is, the question of the monetary realization of profits is, as a consequence, temporarily solved. It would be difficult to predict how long this sort of solution can last since it contains unstable and, in the long run, unsustainable elements and forces. These are to be seen both within the dominant economies and in geopolitical factors, and, perhaps increasingly, within the global reserve army economies of China and India.[4]

3. . . . MEANWHILE IN EUROPE THE STABILITY PACT IS NOT THE MAIN PROBLEM

Europe does not belong to a different narrative (Bellofiore 2004; Halevi and Kriesler 2004). To begin with, the nature of the new American–Asian model is such that Europe plays the role of a residual actor and appears as a loser. The axis USA–Asia requires that the US dollar remain the pivot of the world financial system, even under conditions of systemic but controlled devaluation. This factor, together with the rise of the Asian manufacturing sector, hurts the Old Continent. Within it the weakest areas such as Italy are experiencing a total stall in their economic dynamics. The pain is bound to get worse with the acceleration of the dollar's devaluation. Yet were the new model – which we describe only in the most general terms – to implode, it would bring to a halt the only global economic locomotive still active, notwithstanding its limitations. Europe would simply not be in a position to replace it even if it wanted to. Nor is the idea of a decoupling of Europe from the USA very convincing, as long as the new exporting areas like China and Asia, or Eastern Europe, are closely knit to the USA themselves.

European impotence ensures that the USA will always hold significant blackmailing power. Furthermore, Europe is increasingly taking the social and financial reality of the USA as its model, albeit in contradictory and, sometimes, reluctant terms. Last, Italy, and with a vengeance compared to other European countries, precisely because of its relatively backward conditions, is implementing at a reckless speed the reorganization of financial institutions, of the labor market, of production processes, and of the governance of firms according to criteria imported from Anglo-Saxon capitalism. Indeed, Italy is the last carriage but of the same train!

It is necessary to avoid a serious misunderstanding. We should not believe that the Maastricht Treaty and the Stability and Growth Pact of Dublin and Amsterdam were just mindless or a stupid idea, to quote the former head of the European Commission and Italy's former prime minister, Romano Prodi. Instead, the Maastricht Treaty and the Stability Pact represent the alibi behind which, in Europe, proceeded industrial restructuring, the creation of a financial space, the formation of new regional articulations and the dismantling of the welfare state based on acquired rights. These processes, however, stem from much more substantial factors that are bound to persist, and they will, even in the case of the relaxation – already happening in recent years – of the Treaties' constraints on public finances. These processes not only admit but require divergent dynamics for the different areas of the EU. The divergent dynamics are rendered more dichotomous by the new entrants from Eastern Europe with their disguised unemployment and low wages, and with their skilled labor force.

Our scenario identifies five different areas within the EU and the countries gravitating towards it. A quality-based manufacturing pole is centered on the traditional Franco-German heart of Europe, which therefore includes Belgium but also Austria and, *de facto*, Switzerland's regions of heavy industry. This pole has, through Germany's activity of restructuring, a small industrialized periphery in Eastern Europe, mostly in the Czech Republic and to some extent in Slovakia. The Western European side of this pole still has a substantial system of welfare provision that is being gradually thinned out. We then have a pole based on niche productions of advanced technologies located in the Scandinavian countries, including Finland, where the essential features of the social democratic model seem to be still holding pretty well, but the generalization of such a model to the rest of Europe is out of the question. Then we have the UK, fundamentally a pole unto itself, but with strong ties to the Netherlands and Luxembourg *qua* financial and service centers, linked mostly to Anglo-Saxon capitalism. The fourth pole is centered on Italy and is characterized by an area of relocation of low-level industries, as evidenced by the outsourcing of the small Italian firms in the traditional sectors to countries that were outside the EU, like Romania, and still are, like Albania. The last area is formed by countries such as Spain and Greece. Neither possesses companies and sectors that are crucial to capital accumulation internationally. Spain's major industrial firms are either branches of, or are tied to, multinational companies. Its telecommunication companies developed rent-seeking activities in Latin America, especially in Argentina, and played a significant role in the financial crisis of that country in 2001. But Spain's growth is essentially due to construction and real estate, and is connected, like that of Greece, to an expanding external deficit that is larger, in per capita terms, than that of the USA.

Until now the EU financial system has bankrolled both countries' deficits, but such a situation cannot be assumed to last indefinitely. The new economic geography of Europe both updates and confirms the old one: some countries, like Italy, slide down the ladder, abandoning their previous positions and roles, while at the same time there are tendencies to establish also an imperialist pole centered on 'Mitteleuropa'.

Within this context one cannot bury one's head in the sand and not see that in the first few years of the new millennium, redefining, not just on paper but in practice, the Stability Pact has become the lever with which power relations are exercised and altered. The ways in which countries pretend to apply it, or decide to bypass it, highlight in full the predominantly national dimension of European policy making. The European nation states (countries) constitute the pivot of the political and institutional dimensions of the Continent's and of the EU's class articulations. The most relevant proof of the pivotal role of nation states in Europe comes from the fact that no country, even those where the wage rates are similar, advocates the unification of labor norms. In the core countries of continental Europe, and certainly as far as Germany, France and Italy are concerned, capitalism developed on a neomercantilist basis. Until 1939 such neomercantilism *vis-à-vis* each other was connected to the construction of multiple conflicting imperialist peripheries that were supposed to provide both raw materials and net financial flows to the metropolis. In the post-WWII period the process of European integration emphasized the reciprocal, hence incompatible, neomercantilist orientation of European capitalisms. Indeed, European macroeconomic accumulation was largely based on export-led growth towards Europe itself and even today the macroeconomic performance of Germany is crucially dependent upon its net exports towards the EU. Thus European treaties and agreements always implicitly express the neomercantilist balance of power ruling during the phases that led to the formulation of those very treaties.

In this context, the small countries support the Stability Pact precisely because they went through heavy sacrifices to comply with it. For this purpose they had, as in the Dutch case, to impose sacrifices that redefined the relations with trade unions and social relations within the society. In the Netherlands, for instance, the path to compliance has entailed the mutation of around 40 percent of the total employment into part-time jobs. Neither capitalists nor any standard government would, in all good faith, call this outcome into question and say 'Sorry, we were wrong; let us pay no attention to the Stability Pact for which we put 40 percent of you into precarious occupations'. Thus to fence off the possible repercussions coming from the (large) countries that do not abide by the criteria, is, for the Netherlands, a way of defending the new class articulation achieved through the imposition of those sacrifices.

For France and Germany the situation appears to be altogether different. With the launching of the new single currency these two countries were, without fudging the data, outside the parameters. These two were also the countries that most adamantly opposed, by throwing their weight around, the creation of a truly European budget. They were exercising pressure while they were successfully demanding to be allowed not to respect the rules that they imposed upon the smaller members of the EU, as well as on Italy. It is equally significant that France and Germany are crucial contributors, at the EU level, to the reformulation of the discretional rules in a way that would favor a greater severity regarding the criteria of public debt. The new discretional rules that France and Germany are supporting are constructed on the basis of an ideal culprit, Italy, so that Paris and Berlin can continue to use the Stability Pact as it suits them, while Italy will have to converge towards its parameters being treated as a repeated offender. France, for instance, has already stated that it will not abide by the Pact until 2012. Germany, after years of violating the rules, has shown a rekindled interest in enforcing the Pact, thereby clashing with France. This is due to the powerful export surplus it has obtained within the EU, which has, momentarily, restarted the growth process and, with it, the net fiscal revenues of the German Federal Republic.

It follows therefore that it is impossible to see on what basis of common interests a European form of Keynesianism in the traditional meaning can emerge, leading to a coherent reform of the Pact. There is simply no scope for this kind of action.

Europe has been in effect a unified territory for quite a long time, but not because of the impact of the overarching process of globalization. Rather, what unified the European territory was and is political intervention. It is a unified space in terms of markets that are regularly the target of neomercantilist forays by the very same national capitalisms forming that space. It suffices to look at the German current account surplus of more than $218 billion estimated for 2007 by the OECD. If we now add the Swedish, the Dutch, the Belgian and the Swiss surpluses, we obtain a sum of $187 billion, not far behind the German level. The bulk of these surpluses are realized, in a pure Marxian–Kaleckian sense, within Europe itself, that is through intra-European transactions. This fact points to a problem that, for the Continent, has by far deeper, more structural and graver implications than the supposed constraints of the Maastricht parameters. Indeed, in Europe there is absolutely no mechanism to recycle in a Keynesian manner the current account surpluses of the countries accumulating them. The recycling used to occur quite swiftly before the creation of the European Community. This was in the 1950s, thanks to the European Payments Union set up to receive the counterpart funds of the American Marshall Plan. While the balance of payments issue is unavoidable,[5] the Maastricht parameters can be manipulated and even ignored, as France and Germany (and the UK) have done during the 1990s.

We can rest assured that in the case of the external surplus, too, Germany will never accept the formation of a European-wide clearing union in the way suggested by Keynes during the negotiations at Bretton Woods. The reason is rather elementary. For Germany the surpluses are profits obtained through the external transactions by German companies or by the German affiliates of foreign multinationals. And profits must remain profits: it is not acceptable to 'socialize' them. If one follows our non-'idealistic' reading of Keynes's analytical apparatus and, in this context, sees the anti-Keynesian implications of the surpluses in the current account, it is easy to grasp the present-day impossibility of a European-wide true Keynesianism. Hence our reasoning uncovers the flimsy nature of those analyses that end up merely advocating greater margins for budget deficits and for the public debt in matters of economic policies, and stronger wage demands in matters of social policies and actions.

Our analysis leads us to reject the Stability Pact and the present mechanisms of income distribution without any delusion concerning the possibility today of opening up new spaces for Keynesian policies. We deem that both the Pact and the distributive mechanism at work nowadays are structurally tied to the capital–labor relation that has been established in the European neomercantilist context. Instead our analysis suggests that it is urgent to tackle politically from the left the neglected issue of the structural determination of the productive system – 'what' and 'how' to produce. This alternative discourse and policy project – at the European level – cannot but be grounded on the explicit integration into the conceptual and policy frameworks of class analysis. The renewed central role of class analysis in understanding policies stems from the current configuration of the capitalist system. Indeed, economic policies are framed in a way consistent with the remaking of the immediate valorization process, something that is deepened by what may be labeled as the 'real subsumption of labor to finance' – referring both to the investment in the stock exchange and to the bank debt to sustain consumption. This reality cannot be opposed and reshaped without understanding the changes in the capitalist labor process. Unfortunately most progressive economists in Europe make only a liturgical reference to class, and then proceed to suggest reforms to the existing arrangements as if all that was needed is a team of non-orthodox economic advisors (Bellofiore and Halevi 2006).

4. THE NEW MODALITIES OF THE OLD SYSTEM OF EXPLOITATION

We have already pointed out that, at least as far as the pressure on the labor force is concerned, the so-called European model increasingly appears to be a local adaptation of the Anglo-Saxon model. The long-run growth rate is low and unstable, the composition of demand depends in a growing measure on rising inequalities in the distribution of income, and finance has acquired a commanding role with direct repercussions on firms' corporate governance (Gallino 2005). What is crucial to understand in the present capitalist dynamics is that these factors allow for a 'systematic' control over labor, whatever the skill levels.

On the one hand, the new forms of command over 'flexible' and precarious labor force appear as imposed upon firms by markets' profound unpredictability and fickleness, although, as we have shown, they are also the product of political decisions regarding global macroeconomic management. The monetary and fiscal policies pursued in the eurozone of the EU are certainly playing a role in creating such a situation. Yet beneath those policies lies the harsh substance of the social relations of production. No progressive economic policies can be conceived without first addressing the nature of the social relations of production prevailing today.

On the other hand, the 'fragmentation' of labor and its 'destructuring' are generated from within the firms on the basis of the new microeconomic criteria of corporate governance. All this is deeply affecting the dynamics of valorization directly in the production process. Work is no longer performed according to productivity criteria defined *a priori* in a stable productive and technological context (production as a plan to be sequentially and rigidly implemented). Instead it is being organized around objectives and targets that will be evaluated *ex post* (production becomes a task to perform with flexibility). The penetration of the market into the mechanism of production has been going on at least since the 1980s. At first, the market 'entered' into the process of production with a reorganization of the holdings where each unit is judged on whether or not it is a profit center, and as such it must virtually exchange with the other internal profit centers. More and more the choice to be made is 'make or buy?', that is, to produce internally or to purchase on the market. The process has been accelerated with traditional outsourcing, but becomes dramatic in the late 1990s with in-house outsourcing, where workers of the same production line end up belonging to different ownerships, different contractual frameworks, and are even unionized differently. The new regime is conducive to the expansion of casualization. Living labor itself is treated as if it were a 'commodity' just like any other, to be performed and paid for 'just in time'.[6] It is here that the 'real subsumption of labor to finance' – with wage earners effectively 'incorporated' within the latter thanks to the changes in the pension system, the ensuing redirection of workers' savings towards the financial markets, and in Europe also the reform of the banking system along the lines of the Anglo-Saxon model – may be ideologically exploited by the capitalist class.[7] The wage squeeze and job uncertainties should – according to the ideologues – be counterbalanced by higher returns obtained by investing workers' savings in the stock exchanges.

We therefore have a two-pronged tendency: one sequence goes from the predominance of finance to the control over labor via the volatility of markets and the macroeconomic dynamics; the other sequence goes from the predominance of finance to the control over labor via the internal decentralization of firms. The current worldwide expansion of wage labor – which in itself shows the futility of the arguments that just a few years ago were advanced by the 'end of work' literature – translates itself into a fragmentation of the working class. The latter does not disappear but its social consciousness and strength are dramatically weakened.

In this context it is also important to criticize those who portray contemporary capitalism as increasingly based on non-material, knowledge-intensive, activities. It must be stressed that in Marx the term 'working class' is not a sociological–descriptive concept covering only industrial labor, strictly speaking. More than that: the relevance of the working class does not lie in its numerical expansion as a growingly homogeneous subject. Its importance as a class resides in the fact that the new value, and hence income, produced by productive workers is nothing but the monetary expression of their living labor. This is true even today, when often the increasing centralization of the commanding heights of capital (in both finance and production) is going on hand in hand with a decrease in the size of productive units, and also in the amount of workers employed by the same individual capital. In Marxian terminology, and opposite to what was true until a few decades ago, we are witnessing a 'centralization without concentration'. This means that capital's drive to divide and fragment the working class is much more powerful than ever in the past.[8] After some decades when it decreased as a share in total employment (the 'Fordist' era), nowadays wage labor, the labor dependent upon capital, is significantly expanding again, not only in absolute terms but also as a proportion of total employment – in the world arena as in the 'mature' capitalist countries.

Last, the manufacturing sector has intrinsically an important role in the occupational structure. Although the data may seem to tell a different story, in reality many occupations appear as belonging to the service sectors simply because they have been outsourced by the industrial firms, whereas previously they were integrated into the data on industrial employment proper. 'Manufacturing matters' also in the pure technical productive sense. Without a strong advanced industry nothing can be produced, not even services, since they require significant industrial inputs such as computers. The case of the USA proves this point. 'American' capitalism does have its industrial sector, but it is increasingly located outside the national territory and outside the direct realm of the US dollar. Thus, unless one wishes to maintain that the US balance of payments deficit does not matter, the US case confirms, by default, the national importance of having and nurturing a strong manufacturing sector.[9]

Although 'turbo-capitalism' can coexist both with military Keynesianism and industrial hollowing out, its impact is severe for the population of the country originating it, as argued by the inventor of the term, the former Reagan advisor Edward Luttwak. Similar processes are bound to occur, and indeed are occurring, in Europe as well. Hence the organization of the oppositional struggle must have as the first item on the agenda the social reunification of labor 'from below'. An exclusive focus on economic policies 'from above' is only a necessary but far from sufficient condition to advance the unification of labor. The crucial issue is the centrality of class relations and of the mode of production both within the inquiry of contemporary capitalism and the configuration of alternative economic policies. These twin elements must become the defining elements of any political and economic strategy of the left.

We can now summarize the essence of contemporary capitalism from the point of view of labor. The unstable equilibrium of today's capitalistic growth rests on scared workers (because of the transformations in the labor process and in the so-called labor market), 'terrorized' savers (because of the modifications in retirement systems and the uncertainties related to financial investments), and indebted consumers (because of the increased dependence of consumption expenditure on banks' credit).[10] This is nothing but the dialectical aspect – from the angle of wage earners – of the process centered on the formation and expansion of an industrial reserve army on the world scale, on global migration flows, and on the planetary delocalization of manufacturing industries. In each economic area this harsh global class reality is politically managed according to a different specific macroeconomic dynamics. If in the 1930s state intervention was the condition for restarting the process of expanded reproduction, under contemporary capitalism the management and the very reproduction of 'instability' and even 'crisis' become the political and economic condition for the governance of the phases of accumulation. It is therefore futile to separate growth from instability and crisis in assessing the dynamics of the system.

The Achilles heel of both the post-Keynesian and Sraffo-Keynesian approaches lies precisely in the unwarranted separation between, on the one side, the dynamics of accumulation and, on the other side, the reproduction of instability and crisis, the latter being a condition of the former in these decades – as if a renewed Keynesianism or a wage-led accumulation were possible without at the same time structural transformations pointing towards a break of capitalist social relations.

5. WHAT KIND OF ALTERNATIVE ECONOMIC POLICIES?

Any left-oriented fiscal policy claiming the necessity to expand the share of public expenditure over national income must deal with a radical redefinition of the content and composition of state spending. If our observations are correct, namely that capitalism today is, in its particular way, capable of attaining a form of precarious and part-time 'full employment' on the basis of a flimsy growth process led by military spending and/or by financial, asset-based, bubble Keynesianism, the core of an alternative policy must be that of planning employment, work organization and the economy (based on a 'bottom-up' approach that links planning to class and social struggles, and not on a top-down, bureaucratic and autistic management 'from above'). The need to open up new planning horizons stems also from the fact that decades of restrictive policies have led to bottlenecks on the supply side.

The skeleton of this kind of strategy is well known: public intervention to determine the long-run direction of investment; an active industrial policy together with a selective credit policy; a welfare system providing goods and services 'in kind' on an expanded basis. It is in relation to these objectives that industrial restructuring and conversion ought to be planned. The question of the environment can become the pivot in the formulation of the strategy since addressing the matter seriously raises a number of challenges. Far from being a hands-off affair, the environmental question can be tackled – within the limits of entropy – by means of advanced investment and cutting-edge biotechnologies, and also by restricting the private use of the public space, air, soil and water by the major corporations. This strategy is completely at variance with the institutional privatization of the environment pursued by the EU with its marketable pollution permits. The environmental issue, if addressed seriously, opens up the way to the planning of the modalities of transportation, to a redefinition of the size and role of the usage of private transport, and to the planned reform of urban settings.

In the above context we are convinced of the limited effectiveness of traditional monetary policies based on the unreliable presumption that private investment immediately responds to a reduction in interest rates. And in any case, the issue is not that of an unqualified aggregate expansion of investment but rather that of its qualitative dimensions. Of course, deficit spending contributes to profits in a pure Kaleckian fashion. But we do not believe that a positive effect on employment will automatically follow. Instead, we submit that the impact of deficit spending upon employment will not follow a mechanical pattern. It will rather depend on the independent decisions of industrial and financial capital. By the same token, we do not believe that policies to raise money incomes (through higher wages, transfers, basic income and the like) imply by themselves direct and positive repercussions on the distribution of income in real terms. Firms' real decisions are independent of the money choices of wage earners or households, and this asymmetry is not overcome with more nominal redistribution.

To actively modify income distribution in real terms and to determine not just the total level of employment but also its sectoral allocation, thereby producing a qualitative change in the composition of output, it would be necessary to tie an active demand policy to the structural composition of investment. It must be borne in mind, however, that no economic policy of this nature, including universal welfare based on expanding services in kind, will be possible without introducing, within Europe itself, a segmentation of capital markets, including controls on the nature and on the amounts of capital flows.

One of the features of the dominant economic policy perspectives is the idea that a full-employment policy requires the 'employability' of labor. People must be taught 'how to work'. The mere process of training the labor force is supposed to increase employment and real incomes. The schooling and the university system should, then, be reformed away from education towards vocational training in ways most functional to the (short-term) exigencies of the economy and of the regions. Again, unemployment is no longer seen as a problem originating from the angle of demand: namely that, given the institutional set-up, the level of demand is not sufficient to ensure full employment. Unemployment essentially derives from a supply bottleneck due to mismatching and lack of the required specifications within segments of the labor force. In short, the unemployed have only themselves to blame for their condition.

Our position is against all this. The struggle against poverty and over the distribution of income in real terms goes through the creation of jobs for the people as they are. The aim should be to generate more vacancies than available workers. For this purpose a kind of 'labor plan' is needed, implemented and managed by the state: expansionary monetary or fiscal policies are not enough; there must be direct creation of new occupations, and these can be in sectors that may be at a high labor intensity, even though they need high skills. This is what we label the 'labor plan'.

In this context the best form of 'training' is that of a universally accessible education emphasizing general knowledge and critical faculties, since it is from these two factors that the subaltern classes can become protagonists and grasp the changes continuously occurring in the world we live in. This perspective assumes active agents and is tendentially egalitarian, whereas at best current economic policies limit themselves to a redistribution of a given pool of jobs, favoring the more skilled and thereby deepening inequality. Moreover, our perspective does not endorse a generic full employment, but stresses the quality of the output and of the employment as the counterpart of the protagonism of social subjects. But all this is quite incompatible with the present trends in capitalism, so that the alternative strategy must openly confront how to deal politically with the clash between the needs of the subalterns and the exigencies of capital.

NOTES

* This paper, along with another one entitled 'A Minsky moment' (printed in 2011, see references), was presented in Dijon in 2007. It is important to note that this 'Deconstruction' paper was an English version of a paper in Italian written in 2005 (and published there in 2006), well before the onset of the Great Recession. Ours is not then a belated understanding and rationalization of the crisis. Even with hindsight, we believe we presented a rather perceptive and comprehensive picture of the ascent of the 'new capitalism' and of its contradictions (while also anticipating the now fashionable concept of 'privatized Keynesianism') in the 'Deconstruction' paper. The Minsky-moment paper on the subprime crisis was also quite timely explaining the reasons for its decline and collapse. Our reading of contemporary capitalism and the crisis was very much opposed to most Sraffian and Postkeynesian analyses, which were marred by a too poor distributive and underconsumptionist approach (witness the several polemics we had with Italian economists in books, journals, newspapers since the early 2000s). Most of our analyses later became common sense in the best analyses of the current capitalist phase. Of course, if we would have to write new papers, we would introduce some changes here and there, but the overall interpretation contained in these two papers would remain the same.

1. See Bellofiore and Vertova (2006) for a more detailed analysis.
2. On the resurgence of a 'Minsky moment', see Bellofiore and Halevi (2011). Relative to the original Minsky's argument (see Bellofiore and Ferri 2001), this time the increase of leverage affected mainly households, the driving component of demand was consumption driven by speculative bubbles, and monetary economic policy was for a while effective in boosting effective demand.
3. With the privatization of pension schemes and with the continuation of compulsory contributions, but now to private or corporatized funds, wage earners become captive investors although the decisions about actual financial placements are made by the exceptionally high-paid managers of the now private pension funds. This is not a minor

point. No government favoring the privatization of pension schemes has ever suggested making contributions optional. Hence all the rules and laws regarding compulsory contributions are in place while the flow of funds is redirected towards the privatized institutional investors.

4. A recent study by the Asian Development Bank (2006) has highlighted that the persistence of low wages and an expanding, job-wise unstable informal sector may actually bring down the growth rates of both China and India to the relatively low level of 3 percent per annum, which in per capita terms would be less than 2 percent.
5. The balance of payments deficit is a concrete phenomenon. In Kaleckian terms it states that the consolidated accounts of the capitalist units within a country do not generate net profits in their international transactions. This is true also for the USA, but US capitalism is a world capitalist economy and is not characterized by neomercantilism.
6. In this respect Italy, precisely because it is a periphery in Europe and relatively weak, has been and is an experimental laboratory of anti-labor policies, starting with the 'Pacchetto Treu' of the first Prodi government in the 1996–98 period and then with the so-called 'Legge Biagi' of the second Berlusconi government, maintained by the second Prodi government.
7. On a criticism of the so-called pension-fund capitalism, see Bellofiore (2000).
8. The unity of the working class has however never been the outcome of some spontaneous process: it was and is, always and everywhere, the product of a conscious social and political action against the 'deconstruction' furthered by capital.
9. Of course, if a country loses its industrial base, demand polices in the Keynesian sense by themselves cannot bring it back – and the same is true for Italy now.
10. Actually, 'scared' workers are exactly the 'traumatized' workers whom Greenspan talked about. A more precise definition of 'terrorized' savers would be savers affected by a 'manic-depressive' syndrome.

REFERENCES

Asian Development Bank (2006), *Labor Market in Asia: Issues and Perspectives*, Basingstoke: Palgrave Macmillan.

Bellofiore, R. (2000), 'Il capitalismo dei fondi pensione', *La rivista del manifesto*, **10**: 35–42.

Bellofiore, R. (2004), 'Contemporary capitalism, European policies, and working class conditions', *International Journal of Political Economy*, Special Issue, *The European Economic and Monetary Union in the global economy: is there a deflationary bias?* Summer: 86–104.

Bellofiore, R. and P. Ferri (2001), 'Things fall apart, the centre cannot hold. Introduction to the economic legacy of Hyman Minsky', in R. Bellofiore and P. Ferri (eds), *Financial Keynesianism and Market Instability: The Economic Legacy of Hyman Minsky, Volume I*, Elgar, Cheltenham, UK and Northampton, MA, USA: Edward Elgar, pp. 1–29. Also in R. Bellofiore and P. Ferri (eds), *Financial Fragility and Investment in the Capitalist Economy: The Economic Legacy of Hyman Minsky, Volume II*, Cheltenham, UK and Northampton, MA, USA: Edward Elgar, pp. 1–30.

Bellofiore, R. and J. Halevi (2006), 'Is European Union Keynesian-able? A sceptical view', in E. Hein, A. Heise and A. Truger (eds), *Macroeconomics and Macroeconomic Policies: Alternative Approaches to European Policies*, Marburg: Metropolis, pp. 329–45.

Bellofiore, R. and J. Halevi (2011), 'A Minsky moment? The subprime crisis and the new capitalism', in C. Gnos and L.-P. Rochon (eds), *Credit, Money and Macroeconomic Policy. A Post-Keynesian Approach*, Cheltenham, UK and Northampton, MA, USA: Edward Elgar, pp. 215–32.

Bellofiore, R. and G. Vertova (2006), 'Lost in space? The geographical and political dimension of uneven capitalism development', in G. Vertova (ed.), *Changing Economic Geography of Globalization*, London: Routledge, pp. 23–44.

Gallino, L. (2005), *L'impresa irresponsabile*, Torino: Einaudi.

Halevi, J. (1999), 'The accumulation process in East Asia as compared to the role of Germany in European post-war growth', in R. Bellofiore (ed.), *Global Money, Capital Restructuring and the Changing Patterns of Labour*, Cheltenham, UK and Northampton, MA, USA: Edward Elgar, pp. 86–98.

Halevi, J. and B. Lucarelli (2002), 'Japan's stagnationist crisis', *Monthly Review*, **53** (9): 24–36.

Halevi, J. and P. Kriesler (2004), 'Stagnation and economic conflict in Europe', *International Journal of Political Economy*, Special Issue, *The European Economic and Monetary Union in the global economy: is there a deflationary bias?* Summer: 19–45.

Halevi, J. and P. Kriesler (2006), 'The changing patterns of accumulation and realization in East Asia since the 1990s', CAER Working Paper No. 9, University of New South Wales, Sydney.

2. Breaking the economic dependence of developing countries to promote economic development and full employment: the case of the Maghreb countries

Mehdi Ben Guirat and Corinne Pastoret

Since the collapse of colonial rule, the newly independent countries of the Maghreb (Algeria, Morocco, Tunisia)[1] have remained heavily dependent on their economic relations with Europe. Despite positive growth rates, the Maghreb experiences high levels of unemployment and remains heavily dependent on imports of machinery and technology from European countries. While breaking this subsequent economic dependence requires multiple policies such as monetary and financial reforms (Ben Guirat and Pastoret 2009; Rossi 2009), this chapter argues that regional integration is fundamental to promote diversified economic development and full employment (Prebisch 1959).

Dependency in the Maghreb took many forms in the last centuries; the first section briefly depicts the evolving historical, social, political and economic factors that contributed to the current situation. It also highlights some attempts to resist some economic aspects of what is referred to as Western imperialism and its free-market ideology by promoting state interventionism through public employment policy and redistributive policy (Adams and Page 2003). The ensuing sections propose to deepen the regionalization of the Maghreb countries, in particular through further development of the Arab Maghreb Union (AMU). The achievements and limitations of the AMU, which was created in 1989, are first analyzed. Then further arguments are presented for a deeper regional integration that provides a framework in which macroeconomic policies promoting diversified economic growth and full employment can be implemented, while reducing political and economic dependency on European countries.

HISTORICAL, SOCIAL, POLITICAL AND ECONOMIC DETERMINANTS OF DEPENDENCY IN THE MAGHREB COUNTRIES

Current dependency situations in the Maghreb countries are the results of a historical, political and economic process that unfolded over centuries. Dependency in the Maghreb took place by the 'force of arms', as mentioned in the seminal work of Andre Gunder Frank (1967, p. 21) about economic dependency. In fact, by the end of the nineteenth century, most African countries were either formally colonized or put under the 'protective' authority of several European powers. In the case of the Maghreb countries, their sovereignty was challenged even before they were fully subdued and well before colonization, as France and Italy were mingling in the Maghreb countries' internal affairs. Jamil Abun-Nasr (1987, p. 248) argues that 'after 1830 the character of relations between the rulers of Tunisia, Morocco, and Tripolitania [Algeria being almost fully colonized] and the European powers underwent a change. The consuls of these powers emerged as centers of authority, using the weakness of local rulers or their need for protection in order to advance the national economic interests at the expense of others.' By the early twentieth century, all of the Maghreb was colonized by France, Italy or Spain, and although each power had a different agenda, the general trend was mainly to secure and provide low-cost labor and resources to support economic development on the mainland. To this end, the different local and regional economic structures of the Maghreb at the time were shaped to meet the needs of accumulation of European countries (Amin 1976, p. 16). The Maghreb countries therefore lost control over their productive resources, as a result of economic policies whose aim was not to promote their own economic development.

These imposed policies eliminated any attempt by the Maghreb countries to develop a burgeoning manufacturing industry (especially in the textile sector in the late nineteenth century) and favored stronger investment and resource-shifting policies toward the primary sector. Large pieces of land were expropriated by colonizers and strong farming practices were developed using the available local, cheap and docile labor. Mining activities were also developed on a similar pattern. To this day the Maghreb countries' geo-economical landscape resembles the one established during the colonization years. In fact by the end of that period, the now former colonizers – mainly France and Italy – had contributed to perpetuate very strong dependency relationships of the Maghreb toward their newly defined economic partners across the Mediterranean.

After the Maghreb countries' independence in the 1950s, new forms of economic dependency emerged. Despite the Maghreb's intention as

Table 2.1 Annual average growth rates of real gross domestic product of AMU countries and the EU

Year	1970–80	1980–90	1990–2000	2000–2010
AMU	7.32	1.70	2.97	4.23
Algeria	6.70	2.68	1.57	3.62
Libya	9.14	−1.82	n.a.	4.32
Morocco	5.65	4.24	2.78	4.75
Tunisia	6.84	3.32	5.08	4.66
Mauritania	3.15	1.63	2.57	3.83
EU	3.11	2.57	2.84	1.62

Source: UNCTAD and World Bank.

a region to recover its economic and political sovereignty and to regain control over its productive resources, the task remains unfulfilled. During the 1960s, the states started to became an 'instrument of social transformation, political mobilization and economic distribution' (Yousef 2004, p. 92). Interventionist–redistributive policies aimed at promoting full employment (through the development of a strong public sector), education and health, income redistribution and industrialization by protecting its infant industries from global competition. With these strong government policies, the Maghreb experienced average intermittent levels of economic growth and capital accumulation from the 1960s to the early 1980s and from the 1990s to this day (see Table 2.1). The 1980s saw a sharp economic slowdown in many countries, including the Maghreb, whose annual average output grew by only 1.7 percent from 1980 to 1990.

While growth rates in the AMU region have been positive since the 1960s, they were not sufficient to significantly increase living standards in the region (see Figure 2.1). Indeed, Figure 2.1 specifically shows that the nominal GDP per capita increases by several fold for all the Maghreb countries. Yet it remains under $4000 for all countries except oil-producing Libya, where it is reaching $10 000 per capita.

In association with the relatively mitigated results of their economic development policy, growth in the Maghreb countries was constrained by recursive balance of payments disequilibria. Because AMU currencies do not benefit from the same status and strength as European currencies, the Maghreb countries need to accumulate foreign currencies to pay for the import content of their economic development, while strictly defending fixed parities with European currencies (Thirlwall 2003). As a consequence, they crucially need to export primary goods, or low value added manufactured goods, in order to import high-technology capital goods.

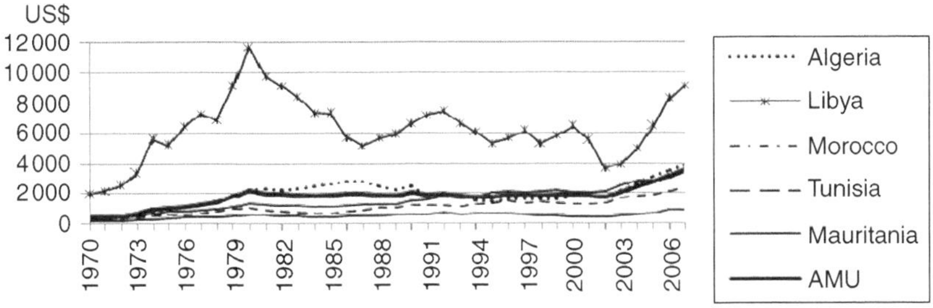

Source: UNCTAD.

Figure 2.1 Per capital nominal gross domestic product, in US dollars at current prices

Some exceptions do exist, though. In Algeria and Libya, oil revenues were able to release the financial constraint during the oil booms in the 1970s, thus further boosting industrialization. But foreign exchange decreased dramatically during the 1980s. With the recent increase in oil prices, new foreign exchange reserves were accumulated again. It is noted that most of these funds were held as official reserves with little use for financing productive investment. In some cases, funds were released for basic infrastructure such as highways; the trans-Maghreb highway has been an ongoing project for more than 25 years now. In the case of Algeria, a large part of the foreign exchange reserves was also used to pay debt contracted during the 1980s.

Maghreb countries' dependency on foreign currencies has led to a continuous deterioration of the terms of trade. These countries and other developing countries in general tend to export goods that have low value added and low income elasticity of demand, while developed countries tend to export goods with a high value added and a high income elasticity of demand (Prebisch 1950). The need to produce and export inelastic primary goods to pay for imports of industrial goods becomes a vicious circle that leads to falling prices of the exported goods. Furthermore, the only adopted compensating policy that could fix this problem is to produce larger quantities. This policy does not correct the decreasing terms of trade by increasing value added, but deepens the problem by exerting a heavier downward pressure on prices. It can therefore be argued that this mechanism breaks the classical idea that specialization and trade create a mutual benefit for the two commercial partners.

In fact, the trade history of the AMU with the EU proves that total free trade between unequal partners is not an ideal situation. The 1980 and 1990s, for example, were characterized by an opening of the trade of the Maghreb countries with the rest of the world and to a limited extent the privatization of their public enterprises. This development strategy favored export-led growth policies with a multiplication of bilateral agreements between the Maghreb countries and Europe. These policies were directed toward one main client, the EU, which is interested in a limited number of commodities, including oil and gas from Algeria and Libya, and the outsourcing of light industry, textiles and some agricultural products. Over time, this has created economies that are not integrated and not diversified, and hence very unstable. As a consequence, productive resources are channeled with the sole aim of satisfying one unique client with very specific demands.

In the case of the Maghreb countries, dependency was not associated with underdevelopment *per se*, since Maghreb countries have experienced continuous economic growth, but dependency resulted from the choice of policies that were not intended for the best interests of their own populations. The Maghreb countries are no longer forced 'by arms' to export their commodities at low prices to European countries, but since their industry and technology are not yet competitive, they need to import machinery and technological goods, and, to this end, they need to export to gain the necessary foreign exchange. To be able to transform their economic structures and diversify their economies, the Maghreb countries 'first' need to meet the demand from European countries and to adapt their economies to these specific productions. But if they do so, they cannot rapidly diversify their economies and will not keep pace with technological change, thus becoming more dependent on European countries.

This vicious circle is one of the manifestations of current economic and financial dependency situations that remain nearly 50 years after the Maghreb countries became independent. In addition, these countries lack bargaining power when trade agreements are discussed. The EU usually favors bilateral trade agreements with individual countries among the Maghreb bloc; this policy creates an imbalance of power that favors the EU. As a consequence, the Maghreb countries need more political power to be able to negotiate fair trade agreements with Europe, in particular by reviving the different AMU political and economic processes. This solution would also reduce their economic and financial dependencies, while improving their integration in the global economy.

THE ARAB MAGHREB UNION AND ITS FAILURE TO PROMOTE REGIONAL INTEGRATION

The Arab Maghreb Union (AMU) was created on 17 February 1989 to build a cultural, political and economic union between Algeria, Morocco, Tunisia, Libya and Mauritania. To this end, these countries agreed to

Table 2.2 Intra-trade within the AMU (%)

1950	1960	1970	1980	1990	2000	2006
4.53	4.58	1.44	0.26	2.86	2.25	2.01

Source: UNCTAD.

sign the Treaty of Marrakech, whose main objectives are: (1) a common market in which goods, services and individuals can freely circulate; (2) the adoption of common economic policies in order to promote agricultural, industrial, commercial and social developments among its members; and (3) the disappearance of tariffs within the economic union and the application of a common tariff for the rest of the world.

Almost 20 years after its creation, the progress of the AMU in terms of regional integration remains limited. In 2006, intra-regional trade represented 2.01 percent, while most of its foreign transactions took place with the EU on the basis of bilateral trade agreements (see Table 2.2). This situation has two main explanations – one purely economic, the other political. There are several political disagreements among AMU countries – in particular, the issue of the Western Sahara.[2] There are also economic reasons mentioned above, related to dependent trade relationships with European countries.

Historically, Europe has been the main trade partner of the AMU but other partners such as North America and China have increased their trade with the AMU (see Appendix, Table 2A.1). For example, AMU exports toward Europe grew from 72 percent of AMU total exports in 1995 to 61 percent in 2006.

Since the creation of the AMU, the structure of its trade with the rest of the world has remained relatively unchanged. As stated in the first section, the Maghreb countries continue to export primary commodities and manufacturing goods with low value added and to import manufactured goods, especially machinery.

While the AMU has mostly experienced trade surpluses since 1995 (see Figure 2.2), a closer look at individual countries indicates that fuel-exporting countries, such as Libya and Algeria, have experienced surpluses, while all the other countries faced trade deficits (see Appendix, Table 2A.2). Higher percentages of export and imports in the 1970s are due to the oil crisis and more favorable trade deals with the European partners at the time. The level of both exports and imports in the AMU has considerably increased since 1995 (see Figure 2.2), as a result of bilateral trade agreements with Europe combined with a boom of fuels

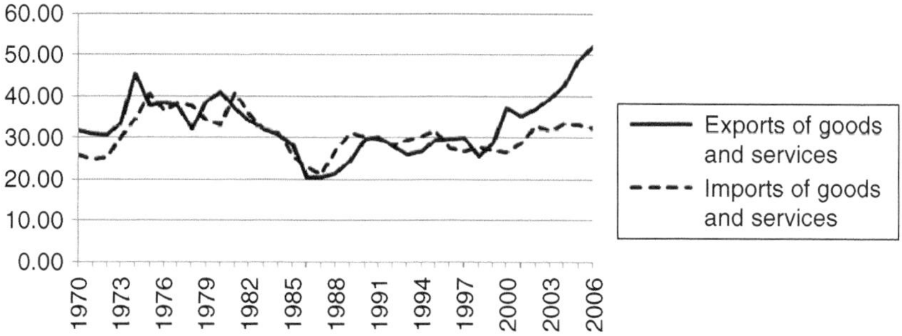

Source: UNCTAD.

Figure 2.2 Evolution of exports, imports and trade balances in the AMU since 1970, as a percentage of GDP

and minerals exports. Since 1995, exports went from $29.4 billion to $46 billion in 2000 and $110.6 billion in 2006. As shown in Figure 2.3, primary commodities account for 81.5 percent of the total exports of the Maghreb countries in 2006. Primary commodities (excluding fuels) went from $3.5 billion in 1995 to $3.4 billion in 2000 to $7 billion in 2006, mostly as a result of an increase in basic food items and ores and metals. The most striking change, compared to the economic situation of the AMU in 1995, is the boom of fuels exports by mostly Algeria and Libya, which grew from $18.3 billion in 1995 to $83.2 billion in 2006. Imports have also nearly doubled since 1995 (see Appendix, Table 2A.2): they grew from $33.3 billion in 2000 to $70.2 billon in 2006. Imports of manufactured goods represent about 70 percent of total imports in 2006 (65.7 percent in 1995); 46.6 percent of these imported manufactured goods are machinery.

The structure of trade between the AMU and Europe has led to a lack of diversification of the Maghreb economies. Individual countries are still relying on exporting primary commodities in order to import manufacturing and technological goods. They continue to allocate a sizable amount of resources in order to satisfy a main client (mostly Europe), even if new partners have emerged, so that their economic growth depends mostly on the state of the European economies and their demand. Furthermore, industries in the Maghreb countries and especially export-oriented industries (e.g. the textile industry or light mechanical and electrical industries in Tunisia and Morocco) are contributing to output growth with a lesser impact due to high international competition from China and Eastern Europe. This fierce international context is creating an industry that is becoming less intensive in labor, an industry with chronic low pay standards and an industry that is reducing social protection.

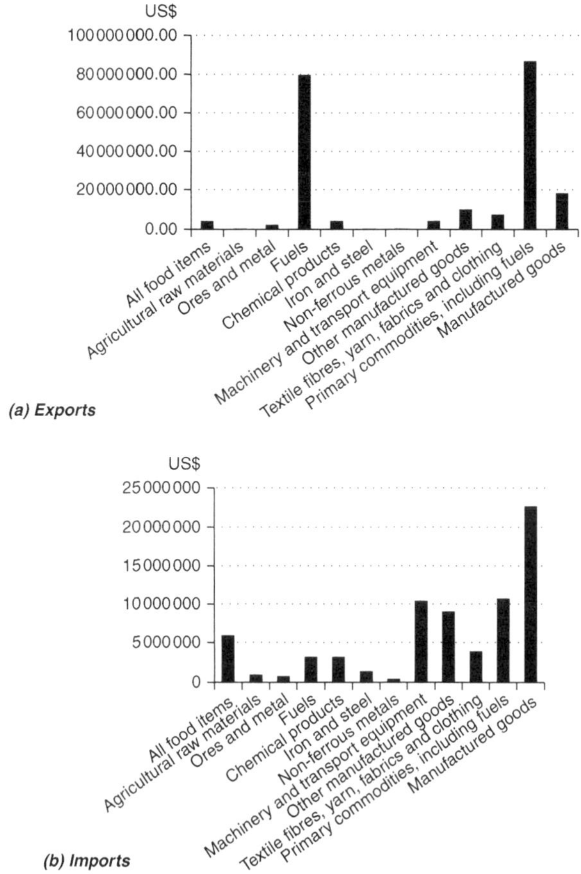

Source: UNCTAD.

Figure 2.3 AMU exports and imports in thousands of US$, 2006

Twenty years later, the Treaty of Marrakech has mitigated results. AMU countries have experienced ‘immiserizing growth’ (Bhagwati 1958, p. 201), which failed to eradicate poverty and unemployment (see Table 2.3), while perpetuating dependency situations between the AMU and Europe. The Maghreb manufacturing sector is particularly at risk, especially its production of technological goods, which is underdeveloped and lacking diversification. Now that the boom of fuel exports is releasing the balance of payment constraint on development (specifically for Algeria and Libya), AMU countries would highly benefit from a restart of the regionalization process.

Table 2.3 Basic indicators

	GDP in billions of dollars in 2006 and 2007	GDP per capita in thousands of dollars 2006 and 2007	Population in millions	Unemployment % in 2007	GDP growth in billions of dollars from 2000 to 2005	Poverty % in 2007
Algeria	131.6	3894.7	34	11.8	5.1	25
Libya	57	9082.5	6	30	4.7	7.4
Morocco	73.5	2326.0	34	9.8	4.3	15
Tunisia	35	3358.0	10.5	14	4.5	7.4
Mauritania	2.7	906.7	3.5	20	4.0	40
AMU	299.8	3511.3	88	13	4.8	17

Source: UNCTAD.

INCREASING REGIONALIZATION TO PROMOTE INDUSTRIALIZATION, TECHNICAL PROGRESS, DIVERSIFIED GROWTH AND FULL EMPLOYMENT

Two main challenges that the AMU countries are facing are their high levels of unemployment and the lack of diversification of their economies. In this last section, it is argued that further regional integration should be strongly encouraged, despite political disputes about the Western Sahara and other issues. Indeed, regional integration would make it possible to break the economic dependency of the Maghreb countries, while supporting the necessary structural transformation of their economies. Regional integration would be the first step to allow AMU countries to regain control over their productive resources, while implementing policies to promote full employment. With the current boom of fuel exports that contributed to weakening the financial constraint on development, now could be the right time to accelerate regional integration and cooperation within the AMU countries, while gaining political power to negotiate fairer trade agreements with Europe and the rest of the world.

Further regional integration will have a beneficial impact on employment and economic development, while reducing economic dependency on Europe. First, a dynamic common market promotes diversified economic growth and domestic industrialization by allowing economies of scale that would otherwise be impossible. However, this common market should not be based on free trade, but on preferential treatments within the union

(Prebisch 1959). In other words, regional integration combines the benefits of export-led models and protectionism without exposing countries to excessive competition from developed economies. Countries are therefore able to regain control over their productive resources and to implement development strategies that go beyond relying exclusively on exports of a limited number of low value added products to developed countries.

In the case of Latin America, Prebisch (1959, p. 268) explained:

> the response . . . should be the enlargement of national markets through the gradual establishment of a common market. But the common market, just as in Europe, cannot be established on the principle of universal multilateralism. Preferential treatment is needed inside the area to promote specialization in industrial products and primary commodities . . . Latin American protectionism and preferences, if kept within reasonable limits, will not hamper world trade. Imports from the center will continue to depend on Latin American exports to them – a clearly passive situation. The only changes – and these will be very important indeed – will take place in import composition, and through them, countries will specialize in industrial products as well as agricultural ones. Without the common market, there will be a continued tendency to try to produce everything – say from automobile to machinery – under the sheltering wing of very high protection.

Further regional integration would promote industrialization and economic development in the AMU: 'most Arab economies are simply too small to be able individually to achieve rapid industrialization or diversified growth. A natural response to these limitations would be to pursue Arab regional economic and trade arrangements' (UNDP 2002, p. 96). In the line of Prebisch, the UNDP (2002) does not consider that multilateralism is the key to economic development. Rather, it advocates regional integration and economic partnerships in order to build virtuous growth triangles, in which countries would combine their capital, labor, natural resources and techniques in order to become competitive in the world economy. In this context growth triangles are defined as

> Capital, labour and natural resources needed to enter regional and world markets can be shared among collaborating countries, with one contributing financial capital and technical know-how, for example, and another providing natural resources and cheap labour unavailable in the first. By combining the endowments of each country, partnerships emerge that bring more growth and prosperity to partners as a group than any could have achieved alone. (UNDP 2002, p. 97)

Virtuous growth triangles would be enhanced if AMU countries collectively supported research, education and infrastructures in order to dynamically create new products to meet the demand of new regional and international markets.

> Beyond comparative advantage, growth triangles can also help to create a competitive edge by focusing partner countries' joint resources, skills and knowledge on creating new products and services demanded by new markets, overcoming possible disadvantages that each may face individually. (Ibid.)

A second major advantage of strengthening regional integration in the AMU is the possibility for Arab countries to regain control over their macroeconomic policy in order to promote full employment. According to Cardoso (1979), unemployment and poverty are the structural consequences of global dependent economic relations between the center and the periphery.[3] He explains that dependency 'in the periphery as well as in the center, produces as it evolves, in a cyclical way, wealth and poverty, accumulation and shortage of capital, employment for some and unemployment for others' (Cardoso 1979, p. xxiii). More specifically, export-led growth strategies in the AMU were associated with high unemployment because the jobs created in the manufacturing sector did not compensate for the loss of jobs in the non-exporting sector. This sector had, indeed, to compete with imports from European countries.

> Countries forced to specialize in these activities through the pursuit of static comparative advantage may find themselves with unemployment owing to their inability to absorb the labor from the activities in which they have a comparative disadvantage. The mutual profitability of free trade argument breaks down. (Thirlwall 2003, p. 43)

Furthermore, most of the exporting industries offer low-paid jobs and have a tendency to repatriate profits abroad. These often off-shore exporting industries contribute to the limited impact of growth on local and regional effective demand. It should nevertheless be pointed out that unemployment in the AMU would have been worse had governments not decided to create public jobs to absorb unemployment, especially from high-skilled workers.

Finally, 'renewed growth is a necessary, although not a sufficient, condition to meet the challenge of full employment, fully use human capabilities and overcome poverty' (UNDP 2002, p. 850). In contrast to neoclassical export-led models that postulate full employment, unemployment in the AMU is a crucial challenge that needs to be addressed immediately. If macroeconomic policy were to remain the same, unemployment would only worsen, as emphasized by the UNDP report (2002, p. 94):

> The challenge of attacking unemployment and poverty by creating productive and gainful jobs for today's openly unemployed plus those newly entering the labour force is enormous, but it is also critical for Arab countries (especially

in environments where formal safety nets are ineffective) – and it must be addressed now because otherwise, the problem will only worsen.

Increasing liberalization and deregulation is therefore not the solution, and in the aftermath of the subprime crisis in the USA, even developed countries agree that state intervention and regulation are necessary to promote stable economic growth and full employment. Besides the promotion of regional integration, AMU countries would benefit from stimulating effective demand through various macroeconomic policies (Cesaratto et al. 2003; Kaldor 1970; Prebisch 1950; Thirlwall 2003), including direct employment policy (Bhaduri 2005; Karimi 2008; Pastoret 2009; Wray 2007), thus increasing the importance of larger local markets as a factor of growth and employment.

CONCLUSION

Despite the decolonization process and the creation of the AMU, the Maghreb countries have not escaped the vicious circles of economic dependency on European countries. While the AMU has experienced economic growth, the same 'old' economic structures have been perpetuated over time, involving exports of primary goods in order to pay for the imports of capital and technological goods from Europe. The growth in the AMU countries might not be sustainable over time, as it fails to eliminate unemployment and poverty. In addition, this situation of dependent economic growth has left AMU countries in a situation where their economies would fall apart if European countries were to face a severe recession.

Developing regional integration would be a crucial step forward in order to break economic and political dependency in the AMU for two main reasons: (1) through the creation of growth triangles, it would allow both economic diversification at the regional level and a more competitive integration of the Maghreb countries into the global economy; and (2) Maghreb countries could regain control over their macroeconomic policy in order to promote full employment and a higher level of regional effective demand to support economic growth.

NOTES

1. The political and economic entity called 'Arab Maghreb Union, AMU' or 'Maghreb Arab Union, MAU' consists of five countries: Mauritania, Morocco, Algeria, Tunisia and Libya. In our analysis we shall refer to only three countries unless stated otherwise. These countries are Morocco, Algeria and Tunisia.

2. A former Spanish colony, the Western Sahara has been claimed by Morocco since the Spanish withdrawal in 1975 while Algeria supports its independence.
3. 'Center' is the developed countries and 'Periphery' is the developing countries.

REFERENCES

Abun-Nasr, J. (1987), *A History of the Maghreb in the Islamic Period*, Cambridge: Cambridge University Press.

Adams, R.H. and Page, J. (2003), 'Poverty, inequality and growth in selected Middle East and North Africa countries, 1980–2000', *World Development*, **31** (12), 2027–48.

Amin, S. (1976), *Unequal Development: An Essay on the Social Formations of Peripheral Capitalism*, New York: Monthly Review Press.

Ben Guirat, M. and Pastoret, C. (2009–10), 'Financial constraints on economic growth in the Maghreb countries: what are the solutions?', *International Journal of Political Economy*, **38** (4), 66–85.

Bhaduri, A. (2005), *Development with Dignity: A Case for Full Employment*, New Delhi, India: National Book Trust.

Bhagwati, J. (1958), 'Immiserizing growth: a geometrical note', *Review of Economic Studies*, **25**, 201–5.

Cardoso, F.H. (1979), *Dependency and Development in Latin America*, Los Angeles, CA: University of California Press.

Cesaratto, S., Serrano, F. and Stirati, A. (2003), 'Technical change, effective demand and employment', *Review of Political Economy*, **15** (1), 33–53.

Gunder Frank, A. (1967), *Capitalism and Underdevelopment in Latin America: Historical Studies of Chile and Brazil.* New York: Monthly Review Press.

Kaldor, N. (1970), 'The case for regional policies', *Scottish Journal of Political Economy*, **85**, 337–48.

Karimi, Z. (2008), 'Financing job guarantee schemes by oil revenue: the case of Iran', Levy Economics Institute Working Paper No. 527.

Pastoret, C. (2009), 'The Argentine Jefes Program: from a post-financial crisis emergency safety net to a long-run policy promoting development', in C. Gnos and L.-P. Rochon (eds), *Monetary Policy and Financial Stability: A Post-Keynesian Agenda*, Cheltenham, UK and Northampton, MA, USA: Edward Elgar, pp. 222–47.

Prebisch, R. (1950), *The Economic Development of Latin America and its Principal Problems*, New York: ECLA, UN Dept. of Economic Affairs.

Prebisch, R. (1959), 'Commercial policy in the underdeveloped countries', *American Economic Review, Papers and Proceedings*, **49** (2), 251–73.

Rossi, S. (2009), 'A common currency for Middle Eastern and North African countries? Lessons from the European Monetary Union', in D. Cobham and G. Dibeh (eds), *Monetary Policy and Central Banking in the Middle East and North Africa*, London: Routledge, pp. 226–45.

Thirlwall, A.P. (2003), *Trade, the Balance of Payments and Exchange Rate Policy in Developing Countries*, Cheltenham, UK and Northampton, MA, USA: Edward Elgar.

UNDP (2002), *Arab Human Development Report: Creating Opportunities For Future Generations*, New York: United Nations Publications.

Wray, R. (2007), 'The employer of last resort programme: could it work for developing countries?', Economic and Labour Market Papers N.2007/5, International Labour Office, Geneva.

Yousef, T. (2004), 'Development, growth and policy reform in the Middle East and North Africa since 1950', *The Journal of Economic Perspectives*, **18** (3), 91–115.

APPENDIX

Table 2A.1 Trade structure of the AMU, by product groups, in thousands of US$

PRODUCT	Total	All food items	Agric. raw materials	Ores & metal	Fuels	Chemical products
	SITC 0 to 9	SITC 0 + 1 + 22 + 4	SITC 2 −22 −27 −28	SITC 27 + 28 + 68	SITC 3	SITC 5
PARTNER						
World	106 184 338.45	4 107 608.24	297 178.03	2 531 070.51	79 101 849.85	3 840 106.16
Developing economies: Africa	3 366 410.59	570 406.50	29 082.60	126 802.87	1 238 338.75	416 571.13
Developing economies: America	3 302 348.49	26 899.68	2062.00	102 521.40	2 772 082.14	354 039.59
Developing economies: Asia	8 571 114.89	210 646.93	36 413.67	408 363.84	4 897 401.73	1 368 019.14
Developed economies: America	20 470 268.54	111 359.17	11 814.92	110 061.55	20 087 798.64	57 900.66
Developed economies: Asia	486 800.92	371 154.81	18 768.49	10 197.94	66 169.16	3 490.58
Developed economies: Europe	65 682 999.20	2 178 914.60	206 456.64	1 401 766.01	49 334 238.51	1 299 428.77
Major petroleum exporters: Developing Africa	1 086 640.44	310 398.21	6 382.25	64 962.51	13 069.16	158 037.64
UMA	2 136 822.63	319 920.97	13 187.33	104 773.09	734 009.83	269 309.87
EU-25	64 424 709.73	2 139 114.90	205 723.98	1 295 159.48	48 318 206.59	1 296 857.14
Eurozone	60 703 320.46	2 019 765.60	203 069.85	1 151 078.90	45 871 626.34	1 241 547.22

Source: UNCTAD.

Iron & steel	Non-ferrous metals	Machinery & transport equip	Other manu-factured goods	Textile fibres, yarn fabrics & clothing	Primary commodities including fuels	Manufactured goods
SITC 67	SITC 68	SITC 7	SITC 6 + 8 less 68	SITC 26 + 65 + 84	SITC 0 + 1 + 2 + 3 + 4 + 68	SITC 5 to 8 less 68
586 990.20	311 035.78	4 390 135.11	10 385 597.73	7 545 169.05	86 037 706.63	18 615 838.99
195 155.40	48 051.28	271 834.03	674 703.68	49 326.63	1 964 630.72	1 363 108.85
2 105.32	347.84	35 316.80	9 147.41	5 049.22	2 903 565.21	398 503.81
64 758.69	20 748.46	60 340.01	185 729.75	42 214.47	5 552 826.17	1 614 088.89
3 121.51	4 510.58	10 609.83	80 539.16	49 179.95	20 321 034.28	149 049.65
–	4 194.02	7 856.71	8 802.60	7 317.61	466 290.40	20 149.90
318 137.36	232 315.75	3 501 123.80	7 684 756.84	6 028 612.93	53 121 375.75	12 485 309.41
58 443.86	7 040.77	147 142.57	361 368.40	26 677.89	394 812.12	666 548.61
156 887.30	46 753.93	177 991.28	516 356.57	22 409.39	1 171 891.23	963 657.72
318 107.77	164 719.90	3 480 715.34	7 636 855.81	6 013 750.88	51 958 204.96	12 414 428.29
312 241.73	163 355.18	3 326 317.74	6 842 745.92	5 272 615.14	49 245 540.69	11 410 610.88

Table 2A.2 Gross domestic products in the AMU by type of expenditure and by kind of economic activity (as percentage of GDP)

	Algeria				
YEAR	1970	1980	1990	2000	2006
COMPONENT					
Gross domestic product (GDP)	100	100	100	100	100
Final consumption expenditure	72.71	56.94	72.82	55.15	40.85
Household consumption expenditure	59.44	43.19	56.57	41.57	28.73
Government final consumption expenditure	13.27	13.75	16.25	13.58	12.12
Gross capital formation	33.15	39.08	28.90	23.52	32.27
Gross fixed capital formation	30.60	33.77	25.59	20.68	24.69
Changes in inventories	2.55	5.31	3.31	2.84	7.58
Exports of goods and services	22.13	34.34	23.38	42.07	49.85
Imports of goods and services	27.46	30.36	25.09	20.74	22.98
Total value added	100	100	100	100	100
Agriculture, hunting, forestry, fishing	13.97	8.53	11.92	8.76	9.42
Industry	37.64	57.63	48.26	56.71	56.27
Mining, manufacturing, utilities	29.55	46.73	37.39	49.32	48.61
Manufacturing	11.77	10.54	11.63	6.03	5.98
Construction	8.09	10.90	10.87	7.39	7.66
Services	48.40	33.84	39.82	34.53	34.31
Wholesale, retail trade and restaurants	19.03	12.52	13.59	12.18	11.38
Transport, storage and communications	6.05	5.07	5.17	6.98	8.40
Other activities	23.31	16.25	21.06	15.37	14.53

Libya					Mauritania				
1970	1980	1990	2000	2006	1970	1980	1990	2000	2006
100	100	100	100	100	100	100	100	100	100
50.74	49.36	72.83	67.04	33.01	69.29	98.54	94.88	101.83	76.91
32.52	27.13	48.43	46.44	18.62	52.94	74.42	78.31	74.19	59.44
18.22	22.23	24.40	20.60	14.39	16.35	24.12	16.57	27.64	17.47
16.52	24.30	18.62	13.04	14.43	22.59	26.79	19.49	18.56	28.99
16.26	23.40	13.87	12.62	17.37	20.64	20.49	13.10	22.36	28.99
0.25	0.90	4.75	0.42	−2.94	1.94	6.30	6.39	−3.81	–
60.99	61.82	39.67	35.25	83.11	42.01	30.38	43.45	35.61	54.91
28.25	35.48	31.12	15.33	30.55	33.89	55.71	57.82	55.99	60.81
100	100	100	100	100	100	100	100	100	100
2.39	1.78	8.67	8.09	4.56	29.27	34.38	37.45	27.65	25.60
68.64	75.87	45.95	53.72	68.07	37.93	24.72	24.23	29.74	26.99
58.48	66.77	40.94	48.01	63.62	31.35	18.23	19.03	23.14	18.22
2.10	1.87	6.30	5.01	2.59	4.94	5.60	8.97	8.98	5.67
10.16	9.10	5.01	5.70	4.45	6.58	6.49	5.20	6.60	8.76
28.97	22.35	45.37	38.20	27.37	32.80	40.89	38.32	42.61	47.41
5.02	4.77	11.94	9.48	7.26	6.20	9.60	9.38	13.91	13.99
5.41	3.46	8.27	6.83	5.01	5.69	7.25	3.39	4.34	6.02
18.54	14.12	25.17	21.88	15.10	20.91	24.05	25.56	24.35	27.40

Table 2A.2 (continued)

	Morocco				
YEAR	1970	1980	1990	2000	2006
COMPONENT					
Gross domestic product (GDP)	100	100	100	100	100
Final consumption expenditure	79.72	80.28	75.48	79.86	77.91
Household consumption expenditure	68.62	63.26	61.11	61.49	61.18
Government final consumption expenditure	11.11	17.02	14.37	18.37	16.74
Gross capital formation	21.67	28.38	29.60	25.52	29.87
Gross fixed capital formation	15.86	23.63	25.48	25.95	28.86
Changes in inventories	5.81	4.75	4.12	−0.43	1.01
Exports of goods and services	19.10	19.01	26.52	27.88	32.52
Imports of goods and services	21.43	27.86	30.86	33.27	39.90
Total value added	100	100	100	100	100
Agriculture, hunting, forestry, fishing	21.74	20.54	20.00	14.22	14.96
Industry	24.02	28.42	28.42	27.69	26.98
Mining, manufacturing, utilities	20.25	22.72	23.51	22.83	21.06
Manufacturing	15.36	16.27	18.03	16.61	16.22
Construction	3.77	5.70	4.90	4.85	5.93
Services	54.23	51.04	51.59	58.10	58.05
Wholesale, retail trade and restaurants	15.10	14.21	14.36	15.77	14.02
Transport, storage and communications	6.66	6.27	6.33	6.57	7.22
Other activities	32.48	30.57	30.89	35.75	36.82

Tunisia					MAU				
1970	1980	1990	2000	2006	1970	1980	1990	2000	2006
100	100	100	100	100	100	100	100	100	100
83.35	76.00	79.98	76.30	78.86	69.94	60.81	74.24	67.32	53.27
66.49	61.54	63.62	60.74	63.76	55.62	43.51	56.61	50.52	39.18
16.86	14.47	16.36	15.56	15.10	14.32	17.31	17.62	16.80	14.09
21.15	29.36	27.07	27.35	23.13	24.18	31.28	26.57	22.05	27.19
20.52	28.30	24.36	25.98	22.20	21.47	27.86	22.81	20.84	24.08
0.63	1.05	2.70	1.37	0.92	2.71	3.42	3.77	1.20	3.11
22.00	40.90	43.56	44.55	50.34	31.70	40.90	29.63	37.17	52.01
26.49	46.25	50.60	48.19	52.33	25.91	33.03	30.27	26.54	32.37
100	100	100	100	100	100	100	100	100	100
19.90	16.81	17.21	13.79	11.97	13.84	9.34	13.55	10.70	10.23
23.07	34.06	32.11	31.90	31.76	40.76	56.26	41.93	45.54	48.52
17.17	27.08	27.67	26.64	25.96	33.59	47.29	34.27	39.46	42.12
10.74	15.34	20.22	21.87	18.38	10.04	9.00	12.51	10.37	9.16
5.90	6.98	4.44	5.26	5.81	7.17	8.97	7.66	6.08	6.40
57.04	49.13	50.68	54.31	56.27	45.40	34.40	44.52	43.76	41.25
22.90	20.89	15.82	16.61	16.75	14.26	10.79	13.54	12.96	11.82
7.17	5.72	7.47	8.87	11.57	6.15	4.82	6.31	7.06	7.76
26.97	22.53	27.38	28.83	27.96	25.00	18.79	24.66	23.75	21.68

Table 2A.3 Trade structure of the AMU with the world and with the EU, by products groups, in thousands of US$

PARTNER: WORLD		FLOW: EXPORTS			
PRODUCT MAU	Total	Primary commodities	Primary comm. excluding fuels	All food items	Food, basic
1995	29423577.58	21905377.48	3533757.79	2421255.95	2339543.57
2000	46070992.67	35681789.31	3447406.28	2267202.30	2200560.90
2006	110635679.78	90263745.27	7070365.01	4098415.36	3969482.08
PARTNER: WORLD		FLOW: IMPORTS			
PRODUCT MAU	Total	Primary commodities	Primary comm. excluding fuels	All food items	Food, basic
1995	32714235.58	11162074.80	9188883.16	7089921.13	6817662.22
2000	33335755.91	10710695.91	7551021.96	5958841.50	5717754.18
2006	70245932.78	20805312.89	12630080.24	9140350.88	8759594.25
PARTNER: EU		FLOW: EXPORTS			
PRODUCT MAU	Total	Primary commodities	Primary comm. excluding fuels	All food items	Food, basic
1995	21233168.79	15815770.05	2115662.75	1388167.12	1363134.30
2000	33129855.38	25078455.55	2162212.63	1418193.02	1391037.49
2006	67943773.60	55387704.43	3685394.31	2139784.89	2098737.02
PARTNER: EU		FLOW: IMPORTS			
PRODUCT ECONOMY	Total	Primary commodities	Primary comm. excluding fuels	All food items	Food, basic
1995	20674205.40	5002937.46	4555948.05	3351368.26	3250215.33
2000	20816806.15	4631116.87	3751937.68	2810784.81	2718971.96
2006	36763898.65	7781722.47	5346580.20	3258731.27	3079544.88

Source: UNDP.

Agricultural raw materials	Ores, metals and precious stones	Manufactured goods	Chemical products	Machinery and transport equipment	Other manuf. goods
207 820.96	904 680.87	7 515 652.71	2 052 662.06	714 427.21	4 748 563.44
217 839.81	962 364.16	10 274 265.95	2 115 737.19	1 698 625.06	6 459 903.71
297 661.04	2 674 288.61	18 773 095.11	3 957 436.19	4 397 379.93	10 418 278.99

Agricultural raw materials	Ores, metals and precious stones	Manufactured goods	Chemical products	Machinery and transport equipment	Other manuf. goods
1 263 753.01	835 209.03	21 551 690.11	3 349 569.44	9 289 579.08	8 912 541.59
890 230.66	701 949.80	22 563 421.81	3 108 412.17	10 441 985.24	9 013 024.40
1 584 975.93	1 904 753.43	48 917 244.55	7 048 656.01	22 782 398.49	19 086 190.05

Agricultural raw materials	Ores, metals and precious stones	Manufactured goods	Chemical products	Machinery and transport equipment	Other manuf. goods
125 471.85	602 023.77	5 416 337.27	873 890.50	552 174.27	3 990 272.51
153 360.93	590 658.68	7 994 140.67	787 411.79	1 524 612.67	5 682 116.21
206 254.83	1 339 354.58	12 513 001.63	1 361 788.85	3 484 772.97	7 666 439.80

Agricultural raw materials	Ores, metals and precious stones	Manufactured goods	Chemical products	Machinery and transport equipment	Other manuf. goods
765 863.65	438 716.14	15 670 508.65	2 587 213.58	6 647 239.34	6 436 055.73
575 598.32	365 554.56	16 146 082.55	2 319 203.57	7 263 398.47	6 563 480.51
1 089 765.49	998 083.44	28 821 438.34	4 662 564.80	13 568 453.95	10 590 419.58

3. The redistribution conflict in the 'patrimonial regime' through a stock–flow consistent model

Mickaël Clévenot and Yann Guy[1]

The financial liberalization, undertaken at the end of the 1970s in the USA and in the UK was followed in the mid-1980s by a large majority of countries. In France, liberalization of the stock accounts was completed in 1989. Some laws organizing national market liberalization, from 1984 onwards, had previously been passed. The impact of financial liberalization remains ambiguous considering the diversity of results. In Japan, it brings to mind the deflationary crisis of the 1990s. In all countries, it led to more or less pronounced banking crises (Ben Gamra and Clévenot 2006). In the medium term, the US and the UK experiment looks positive, whereas France is suffering from slow growth. Financial liberalization seems to require an institutional environment that is not present everywhere. In other words, the new institutional hierarchy imposed by finance does not spontaneously meet the complementarities that are necessary to fulfil a finance-led accumulation pattern. These conditions will be tested on models of closed economies. Standard models fail to apprehend correctly the formal treatment of accumulation pattern controlled by stock effects. The neoclassical–Keynesian synthesis models produce many inconsistencies as regards currencies and financial assets, particularly in stock–flow relations, due to a non-existent accounting consistency and unaccounted-for stock effects, which are however implicit in the definition of equilibrium link flows (Taylor 2004a, 2004b). In neoclassical models with rational expectations, at the equilibrium there is no difference between flows and stocks; that is, either a flow or a stock equilibrium is defined, but there is no interaction between the two (Foley 1975).

Regulation theory teaches us that switching from the Fordian regime to the patrimonial regime entails both an inversion of the institutional hierarchy and the formation of new complementarities. However, the formal representation of financialized capitalism established by regulation authors is not fully satisfactory either. Thus, in this chapter, these relations are modelled thanks to stock–flow consistent (SFC) macroeconomic models. From the initial model set up by Lavoie and Godley (2001), the locking-up variables in income distribution as well as the behavioural equations are modified in order to represent institutional inversion phenomena. Firms' stockholding behaviour is also taken into account. The new model is then presented in three versions, in order to establish the installation requirements of a new coherence faced with the new political deal, increasing financial power and weakened worker power.

1. REPRESENTATIONS OF FINANCE-LED CAPITALISM

1.1 Theoretical Presentation of Financialized Capitalism

Aglietta (1998) is the first economist in France who tried to provide a comprehensive representation of financialized capitalism, named patrimonial capitalism. To explain the American performances, the regulationist author advanced the notion of a mode of accumulation based on finance. The reconfiguration of capitalism was carried out from an inversion of the Fordist institutional hierarchy (see Amable 2005 for the notion of institutional hierarchy). The then dominating wage–labour nexus became a variable subordinate to the constraints imposed by monetary regime and finance, which used to stand for the adjustment variables of the former period. The performances of the patrimonial regime were then explained by the adequacy of the mode of regulation to the accumulation pattern.

This idea caused many reactions in so far as the existence of an accumulation pattern implies its diffusion to other economies, including the French one. In theory, exporting the American regime supposes a major questioning of the social relations prevailing in France since the postwar period, since it implies a substantial modification of the welfare system. From this perspective, the patrimonial accumulation pattern existing in the USA has important implications for French political economy. The weakness of the French economy over a major part of the 1990s could thereby be explained by the late adoption of new working rules for a finance-dominated economy (Aglietta 2000).

In order to develop this, regulationist authors implemented several modelling processes. However, the formalization of a financialized accumulation pattern, of which the USA in the years 1990–2000 was supposed to be an archetype (Aglietta 1998), was achieved with too partial a description of the wealth effects (Boyer 2000). When the financial aspects were more precisely handled, the macroeconomic closure was lacking (Aglietta and Breton 2001; Aglietta and Rebérioux 2004). Yet the financialization effects required special attention.

This dissatisfaction led economists to resort to formalizations borrowed from the SFC approach, developed by Lavoie and Godley (2001). Their field of analysis was amended and extended in order to be able to test the consistency of the 'patrimonial regime'. Although it was not its first purpose, this approach, known as the 'stock–flow consistent approach to macroeconomic modelling' (SFC), seems able to meet the requirements of a macroeconomic analysis that fully takes into consideration financial interactions. The modifications concerned some behavioural equations, and more especially modifications in the distributive aspects, so as to reveal hierarchical and institutional complementarity phenomena. The field of analysis was extended to more financial aspects, such as the increase in securities issuing, the increase in households' equities and the rise in shareholder pressure or share buybacks by firms, while preserving the more traditional aspects of economic policy.

1.2 Formalization of the Institutional Hierarchy and Complementarity

The Fordist crisis, which started in the late 1960s, gave rise to significant economic, institutional and political modifications. The transformations of the accumulation pattern led to a structural crisis because of the inadequacy of the regulation mode. During the crisis, all the institutions were affected: state interventions, competition, international regime, the monetary system and wage relations. The modelling efforts will focus on these last two institutions. Modelling is limited to a closed economy, so that the globalization implications cannot completely be dealt with.

The monetary system has experienced very important evolutions on both sides of the Atlantic. Since 1979, policies against inflation and the abandonment of the fixed exchange rate regime (1971) have supported the transition from indebtedness regimes to stock market regimes, generating an inversion of the institutional hierarchy. Inflation has revealed the social conflict between capital and labour. Employment now constitutes the adjustment variable, instead of monetary policy. The rise of unemployment in the late 1970s and during the 1980s established an unfavourable situation for the wage interest.

With the sustained and non-inflationary high growth in the USA during the 1990s, it was reasonable to think that this country had come out of the Fordist crisis – in other words that the mode of regulation was adapted to the new accumulation pattern. This new social and political configuration during the 1990s appears to explain a new lease of life in the USA, while it

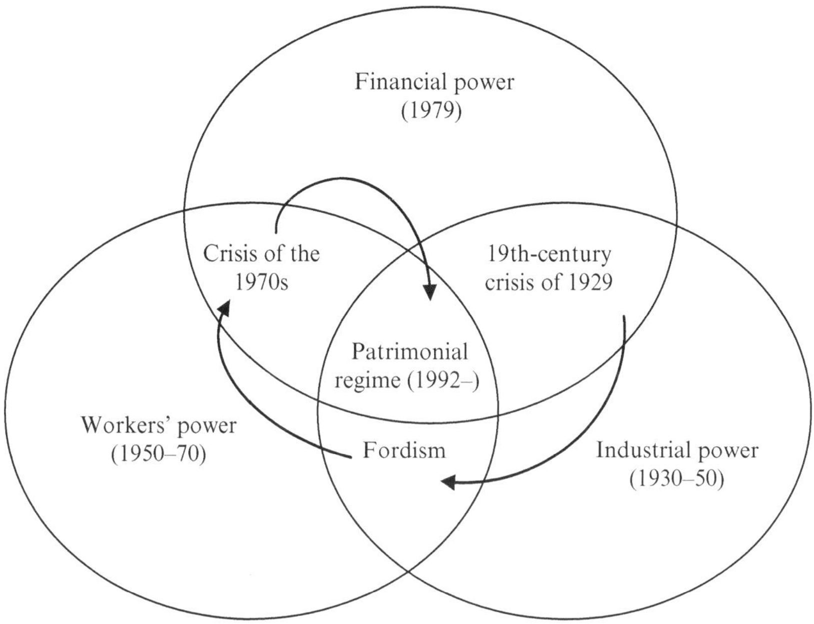

Figure 3.1 Evolution of conflicting solidarity between three social groups

seems rather negative in France. An explanation of this divergence will be attempted in this chapter.

The basic assumption consists in supposing that the accumulation pattern in France and in the USA, imposed by finance, has the same attributes and that the difference between the two economies depends mainly on the mode of regulation. The difficulty is then in formalizing the social power struggle, because institution hierarchy follows from this power struggle.

The social conflict is shaped by the former institutions and social history of the political economies in which it occurs. Thus, modifying the institutions is both an expression of and a limit to this capacity of transformation. Their representation can help us to understand what is at stake in the conflict, and possibly how a new *status quo* could be established. Figure 3.1 represents these evolutions more simply.

Capitalism has been through several phases of revival and stabilization of the social conflict. Figure 3.1 allows us to represent five different situations. The first one corresponds to a crisis in which no agreement is possible between the three social groups. Modelling can illustrate this situation by an overdetermination of distribution relations leading to a structural instability such as those disclosed in the Harrod–Domar model.

Three intermediate situations, known as social conflict stabilization, are possible. An agreement between financiers and industrialists is feasible, as it was during the second half of the nineteenth century. The payroll is then subordinate to financial profitability requirements, as well as the demands related to the financing of capital accumulation. In these conditions, wages constitute a remainder truly dependent on the economic situation (competing wage convention – Boyer 1978). Once industrialization is well established and as soon as luxury consumption no longer manages to satisfy the outlet needs for the industry, the institutions of 1930s capitalism clearly appear conflicting. This type of crisis gave rise to the Fordist period: an 'agreement' between employees and industrialists against financiers. With the Fordist crisis, workers' power, which tended to free itself from the other two social groups, was deeply impaired, while industrial power was reconstructed and financial power continued to recover its strength before the Second World War. However, weak wage incomes penalized this growth through consumption. To cancel this risk, depending on the viability of an accumulation pattern, it is necessary to define allowances that will allow wage-related demand to be maintained at a satisfactory level. Indebtedness and price-cutting of capital goods, as features of the global economy, are involved in maintaining purchasing power. Nevertheless, with the given model, where households cannot get into debt in a closed economy, only financial incomes can offset low wages. This situation corresponds to the theoretical structure of patrimonial capitalism. From a social point of view, this configuration constitutes a singular situation in which a balance between the three social groups can be reached.

This situation would be possible because of weak workers' power, enabling reforms that would institutionally validate the position of workers' power, like wage flexibilization of the wage–labour nexus and liberal management of social protection. These modifications would increase long-term saving, which increases firms' capital stock, and would reinforce the productive discipline through market vigilance and hostile operations. Financiers organize these transformations for the benefit of the financial capital holders among whom an increasingly significant part of employees are found. From a macroeconomic point of view, the reduction of wages is offset by allowances of financial origin (dividends and capital gains in this model).

The different configurations are justified by the concepts that theoretically found the consistency of the finance-led regime in a regulationist approach: institutional hierarchy and complementarity. Institutional hierarchy is represented by the methods of income distribution, while the complementarities are transcribed in the consumption function. The variable that carries the distribution closure identifies the social group in a weak position. The group, whose incomes are established as a fixed share of GDP or investment, determines degrees in the social hierarchy. It is thus possible to define the balance of power between the three actors in the model: households, firms and shareholders. These various rules of income distribution, incorporated in a specific institutional structure, generate more or less coherent situations, according to the determination rules of the consumption level. The most coherent financialized regime is represented by weak workers' power, an intermediate situation for industrial power and a dominant position for the financiers. In this configuration, wages are less important but financial incomes are higher. As a consequence, the propensity to spend wage incomes and financial incomes must change so that the rise in financial incomes can compensate for the fall in wages in the definition of the consumption level. In the case of a wage reduction imposed by an increase in dividends, consumption and growth can be maintained, whereas in a more Fordist regime, where demand remains largely defined by wage incomes, consumption and growth would decrease. Institutional inconsistencies thus contribute to explaining the divergences concerning the evolution of the French and American economies faced with the rise of finance. In all configurations, wages are totally subordinate. They constitute a remainder. Profits should take this form in a traditional conception of the economy. In the following section, these questions will be examined in more detail.

2. PRESENTATION OF THE MODEL

First we present the model accounting framework; then models are presented through their equations and their various closures.

2.1 The Social Accounting Framework

The model represents a closed economy, made up of 31 equations. Three agents are present: households, companies and banks. The households have three types of earnings, wages (*Wd*), dividends (*Fdm*) and interest paid by the banks that remunerate their deposits ($rm*Md_{(-1)}$). Companies receive the proceeds from their production (*GDP*), plus the dividends from their stockholding (*Fde*). Companies can buy back part of their own equities. The interest of such a transaction lies in the possibility of exploring the consequences of equity repurchase policy such as they were implemented in the USA[2] and more recently in France. Company savings, or retained profit (*Fu*), increase in debt (ΔLs) and new issues of securities ($pe*\Delta es$) are the resources that ensure the financing of productive and financial capital.

Table 3.1 Income statement

	Uses			Resources		
	Households	Companies	Banks	Households	Companies	Banks
Services and goods	Cd	Id			PIB	
Wages		Ws		Wd		
Dividends		Fd		Fdm	Fde	
Interests			$rm * Md_{(-1)}$	$rm * Md_{(-1)}$		
		$rl * Ld_{(-1)}$				$rl * Ld_{(-1)}$
Self-financing		Fu			Fu	
Deposits	ΔMd					ΔMs
Loans			ΔLd		ΔLs	
Equities	$pe * \Delta Edm$	$pe * \Delta Ede$			$pe * \Delta Es$	

Table 3.2 Balance sheets

	Assets			Liabilities		
	Households	Companies	Banks	Households	Companies	Banks
Fixed capital		K				
Deposits	Md					Ms
Loans			Ls		Ld	
Equities	$pe * Edm$	$pe * Ede$			$pe * Es$	
Wealth				V	Ve	0

Banks receive the debtor interest paid by companies ($rl * Ld_{(-1)}$). They lend money with household deposits (ΔMs). Households can use their incomes in three different ways: consumption (Cd), deposits (ΔMd) and equities ($\Delta Edm * pe$); see Table 3.1.

Companies pay wages (Ws), distribute dividends (Fd) and interest ($rl * Ld_{(-1)}$). They buy part of the equities on the stock market ($pe * \Delta Ede$). They finance investment (Id). Banks pay deposits interest to households ($rm * Md_{(-1)}$) and provide credit to companies (ΔLd).

The balance sheet (Table 3.2) describes the evolution of the asset stock of the various agents. Households' wealth (V) is composed of deposits and equities. The wealth of companies (Ve) comprises physical and financial assets ($pe * Ede$) minus liabilities: indebtedness and issued equities. Banks hold the loans to companies (Ls). Households' deposits are included in banks' liabilities.

2.2 Equations of the Model

The equations presented are successively those of the financial bloc, the demand bloc, the macroeconomic closure and distribution aspects. In this respect, only the first version of the model is described. The other configurations are specified in the Appendix 1.

The financial bloc

The first three equations represent the companies' behaviours in term of gross equity issue (1), firms' equity demand (2) and households' demand (3). Equation 3.1 defines companies' equity issuing. It is borrowed from Kaldor by Godley (1999). It corresponds to a fixed ratio between investment and equity issuing. This strict formalization is abandoned. The writing chosen for the equation takes as a starting point the econometric results established for France (Clévenot et al. 2010). It indicates the presence of a positive effect between the possibilities of firms' indebtedness refunding and equity issuing ($\tau_1 > 0$), as well as a positive elasticity regarding the debtor interest rate indicating a logical phenomenon of arbitration between the various sources of financing ($\tau_2 > 0$).

$$\frac{\Delta Es * pe}{\mathrm{I}} = \tau_1 * \left(\frac{L_{(-1)}}{Fu}\right) + \tau_2 * rl + \tau_0 \qquad (3.1)$$

Companies' stockholding behaviour is also inspired by the econometric results obtained for France. The variation of desired quantities of equities on the total assets of companies is defined by a positive relation between the profitability of the equities previously held ($\tau_1 * ree_{(-1)}$) and a positive relation with the return on investments ($\tau_2 * rcf$), which represents financing capacity.

$$\frac{\Delta Ede * pe}{((Ede * pe) + K)} = \eta_1 * ree_{(-1)} + \eta_2 * rcf_{(-1)} + \eta_0 \qquad (3.2)$$

Households' demand for equities is drawn up according to portfolio behaviour *à la* Tobin. It allows us to define the price of equities. One supposes a negative relationship with the deposits' profitability ($\psi_1 < 0$), a positive elasticity regarding the return on equity previously held by households ($\psi_2 > 0$) and a negative effect, related to a demand for liquid assets ($\psi_3 < 0$).

$$\left(\frac{pe * Edm}{V}\right)^* = \psi_1 * rm + \psi_2 * rem_{(-1)} + \psi_3 * \left(\frac{Yhr^*}{V^*}\right) + \psi_0 \qquad (3.3)$$

The three following accounting equations allow us to endogeneize the overall equity demand (*Ed*), which corresponds to the demand of households (*Edm*) and companies (*Ede*). The net equity supply of the companies (*Ese*) is obtained by subtracting the companies' demand (*Ede*) from gross equity issuing (*Es*). Lastly, households' demand is logically equivalent to the net supply of firms (3.6).

$$Ed = Edm + Ede \tag{3.4}$$

$$Ese = Es - Ede \tag{3.5}$$

$$Edm = Ese \tag{3.6}$$

The variation of households' deposits (ΔMd) is determined by an accounting equation that shows that deposits correspond to a balance between the different household incomes. The variation of households' wealth (ΔV) corresponds to an increase in saving, that is, unused incomes, from which it is necessary to take away the uses related to financial accumulation ($\Delta Edm * pe$), which reduce households' cash as well as capital gains, which are already considered in the evolution of wealth ($\Delta pe * Edm_{(-1)}$).

$$\Delta Md = \Delta V - pe * \Delta Edm - Edm_{(-1)} * \Delta pe \tag{3.7}$$

Companies' debt (ΔLd) also corresponds to a 'buffer', namely an adjustment variable that allows companies to fill in the weakness of their financing sources for investment, if necessary, when self-financing (*Fu*) and new net equity issue are not enough ($\Delta Ese * pe$). The accounting structure is fixed so that the amount of money supplied by households through the banks exactly corresponds to the needs of companies, without writing the explicit equation of this equality ($L = M$), which rises from the accounting balance of the model and which can be checked at the time of simulations.

$$\Delta Ld = I - Fu - \Delta Edm * pe - Fde^{3} \tag{3.8}$$

The amount of deposits anticipated by households (Md^*) fits with the difference between their level of expected wealth (V^*) and the amount of their financial saving ($Edm * pe$).

$$Md^* = V^* - (Edm * pe) \tag{3.9}$$

Debtor interest rate is equal to credit interest rate so as to avoid mentioning banking profits which would complicate the model. The debtor rate is exogenous.

$$rm = rl \tag{3.10}$$

The two following equations represent the capital gains realized respectively by households and companies.

$$CGm = \Delta pe * Edm_{(-1)} \tag{3.11}$$

$$CGe = \Delta pe * Ede_{(-1)} \tag{3.12}$$

Equations (3.13) and (3.14) establish the amount of dividends received by households and companies, which corresponds respectively to the share of equities held by households and by companies.

$$Fdm = Fd * \left(\frac{Edm}{Es}\right) \tag{3.13}$$

$$Fde = Fd * \left(\frac{Ede}{Es}\right) \tag{3.14}$$

Equations (3.15) and (3.16) establish the rate of profitability of the equities held by households (*rem*) and by companies (*ree*).

$$ree = \frac{(Fde + CGe)}{(pe_{(-1)} * Ede_{(-1)})} \tag{3.15}$$

$$rem = \frac{(Fdm + CGm)}{(pe_{(-1)} * Edm_{(-1)})} \tag{3.16}$$

The evolution of effective wealth (ΔV) results from households' saving, to which capital gains are added. Expected wealth level corresponds to the previous wealth level into which household saving is incorporated, namely expected incomes minus consumption plus capital gains.

$$\Delta V = Yhr - Cons + CGm \tag{3.17}$$

$$V^* = V_{(-1)} + Yhr^* + CGm - Cons \tag{3.18}$$

The demand bloc

Two specifications are chosen to define consumption. In the first two patterns, it is identical (3.19′ and 3.19″). Household consumption is related to two propensities, first to use up expected incomes ($\alpha_1 * Yhr^*$) and second to spend wealth ($\alpha_3 * V_{(-1)}$).

$$Cons = \alpha_0 + \alpha_1 * Yhr^* + \alpha_2 * V_{(-1)} \tag{3.19'}$$

In the last pattern, the propensity to spend incomes is reduced ($\alpha_1 = 0.8$, $\alpha_{11} = 0.7$), so as to reveal the institutional complementarity necessary to the consistency of finance-led regime induced by the modification of institutional hierarchy. The propensity to use up dividends and wealth does not change ($\alpha_{12} = 0.8$, $\alpha_2 = 0.05$). On the other hand, the propensity to spend monetary incomes is reduced ($\alpha_{13} = 0.5$), in order to diminish the effect of a rise in activity induced by the increase in monetary incomes after the rise in interest rates.

$$Cons = \alpha_0 + \alpha_{11} * W_{(-1)} + \alpha_{12} * Fd_{(-1)} + \alpha_{13} * rl * L_{(-1)} + \alpha_2 * V_{(-1)} \tag{3.19''}$$

The regular income follows the Haig–Simon definition chosen by Godley. It corresponds to the addition of the resources drawn from dividends as well as of the interest received by households from their deposit.

$$Yhr = W + Fdm + rm * M_{(-1)} \tag{3.20}$$

Expectations are very rough compared to models with microeconomic foundations, but it is a theoretical choice, meaning that at agglomerate level, there are regularities between various ratios. Expected income rises like the projection of past incomes multiplied by the effective growth rate of previous income.

$$gy = \frac{\Delta Yhr}{Yhr_{(-1)}} \tag{3.21}$$

$$Yhr^* = (1 + gy_{(-1)}) * Yhr_{(-1)} \tag{3.22}$$

The rate of capital accumulation determines the companies' demand for investment. This equation retains an acceleration effect by demand ($\phi_3 = 0.015$) and financial variables, the elasticity regarding profit rate ($\phi_1 = 0.5$), the elasticity regarding indebtedness ratio ($\phi_2 = 0.25$) as well as a positive constant ($\phi_0 > 0$).

$$g = \phi_1 * rcf_{(-1)} - \phi_2 * \left(\frac{L_{(-1)}}{K_{(-1)}}\right) + \phi_3 * \left(\frac{\Delta PIB}{PIB_{(-1)}}\right) + \phi_0 \tag{3.23}$$

Investment level rises from the rate of accumulation applied to capital stock at a previous period.

$$I = g * K_{(-1)} \tag{3.24}$$

$$K = K_{(-1)} * (1 - \delta + g) \tag{3.25}$$

Macroeconomic closure and distribution aspects

Distribution aspects are essential in the modelling of the inversion of institutional hierarchy. As a consequence, two equations are modified according to configurations, the gross profit equation (3.28‴), and the retained profits equation (3.29). The equation defining dividends does not evolve but the relationship between industrialists and financiers is modified through the equation of self-financing (3.29). The equation of wages is endogeneized, which underlines the wages' subordination in incomes distribution.

GDP corresponds to the sum of firms' investment and households' consumption.

$$PIB = Cons + I \tag{3.26}$$

Wages in this series of models are defined as would-be profits, in the form of a remainder. They are established by a balance between GDP and profits. Wages can then be defined as hierarchically inferior to self-financing (industrial power) and dividends (financial power).

$$W = PIB - Ft \tag{3.27}$$

Determining self-financing and gross profit equations will thus make it possible to fix the dominant social group of the model. In the first and last configurations, profits are defined in an accounting way as the sum of self-financing, dividends and debt burden. In the second one, they are established like a proportion of GDP. They are defined like wages (ι_1 =0.33).

$$Ft = Fu + Fd + rl * L_{(-1)} \tag{3.28$'$}$$

$$Ft = \iota_1 * PIB - W_0 \tag{3.28$''$}$$

$$Ft = Fu + Fd + rl * L_{(-1)} \tag{3.28$'''$}$$

The distribution of dividends is proportional to the gross profits level after debt repayment. The rule of dividends distribution is represented by (1 − *sf*). This expression underlines the pressure exerted by shareholders.

$$Fd = (1 - sf) * (Ft - rl * L_{(-1)}) \tag{3.29}$$

Self-financing in the first configuration is proportional to the investment observed in the previous period ($\vartheta_1 = 0.33$). In the second one, it is established like a remainder on the basis of gross profits, minus dividends and debt burden. In the last one, it is defined like wages by a proportion of GDP (υ_1=0.1).

$$Fu = \vartheta_1 * I_{(-1)} - W_0 \quad (3.30')$$

$$Fu = Ft - Fd - rl * L_{(-1)} \quad (3.30'')$$

$$Fu = \upsilon_1 * PIB_{(-1)} - W_0 \quad (3.30''')$$

Finally, one can establish the rate of profit as a ratio of profit over capital stock.

$$rcf = \frac{Fu}{K_{(-1)}} \quad (3.31)$$

The combination of these various methods of income distribution is supposed to help define the power of various social groups. Employees are the weakest. The relative position of industrialists and financiers must then be established.

In the first case, self-financing is imposed by industrialists as a fixed proportion of investment. Their situation is intermediate, they keep a decision margin but they don't enjoy growth directly. Defined in an accounting way, gross profit transfers the requirements of income distribution closure to employees. In the second case, gross profit is defined proportionally to GDP, which could lead one to believe that industrialists are dominant, but self-financing is defined as a remainder. Industrial power is thus limited and financiers are dominant in this configuration. It is the most financialized regime of the three. The importance of gross profits contributes to the reinforcement of paid dividends. In the last case, power is better distributed between industrialists and financiers since retained profit is directly fixed to GDP, industrialists can take advantage of the growth for investment financing. The accounting definition of gross profit makes it possible to transfer financial pressure on employees. This is the closest configuration to the patrimonial regime described by Aglietta (1998). In addition, the equation of consumption has been modified. Consumption is less dependent on wage incomes. Shareholders' pressures should thus less affect households' consumption.

The presentation of the results is graphically carried out, generally over 100 periods. These periods cannot be assimilated to years because the behavioural functions are established in an *ad hoc* way, so as to allow the different models to converge towards a steady position. It is the cost of the models' complexity. What is gained with macroeconomic closure, integration of financial phenomena and accounting coherence is lost with the consistency of behavioural functions. To remedy these disadvantages, models are retained only when they present good properties in terms of stability. Simulations are carried out on underlying models that are coherent from the macroeconomic point of view.[4] The interpretation of the results is carried out according to three periods: short, average and long term. In the short term, evolutions are described directly after the shock. In the medium term, the process of adjustment is studied. In the long term, the shock has been absorbed and the model becomes stable. Depending on the shocks, presentations can require fewer than 100 periods. In these cases, the periods covered by graphs are reduced to better perceive medium-term changes.

Simulations constitute the way to solve the model in its different closures. Simulations consist in modifying an exogenous parameter of the model and in observing the model behaviour after the shock. The graphs represent a deviation from baseline in percentage through the following formula:

$$\left(\frac{(X_1 - X_0)}{X_0}\right) * 100$$

Variable X, shocked in scenario 1, has notation X_1. The value of the initial variable has notation X_0. Some macroeconomic or financial variables are presented in order to clarify the model behaviour. Each configuration is illustrated by two graphs vertically organized so as to compare the different definitions.

3. SIMULATIONS OF THE MODELS (SEE APPENDIX 2)

Scenario 1: Increase in Wages

Wage increase is simulated by a final reduction of undistributed profits equivalent to 1 per cent of GDP for the year 2005. In that way, the opposition between wage and profit is underlined. As a matter of fact, it is not possible to operate differently considering the definition of wages as remainder of profits compared to GDP. One of the results in term of interest conflict also resides in the reduction of financial wealth importance, reducing the power of finance in proportion. In all configurations, contradictory evolutions in the short and the long run can be observed. The revival effect induced by wages dominates in the short run, while financial effects of supply recession dominate in the medium- and long-run evolutions. The sign of the evolutions of the three models is identical, but the level of each configuration can be rather different. Some symmetry can be observed in the first two regimes; the last one is on the contrary more asymmetric with a large divergence between the short and the long run. In Configuration 1, after five periods, the wages have increased by more than 20 %, consumption is up at 17 % and GDP at 12 % above baseline progression. Profits are reduced through the reduction in self-financing caused by the rise in wages. Gross profits are also relevant since they are established as the sum of dividends, interest paid and self-financing. Reduction in gross profits involves a reduction in dividends. Investment is reduced, faced with both indebtedness increase and profit reduction, although the positive acceleration effect maintains it during the first periods after the shock, close to baseline progression. The explosion of wages is explained by the shock but also by the rise in GDP. As gross profits do not depend directly on GDP, their increase is less significant, which increases wages in proportion. The logic of the model, structurally unfavourable to employees, is reversed in this case. The different impacts for Configuration 2 are easily explained. The shock relates to gross profits, which divides the impact of the shock on self-financing by approximately 3. The ratio between gross profits and undistributed profits is one to three. In the last configuration, the effects of wage rises are very quickly cancelled out. The reduction of dividends cannot be compensated by the rise in wages.

Scenario 2: Increase in Equity Issuing

The increase in equity issuing is simulated by a positive variation of the constant τ_0 in equation (3.1). It leads to an increase in the equity financing of investment equivalent to 1 per cent of the investment for 2005. The raising of the constant is permanent. The expected effects are an indebtedness reduction and an increase in investment and growth. These are precisely the results obtained in the three configurations. A negative effect can be noted: the dilution effect related to the increasing equity issuing but a volume effect can compensate for this fall in prices.

The evolutions are very close for all configurations. Investment is the first element that pushes growth. It is due to indebtedness reduction and to the increase in retained earnings. In the first configuration, gross profits increase less quickly than GDP, which leads to a clear rise in wages, which maintains demand from employees. The virtuous sequence between consumption and investment is set up. In the second configuration, the distributed profits increase most quickly after investment. The rise in gross profits also induces an increase in undistributed profits. A less important driving force is observed for the third configuration. Investment slightly deviates from the other variables, contrary to the first two configurations. Consumption is lower than in the baseline during the first periods following the shock, whereas wages and distributed dividends increase, yet less markedly than in previous situations. At the same time, monetary incomes decrease, and shareholders sustain capital losses.

Scenario 3: Increase in Households' Equities

The rise in household shareholding is simulated through the increase in ψ_0, the constant in equation (3.3), which determines the household portfolio behaviour. This variation aims at increasing by 1 per cent the share of equities in household financial capital. It goes from approximately 43 % to more than 44 %. Contrary to preceding scenarios, this shock generates effects that are specific to each configuration, with a surprising effect for the first one, namely an evolution that becomes negative in the long run. In spite of some contradictory oscillations in the medium run, the two following ones converge in the long run towards the expected results, yet with weak effects on growth, since after 40 periods GDP is only 1 per cent above the reference scenario. For more financial aspects, the evolution of equity prices is opposed to the evolution of the total portfolio of equities held, which is explained by diversification phenomena generated by the stability of actors' portfolio behaviour.

Configuration 1 diverges from expectations. Immediately after the shock, investment decreases while an increase in indebtedness can be noticed, in opposition to the intuition of an increase in firms shareholders' equity. During the very first periods, firms increase their financial investments because of the rising equity prices initiated by the increase in households' demand. Real economy and financial economy are opposed. This first movement is symmetrical to an increase in wages, consumption and GDP. It is induced by the reduction of self-financing caused by investment reduction. Undistributed profit depends on the previous period investment. The reduction in self-financing negatively affects gross profits, which increases wages. Investment is restored by demand acceleration effects as well as profit recovery and debt reduction. Yet growth does not become stable, but plummets. Consumption alone cannot lead investment. The fixing of self-financing on former investment harms the capacity of finance, which results in an inescapable increase in indebtedness. In Configuration 2, short-run indebtedness, caused by firms' financial investments, increases again. The definition of self-financing less unfavourable to firms in the last configurations allows to reduce the debt and finally to revive investment.

Scenario 4: Increase in Dividends

The increase in dividends is simulated by the reduction of (*sf*) in equation (3.29) establishing the distribution of profits. Dividends initially represent 18 % of GDP, that is, 64 % of gross profits. The shock consists in increasing them by 1 per cent of GDP. Dividends then reach 19 % of GDP. The expected results are related to the nature of the model. The rise in dividends is financed either by a reduction in self-financing or by a cut in wages. The question posed here is whether the fall in investment in the first case or of consumption in the second one will be compensated by an increase in firms' and households' financial funds. The last configuration is not ambiguous. In the short and the long run alike, the increase in dividends can compensate for the cut in wages. This process is facilitated by the modification of the consumption equation where the propensity to consume wages has been reduced. The fall in earned incomes affects consumption less strongly. Moreover, the way of establishing profits does not penalize firms' accounts since the shock is transferred to wages. Indebtedness is reduced, which supports investment. In addition, the impact of increased dividend on firms is limited in so far as firms also take advantage of this rise, as do shareholders. In the second configuration, undistributed profits are used to finance the rise in dividends. Consumption is led by financial incomes, but firms' accounts are penalized. The increase in investment cannot be maintained. GDP evolution, which is confused with wages evolution, becomes clearly negative shortly before the fortieth period. In Configuration 1, total evolution is symmetrical. Adjustment focuses on wages, while firms defer all their financial constraints on employees. Consumption follows decreasing wages. Conversely, firms invest more because of the reduction of their indebtedness level, partly due to the rise in dividends, which depends on gross profits. The reduction in wages inflates gross profits, which explains the surge of dividends. Maintaining investment helps to contain the fall of activity. The rise in dividends finally manages to compensate for the cut in wages. The total demand is revived five periods after the shock and recovers a level close to the baseline at the 25th period.

Scenario 5: Share Buybacks by Firms

In this last scenario, the variation of the constant η_0 increases by 1 per cent of firms' shareholding. The share buyback policies have become numerous. Through these policies, firms try to increase shareholder value, to protect themselves against unfriendly takeovers and to increase their absorption capacity. All these elements of industrial economy cannot be recalled within the chosen macroeconomic structure. Attention is focused on the macroeconomic consequences of such practices. Effects are unspecified *a priori*, because the cash used in share buybacks is of course not used for productive investment, but income flows could be used for sellers' consumption. At the macroeconomic level, this leak effect disappears. By contrast, the increase in equity prices constitutes a potential escape, a kind of inflation, if it does not correspond to an equivalent increase in produced value when equities are resold.[5]

This ambivalence shows through in all configurations where the first movement is a decline in activity related to the increase in indebtedness. The question of the debt ratio used, debt over fixed capital stock, can be asked in so far as an increase in financial wealth is noticed at the same time. A financial illusion process could arise in reality, especially in a context of regular increase in equity prices that would not penalize investment and could generate cumulative dynamics, which does not appear in the model. In Configuration 1, the positive effects of share buyback appears after 40 periods; in the second one, it is necessary to wait 75 periods. The coherence of the third configuration seems stronger. Positive effects appear after 15 periods. Configuration 2 is the easiest to interpret. Financial investment generates indebtedness, which penalizes physical investment. Once the first shock wave is absorbed, indebtedness decreases and the rate of profit is stabilized, whereas wages, consumption and growth continue to fall. Thereafter, the reduction of indebtedness allows a resurgence of investment. This stimulates growth, wages, dividends and consumption. Economy breaks the deadlock. The procyclic nature of the model explains the crisis intensity. Gross profits fixed on GDP collapse with GDP. Undistributed profits follow suit and also suffer from the rise in indebtedness. In Configuration 1, undistributed profits are fixed on past investment, which can contain cumulative fall. Gross profit corresponds to the sum of distributed and undistributed profits, together with debt service. The fall in undistributed profits is controlled, while debt service increases. On the other hand, consumption and GDP evolve more favourably than in the short run in Configuration 2, but are less enduring. The good performance of gross profits gives rise to important dividends, which allow consumption resurgence. Configuration 3 experiences a short-term evolution less unfavourable than the first one, but its long-term evolution is less sustained. After the shock, it is the only one to maintain consumption. Gross profits are slightly reduced. This involves wage increase, reinforced by the increase in monetary incomes.

Investment decline is partially compensated by the maintenance of consumption. The shock is quickly absorbed because of the weak impact on investment and consumption. Indebtedness is less strongly reduced than in Configuration 3, which explains the very gentle investment curve. Finally, the differences between the many configurations seem to be summed up through the significance of equity prices evolution. The most developed financial wealth is, the most reduced indebtness gets. As a consequence, growth is encouraged.

CONCLUSION

The method developed by the SFC approach seems able to explain the specificities of finance-led capitalism. Structural models can clarify all the different flows and stocks links, as well as the influence of wealth effects and leverage. Regulation theory specifies the transformations that have taken place in contemporary capitalism through the inversion of institutional hierarchy, the rise of financial power and the backward flow of workers' power.

The most salient results of these various experiments relate to the opposition between wage increase, which plays a negative part as expected in a financialized regime, together with the rise in dividends, which on the contrary acts positively in two cases out of three. These contradictory evolutions can provide theoretical elements to explain the divergences between France and the USA, within the context of a closed and financialized economy. France is faced with an absence of consistent institutions, which concerns at the same time its economy structures, its place in the world economy as well as its regulation mode, inherited from the Fordist period.

From an economic point of view, France has gone into financialization. However, from a political point of view concerning the mode of regulation, there is resistance to the complete adoption of a financialized regime. The increase in ensuing inequalities and the excluding nature of a finance-led regime both generate political resistance. Consequently, France has entered a financialized accumulation pattern, which is restrained by extra-economic elements and which does not prevent a reduced and profitable capital accumulation but keeps full employment at bay. In order to attain a sustained high growth within a context of increasing financialization, some institutional complementarities must emerge. In their absence, the financial burden penalizes economic growth. In the model presented in this chapter, firms profit from financial dynamics, as do shareholders. Thus, when firms are not penalized by the form of income distribution, growth can be more constant.

However, these results are conditioned by a strong household involvement in the financial market. Yet this is very uneven, even in the USA. In France, this involvement is at a lower level, but it is just as concentrated. Financial wealth effects have indeed appeared in the USA, but real-estate wealth effects have been more powerful, relegated by a rising households' debt. So as to identify an accumulation pattern, it is necessary to establish the dynamic coherence of the American economic system. With this intention, the international regime question, which is not treated in present closed models, cannot be avoided. Consequently, even if these models may account for the first regulationist intuitions about the existence of a patrimonial regime, they cannot describe the reality of the American macroeconomic closing in such a restricted context. To explain the working of the American economy, the model should be open; households should be able to incur debt and to hold houses and financial assets.

From a theoretical point of view, the model meets some limits. Concerning the treatment of equity prices, a model with endogenuously determined equity prices has been tested, but it generates some paradoxical portfolio behaviours. An exogenous determination of equity prices should be tested. The theoretical context of endogenous money is not fit to describe a financialized regime where companies undergo financial constraints. Finally, to improve the model, it would be interesting to introduce two types of households (poor and rich). The first type would depend on wages and the second on dividends and capital gains. In addition, two sectors could be brought in, small and big companies, differentiated by their access to equity finance and by their participation in general to stock market dynamics.

NOTES

1. Many thanks to Isabelle Métais for her invaluable help in translating this chapter.
2. In the USA, net equity issues have been negative since the mid-1990s. The argument specifying that liberalization would make it possible to reduce financing costs is thus called into question. This flaw emphasizes a second aspect of financial liberalization: the capacity to operate quick capital restructuring. This element constitutes the central point of contemporary financial logic: financial capital liquid assets.
3. Equation 3.8 should be written as follows: $\Delta Ld = I - Fu - \Delta Ese * pe - Fde$, where the needs for external financing are represented by the difference between the level of investment minus self-financing and the net issuing of firms. However, it is written using the net equity household purchases, which is equivalent from an accounting point of view, but it reduces the difference with initial values because of calibration difficulties, so that the equality $Ld = Md$ is immediately observed, allowing us to validate the accounting consistency of the model. Otherwise, convergence is underlying and not instantaneous. In order to correct this calibration problem, this option is chosen.

4. They do not present any anomaly in relative level: shares of wage in GDP, of investment and of equity prices, and their respective quantity, are always positive at the time of the shocks. The level of relevant ratios is defined by the parameters' value, and all the models' variables; see Appendices.
5. If an important gap is observed between fundamental and nominal equity values at the time of equity resale, a depreciation process can occur. The rise in equity prices is driven by demand while launching pension funds. Once it is ripe, the capitalized pension system can involve a fall in equity prices or inflation because of share selling, with the same result regarding purchasing power.

REFERENCES

Aglietta, M. (1998), 'Le Capitalisme de demain', *Note de la fondation Saint-Simon*, no. 101, novembre.

Aglietta, M. (2000), 'Shareholder value and corporate governance: some tricky questions', *Economy and Society*, **29** (1), 146–59.

Aglietta, M. and Breton, R. (2001), 'Financial systems, corporate control, and capital accumulation', *Economy and Society*, **30** (4), 433–66.

Aglietta, M. and Rebérioux, A. (2004), *L'instabilité du capitalisme financier*, Paris: Albin Michel.

Amable, B. (2005), *The Diversity of Modem Capitalism*, Oxford: Oxford University Press.

Ben Gamra, S. and Clévenot, M. (2006), 'Libéralisation financière et crises bancaires dans les pays tiers. La prégnance du rôle des institutions', CEPN Working Paper No. WP2006-08. Available at http://www.univ-paris13.fr/CEPN/wp2006_08.pdf.

Boyer, R. (1978), 'L'évolution des salaires en longue période', *Economie et Statistique*, no. 103, 27–57.

Boyer, R. (2000), 'Is a finance-led growth regime a viable alternative to Fordism? A preliminary analysis', *Economy and Society*, **29** (1), 111–45.

Clévenot, M., Guy, Y. and Mazier, J. (2010), 'Investment and rate of profit in a financial context. The French case', *International Review of Applied Economics*, **24** (6), 693–714.

Foley, D.K. (1975), 'On two specifications of asset equilibrium in macroeconomic models', *Journal of Political Economy*, **83** (2), 303–24.

Godley, W. (1999), 'Money and credit in a Keynesian model of income determination', *Cambridge Journal of Economics*, **23** (4), 393–411.

Lavoie, M. and Godley, W. (2001), 'Kaleckian models of growth in a coherent stock–flow monetary framework: a Kaldorian view', *Journal of Post Keynesian Economics*, **24** (2), 277–312.

Taylor, L. (2004a), 'Exchange rate *in*determinacy in portfolio balance, Mundell–Fleming and uncovered interest rate parity models', *Cambridge Journal of Economics*, **28** (2), 205–27.

Taylor, L. (2004b), *Reconstructing Macroeconomics: Structuralist Proposals and Critiques on the Mainstream*, Cambridge, MA: Harvard University Press.

APPENDIX 1 SUMMARY OF THE THREE CONFIGURATIONS

(3.1) $$\frac{\Delta Es * pe}{I} = \tau_1 * \left(\frac{L_{(-1)}}{Fu}\right) + \tau_2 * rl + \tau_0$$

(3.2) $$\frac{\Delta Ede * pe}{((Ede * pe) + K)} = \eta_1 * ree_{(-1)} + \eta_2 * rcf_{(-1)} + \eta_0$$

(3.3) $$\left(\frac{pe * Edm}{V}\right)^* = \psi_1 * rm + \psi_2 * rem_{(-1)} + \psi_3 * \left(\frac{Yhr^*}{V^*}\right) + \psi_0$$

(3.4) $$Ed = Edm + Ede$$

(3.5) $$Ese = Es - Ede$$

(3.6) $$Edm = Ese$$

(3.7) $$\Delta Md = \Delta V - pe * \Delta Edm - Edm_{(-1)} * \Delta pe$$

(3.8) $$\Delta Ld = I - Fu - \Delta Edm * pe - Fde$$

(3.9) $$Md^* = V^* - (Edm * pe)$$

(3.10) $$rm = rl$$

(3.11) $$CGm = \Delta pe * Edm_{(-1)}$$

(3.12) $$CGe = \Delta pe * Ede_{(-1)}$$

(3.13) $$Fdm = Fd * \left(\frac{Edm}{Es}\right)$$

(3.14) $$Fde = Fd * \left(\frac{Ede}{Es}\right)$$

(3.15) $$ree = \frac{(Fde + CGe)}{(pe_{(-1)} * Ede_{(-1)})}$$

(3.16) $$rem = \frac{(Fdm + CGm)}{(pe_{(-1)} * Edm_{(-1)})}$$

(3.17) $$\Delta V = Yhr - Cons + CGm$$

(3.18) $$V^* = V_{(-1)} + Yhr^* + CGm - Cons$$

(3.20) $$Yhr = W + Fdm + rm * M_{(-1)}$$

$$(3.21)\quad gy = \frac{\Delta Yhr}{Yhr_{(-1)}}$$

$$(3.22)\quad Yhr^* = (1 + gy_{(-1)}) * Yhr_{(-1)}$$

$$(3.23)\quad g = \phi_1 * rcf_{(-1)} - \phi_2 * \left(\frac{L_{(-1)}}{K_{(-1)}}\right) + \phi_3 * \left(\frac{\Delta PIB}{PIB_{(-1)}}\right) + \phi_0$$

$$(3.24)\quad I = g * K_{(-1)}$$

$$(3.25)\quad K = K_{(-1)} * (1 - \delta + g)$$

$$(3.26)\quad PIB = Cons + I$$

$$(3.31)\quad rcf = \frac{Fu}{K_{(-1)}}$$

Configuration 1

$$(3.19')\quad Cons = \alpha_0 + \alpha_1 * Yhr^* + \alpha_2 * V_{(-1)}$$

$$(3.28')\quad Ft = Fu + Fd + rl * L_{(-1)}$$

$$(3.30')\quad Fu = \vartheta_1 * I_{(-1)} - W_0$$

Configuration 2

$$(3.19')\quad Cons = \alpha_0 + \alpha_1 * Yhr^* + \alpha_2 * V_{(-1)}$$

$$(3.28'')\quad Ft = \iota_1 * PIB - W_0$$

$$(3.29'')\quad Fd = (1 - sf) * (Ft - rl * L_{(-1)})$$

$$(3.30'')\quad Fu = Ft - Fd - rl * L_{(-1)}$$

Configuration 3

$$(3.19''')\quad Cons = \alpha_0 + \alpha_{11} * W_{(-1)} + \alpha_{12} * Fd_{(-1)} + \alpha_{13} * rl * L_{(-1)} + \alpha_2 * V_{(-1)}$$

$$(3.28''')\quad Ft = Fu + Fd + rl * L_{(-1)}$$

$$(3.29)\quad Fd = (1 - sf) * (Ft - rl * L_{(-1)})$$

$$(3.30''')\quad Fu = \upsilon_1 * PIB_{(-1)} - W_0$$

APPENDIX 2 SCENARIOS

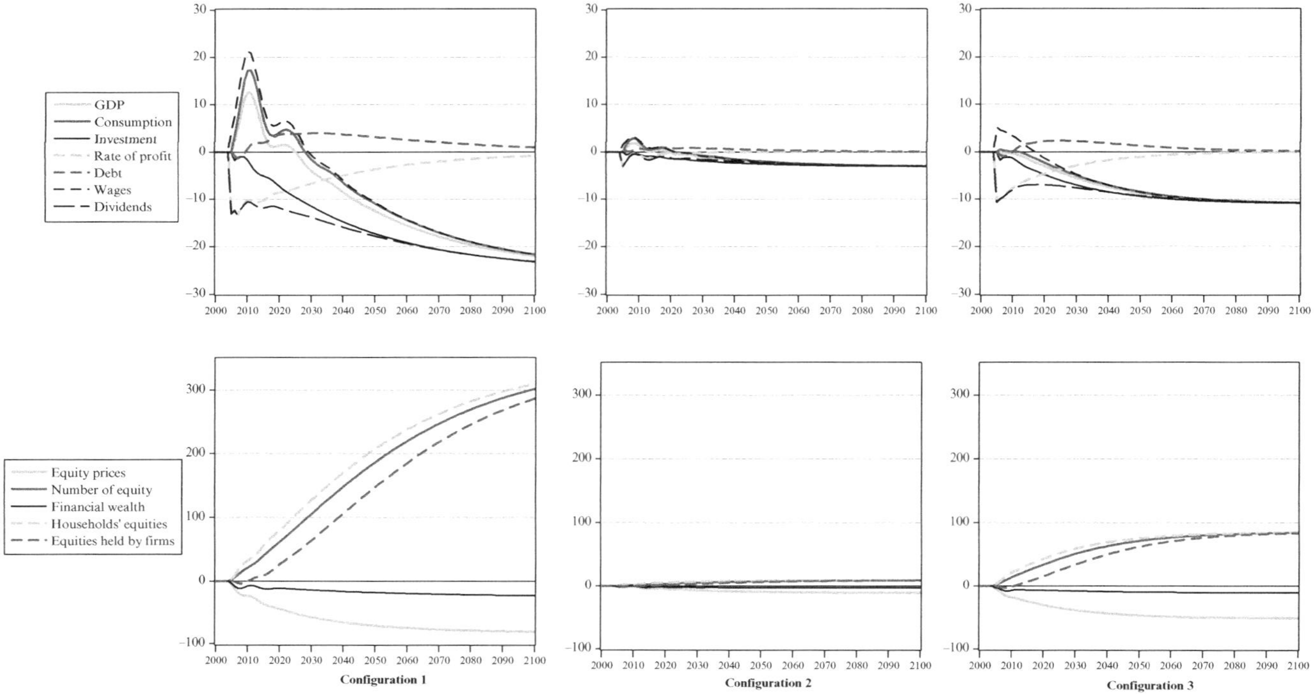

Figure 3A.1 Increase in wages equivalent to 1 per cent of GDP

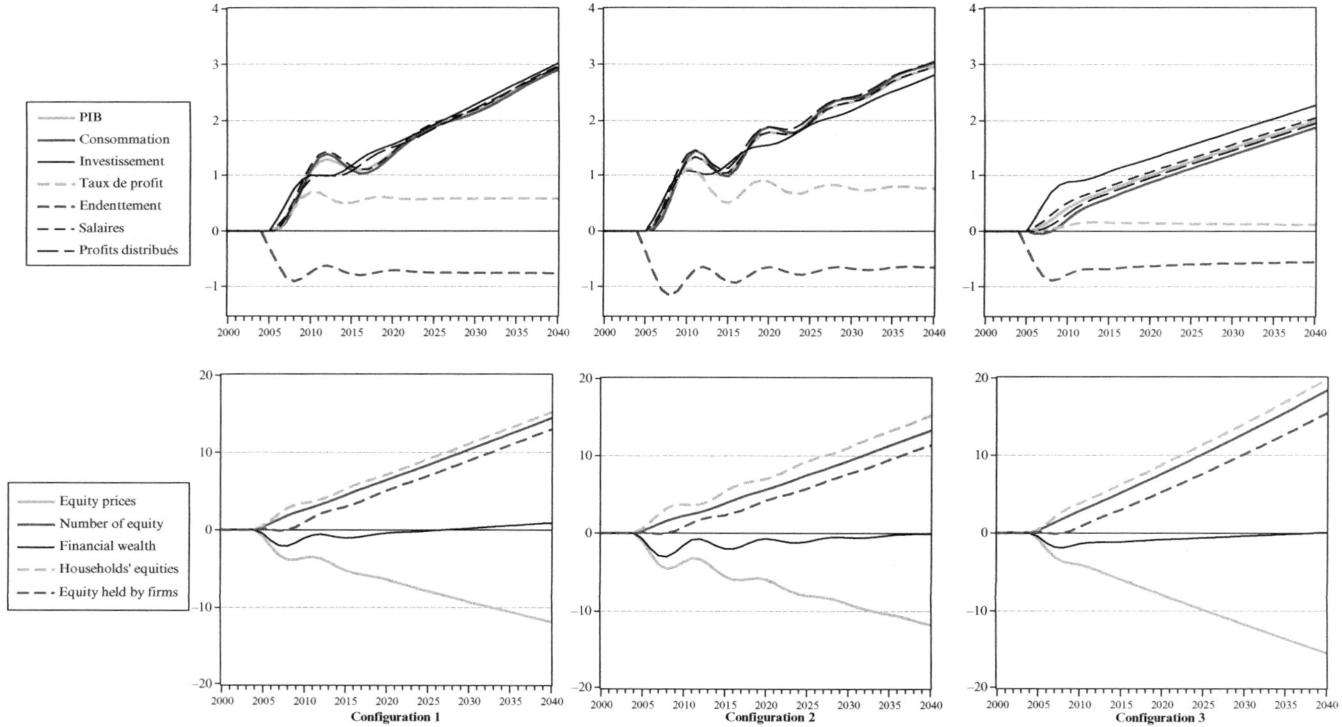

Figure 3A.2 Increase in equity issuing equivalent to 1 per cent of GDP

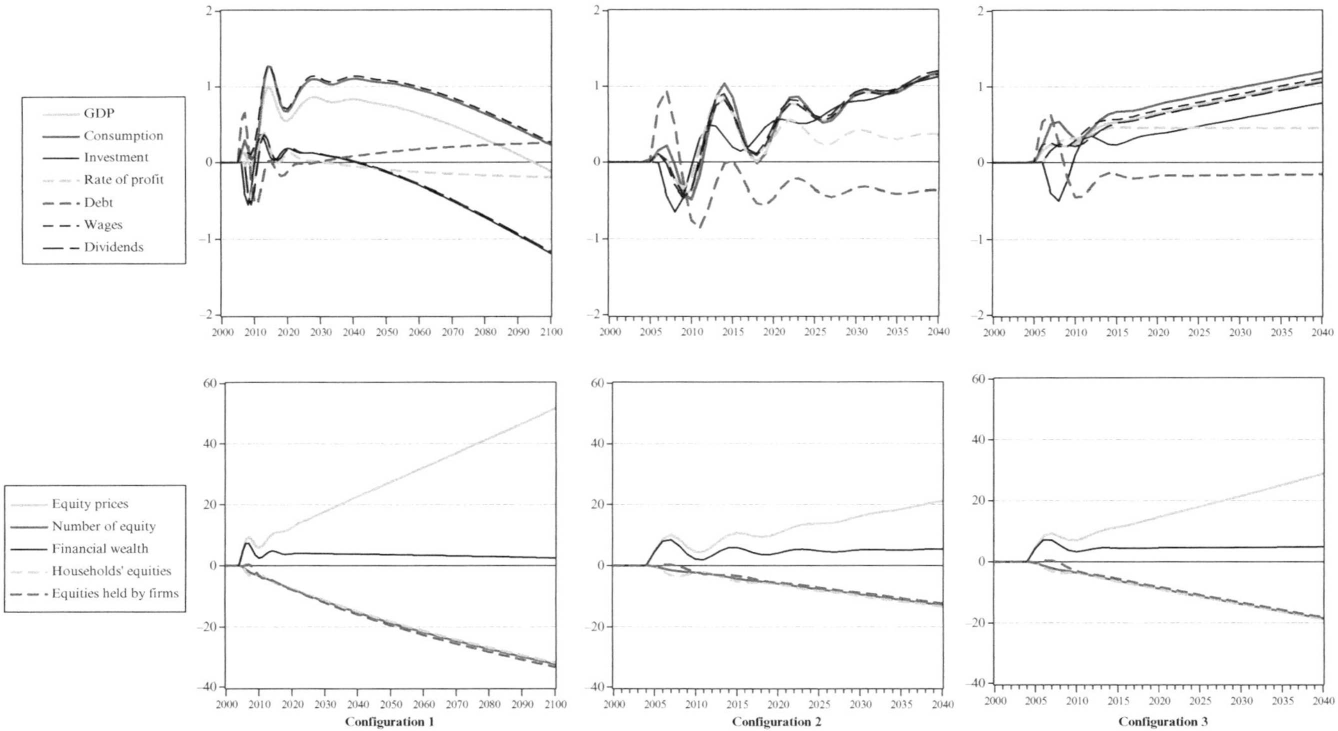

Figure 3A.3 Increase in households' equities equivalent to 1 per cent of their financial wealth

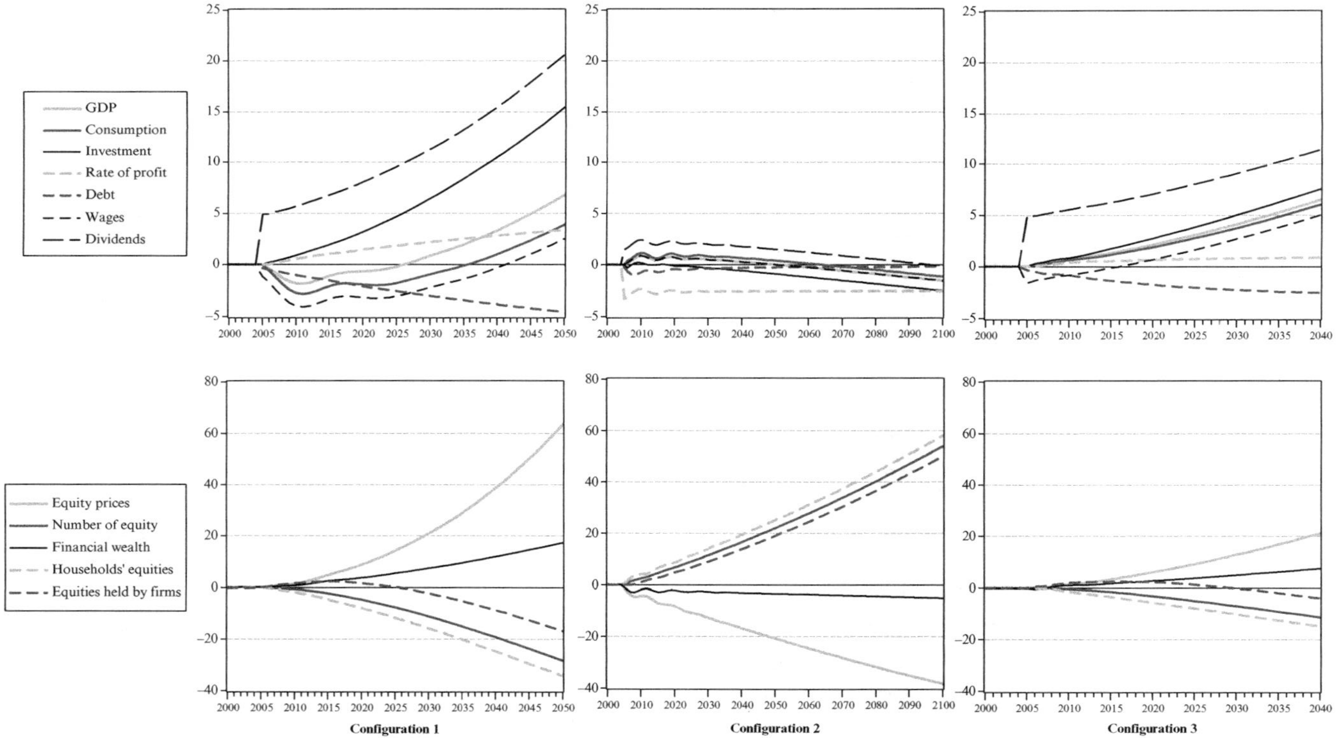

Figure 3A.4 Increase in dividends equivalent to 1 per cent of GDP

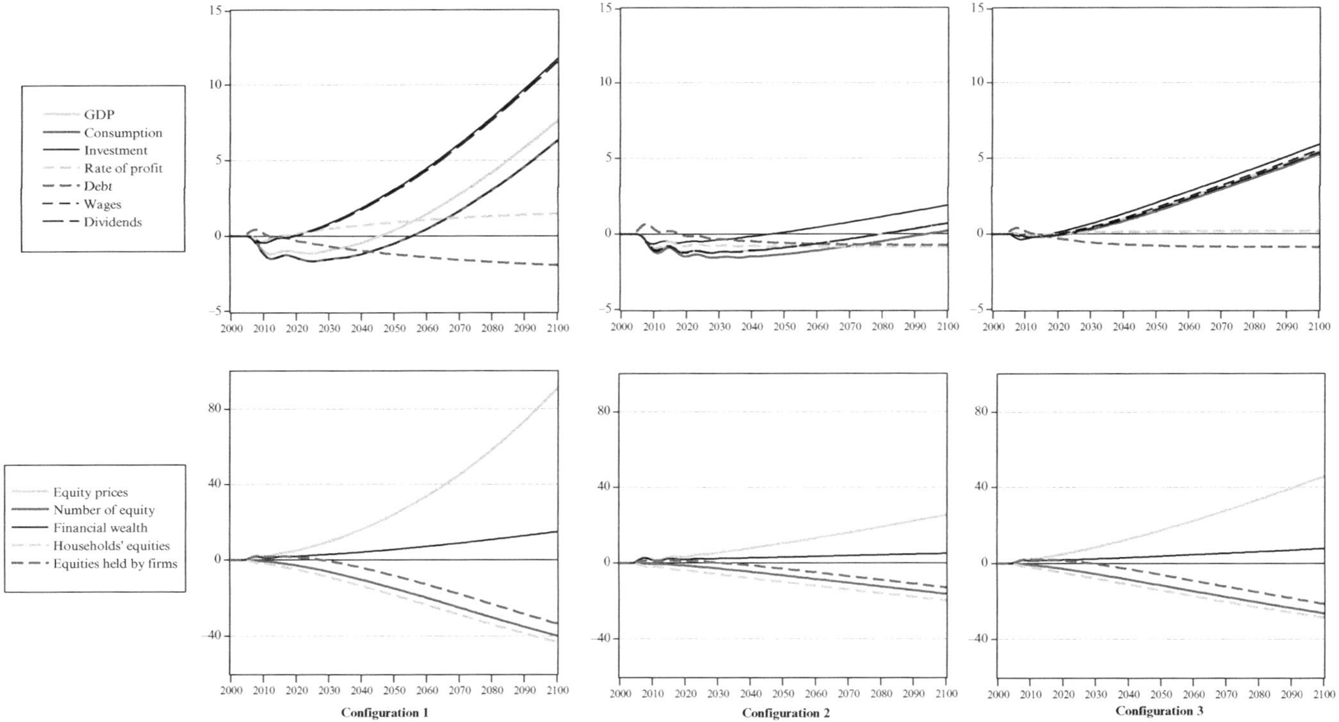

Figure 3A.5 Increase of 1 per cent in share buyback by firms

4. Income distribution, growth and financialization: the Italian case

Domenica Tropeano

INTRODUCTION

The recent performance of the Italian economy has been very weak. The main stylized facts are the slow growth of output and investment, the fall in the export share, the worsening in the distribution of income and the fall in labour productivity. Many explanations have been proposed, though mainly on the microeconomic level. In what follows I shall deal with the issue of whether Italy's bad economic performance is related to financialization, the country having entered into a phase of deep structural changes involving both trade and financial liberalization. In the first section I shall briefly review the recent literature on financialization, from the macroeconomic side, to see whether this approach could be applied to the Italian case. In the second section I shall show the main trends in macroeconomic aggregates and distribution of income in Italy and discuss the debate on these themes. In the third section I shall propose a very simple model of financialization, which could eventually apply to the Italian case. In that model, financialization would work through an increase in the target rate of return. The conclusions of that model, however, do not fit the Italian case well. In the last section I shall examine another story, mainly dealing with monopoly power and classical competition among capital. According to the last story, financialization, interpreted as the changed attitude of firms towards investment, share issues and dividends, might be a consequence rather the origin of the problem. Conclusions will follow.

1. FINANCIALIZATION IN MACROECONOMIC MODELS

In the macroeconomic literature on financialization there are two main approaches. First, financialization is defined as a growing rate of return on financial assets relative to real assets, that is an increase in the real long-term rate of interest or in the yield of financial activities. Another strand of literature, fast growing recently, deals with the change in the corporate governance of enterprises, the so-called shareholder value orientation. In particular it focuses on the increase in the dividends distributed, on the fall in the rate of issue of new shares and on the repurchase of their own shares by enterprises. These changes are incorporated in standard macroeconomic models and their effects on the accumulation of capital and its profitability are examined (see Stockhammer 2005–06; Skott and Ryoo 2007; Hein and van Treeck 2007; Aglietta and Breton 2001; Boyer 2000).

In Kaleckian models the usual investment and saving functions are rewritten by taking into account those changes, and the usual comparative statics derivatives are calculated. They show what happens to the endogenous variables of the model with respect to a change in shareholder orientation. Since this change affects both the investment and saving functions, the result is that an equilibrium between saving and investment at a higher level of output is possible provided that the decrease in investment is compensated by an increase in consumption out of wealth (coming from the increase in distributed dividends). If instead the propensity to consume out of wealth is low, a lower accumulation rate will prevail.

Most of the arguments used can be represented graphically by means of a diagram in which the rate of profit is a function of rate of growth of saving and of investment (see Lavoie 1995a). To a certain equilibrium between saving and investment corresponds a certain equilibrium rate of profit. If the curves shift, then a new equilibrium point will be reached at a higher or lower rate of growth of saving and investment and a new equilibrium rate of profit will result.

By means of this graphical representation the main supposed changes related to financialization are examined. The so-called shareholder value orientation is simply represented as a downward shift in the investment function. Other things being equal, this means a lower saving–investment equilibrium and a lower rate of profit.

The other change is an increase in the dividend rate. This is simply accounted for by assuming that dividends are a negative item in the saving function of entrepreneurs, which at least in some models are the unique figures to save. However, if those dividends are used to demand more goods, consumption will increase as well.

As Skott and Ryoo (2007) point out, if a change in the new issue policy and a decrease in retained earnings are the main consequences of financialization, in this type of model the effect on the rate of accumulation and the rate of profit must be positive. In fact, all these things simply amount to a reduction in the savings ratio. However, in models where capacity is underutilized and labour supply is elastic, a reduction in the savings ratio will increase aggregate demand and output.

If all these things happen, according to the most common definition of the investment function, the investment curve should shift upwards too. In fact the profit share rises, as does the ratio of price of shares to reproduction cost of capital, and the rate of utilization rises as well. In such a context investment should increase too. Empirically, however, this does not happen, and to reach the desired conclusions one has to assume that, although investment is a function of all these things, the relative parameters are very low and shareholders' value orientation simply means a downward exogenous shift in the investment function.

For example, in the model by Stockhammer (2005–06) it is assumed that shareholders prefer profits to growth and this is embedded in the production function. A growing weight of shareholders means that a point in the preference function of firms where higher profits and lower investment is chosen. As Skott and Ryoo (2007) write, in this case rather than explaining the stylized facts they are simply assumed as basis for the analysis. In this model the outcome of a lower growth of investment and a higher rate of profit is simply supposed to exist and introduced in the production function rather than explained by the model.

In Hein and van Treeck (2007) dividends are explicitly introduced in the saving function of the entrepreneurs and an increase in these has a depressive effect on output if the propensities to consume out of wealth are low. Hein and van Treeck (2007) consider whether the increase in dividends will be transferred to prices or not. According to different parameter values, an outcome compatible with the stylized facts of higher profits and lower investment can occur. This happens when, the increase in capacity utilization notwithstanding, firms decide not to invest given the weight of the dividends distributed. Thus capacity utilization and profits are high while investment grows at a low rate. The high capacity utilization is due to the higher demand, which stems out of wealth effects as usual. Thus both the profit rate and the rate accumulation move parallel to each other, as in all the models based on steady-state growth in the Cambridge tradition. Only investment grows less; that is the rate of profit may be lower than the rate of change in the capital stock. In most models, as Skott and Ryoo (2007) point out, it is not clear what happens to the prices of shares and why Tobin's *Q* does not work, Boyer (2000) keeps it fixed and Stockhammer (2005–06) does not consider it at all.

The problem is that, if shareholder value orientation simply means a shift in the investment function, one wonders why have such an investment function. If, as is commonly assumed, investment is rather insensitive to increases in the share of profits, capacity utilization and the *Q* ratio, then the next question to ask is for how long an expansion fuelled only by consumption might last. In medium-term models this question may be ignored but the same is not true in the long term.

The assumption of shareholder value orientation is simply used as a *deus ex machina* to make the models match the empirical evidence. In practice, this amounts to denying any validity, under present historical conditions, to the investment functions. Then why do we still use them?

Another issue is how changes in the dividend and new issue policies of corporations are introduced into the analysis. Although most scholars dealing with the issue of financialization refer to Lazonick's definition of the present era as one of 'downsize and distribute' rather than 'retain and grow', nobody asks how these increased profits to be distributed are obtained. The underlying assumption is that the share of retained profits falls so as to allow a greater part of them to be distributed. The question that is not on the agenda is how the increase in the profit share and rate has been obtained. The question answered instead is what happens if a greater part of profits is not retained within the firm but distributed as dividends to the shareholders. But a sensible assumption would be that the target rate of return of enterprises has increased. Moreover, if they downsize, this has important implications for the composition of aggregate demand. The most common consequence is a fall in the level of wages paid. Thus opposite tendencies prevail at the top and at the bottom of the production chain. At the top, concentration increases, while at the bottom, increased competition depresses wages (see Milberg 2006). All these things are neglected in the most used aggregate models, which are by definition one-sector models.

In the rest of the chapter, which refers to the present situation in Italy, the issue of financialization is dealt with in an open-economy context by focusing on the increase in the target rate of return of enterprises, favoured by various circumstances, among which are the change in the financial norm at the world level, the opening of the economy to foreign trade, the privatization of public enterprises and the change in the regulation of labour markets. Thus the effect of shareholder orientation on dividends and new issues is ignored in the first instance.

2. CHANGES IN INCOME DISTRIBUTION AND SLOW GROWTH: THE CASE OF ITALY

The present state of the Italian economy is not encouraging. The country is often described as being in a state of economic decline. There is no agreement, however, on what is meant by this phrase. The most commonly mentioned circumstances are the slow growth of output and capital accumulation, the fall in the productivity of labour and the fall in the share of exports. Moreover, in the last decade there has been a shift in the distribution of income with a rise in the share of profits and a fall in the share of wages. All this has happened just when the Italian economy has undergone a process of financial opening, trade liberalization and internal economic reforms aiming at improving efficiency and performance. Among the latter the most important one has been the privatization of previously state-owned enterprises. The introduction of the euro and its appreciation until now has contributed to the difficulties encountered by the exporting industries.

At the same time the economy has experienced a process of deindustrialization and tertiarization common to many other European countries but with some peculiar characteristics. The weight of the industrial sector calculated as a percentage of its value added to GNP has decreased, while that of various types of service sectors has increased. Recently this process has accelerated and now the industry accounts for roughly 30% of GDP.

At the same time a change in the distribution of income has taken place. The share of wages has fallen while that of profits has increased. This fact has been empirically ascertained by a number of recent studies (Levrero and Stirati 2005; Prezioso 2005; Torrini 2005a, 2005b; Daveri and Lasinio 2005). The methodology employed in these studies varies but the results are the same. They differ in the interpretation of the results. Torrini (2005b) and Daveri and Lasinio estimate a neoclassical production function, which could allow for changing factor shares. Prezioso (2005) calculates that the wage share has fallen five percentage points in the last 20 years. The fact is remarkable because during the same period total employment has been rising by 21.1%. Levrero and Stirati (2005) calculate also the wage share for the same period and find that it has fallen; they also calculate the rate of profit by dividing the profits by the value of capital and find that this has risen, which is particularly remarkable for the services sector.

Prezioso (2005) calculates the mark-ups for two series of prices, consumption good prices and industrial products. In the industrial sectors the mark-up over variable costs has decreased. However, this fall has not benefited workers because fixed costs have increased, namely the costs of scrapping old machinery and replacing it. The average time use of plants has greatly decreased. The mark-up has not increased, although the rate of increase of prices has been higher than that of labour costs. Notably the price of exports in Italy has been higher than that of foreign competitors, even European ones. The rate of growth of industrial prices has been higher than that of the same goods in France, Germany and Spain. The conclusion that Prezioso draws is that the rise in the mark-up has contributed to the slow growth of output since the average propensity to save out of profits is usually lower that that out of wages. In Kaleckian types of model the value of the multiplier falls as the mark-up rises (for a restatement of this proposition see Vera 2006). To this it must be added that the main sources of output growth in the same period have fallen, namely state expenditure and exports. State expenditure has been cut to reduce the debt and meet European targets; exports fell because of the decline in the industrial sector. Thus aggregate expenditure has been reduced, as has the multiplier through the rise in mark-up. The lower expenditure has had a smaller effect than in the past on output.

Levrero and Stirati (2005) offer the same type of empirical evidence as to the changes in distribution of shares. They offer a slightly different explanation of the fall in the profit share of the industrial sector with respect to that of the services sector. They argue that, if the mark-up and then the profit rate increase in one sector, whose products are used as inputs by the other sector, the profit rate in the latter must necessarily decline independently of the differences in the market structure. This would happen just because of input–output linkages. Many scholars also claim that the loss of competitiveness of the Italian exporting industries is due to the higher prices of the services employed in the production of industrial goods and thus to the inefficiency of the non-traded sectors, which are not exposed to international competition. However, a closer examination of the weight of intermediate inputs from these sectors over total costs of the industrial sector casts some doubts on this explanation (see Schiattarella 2007). The same result has been reached by using a different method by Daveri and Lasinio (2005).

Another open issue is the source of higher mark-up in the services industries. Services is a wide sector where there are both traditional low-productivity sectors and innovative high-productivity firms. The productivity of labour in low-productivity firms has always been lower than in the traded goods sector, and recently it has declined further. However, the mark-ups are also high in services enterprises that have been privatized and have a high productivity of labour, such as telecommunications, banking and finance, and new services to enterprises. For the branches, whose productivity has fallen, the higher mark-up is due to recharging on prices the increase in costs; for the other more efficient ones, the high mark-up comes from the choice of not granting to labour its share of productivity improvements. This could fit well with the motivation given in the financialization literature. The owners and controllers of those big firms aim at a high stock market valuation and to get it they have to show high net profit figures in their balance sheets. They need also to have high margins to be able to distribute dividends. High profit margins and high dividends are also necessary to be able to resell the firm with a capital gain after some time.

The return on capital has actually been higher in the newly privatized industries, irrespective of their belonging to the manufacturing or service sectors. Torrini (2005b) calculates the return on capital as the profits net of depreciation divided by capital value at replacement costs. He finds that, starting from a base value of 1.00 in 1989, the rate of return on capital in the manufacturing sector has been falling throughout the period 1989–2001, reaching 0.52 in 2001, while, over the same period, it has been rising from 1.00 to 2.21, 1.65, 1.30 respectively in the three sectors energy, transportation and finance (see Torrini 2005b, table 5, p. 24). In this case, although the ratio of price of shares to the cost of reproduction of capital (Tobin's *Q*) rises, no increase in investment occurs because the required high rate of return is possible only in high oligopolistic sectors where entry is legally regulated and requires enormous financial means. The option of setting up a new firm rather than acquiring an existing one is not available in these cases. This means that investment is replaced by mergers and acquisitions, which in turn require high borrowing. Further those mergers and acquisitions boost the price of shares of the firms to be acquired. In the traded goods sector, the labour saving technical progress may displace workers while in the non-traded sectors the expansion of overhead labour may increase employment, although only for low-skilled workers. The combination of all these changes may cause a shrinking of the labour share and a rise in the average rate of profit without an increase in the rate of growth of output.

The increase in the target rate of return in one sector, according to Lavoie and Ramirez (1997), should reduce the rates of accumulation and the rates of growth in all sectors both in the short run and in the long run. The model, however, is one in which capital accumulation depends on the utilization of capacity and nominal wages are fixed. The mark-up is fixed and the paradox of costs holds. In the present environment, maintaining a certain profit margin in adverse circumstances is possible if an adequate restructuring of the production is undertaken, for example through foreign outsourcing to low-wage countries. This implies the assumption that both nominal wages and mark-ups are flexible. In this way a low accumulation of capital and low growth rates may be compatible with a higher target rate of return and also a higher *ex post* realized rate of return at least in the sectors towards which the new investment is flowing.

3. FINANCIALIZATION AND THE ITALIAN CASE: THE EFFECTS OF AN INCREASE IN THE TARGET RATE OF RETURN

As we have seen in the preceding section, the empirical studies on the Italian economy we have cited all agree that the mark-up has increased, particularly from 1992 onwards, though with different trends in different productive sectors. Thus the main issues discussed in the macroeconomic literature on financialization, namely the consequences of different attitudes of managers towards retaining profits and new issues or the wealth effects on consumption, are not relevant in the Italian case. The reason may be that most Italian firms are small; thus they are not concerned with the problems of medium-sized and big corporations. Moreover, the wealth effects on consumption have virtually vanished after the lowering of the interest rate on debt and its sale abroad, while they were important in the 1970s and the 1980s. However, I argue that financialization may still be important in the Italian case if attention is devoted to the issue of the increase in the target rate of return, which may be the consequence of financial opening and of a different sensitivity to this issue.

In order to explain the macroeconomic consequences of an increase in the financial norm on output growth and the rate of profit, I shall use an old model developed by Lavoie (1995). In particular, I shall draw on the so-called neo-Ricardian variation on this model. The object of Lavoie's model is to study the effects of an increase in the rate of interest. The object of Lavoie's work was the increase in the real rate of interest on the rate of profit and the growth rate of output. He uses the same model with a few variations to show the different positions on the subject of Cambridge theorists, Kalecki, neo-Ricardians and at the end he develops a variant that is called the Minsky–Steindl model. In the tradition stemming from Cambridge and Kalecki, a rise in the rate of interest should simply lead to a fall in the rate of growth and the rate of profit. Some neo-Ricardians following Sraffa's idea that the increase in the long-run rate of interest should lead to an increase in the desired rate of profit or normal rate of profit argue like this, distinguishing, however, between the *ex ante* and the *ex post* rate of profit. At the end Lavoie develops a sort of Minsky–Steindl model in which wealth effects are considered and entrepreneurs are allowed to save; in this model, it is shown that an increase in the real rate of interest may have effects of different type on the rate of accumulation and the rate of profit according to the values assigned to the parameters of the model.

The claim that an increase in the financial rate of return should increase the normal rate of profit in Sraffa is not based on macroeconomic considerations. Thus it is not necessary to develop a complicated macroeconomic model to see what happens to the accumulation of capital. An increase in the financial norm could have macroeconomic effects even if all the other ingredients used by Lavoie (1995), such as the propensity to save out of profits, out of wealth and so on, were omitted from the model. The inclusion of all these ingredients obviously changes the equilibrium point between saving and investment, and may give rise to different results. The tendency of the normal rate to equate to the changed rate of return on financial assets does not necessarily depend on the saving and investment propensities of capitalists, shareholders and bondholders. It could exist even in an economy that is not so sophisticated in this respect. Italy is a case in point. Thus in order to see the macroeconomic effects of a change in the perceived rate of return on financial assets it is not necessary to have a model in which all these different propensities to save and to invest are specified. A change in the perceived return on financial assets might have macroeconomic effects even in an economy with a much simpler financial structure. For this reason I shall use the most simple model developed by Lavoie (1995a) with reference to the neo-Ricardian position.

In Lavoie (1995a), the Kaleckian model consists of an investment equation depending on the differential between the expected rate of profit and the interest rate and of a saving equation derived from the Cambridge equation. The demand for investment depends on the expected rate of profit and on the interest rate, and on a parameter γ that describes the expected future sales growth.

$$g_i = \gamma + g_r(r_e - i) \tag{4.1}$$

where $r^e - i$ is the difference between expected rate of profit and the real interest rate.

The saving equation will be equal to the Cambridge equation:

$$g_s = s_p r \tag{4.2}$$

The combination of equations 4.1 and 4.2 under the assumption that the expected and realized profit rates are the same allows us to obtain an equation for the rate of profit as a function of exogenous variables and parameters.

$$r = \frac{\gamma - g_r i}{s_p - g_r} \tag{4.3}$$

Lavoie (1995) adds another equation, which defines the profit rate from the standpoint of costs. From this point onwards it will be termed the 'price cost margin equation' and its graphical representation is called the 'price cost margin curve'. Thus the rate of profit defined as profit over capital is as follows:

$$r = \frac{\pi}{K} = \left(\frac{\pi}{Y}\right)\left(\frac{Y}{C}\right)\left(\frac{C}{K}\right) = mu\left(\frac{1}{v}\right) \tag{4.4}$$

Profits over capital are equal to the ratio of profits to output multiplied by the ratio of output to capacity output and to the ratio of capacity output to the stock of capital. m is the share of profits u the rate of capacity utilization and v the capital–output ratio, assumed as given.

Equation 4.4 can be rewritten in the following way:

$$u = \left(\frac{v}{m}\right)r \tag{4.5}$$

Lavoie then recalls that for a rate of profit given by the effective demand constraint of equation 4.3 the rate of capacity utilization u depends on the margin of profit m, that is, on the mark-up over costs set by the firms. The price is determined by the following equation:

$$p = (1 + \theta)w/y \tag{4.6}$$

where p is the price level, θ the mark-up w the nominal wage rate and y the average labour productivity. The mark-up and the share of profit are related to each other in the following way:

$$m = \frac{\theta}{1 + \theta} \tag{4.7}$$

According to Kalecki's original thought, the mark-up should be fixed.

Lavoie (1995a) reformulates this model in order to take into account the neo-Ricardian critique and the reformulation as follows. The main objection of the neo-Ricardians is that investment does not depend on the actual rate of profit or on the interest rate, but rather investors, when making their decisions, look at the natural or normal rate of profit (on this, see Lavoie 1995b). The normal rate of profit r_n should be equal at least to the opportunity cost of alternative investments such as the real interest rate i and to the normal profit of enterprise npe. Thus the equation for the normal rate of profit is the following:

$$r_n = i + npe \tag{4.8}$$

This equation may be linked to the cost-plus pricing model. In fact in target return pricing the margin of profit is set to a level that provides a normal rate of profit when firms produce at the normal standard degree of capacity utilization. In terms of the previous model this implies that

$$r_n = \frac{mu_n}{v} \tag{4.9}$$

By combining the last two equations we see that

$$m = m_0 + m_i i \tag{4.10}$$

We can see that the profit margin becomes a positive function of the real interest rate.

We then define:

$$m_0 = (npe)\, v/u_n \tag{4.11}$$

and

$$m_i = v/u_n \tag{4.12}$$

The real wage would be defined by the following equation:

$$w/p = y(1 - m) \tag{4.13}$$

Lavoie also considers the neo-Ricardian claim that the investment function does not depend on the current rate of profit but on the normal one, and replaces the investment function of the previous model with the following:

$$g_i = \gamma + g_r(r_n - i) = \gamma + g_r(npe) \tag{4.14}$$

In this case the g_i curve becomes a straight line (see Figure 4.1). Lavoie shows that in that case an increase in the normal rate of profit will cause a rotation downwards in the profit cost curve since the mark-up increases, and even if the investment line does not move at all, a fall in the utilization of capacity. The realized *ex post* rate of profit would not change after the revision in the normal rate of profit.

If applied to the Italian case, this means that the increase in the financial norm has increased the mark-up on costs, thus causing a fall in the realized utilization rate. The equilibrium between saving and investment has not changed. This means that the change in the financial norm has had no effect at all on the rate of growth of output and the rate of profit. Of course this happens only under the assumption that the investment equation is a

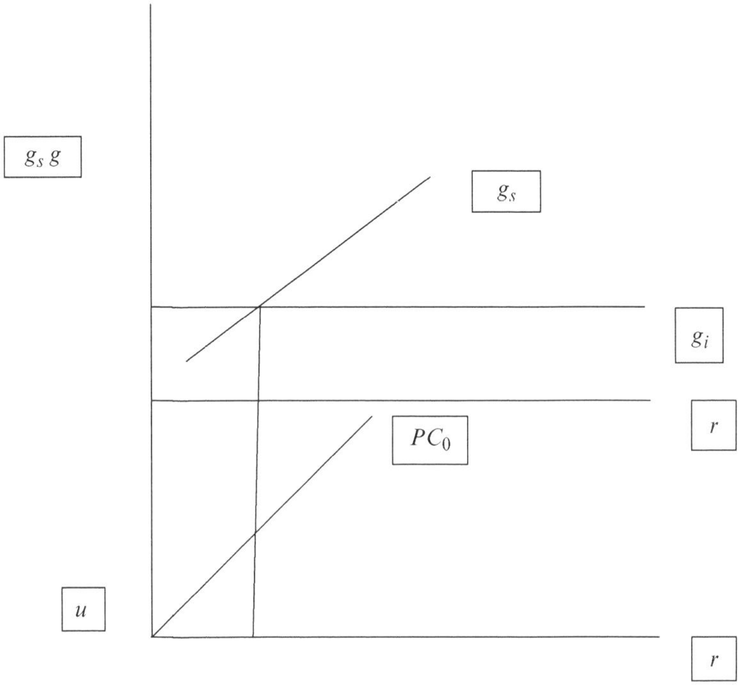

Figure 4.1 *Equilibrium between saving and investment and price cost margin*

straight line. If investment had been lower, then a fall in the rate of growth of output and in the realized rate of profit would have occurred.

A different picture emerges if we expand the same model to an open economy. This requires that in the saving equation we take into account the current account of the balance of payments. In an open economy the saving–investment equation is replaced by an equation that has on the right side the sum of investment and the current account balance. If we assume, as usual, that the current account depends on the level of the real exchange rate we get the following equation for savings:

$$g^s = s_p r + CA(h) \tag{4.15}$$

The real exchange rate h is defined as the ratio of the nominal exchange rate multiplied by the foreign price level divided by the domestic price level:

$$h = \frac{eP^*}{P} \tag{4.16}$$

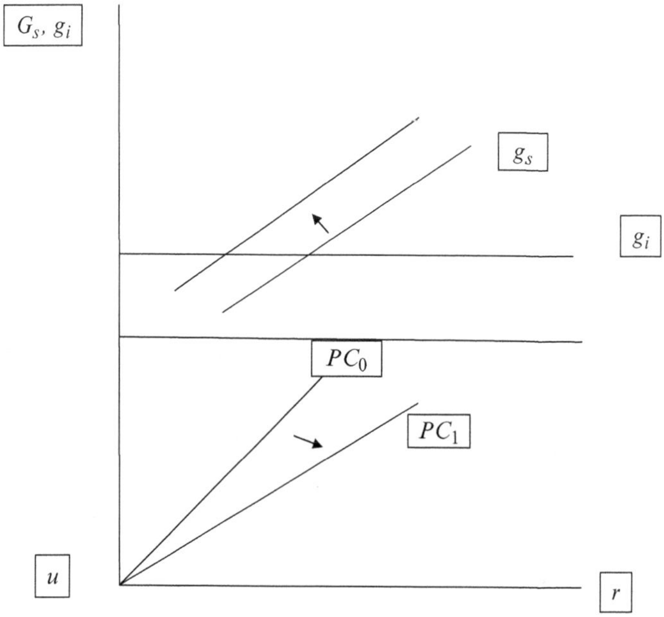

Figure 4.2 Equilibrium between saving and investment and price cost margin in an open economy after an appreciation of the currency

We assume as in the preceding model that mark-up is fixed, inflexible and exogenously determined by the conditions on financial markets. Thus we do not assume that domestic firms' profitability depends positively on the exchange rate. If the exchange rate appreciates, domestic firms do not reduce their mark-up in order to maintain competitiveness. This contrasts with other views on the issue of mark-up and competitiveness (see Blecker 1989), but it reflects more closely the behaviour of Italian exporting firms (see Bugamelli and Tedeschi 2007).

Now we see graphically the consequences of a higher target rate of return and of a nominal appreciation. We observe that the saving curve goes up, thus reducing the rate of profit *ex post*, while the rise in the mark-up makes the price cost margin curve *PC* rotate downwards (see Figure 4.2).

In the case in which the target rate of return is raised and a nominal appreciation occurs, the saving curve should shift to the left because of the lower value of *e*, the nominal exchange rate, and the higher value of *P*, the price of domestic goods. This amounts to a real appreciation of the domestic currency. In a closed economy, instead, under these conditions, an increase in the target mark-up would have led only to a decrease in capacity utilization while the rate of profit *ex post* would have stayed constant. In fact, if we assume that the investment line does not move, the higher desired target rate of return will only affect utilization of capacity but it will not lower the realized profit rate. The effect of an appreciation would be a fall in the rate of profit (see Figure 4.2). The final result of a constant rate of growth and an unchanged rate of profit, though with lower utilization rate, does not fit well the current situation of the Italian economy, as we have seen in the last section. In fact the rate of profit has increased while the rate of growth has decreased.

Lavoie (1995a) asserts that the normal rate has nothing to do with the realized *ex post* rate of profit and therefore it is used as a substitute for the mark-up that firms impose on variable costs. Once the normal rate of profit has been revised, the mark-up in the whole economy must increase while the real wage and the utilization rate must fall. In the model the revision of the normal rate of profit is equivalent to an increase in the mark-up, which makes real wages fall and the profit share increase leaving the rate of profit unchanged. This means that firms will produce less, thus reducing the utilization of their plants, but their monetary revenues will be unchanged. Monetary profits will remain constant and thus saving, which is equivalent in the Cambridge tradition to the capitalists' savings out of profits as households do not save. Because of the equilibrium condition of saving and investment it follows that also investment does not change. In the upper part of the graph nothing changes. The change in the normal rate of profit affects the mark-up and the price cost margin equation whose slope depends on m, the share of profits, which has increased. In the end the firms do not succeed in achieving a higher rate of profit.

The inclusion in a steady-state growth model of the normal rate of profit does not change in meaningful ways the behaviour of the model. The reason that has been highlighted by Pivetti (2007) is that it is impossible to reconcile the profit rate determination through capital accumulation that is typical of the Cambridge tradition with the determination through financial conditions and in particular the long-term real interest rate. This is exactly what has been attempted in the model by Lavoie (1995a).

4. AN ALTERNATIVE STORY: MONOPOLY POWER, CLASSICAL COMPETITION AND FINANCIALIZATION

An alternative explanation of the changes in the distribution of income in Italy and of the evolution of the macroeconomic aggregates could be based on a model in which mark-up pricing coexists with classical competition (see Dutt 1995, 1997). In this model the rate of growth of output would depend on the rate of capital utilization (average) and on the rate of profit. Thus the accumulation of capital would depend on the utilization and profit. The allocation of a given capital among sectors would depend instead upon the profit rate differentials among sectors. The last feature would reintroduce some form of classical competition in the model. There is a mechanism, however that ensures in the long run equalization of profit rates and convergence to the steady-state rate of growth. The rate of growth is defined as follows:

$$g = (g_1K_1 + g_2K_2)/(K_1 + K_2) = \tau_0 + \beta_1 u + \beta_2 r \quad (4.17)$$

where

$$u = (P_1/P_2)^0 u_1 k_1 + u_2 k_2 \quad (4.18)$$

and

$$r = r_1 k_1 + r_2 k_2 \quad (4.19)$$

where

$$u_i = X_i/K_i,\ k_i = K_i/K_1 + K_2 \quad (4.20)$$

and $(P_1/P_2)^0$ is the initial price ratio.

If the allocation of investment between sectors is governed by the profit rate differential:

$$g_1 - g_2 = \mu(r_1 - r_2) \quad (4.21)$$

In the short run, given the stocks of capital, the market for each good clears through output adjustments. In the long run the stocks of capital in the two sectors change. Of course if there is no possibility of free entry in the second sector, the profit rates in the long run would not be equalized.

The implications of the model are the following, according to Dutt (1995). The relative price both in the short and the long run is determined by each sector's degree of monopoly and by technical parameters. This would be in contrast to the classical approach where prices are determined assuming equalized rates of profit, given input–output relations and distributional parameters. In this type of model the allocation of capital among sectors would depend on the relative profitability of the sectors, and the movement of capital would produce in the long run the equalization of profit rates. In this case no change in the target rate of return would be necessary to explain the trends in the accumulation of capital, output growth and the distribution of income. The profit rate differential would be sufficient to cause the higher rate of growth in newly privatized sectors with respect to old industrial sectors. In this case, however, no equalization of profit rates would be attainable even if free capital mobility were assumed. The reason is that the sectors with higher returns are monopolistic ones, this means that there are barriers to entry. The only thing that can be done is to purchase a stake in them order to control them. The attempt to purchase them would only cause a rise in the prices of their shares and thus in the value of their capital in the stock exchange. The rate of profit in some sectors could be persistently higher than in other sectors and higher than the average rate of growth.

CONCLUSIONS

I have recalled some stylized facts regarding the Italian economy. In particular, in the last 20 years the rate of profit and the share of profit have gone up, output growth and investment have slowed down and the export share has fallen. We have discussed whether the decline of the Italian economy could be linked to the financialization process. Usually the literature on financialization focuses on changes in the investment attitude of corporations such as the increase in distributed dividends and the fall in new issues of shares. I have argued that, even in a country where all these things have happened to some extent and later than in the rest of the world, financialization may have deep effects by changing the perceived financial norm. If this financial norm affects the target return on capital, macroeconomic effects may be very important even without explicitly taking into account all the other things.

By drawing on a model by Lavoie (1995a), I have shown that an increase in the target rate of return would leave unchanged the rate of accumulation, the rate of growth and the realized rate of profit while reducing the capacity utilization. If we extend the same model to an open economy and assume that an appreciation of the currency occurs, a fall in the rate of growth, accumulation and in the realized rate of profit would follow. This picture, however, does not fit well with the stylized facts mentioned above. In Italy, the rate of growth and the capital accumulation have slowed down while the rate of profit and the profit share have clearly increased. The increase concerns the average profit share and the average profit rate, while indeed the profit rate is declining in the manufacturing sectors and rising in the services sector. The profit rate is declining in the manufacturing sector, due to the increase in fixed costs for a more rapid replacement of the old capital stock. This decline does not depend on the utilization rate. I have pointed out that the main shortcoming of this type of modelling is that two alternative explanations of the profit rate are mixed up – the one that makes the profit rate depend on capital accumulation and the one that links it to the long-run real interest rate or to any exogenous financial norm. The relevance of this explanation should therefore be assessed by building other types of models based on the monetary theory of distribution.

In the second part of the chapter a different interpretation is presented, which is no longer based on the financialization hypothesis but rather on the increase in the degree of monopoly in the Italian industrial sectors, given the increase in the mark-up. This process would have been favoured by the privatization process of previously public enterprises. I show what might have happened by using a model by Dutt (1995) with two sectors. The stock of capital is fixed in the short run while the rate of growth depends on the total utilization of capacity and the average rate of profit. In the long run, however, while the accumulation of capital is still governed by aggregate utilization and profitability, the allocation of capital among sectors and their growth depends on the profit rate differential. In the steady state, this differential would tend to zero. That model allows for movement of capital within the sectors, which is a persistent tendency of the Italian economy with a falling manufacturing share over total industrial output. The disturbing feature in that model is that the capital flows among sectors are triggered by price differentials determined according to neoclassical lines. In this case, financialization would be a side effect of the increase in monopolistic competition.

A more realistic approach to the problem of changes in income distribution and growth in Italy should start from a monetary theory of distribution, in which the rate of profit is only determined by the long-run rate of interest or any exogenous financial norm, and allow for the possibility of capital flows among sectors triggered by profit rate differentials with underlying changes in the productive structure. In the end only the sectors that manage by using different tools to get a rate of profit as high as the exogenous real interest rate or the exogenous financial norm will survive.

ACKNOWLEDGEMENT

Thanks to Paolo Ramazzotti for reading and commenting on the chapter.

REFERENCES

Aglietta, M. and R. Breton (2001), 'Financial systems, corporate control and capital accumulation', *Economy and Society*, **30** (4), 433–66.

Boyer, Robert (2000), 'Is finance-led growth a viable alternative to Fordism? A preliminary analysis', *Economy and Society*, **29** (1), 111–45.

Blecker, Robert A. (1989), 'International competition, income distribution and economic growth', *Cambridge Journal of Economics*, **13** (3), 395–412.

Bugamelli, Matteo and Roberto Tedeschi (2007), 'Le strategie di prezzo delle imprese esportatrici italiane', *Politica Economica*, **3**, 321–49.

Daveri, Francesco and Cecilia Jona-Lasinio (2005), 'Italy's decline: getting the facts right', IGIER Working Paper No. 301, December.

Dutt, A. (1995), 'Monopoly power and uniform rates of profit: a reply to Glick–Campbell and Dumenil–Levy, *Review of Radical Political Economics*, **27**, 142–53.

Dutt, A. (1997), 'Profit rate equalization in the Kalecki–Steindl model and the "over-determination" problem', *The Manchester School*, **65** (4), 443–51.

Hein, Eckhard and Till van Treeck (2007), '"Financialisation" in Kaleckian/post-Kaleckian models of distribution and growth', Working Paper 7/2007, Macroeconomic Policy Institute, Hans Boeckler Foundation.

Lavoie, Marc (1995a), 'Interest rates in post-keynesian models of growth and distribution', *Metroeconomica*, **46** (2), 146–77.

Lavoie, Marc (1995b), 'The Kaleckian model of growth and distribution and its neo-Ricardian and neo-Marxian critiques', *Cambridge Journal of Economics*, **19** (6), 789–818.

Lavoie, M. and P. Ramirez-Gaston (1997), 'Traverse in a two sector Kaleckian model of growth with target return pricing', *Manchester School of Economic and Social Studies*, **65** (2), 145–69.

Levrero, Sergio and Antonella Stirati (2005), 'Distribuzione del reddito e prezzi relativi in Italia 1970–2002', *Politica Economica*, **3**, 401–34.

Milberg, W. (2006), 'Pricing and profits under globalized competition: a post Keynesian perspective on U.S. economic history', SCEPA Working Paper 2006–5.

Pivetti, Massimo (2007), 'Distribution, inflation and policy analysis', *Review of Political Economy*, **19** (2), 243–7.

Prezioso, Stefano (2005), 'Prezzi, distribuzione e ristagno: una nota', *Politica economica*, **1**, 103–30.

Schiattarella, Roberto (2007), 'Rendite e competitivita', paper presented at the Conference Aissec Parma, June.

Skott, Peter and Soon Ryoo (2007), 'Macroeconomic implications of financialization', Working Paper, University of Massachusetts at Amherst.

Stockhammer, Engelbert (2005–06), 'Shareholder value orientation and the investment–profit puzzle', *Journal of Post-Keynesian Economics*, **28** (2), 193–215.

Torrini, Roberto (2005a), 'Quota dei profitti e redditivita' del capitale in Italia', *Politica Economica*, **1**, 7–42.

Torrini, Roberto (2005b), 'Profit share and returns on capital stock in Italy: the role of privatisations behind the rise of the 1990s', CEP Discussion Paper No. 671, January.

Vera, Leonardo (2006), 'Representative agent meets class structure: imperfect competition and the balanced-budget multiplier', *Cambridge Journal of Economics*, **30** (5), 783–96.

5. Faith-based macroeconomics: a critique of recent developments in NAIRU estimation

Dany Lang and Mark Setterfield

1. INTRODUCTION

The idea of a non-accelerating inflation rate of unemployment (NAIRU) is a well-established but controversial feature of modern macroeconomics. The NAIRU codifies a pre-Keynesian vision of the economy, according to which money is neutral and aggregate demand is irrelevant for the determination of output and employment, at least in the long run. Although critics of the NAIRU question its very existence (see, e.g., Galbraith 1997; Lang 2007), the concept has made deep inroads into macroeconomic policy circles, and there exists an extensive empirical literature that purports to identify the precise value of the NAIRU that policy makers should incorporate into their decisions.

Our concern in this chapter is with recent developments in the literature that seeks to estimate the value of the NAIRU. A necessary condition for the existence of a NAIRU is dynamic homogeneity: the 'Phillips curve' should be homogeneous of degree one in lagged and/or expected inflation. But contemporary approaches to estimating the NAIRU typically assume rather than test for dynamic homogeneity, thus assuming (rather than testing for) the existence of a NAIRU. We argue that these developments remove the NAIRU from the domain of testable hypotheses and transform the concept into an article of faith. In terms of the Popper–Lakatos tradition in the methodology of science, this makes the contemporary empirical NAIRU literature a degenerative research programme.

The remainder of our chapter is organized as follows. Sections 2 and 3 review conventional and more recent methods for estimating the value of the NAIRU, respectively. It is shown that the modern empirical NAIRU literature has engaged in an implicit retreat from hypothesis testing – specifically, testing for the existence of a NAIRU. This has occurred at a time when efforts directed at testing ought to have been redoubled, by virtue of the consistency of a competing hypothesis – which yields radically different implications for the role of money and aggregate demand in the economy – with the null hypothesis that was formerly understood to denote the existence of a NAIRU. Section 4 then reflects on the methodological implications of the retreat from hypothesis testing in modern methods of NAIRU estimation. It is argued that this retreat from testing makes the contemporary empirical NAIRU literature degenerative, and 'elevates' the NAIRU concept into the realm of faith-based macroeconomics. Finally, Section 5 offers some conclusions.

2. ESTIMATING THE NAIRU USING THE 'PHILLIPS CURVE'

The conventional approach to estimating the NAIRU involves initial estimation of a reduced-form expression derived from structural wage- and price-setting equations. This expression takes the form of a conventional 'Phillips curve' that can be written as:

$$p = \alpha + \beta p^e + \sum_{i=1}^{n} \gamma_i p_{-i} - \delta U + \eta \tag{5.1}$$

where p is the rate of inflation, p^e denotes inflation expectations, U is the rate of unemployment and η captures transitory supply shocks.

The Phillips curve in equation (5.1) exemplifies what Gordon (1997, 1998) and Dew-Becker and Gordon (2005) describe as the canonical 'triangular' model of the inflation process, expressing inflation as resulting from: inflation inertia and/or expectations; demand-side forces (captured by U); and supply-side forces (captured by η). It can be thought of as a useful 'organizing concept' in macroeconomic theory, emerging in one form or another from a wide variety of otherwise competing traditions in macroeconomics.

Under the equilibrium conditions $p = p^e = p_{-i} = p^*$ (for all $i = 1, \ldots, n$) and $\eta = 0$, we obtain the long-run Phillips curve:

$$p^* = \frac{\alpha - \delta U}{1 - \left(\beta + \sum_{i=1}^{n} \gamma_i\right)} \tag{5.2}$$

In general – that is, when the denominator in (5.2) is non-zero – equation (5.2) implies a trade-off between inflation and unemployment. The idea of a NAIRU (or alternatively, a natural rate of unemployment) emerges as a specific form of the equilibrium solution to (5.1),[1] that arises when we observe 'dynamic homogeneity' in the inflation process – or in other words, when

$$\beta + \sum_{i=1}^{n} \gamma_i = 1 \tag{5.3}$$

Given dynamic homogeneity, imposing the equilibrium conditions $p = p^e = p_{-i} = p^*$ (for all $i = 1, \ldots, n$) and $\eta = 0$ on equation (5.1) now yields:

$$U = \alpha/\delta = U_n \tag{5.4}$$

where U_n is the NAIRU. The long-run Phillips curve in equation (5.4) now implies that there is no long-run relationship between unemployment and inflation. Instead, as equation (5.4) indicates, the long-run rate of unemployment is always consistent with the NAIRU – which is understood to be a unique equilibrium rate of unemployment determined on the supply side of the economy, independently of the actual rate of unemployment – regardless of the rate of inflation. Given equation (5.4), it is a straightforward matter to establish the precise value of the NAIRU using the estimation coefficients $\hat{\alpha}$ and $\hat{\delta}$ as approximations for the parameters α and δ, respectively.

The preceding analysis reveals the advantage of the conventional Phillips curve approach to estimating the value of the NAIRU. The process begins with a 'generic' Phillips curve that nests competing hypotheses about the precise relationship between p and U, of which the 'NAIRU hypothesis' (NAIRUH) – that there is no long-run relationship between p and U – is just one. The concept of a NAIRU then emerges under specific conditions that are testable. In short, the approach taken above renders the NAIRUH a testable hypothesis. Certainly, the power of the resulting test of H_0: $\hat{\beta} + \Sigma_{i=1}^{n}\hat{\gamma}_i = 1$ is open to question. Hence Setterfield and LeBlond (2003), using contemporary US data, show that failure to reject the null hypothesis of dynamic homogeneity is associated with large Type II errors. Nevertheless, the methodological point remains that the procedure for estimating the NAIRU outlined above keeps the NAIRUH firmly within the realm of testable hypotheses.

3. RECENT DEVELOPMENTS IN NAIRU ESTIMATION

More recently, the preferred approach to estimating the value of the NAIRU has moved away from the practices outlined above. In its efforts to estimate the NAIRU, the contemporary literature places emphasis on the use of more or less elaborate statistical methods designed to extract the trend rate of unemployment from an unemployment time series. To some extent these recent practices have been well motivated. Hence the procedure described in the previous section produces a single point estimate of the NAIRU (from equation (5.4)) for the entire range of data used to estimate equation (5.1). It has long been claimed, however, that the value of the NAIRU can change over time. Allowing for this time variation in the value of the NAIRU is an important motivating factor in the new empirical NAIRU literature. But unfortunately, as will become clear in what follows, the contemporary literature has – unwittingly or otherwise – undermined the status of the NAIRUH as a testable hypothesis, elevating it instead to the status of an article of faith.

There are two strands of the contemporary literature referred to above. The first, and less sophisticated, strand – which is increasingly evident in undergraduate macroeconomics textbooks (see, e.g., Mankiw 2006, figure 6.1, p. 160) – involves calculating a moving average of the actual unemployment rate and simply calling this trend a NAIRU.[2] Although this type of exercise may serve to inculcate undergraduates with the language of 'modern macroeconomics', the problem with this approach is obvious. Both the concept and the value of the NAIRU emerge by definitional fiat, and not as the result of any identifiable hypothesis about the behaviour of the unemployment rate that can be subject to testing.

The second, more sophisticated, strand of the contemporary empirical NAIRU literature employs statistical filters (usually either a Hodrick–Prescott filter or a Kalman filter) to extract a trend rate of unemployment from an unemployment time series generated by a statistical model. This second strand is exemplified by Ball and Mankiw (2002). Ball and Mankiw begin by estimating an equation of the form:

$$\Delta p = \alpha - \delta U + \eta \qquad (5.1')$$

Under the equilibrium conditions $\Delta p = \eta = 0$, the now familiar NAIRU result in equation (5.4) emerges from (5.1′). This, in turn, can be rewritten as

$$\alpha = \delta U_n$$

Substituting this last expression into Ball and Mankiw's original estimating equation and rearranging, we arrive at

$$U_n + \eta/\delta = U + \Delta p/\delta$$

The right-hand side of this expression can easily be calculated using time series data for U and Δp and by using $\hat{\delta}$ as an approximation for δ. Ball and Mankiw (2002) then contend that since η/δ will exhibit high-frequency variation while U_n will exhibit low-frequency variation, it is possible to extract the (time-varying) value of U_n from the calculated series $U + \Delta p/\hat{\delta}$ using any standard statistical method for extracting a trend from a time series. As intimated above, their preferred method of extracting this trend involves use of a Hodrick–Prescott filter. On this basis, Ball and Mankiw (2002) calculate what they identify to be the value of a time-varying NAIRU for the US economy for the period 1960–2000. They claim that this time-varying NAIRU first rose (between 1960 and 1980) and subsequently fell, much as the actual rate of unemployment first rose and then fell during the period of their investigation. The implication is that the 'evolution' of the time-varying NAIRU explains changes in the actual rate of unemployment over several successive business cycles in the US economy.

The problem with this approach to 'estimating the NAIRU' is at once simple but important: by estimating (5.1′) (in which the dependent variable is Δp) rather than (5.1), the dynamic homogeneity in equation (5.3) that was revealed in the previous section as a necessary condition for the existence of a NAIRU has been imposed upon the estimating equation from the outset. In other words, Ball and Mankiw assume rather than test for the dynamic homogeneity necessary to empirically validate the Phillips curve in equation (5.1′) that they estimate, and in the process they assume rather than test for the existence of a NAIRU. The trend they extract from the time series $U + \Delta p/\hat{\delta}$ is labelled a NAIRU, but the authors provide no statistical evidence to suggest that their interpretation of this trend (as being a NAIRU) is consistent with the underlying data. In other words, for all its seeming sophistication, the basic problem with the second strand of the contemporary empirical NAIRU literature is much the same as the problem with the first strand discussed earlier: a purported value of the NAIRU emerges from a process in which testing for the very existence of a NAIRU – a contested concept – is conspicuous by its absence.

4. IS THE NAIRU HYPOTHESIS DEGENERATIVE?

The essential problem with the literature reviewed in the previous section is that, literally interpreted, it does nothing more than extract a long-run trend from a macroeconomic time series and then designate this trend as representing the NAIRU. This designation is either completely arbitrary (as in the case of the less sophisticated strand of the literature) or true by assumption (as in the case of the more sophisticated strand, that assumes rather than tests for dynamic homogeneity). But the designation of trend unemployment as a unique and stable supply-determined equilibrium rate of unemployment consistent with stable inflation is nothing more than that – a designation. It provides no test through which the concept of the NAIRU could, in principle, be falsified. In short, modern methods of estimating the NAIRU elevate the NAIRUH beyond the status of a testable hypothesis to that of an article of faith. In other words, what we are dealing with here is what can be called 'faith-based macroeconomics'.

Unfortunately, things get worse for the NAIRUH. At the same time that the NAIRU literature has retreated from treating the NAIRU as a testable hypothesis, the usefulness of the 'dynamic homogeneity' test described above has been undermined by the idea of hysteresis in the NAIRU. To see this, note that on the basis of (5.4), we have $\delta U_n = \alpha$. Substituting into (5.1) and rearranging, we arrive at

$$p = \beta p^e + \sum_{i=1}^{n} \gamma_i p_{-i} - \delta(U - U_n) + \eta$$

or

$$U - U_n = \Omega\left(\beta p^e + \sum_{i=1}^{n} \gamma_i p_{-i} - p\right) + \varepsilon \tag{5.5}$$

where $\Omega = 1/\delta$ and $\varepsilon = \eta/\delta$. Equation (5.5) is essentially a Lucas supply function, which suggests that, given dynamic homogeneity as in (5.3), it is only possible for unemployment to vary from the NAIRU if $p \neq p^e \neq p_{-i}$ (for all $i = 1, \ldots, n$) or $\eta \neq 0$, events that are understood to represent transitory (disequilibrium) conditions. Hence in the long run, the actual rate of unemployment is anchored at the NAIRU regardless of the rate of inflation.

But notice that this last statement only implies that there is no trade-off between inflation and unemployment if we assume that

$$\dot{U}_n = 0 \tag{5.6}$$

Equation (5.6) can be considered the 'missing equation' of NAIRU analysis (see Lavoie, 2006). But suppose, in fact, that

$$\dot{U}_n = f(U - U_n) \tag{5.7}$$

where $f' > 0$. Equation (5.7) characterizes a NAIRU that is path dependent: its value changes if the actual rate of unemployment differs from the NAIRU at any point in time.[3] In the NAIRU literature, equation (5.7) is usually understood to connote the existence of hysteresis in the NAIRU.[4] Notice that we are still referring to the existence of something called a NAIRU and (most importantly for our purposes) we are still assuming dynamic homogeneity. All we are proposing is that equation (5.6) (the missing equation of NAIRU analysis) be replaced with equation (5.7). What are the consequences of this?

To answer this question, suppose that for the sake of simplicity we linearize equation (5.7), writing:[5]

$$\dot{U}_n = \theta(U - U_n) \tag{5.7'}$$

Substituting (5.5) into (5.7′), we arrive at:

$$\dot{U}_n = \theta\Omega\left(\beta p^e + \sum_{i=1}^{n}\gamma_i p_{-i} - p\right) + \nu \tag{5.8}$$

where $\nu = \theta\varepsilon$. What equation (5.8) tells us is that any increase in p above its current equilibrium value will reduce the value of NAIRU.[6] Since the NAIRU is the long-run equilibrium rate of unemployment, and since $U = U_n$ is consistent with stable inflation,[7] we are back to the sort of long-run trade-off between unemployment and inflation originally described in (5.2). But this time, we are using the concept of a NAIRU and are assuming dynamic homogeneity in the inflation process. In other words, the hysteresis hypothesis is consistent with dynamic homogeneity in the inflation process, but yields a predicted long-run relationship between inflation and unemployment that is completely at variance with that of the NAIRUH. Clearly, then, dynamic homogeneity – even if the empirical NAIRU literature were still eager to test for rather than simply assume its existence – is not enough to establish the existence of a unique NAIRU that is invariant with respect to the rate of inflation.

What this means is that just as NAIRU proponents have retreated from directly testing for dynamic homogeneity and hence the existence of a NAIRU, the validity of this traditional test for the existence of a NAIRU has been undermined by the emergence of a competing hypothesis. This competing hypothesis, which postulates the dependence of the NAIRU on the actual rate of unemployment as in equation (5.7), rather than the independence of the NAIRU from the actual rate of unemployment as in equation (5.6), is fully compatible with the dynamic homogeneity condition specified in the null hypothesis of the traditional test for the existence of a NAIRU. But it yields completely different implications for the long-run relationship between unemployment and inflation. The question at this remove, then, is not just whether but how to test for the existence of a NAIRU.[8] And in a discipline that values generating testable hypotheses as a hallmark of scientific progress, we have to ask: what is the scientific status of such a concept?

For economists such as Blaug (1994), who self-identify with the Popperian and Lakatosian projects in the methodology of science, generating new testable hypotheses that are exposed to the potential for falsification is an essential feature of any scientific research programme that is 'progressive' rather than 'degenerative'. This methodological position is, of course, contestable. For instance, a number of the contributions to Backhouse (1994) recommend that economists adopt views of their discipline and/or its object of analysis – and corresponding methodological strictures – that depart radically from those associated with the Popper–Lakatos brand of positivism. But as long as the economics profession (or large tracts of it) continues to at least tacitly identify with the Popper–Lakatos tradition,[9] then it remains reasonable to use the standards of this tradition above all others as yardsticks by which to judge the practices of economists – including those of NAIRU proponents. Hence the essential claim of this chapter is that recent developments in the empirical NAIRU literature fall short of the standards of a progressive research programme. As established above, new testable hypotheses that seek to establish the existence of a NAIRU are sorely needed if the original concept of the NAIRU (that of a unique supply-determined equilibrium rate of unemployment consistent with stable inflation) and the associated NAIRU hypothesis (that there is no long-run trade-off between unemployment and inflation) are to be upheld in the face of a competitor hypothesis (based on the concept of hysteresis). But rather than developing new testable hypotheses, the modern empirical NAIRU literature has largely retreated from testing altogether. Not even the null hypothesis of dynamic homogeneity is regularly tested:[10] instead, even in the more sophisticated strand of the contemporary empirical NAIRU literature, it is typically assumed to be a property of the object of analysis. This faith in the NAIRU hypothesis is perhaps charming,[11] but it is difficult to reconcile with the pursuit of science as envisaged by the Popper–Lakatos tradition. Instead, the characteristics of the contemporary empirical NAIRU literature highlighted above mark the latter out – despite its seeming statistical sophistication – as a degenerative rather than progressive research programme.

5. CONCLUSION

This chapter draws attention to some recent developments in the empirical NAIRU literature. Despite the seeming sophistication of much of this literature, it can ultimately be characterized as embracing 'measurement without testing'. More specifically, the contemporary empirical NAIRU literature is long on the use of statistical filters to derive trends from unemployment time series, but extremely short on hypothesis testing designed to establish – according to recognizable statistical criteria – whether or not the trends so described constitute time-varying NAIRUs. Instead, the property of dynamic homogeneity – that could, in principle, be used to establish a testable hypothesis that would either verify or falsify the existence of a NAIRU – is simply assumed to hold, and is imposed upon the data in the course of what is then assumed to constitute a process of measuring the 'NAIRU'. Now, the traditional test for the existence of a NAIRU, based on verifying dynamic homogeneity, is by no means powerful or conclusive. As was discussed earlier, it is plagued by large Type II errors, whilst an alternative hypothesis to the NAIRUH (based on hysteresis) is also consistent with dynamic homogeneity, but yields a predicted long-run relationship between unemployment and inflation that is totally at variance with that of the NAIRUH. These observations, however, should motivate a redoubling of efforts directed at testing – specifically, the development of new tests that are capable of both verifying the existence of a NAIRU and distinguishing the NAIRUH from competitor hypotheses. They do not justify the abandonment of testing, which serves only to 'elevate' the NAIRUH out of the realm of testable (or tested) hypotheses and into the realm of articles of faith.

But in actual fact, this latter development is exactly what has happened. This is not consistent with the behaviour of a progressive research programme, and it is this observation that leads us to identify moden empirical NAIRU analysis as degenerative. If macroeconomists want to be taken seriously, faith-based developments of this kind cannot be accepted as legitimate and really should be avoided in future research.

NOTES

1. We do not differentiate between the NAIRU and the natural rate of unemployment (NRU) in this chapter, because there is no analytical difference between the way that these concepts are derived from equation (5.1). As such, we refer exclusively in what follows to the concept of the NAIRU.
2. See also CEPR (1995, n. 20).
3. See, for example, Jenkinson (1987) for an early but useful survey of the channels through which the actual rate of unemployment can impact upon on the structure of the labour market and hence the long-run equilibrium rate of unemployment.
4. Strictly speaking, this is something of an abuse of terminology, since hysteresis is a specific form of path dependence (rather than a synonym for path dependence), 'true' hysteresis involving (among other things) discontinuities, which would imply that the

function f (.) in (5.7) is non-linear. See, for example, Lang (2004) and Lang and De Peretti (2009) for a discussion of proper and improper uses of the term hysteresis in macroeconomics, and their application to the NAIRU.

5. In light of what was said in the previous note, note that, in so doing, we cannot claim to be modelling 'true' hysteresis here. Instead, the term 'hysteresis' must be interpreted as a euphemism for path dependence in what follows – thus replicating a common (but unfortunate) trait of the NAIRU literature.
6. Notice that any increase in the current rate of inflation will suffice to produce this result. Even if the increase in inflation is anticipated, inertia in the inflation process will ensure that $\dot{U}_n \neq 0$ in (5.8). Of course, in the absence of inertia (i.e. if $\gamma_i = 0$ for all i), and assuming that we continue to observe dynamic homogeneity (which would now imply that $\beta = 1$), only an unanticipated increase in the rate of inflation would suffice to change the value of the NAIRU. The frequency with which unanticipated inflations occur depends, in part, on the process by which decision makers form expectations. Note, however, that absent perfect foresight, the capacity for expectational error is always present, and so, by extension, is the capacity for 'hysteretic' changes in the value of the NAIRU as described in equation (5.8).
7. Recall the first of the equilibrium conditions that was used to derive the result in (5.4) above.
8. Note that calculating the trend rate of unemployment and then insisting that this must be a NAIRU because inflation increases/decreases when unemployment is below/above the trend value does not suffice to solve this problem, for the simple reason that we would get much the same result from a standard (negatively sloped) Phillips curve. Hence note from (5.1) and (5.2) that:

$$\frac{dp}{dU} = -\delta$$

whereas:

$$\frac{dp^*}{dU} = \frac{-\delta}{1 - \left(\beta + \sum_{i=1}^{n} \gamma_i\right)}$$

Assuming that $\beta + \Sigma_{i=1}^{n}\gamma_i < 1$ – as is consistent with the traditional, negatively sloped Phillips curve we are modelling here – we can see that the increase in long-run inflation resulting from a decrease in unemployment is some multiple of the increase in short-run inflation. In other words, starting from an initial point on the long-run Phillips curve in (5.2) (consistent with constant inflation), any decrease in unemployment below its current value will see inflation rise initially and then keep rising over time. So simply noting that inflation rises/falls as unemployment falls/rises does not establish the existence of a unique rate of unemployment consistent with stable inflation: there will always be a succession of increases (decreases) in inflation following a reduction (increase) in unemployment, even if we do not observe dynamic homogeneity. As such, the observation of successive increases/decreases in inflation following a change in unemployment does not, in and of itself, establish that the Phillips curve is vertical at the original rate of unemployment. What really distinguishes the NAIRUH from the standard Phillips curve is that, according to the NAIRUH, starting from a position consistent with constant inflation, any permanent decrease in unemployment will cause inflation to keep rising indefinitely (the so-called accelerationist hypothesis), whereas according to the standard Phillips curve, the increase in inflation will be finite (inflation will eventually reach a new steady state value, consistent with (5.2)). And according to Fair (1999, 2000), evidence supports the idea that following a reduction in unemployment, the observed increase in inflation is strictly finite. At the end of the day, then, rather than rescuing the NAIRUH, we arrive via this line of reasoning at a result that delivers yet another blow to the hypothesis.

9. The number of contributions to Backhouse (1994) that remain in thrall to this tradition is testimony to its lasting effect on the practice of economics. See, for example, Setterfield (1999). Note also that even economists who eschew formal methodological enquiry may be said to tacitly identify (or be allied) with the Popper–Lakatos tradition. It is instructive to note, in this regard, Blaug's (1994, p. 131) approving remarks about the work of Mayer (1993).
10. Interestingly, it is questionable to what extent it ever was. Hence see Stanley (2005, pp. 617–18) for one indication of the infrequency with which actually testing for the existence of the NAIRU has been a central feature of the empirical NAIRU literature.
11. It might be considered more so were it not for the macroeconomic policy positions that NAIRU theory supports, which critics of the NAIRU identify as severely detrimental to the real economy.

REFERENCES

Backhouse, R.E. (ed.) (1994), *New Directions in Economic Methodology*, London: Routledge.

Ball, L. and Mankiw, N.G. (2002), 'The NAIRU in theory and practice', *Journal of Economic Perspectives*, **16**, 115–36.

Blaug, M. (1994), 'Why I am not a constructivist: confessions of an unrepentant Popperian', in R.E. Backhouse, (ed.), *New Directions in Economic Methodology*, London: Routledge, pp. 109–36.

CEPR (1995), *Unemployment Choices for Europe*, London: Centre for Economic Policy Research.

Dew-Becker, I. and Gordon, R.J. (2005), 'Where did the productivity growth go? Inflation dynamics and the distribution of income', *Brookings Papers on Economic Activity*, **0** (2), 67–127.

Fair, R. (1999), 'Estimated inflation costs had European unemployment been reduced in the 1980s by macroeconomic policies', *Journal of Macroeconomics*, **21**, 1–28.

Fair, R. (2000), 'Testing the NAIRU model for the United States', *Review of Economics and Statistics*, **82**, 64–71.

Galbraith, J.K. (1997), 'Time to ditch the NAIRU', *Journal of Economic Perspectives*, **11**, 93–108.

Gordon, R.J. (1997), 'The time-varying NAIRU and its implications for economic policy', *Journal of Economic Perspectives*, **11** (1), 11–32.

Gordon, R.J. (1998), 'Foundations of the goldilocks economy: supply shocks and the time-varying NAIRU', *Brookings Papers on Economic Activity*, **0** (2), 297–333.

Jenkinson, T. (1987), 'The natural rate of unemployment: does it exist?', *Oxford Review of Economic Policy*, **3** (3), 20–26.

Lang, D. (2004), *Hysteresis in Unemployment*, Thèse de Doctorat, Université de la Méditerranée.

Lang, D. (2007), 'Can the European construction really continue relying on the NAIRU?', in E. Hein, A. Heise, J. Priewe and A. Truger (eds), *European Integration in Crisis*, Marburg: Metropolis, pp. 221–45.

Lang, D. and De Peretti, C. (2009) 'A strong hysteretic model of Okun's Law: theory and a preliminary investigation', *International Review of Applied Economics*, **23** (4), 445–62.

Lavoie, M. (2006), 'A post-Keynesian amendment to the New Consensus on monetary policy', *Metroeconomica*, **57** (2), 165–92.

Mankiw, N.G. (2006), *Macroeconomics*, 6th edn, New York: Worth.

Mayer, T. (1993), *Truth versus Precision in Economics*, Aldershot, UK and Brookfield, US: Edward Elgar.

Setterfield, M. (1999), 'Review of *New Directions in Economic Methodology* edited by R. Backhouse', *Review of Social Economy*, **57** (3), 405–10.

Setterfield, M. and LeBlond, K. (2003), 'The Phillips curve and US macroeconomic performance during the 1990s', *International Review of Applied Economics*, **17**, 361–76.

Stanley, T.D. (2005), 'Integrating the empirical tests of the natural rate hypothesis: a meta-regression analysis', *Kyklos*, **58**, 611–34.

6. Still unemployed, after all these wage cuts. Labor in Europe

Engelbert Stockhammer

INTRODUCTION

Much as in the rest of the world, the late 1970s and early 1980s marked a watershed in European politics. Unlike in the USA or the UK, neoliberalism in continental Europe did not come with an outright assault on labor unions. Notably, important transformations were initiated not by national governments, but by supranational organizations and central banks. The Single European Act, signed in 1986 and effective in 1992, opened national economies and established a competition policy that rules out industrial policy and prevents state-owned enterprises from being subsidized for employment policy. International capital flows were liberalized as part of the European Monetary System (EMS). The Bundesbank dominated the EMS throughout the 1980s and dictated a high real interest rate, which high-inflation countries had to top in order to maintain stable exchange rates. In the 1990s the Bundesbank was succeeded by the European Central Bank, and the Stability and Growth Pact (SGP) shaped monetary and fiscal policies.

One of the most important outcomes of these policies was the rise and the persistence of unemployment. Unemployment in the euro area was around 2 percent in 1970 but increased to (and above) 8 percent after 1981. A second important development has received less publicity: wage growth has consistently lagged behind productivity growth in this period, which amounts to a substantial redistribution of income between capital and labor.[1]

Critical economists have frequently blamed monetary and fiscal policies for these developments, but few quantitative assessments of their relative impact exist. Ideally one would like to use a post-Keynesian consensus estimate for, say, the fiscal multiplier and the effect of a change in interest rates on demand. However, it turns out that no such consensus estimates exist. Indeed, it seems that post-Keynesian economists are hesitant to put figures on these effects. Consequently this chapter will take such figures somewhat selectively from the literature, using mainstream research, and drawing on previous work of my own and common sense. This chapter offers a preliminary assessment rather than precise (or original) results. Rather than deliver definitive answers, the task at hand is to propose a framework for future analysis. While frequently referring to 'Europe', our discussion is indeed limited to the euro area.

The chapter is structured as follows. The following section critically reviews the mainstream flexibility story. In section 2 the economic performance of the euro area is discussed. Sections 3, 4 and 5 assess the demand effects of monetary policy, of fiscal policy, of a change in the wage share respectively and make some (ultimatively inconclusive) comments on the effects of financialization. Finally, section 6 summarizes the key findings and derives policy conclusions.

1. THE MAINSTREAM STORY: INFLEXIBLE LABOR MARKETS

The OECD–IMF–EC explanation of Europe's unemployment claims that the root of the current economic malaise is inflexibility of labor markets, because it allows insiders to maintain wages above market-clearing levels. Discussing the subtleties and contradictions of this literature is beyond the scope of this chapter. There is rich evidence that labor market institutions are unable to explain changes in unemployment. One of the most comprehensive studies was recently presented by Baker et al. (2005, p. 107), who find 'no meaningful relationship between [the] OECD measure of labor market deregulation and shifts in the NAIRU'. Earlier, Madsen (1998, p. 862) concluded from a panel analysis that 'the Layard and Nickell model seems unable to explain the increase in European unemployment'. Ball (1999, p. 191) investigated monetary policy during recessions and finds that 'labor market policies are not important causes of the unemployment successes and failures since 1985'. In a time series analysis covering the large European economies and the USA Stockhammer (2004a) finds no evidence that labor market institutions drive unemployment, with the possible exception of the tax wedge. Moreover, some OECD (1998, 1999) studies found no effect of employment protection or minimum wages on aggregate unemployment. It is notable that the literature mentioned above is routinely ignored in publications by the OECD, the IMF and the EC.

2. THE MACROECONOMIC PERFORMANCE OF THE EURO AREA

One implication of the IMF–OECD explanation is that one would expect high unemployment to go hand in hand with high wages. Indeed, unemployment in these models is caused by wages being set 'too high', thus pushing up the NAIRU. However, this is squarely at odds with the factual development of the European economies. Figure 6.1 plots the development of the rate of unemployment and the (adjusted) wage share from 1971 to 2004. Ignoring differences between the CPI and the GDP deflator, the adjusted wage share is equivalent to the real unit labor costs in the business sector. An increase means that wages are growing faster than productivity. The graph illustrates that unemployment has risen and wages have fallen (relative to productivity) in Europe since 1980. Indeed, the (adjusted) wage share has fallen by around 10 percentage points since 1980.

Table 6.1 summarizes the macroeconomic performance of the euro-12 area (as calculated by the OECD). Period I (1970–80) covers the decade prior to neoliberalism characterized by (often inconsistent) Keynesian policies. Period II (1981–92) covers a period of contested European integration with the establishment and the crisis of the EMS. The year 1992 marks the signing of the Maastricht Treaty (although it did not become effective until 1994) as well as the implementation of the Single Market. In Period III (1993–2004) European integration dominated national policies.

Figure 6.1 Unemployment rate and (adjusted) wage share in the euro-12

Table 6.1 Economic performance of the Euro 12 area

	Period I 1970–80	Period II 1981–92	Period III 1993–2004	Period II – Period I	Period III – Period II
GDP growth	3.02%	2.49%	1.88%	−0.53%	−0.60%
Real long interest	0.57	4.89	3.55	4.32	−1.34
Real short interest	−0.25	4.59	2.18	4.84	−2.40
Primary budget surplus (% GDP)	−0.12	−0.61	0.78	−0.49	1.39
Adjusted wage share	72.40	68.99	65.81	−3.41	−3.18

Source: OECD Economic Outlook Dataset (No. 81), except for adjusted wage share (at factor costs): AMECO database (May 2007 version).

Fiscal policies in particular were geared towards meeting the Maastricht Convergence Criteria and the Stability and Growth Pact respectively. The data show a substantial slowdown of GDP growth, falling from 2.5 to 1.9 (see Table 6.1). It is remarkable that labor productivity growth also slowed down, despite the Single Market, which was promised to generate substantial productivity gains (Emerson et al. 1988).

3. MONETARY POLICY

To assess the monetary policy stance, the *ex post* real values for short-term and long-term interest rates are reported. The short rate is closer to the Central Bank's policy instrument; the long rate should be more relevant for investment decisions. Real interest rates increased by some 4 percentage points in the early 1980s. From the 1981–92 period to 1993–2004 they fell, but stayed above the levels of the 1960s and 1970s until the early 2000s. Thus the run-up to the euro therefore did indeed benefit those countries that had suffered high interest rates in the 1980s to maintain the exchange rate to the Deutschmark. Although it may sound surprising, for the euro area as a whole monetary policy cannot be regarded as tight since 1993, if compared to the 1980s. However, the 1980s were a period of extraordinarily tight monetary policy by postwar standards. Monetary policy is still tight in the sense that interest rates are higher than growth in the 1990s.

While post-Keynesians have frequently criticized restrictive monetary policy for high unemployment, I have failed to find estimates of how much of the unemployment is due to monetary policy. Indeed, it is hard to quantify the effect of monetary policy on output because the effect of interest rates is 'tenuous', as Taylor (1999) put it. While macroeconomic simulation models such as VARs (vector autoregressions) tend to find substantial interest rate effects, the empirical research on consumption and investment usually fails to deliver support for these strong effects (Taylor 1999). The effect seems to be there in the grand picture (i.e. system estimations or simulation) but hard to pin down in detail (in particular when it comes to investment). The ECB itself put the effect of a 1 percent point increase in the interest rate (after three years) at −0.71 percent to −0.29 percent of GDP (ECB 2004, p. 48). The models from which these effects emerge are typically loaded with long-term restrictions that would be unacceptable to post-Keynesian economists. Moreover, the precise timing of monetary policy is probably very important (as American new Keynesians have long pointed out).[2] Below we shall use the assumption of a 0.5 effect of a one percentage point increase in real interest rates on GDP growth.[3]

4. FISCAL POLICY

While we have a reasonably clear and exogenous measure for monetary policy, the interest rate, the same is not the case for fiscal policy. The government's fiscal balance is itself endogenous to the state of the economy. Simply put, if the deficit is high, it is hard to tell whether fiscal policy has been expansionary or the economy is merely in a recession. This poses a severe problem in estimating multiplier effects. Table 6.1 presents two measures for fiscal policy: the primary budget surplus (i.e. budget surplus without interest payments) and the growth rate of real government consumption. Since the budget surplus as well as the primary budget surplus are positively correlated with GDP growth, one would expect that they are affected by GDP growth as well as themselves affecting GDP growth. Automatic stabilizers seem to be operating in the euro area, which creates serious problems for the empirical identification of multiplier effects.

Unlike monetary policy, fiscal policy is not *en vogue* among new Keynesians, so the mainstream literature is much thinner on this issue. Still, there are some estimates of the multiplier at hand. Hemming et al. (2002) offer a survey of the literature that concludes that 'short term multipliers average around one half for taxes and one for spending' (Hemming et al. 2002, p. 36). Many new Keynesian models impose long neutrality via an implicit NAIRU. Most post-Keynesian would probably think that multipliers are substantially higher for a relatively closed economy such as the euro area.

A simple guesstimate of the effect is to assume a multiplier of one on the primary budget deficit (interest payments would thus be allowed to have a different multiplier). An increase in the primary budget deficit leads to a corresponding decrease in GDP. This approach has the advantage of convenience, but obviously does lack elegance or sophistication.[4]

5. CHANGES IN INCOME DISTRIBUTION

One factor in the decline of demand has been the decline of the wage share. Kaleckians have long argued that wage restraint will dampen demand because of the decline in consumption expenditures. More generally, a decline of the wage share will push the various components of aggregate demand in different directions. First, it will likely have depressing effects on (private) consumption expenditures because wage income is typically associated with a higher consumption propensity than profit income. Second, it will have an expansionary effect on investment as profitability is rising. Third, it will have a positive effect on net exports because the falling wage share is equivalent to a fall in unit labor costs, which are a measure of price competitiveness. The overall or net effect is thus *a priori* indeterminate and depends on the specific size of the respective effects (Blecker 1999; Bhaduri and Marglin 1990). Table 6.2 summarizes the results of Stockhammer et al. (2007), who estimated such a model for the euro area. They find that, with minor differences in the method of calculation, an increase in the wage share by one percentage point leads to an increase in (private excess) demand by 0.17 percent of GDP. This estimate is the lower bound of the actual effect as it does not account for second-round effects such as the effect of increased demand on investment.

Table 6.2 Private excess demand (in percentage points of GDP) caused by a 1 percentage point increase of the wage share

	Effects in 2005	**Effects at mean levels**
Consumption	0.43	0.37
Investment	−0.07	−0.07
Domestic excess demand	*0.35*	*0.30*
Net exports	−0.16	−0.11
Private excess demand:	**0.17**	**0.19**

Note: Private excess demand is the sum of the effects of a change in income distribution on consumption, investment and net exports given the level of income.

Source: Based on Stockhammer et al. (2009), Table 7.

In recent years a growing empirical literature has been investigating similar models: Bowles and Boyer (1995); Stockhammer and Onaran (2004); Naastepad and Storm (2006/07); and Hein and Vogel (2008) offer studies on several other countries. For most countries a similar picture emerges. The consumption effect typically outweighs the investment effect and the size (and the sign) of the overall net effect crucially depends on the openness of the economy. In other words, small open economies are likely to be profit led, because foreign trade constitutes a much larger share of their GDP.

6. FINANCIALIZATION AND OTHER INFLUENCES ON PRIVATE INVESTMENT

Remarkably, investment has stagnated despite a substantial rise in profitability, which, at least in Marxian and classical economics, is a key determinant of investment. As depicted in Figure 6.2, the ratio of investment to profits shows a declining trend. In Germany in 1970 investment amounted to 80 percent of profits, whereas in 2000 the value had fallen to around 60 percent. All countries show a similar trend. If the investment–profit ratio had stayed constant, investment would almost be twice as high as it is now.

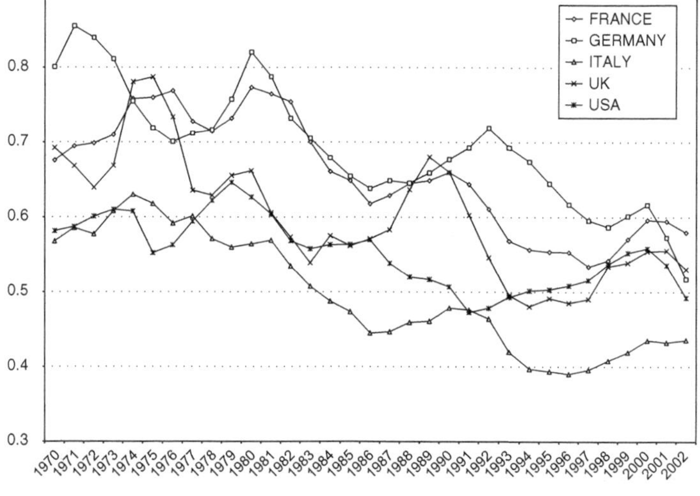

Source: Stockhammer (2006).

Figure 6.2 Investment – operating surplus ratio for major economies

In part these changes in investment behavior may be due to high real interest rates and to slow growth itself. However, post-Keynesians and Marxists tend to see accumulation as the cause rather than the effect of growth. An appropriate discussion of the issue is outside the scope of this chapter. Duménil and Lévy (2001) present calculations showing that after-interest payments profits did not increase as strongly as operating surplus would suggest. If so, this may be part of the explanation. Stockhammer (2004b, 2006) argues that shareholder value orientation has altered investment behavior and finds that on average around one-third of the slowdown of accumulation since the 1960s is explained by financialization (which is defined with respect to the financial activities of non-financial businesses for this purpose). However, the effects differ substantially between countries.

There are other factors that may have contributed to insufficient demand. Globalization in the form of relocation of production may also have reduced domestic investment by substituting it with foreign direct investment.[5] For lack of well-motivated figures that could be used for the comparative effects of financialization and globalization, they will be excluded from our calculations of the effects on demand. This section thus only serves as a reminder of what has been left out.

7. A PRELIMINARY QUANTITATIVE ASSESSMENT

We now turn to an assessment of the size of the effects of changes in monetary policy, fiscal policy and income distribution on aggregate demand in Europe. It must be emphasized that these are to be understood as a first attempt to systematize previous research and put it together from a Keynesian perspective, rather than definitive assessment. It is an attempt to take stock and an invitation for future to refine the methods of such a calculation.

The calculations on the effects of monetary policy fiscal policy and the decline in wage share are summarized in Table 6.3. We assume that a change in the real long-term interest rate has a negative effect on GDP of 0.5. Monetary policy tightened in the 1980s (Period II) compared to the 1970s (Period I) and had a negative effect of some 2.16 percentage points of growth (per annum) in the 1980s. Monetary policy then loosened in the 1990s (Period III), having an expansionary effect of 0.67 percentage points of GDP compared to the 1980s. Note, however, that monetary policy still had a contractionary effect compared to the 1970s.

For fiscal policy a mulitiplier of 1 on the primary budget surplus is assumed. Fiscal policy had a moderately expansionary effect of half a percentage point in the 1980s (Period II) and turned strongly contractionary

Table 6.3 *Demand effects of changes in monetary policy, fiscal policy and income distribution in the 1980 and 1990s*

	Implied effect on demand				
	Period II – Period I	Period III – Period II	Assumed effect on Y	Period II compared to Period I	Period III compared to Period II
(1) Real long interest	4.32	−1.34	*−0.5*	−2.16	0.67
(2) Real short interest	4.84	−2.40	*−0.5*	−2.42	1.20
(3) Primary budget surplus (% GDP)	−0.49	1.39	*−1*	0.49	−1.39
(4) Growth govt consumption	−1.4	−0.4	*0.3*	−0.42	−0.12
(5) Adjusted wage share	−3.41	−3.18	*0.02*	−0.07	−0.06
Sum of effects on GDP growth (rows 1 + 3 + 5)				−1.74	−0.79
Actual change in GDP growth				−0.53%	−0.60%

Note: All effects are compared to the previous period and are per annum.

in the 1990s (Period III), having a negative effect of 1.4 percent of GDP.[6] The effect of wage policy is comparably small with a steady −0.1 percent. The wage share has declined steadily throughout the 1980s and 1990s. It had a rather small overall effect on demand.

With a value of −1.74 percent (in annual growth), our calculations over-explain the slowdown in growth (−0.53) substantially in the 1980s (Period II) and get the order of magnitude of the slowdown in 1990s right (−0.79 and −0.6 for the calculated and actual change respectively). It is thus likely that the multipliers used are not accurate or that important aspects of the story are missing. Presumably both are the case. The results are merely first attempts to quantify the relevant effects. For each effect on demand growth there are two possible mistakes. Either the wrong variable is looked at or the effect may be in need of improvement. For monetary policy and wage policy, the variable will be rather uncontested, but for fiscal policy the choice is less clear cut. The effects (multipliers) will undoubtedly cause disagreement. In particular, the question is to what extent the ECB's estimates should be used in such a context.

The present mainstream literature is much fonder of monetary policy than of fiscal policy. Arguably, this is due to theoretical considerations

Table 6.4 Demand effects with modified multipliers

	Implied effect on demand				
	Period II – Period I	Period III – Period II	Assumed effect on Y	Period II compared to Period I	Period III compared to Period II
(1) Real long interest	4.32	−1.34	*−0.3*	−1.30	0.40
(2) Real short interest	4.84	−2.40	*−0.3*	−1.45	0.72
(3) Primary budget surplus (% GDP)	−0.49	1.39	*−1.2*	0.59	−1.67
(4) Growth govt consumption	−1.4	−0.4	*0.3*	−0.42	−0.12
(5) Adjusted wage share	−3.41	−3.18	*0.02*	−0.07	−0.06
Sum of effects on GDP growth (rows 1 + 3 +5)				−0.78	−1.33
Actual change in GDP growth				−0.53%	−0.60%

(namely the monetarist legacy) rather than to empirical findings. Existing empirical studies on monetary and fiscal multipliers may consequently be biased upwards and downwards respectively. As this will be reflected in our calculations, Table 6.4 repeats the calculation, trying to compensate for these biases. It is assumed that the effect of (a one percentage point) change in the (real) interest rate is 0.3 percent of GDP (rather than 0.5 percent) and that the fiscal multiplier is 1.2 (rather than 1). Both are modifications that do not lie outside the range of estimates surveyed earlier.

With these modified multipliers the results are then more in line for the 1980s (−0.78 calculated versus −0.53 actual), but not for the 1990s (−1.33 calculated versus −0.6 actual). Again the calculated effects are only a coarse match for actual developments. However, the broad trends are clear: monetary policy has had strong negative effects on demand growth in the 1980s and fiscal policy had strong negative effects in the 1990s.

8. CONCLUSION

Rejecting the inflexible labor markets story, the chapter aimed to contribute to an alternative explanation of European unemployment from the empirical side. As a first step our assessment is crude and often little more than a literature review. Monetary policy was extraordinarily tight in the 1980s and eased in the 1990s, but interest rates remain higher than growth rates. The effect of interest rates on growth is 'tenuous'. Fiscal policy was tight in the 1980s compared to the 1970s, and was further tightened in the 1990s. The euro area in the late 1990s has had significant primary budget surpluses and it seems that government spending has robust effects. Thus the creation of the euro and the SGP seem to have eased monetary policy somewhat (for southern European countries), but tightened fiscal policy substantially. While it is probably fair to say that monetary policy played a major role in the increase in unemployment in the 1980s and a minor role in the 1990s, fiscal policy can be considered a major cause of unemployment in the 1990s.

Investment behavior has changed. While some three-quarters of profits were reinvested in the 1970s, only about half of them are reinvested in the early 2000s. Therefore autonomous changes in investment behavior have probably contributed substantially to unemployment in the 1980s as well as the 1990s, but have been left out of this analysis. Prime candidates for such changes are financialization and relocation.

These qualifications call for further research. However, the crude picture painted already allows for some policy conclusions. First, fiscal policy has been unduly restrictive in the past, contributing substantially to unemployment. The political reason for budget cuts of course was the SGP. It has to be reformed so as to allow the state to play an active role. In parallel, tax systems have to be restructured so as to respond to the rising share of financial incomes and wealth. Second, Europe has experienced two decades of wage restraint – with no improvement of economic performance. It is time to realize that more of the same medicine that has not worked in the past is unlikely to work in the future. Lower wages lead to higher profits, not to more employment.

ACKNOWLEDGMENTS

Earlier versions of this chapter were presented at the URPE Session 'Labor in the Age of Neoliberal Globalization' at the ASSA, Boston, 2006, and the conference 'Post Keynesian Economic Policies', Dijon, 2007.

NOTES

1. Mainstream research institutions only started to take this issue seriously in 2007 (IMF 2007; OECD 2007).

2. Ball (1999) found strong effects of monetary policy during a recession on unemployment.
3. Note that we interpret this as a long-run effect, whereas the ECB, on which it is based, interprets it as a short-run effect. Often long-run neutrality is imposed. De Grauwe and Costa Storti (2004) offer an interesting meta-analysis of this literature.
4. Stockhammer (2008) reports an effect of the growth of public consumption on the growth of GDP based on estimates for the euro of around 0.6. For econometric analysis the growth of government consumption can be considered a cause (rather than an effect) of GDP growth, because automatic multipliers mostly operate through transfers and taxes. The implied static multiplier is rather high (around 2.5) and it turns out that the results are rather sensitive to the time period. Taking the estimates at face value, the reductions in the government spending from period 1970–80 to 1981–92 and 1981–92 to 1993–2004 imply growth effects of −0.76 and −0.39 percentage points per annum respectively. In the calculations in the text we shall therefore use a more conservative value of half that estimate.
5. Falk and Wolfmayr (2005) investigate outsourcing measured as intermediate inputs originating from the same industry by means of a sectoral panel study and find that 'the observed change in EU outsourcing between 1995 and 2000 alone accounts for an employment reduction of 0.26 percentage points per year' (p. 16).
6. This finding depends on the measure for fiscal policy. The decline of government consumption, another possible indicator, has been strong in Period II and moderated thereafter. Table 6.3 also indicates the effects of fiscal policy based on government consumption assuming a dynamic multiplier of 0.3 (which corresponds to a static multiplier of roughly 1.3).

REFERENCES

Baker, D., Glyn, A., Howell, D. and Schmitt, J. (2005), 'Labor market institutions and unemployment: a critical assessment of the cross-country evidence', in David Howell (ed.), *Fighting Unemployment. The Limits for Free Market Orthodoxy*. Oxford: Oxford University Press, pp. 72–118.

Ball, Lawrence (1999), 'Aggregate demand and long-run unemployment', *Brookings Papers on Economic Activity*, **2**, 189–236.

Bhaduri, A. and Marglin, S. (1990), 'Unemployment and the real wage: the economic basis for contesting political ideologies', *Cambridge Journal of Economics*, **14**, 375–93.

Blecker, R. (1999), 'Kaleckian macromodels for open economies', in J. Deprez, and J.T. Harvey (eds), *Foundations of International Economics: Post Keynesian Perspectives*, London and New York: Routledge, pp. 116–49.

Bowles, S. and Boyer, R. (1995), 'wages, aggregate demand, and employment in an open economy: an empirical investigation', in G. Epstein and H. Gintis (eds), *Macroeconomic Policy after the Conservative Era: Studies in Investment, Saving and Finance*, Cambridge, Cambridge University press, pp. 147–73.

De Gauwe, P. and Costa Storti, C. (2004), 'The effects of monetary policy: a meta analysis', CESifo Working Paper 1224.

Duménil, G. and Lévy, D. (2001), 'Costs and benefits of neoliberalism: a class analysis', *Review of International Political Economy*, **8** (4), 578–607.

ECB (2004), *The Monetary Policy of the ECB*, Frankfurt: ECB.

Emerson, M., Aujean, M., Catinat, M., Goybet, P. and Jacquemin, A. (1988), *The Economics of 1992*, Oxford: Oxford University Press.

Falk, M. and Wolfmayr, Y. (2005), 'The impact of international outsourcing on employment: empirical evidence for EU countries', paper presented at the workshop 'Relocation to CEECs: who gains, who loses?', Hamburg, September.

Hein, E. and Vogel, L. (2008), 'Distribution and growth reconsidered – empirical results for Austria, France, Germany, the Netherlands, the UK and the USA', *Cambridge Journal of Economics*, **32** (3), 479–511.

Hemming, Richard, Kell, Michael and Mahfouz, Selma (2002), 'The effectiveness of fiscal policy in stimulating economic activity – a review of the literature', IMF Working Paper No. 208.

IMF (2007), 'The globalization of labor', in *World Economics Outlook*, April, Washington: IMF, ch. 5.

Madsen, J. (1998), 'General equilibrium macroeconomic models of unemployment: can they explain the unemployment path in the OECD?', *Economic Journal*, **108**, 850–67.

Naastepad, R. and Storm, S. (2006/07), 'OECD demand regimes (1960–2000)', *Journal of Post-Keynesian Economics*, **29** (2), 213–48.

OECD (2007), 'OECD workers in the global economy: increasingly vulnerable?', *OECD Employment Outlook*, Paris: OECD, ch. 3.

OECD (1998), 'Making the most of the minimum: statutory minimum wages, employment and poverty', *OECD Employment Outlook*, Paris: OECD, ch. 3.

OECD (1999), 'Employment protection and labour market performance', *OECD Employment Outlook*, Paris: OECD, ch. 2.

Stockhammer, Engelbert (2004a), 'Explaining European unemployment: testing the NAIRU story and a Keynesian approach', *International Review of Applied Economics*, **18** (1), 3–24.

Stockhammer, E. (2004b), 'Financialization and the slowdown of accumulation', *Cambridge Journal of Economics*, **28** (5), 719–41.

Stockhammer, Engelbert (2006), 'Shareholder value-orientation and the investment–profit puzzle', *Journal of Post Keynesian Economics*, **28** (2), 193–216.

Stockhammer, Engelbert (2008), 'Effects of European integration on Austria's economy', *International Review of Applied Economics*, **23** (1), 19–40.

Stockhammer, E. and Onaran, Ö. (2004), 'Accumulation, distribution and employment: a structural VAR approach to a Kaleckian macro-model', *Structural Change and Economic Dynamics*, **15** (4), 421–47.

Stockhammer, E., Onaran, Ö. and Ederer, S. (2009), 'Functional income distribution and aggregate demand in the Euro area', *Cambridge Journal of Economics*, **33** (1), 139–59.

Taylor, Mark (1999), 'Real interest rates and macroeconomic activity', *Oxford Review of Economic Policy*, **15** (2), 95–113.

7. Labour market and monetary macroeconomics

Vincent Vernay

INTRODUCTION

When asked whether there is a labour market, most economists would answer yes. And yet it is not certain that there is a market mechanism for labour that can explain the formation of wages.

Before analysing the labour market further, Section 1 sets out the standard presentation of a large majority of economists on this issue. This presentation is based on neoclassical theory in which the existence of such a market is not in doubt. In keeping with its assumptions, mainstream economic thought considers that any study of the labour market can be based on individual behaviour only: the analysis, although heralded as macroeconomic, remains grounded in microeconomics. The market, as it is understood by mainstream theorists, takes on highly specific characteristics. The actions occurring there are of the nature of transfers between two economic agents – workers and firms. Workers offer their productive services[1] against an amount of money that firms make over to them. When analysed like any other goods market, the 'neoclassical' labour market is one component of a general equilibrium model of markets and the place where labour is bought and sold. For neoclassical economists, money is a commodity whose function is to serve as an intermediary in exchange. Considering money to be endowed with purchasing power, the neoclassical analysis views the remuneration of workers as a form of purchase.

At first glance, post-Keynesian economists seem to reject the mainstream view. However, this is not a categorical rejection. Section 2 shows that for Lavoie (1992) the labour market 'does not really exist' (p. 217). Certain post-Keynesian economists' criticism of the 'neoclassical' labour market appears to be only partial, then, because their analyses still bear the imprint of the microeconomic view. However, they do provide food for thought about the operation by which wages are determined, an operation that, they argue, involves factors other than economic ones (balance of power, bargaining processes).

In the last section, Schmitt's theory of money emissions provides a more precise grasp of the role and place of the labour market in the economic system. The foundations of macroeconomics are not microeconomic. Contrary to neoclassical economists' assertions, the formation of wages is not the result of a transfer between two forms of wealth existing prior to production. Production is considered as the primary economic operation and relative exchanges give way to absolute exchanges. Labour, once explained, can no longer be considered as something that is exchanged on a market. It will be seen that the formation of wages is not a matter of a relative exchange of labour against money but of an absolute exchange that workers engage in with themselves. It will be seen that, money being bank money, workers convert their labour into a physical product that is itself converted into a money wage through firms and banks. So workers do not sell their labour to anyone and their income does not consist of wealth somehow produced outside of their productive activity.

1. THE LABOUR MARKET VIEWED BY NEOCLASSICAL THEORY

The framework of the neoclassical analysis is purely microeconomic. The macroeconomic model it aims to build is the result of aggregating individual behaviour. In describing a world where everything is given at the outset and where agents are endowed with goods and abilities to provide market services, neoclassical economists liken production to a simple relative exchange.

The general equilibrium of markets forms the structure behind neoclassical reasoning. The labour market is one of its components. It is the place where labour is bought and sold. Labour, a service sold by workers, is sold in exchange for an amount of money that firms make over to them. The relationship that is established between the two commodities of labour and money is that of a transfer – and so payment of workers is a relative exchange.

However, to be able to buy labour on a market, entrepreneurs must have money endowed from the outset – that is, before any production of goods and services – with purchasing power. Entrepreneurs' spending of money to pay workers is then a simple transfer of pre-existing purchasing power.

Neoclassical economists consider the economy as two spheres, real and monetary, where money and output are not associated.

1.1 From Microeconomic Foundations to Macroeconomics

Neoclassical theory analyses the economy as a set of individuals whose aim is to maximize their satisfaction. From this perspective, economic agents set about trading on a series of markets.

The approach taken by this strand of thought is entirely individualistic: economic agents are autonomous, independent and perfectly rational. And so it goes without saying that, for neoclassical economists, the primary subject of study of economics is the individual and the validity of economic theory cannot be vouchsafed otherwise. 'The actions of groups, organizations, communities, nations, and societies can best be understood by focusing attention on the incentives and actions of members' (Alchian and Allen 1969, p. 19). Economic principles are based on postulates established from individual behaviour.

In developing a macroeconomic theory, neoclassical economists and subsequently new Keynesians were to abide by this idea that the starting point must be the study of individual behaviour. Their objective was to lay down the microeconomic foundations of macroeconomics. For economists of these two schools, there was no question that this was the right road to go down.

'Can macroeconomic phenomena be understood independently of the underlying microeconomic phenomena? Clearly not' (Malinvaud 1991, p. 22; our translation). A macroeconomic model must be constructed by an aggregative process. And this aggregation is done by straightforward summation. Mankiw (1994) asserts as much.

> When we study the economy as a whole, we must consider the decisions of individual economics actor . . . Because aggregate variables are simply the sum of the variables describing many individual decisions, macroeconomics is inevitably founded in microeconomics. (Mankiw 1994, p. 14)

To found a macroeconomic analysis, for neoclassical and new Keynesian economists, one must start from the behaviour of economic agents. There are no two ways about it. But that implies that one can establish a behavioural macroeconomics. 'Macroeconomics studies the behaviour of economic agents, behaviour that is summarized by magnitudes termed aggregates' (Begg et al. 1996, p. 15; our translation). These aggregate magnitudes are invariably based on a study of individual behaviour. Consequently, they are subjective and non-measurable data.

Our final observation relates also to the labour market as it is apprehended by neoclassical economists. 'Global' supply and demand are the sum of the individual supply of and demand for labour. Such aggregation of the individual supply of and demand for labour is made possible by assuming that economic agents all behave in the same way. Neoclassical economists thus define the behaviour of a representative economic agent and assume that all agents behave likewise. It appears that since the individual supply of and demand for labour are based on the behaviour of economic agents, the same must be true of 'global' supply and demand. As Guitton (1984) emphasizes, 'aggregation expresses identical data in another way: there can be no difference between the two expressions' (p. 23; our translation). Can we settle for this definition of macroeconomics as the sum of microeconomic components? If the definition were correct, then as Schmitt (1984) argues, 'the subject matter of macroeconomics would be identical to the subject matter of microeconomics, the only difference being in that the magnitudes are taken in isolation or in their summation' (p. 354; our translation). But might it not be thought that macroeconomics has a dimension of its own? That its foundations are to be sought elsewhere than in an analysis of individual behaviour? For this, we need to dwell on the term 'globality'. For neoclassical theory, aggregation of individual supply of and demand for labour yields the 'global' supply and demand. But for Schmitt (1984), 'a "globality" is a whole, a totality, something indivisible. A magnitude obtained by aggregation, or an aggregate, is on the contrary a sum that can be freely divided since it was obtained by adding its components' (p. 354; our translation). This is why macroeconomic magnitudes are 'global' and are different from microeconomic magnitudes.

The final section follows another avenue of enquiry concerning the foundations of macroeconomics. For now, since for the two main strands of economics a valid economic theory can be constructed solely by starting with individual behaviour, we need to see how the actions of economic agents are coordinated. Let us take a closer look at the major feature of the analysis, the market.

1.2 A Market Defined

Before going any further in analysing the labour market, let us try to understand the core concept of mainstream economic thought – the market.

Neoclassical theory defines a market as a place where buyers and sellers of the same commodity come together. From this convergence of supply by sellers and demand from buyers there arises a price, that of the commodity exchanged. In reality, there is not one object being exchanged on a market but two. That seems logical enough: an exchange by definition presupposes that there are two commodities. Suppose there are two individuals A and B and two commodities a and b. A is a seller of commodity a and B is a buyer of the same commodity a. If B wants to buy commodity a, he will have to give up commodity b in consideration, and commodity b will be bought by A. It can be seen, then, that on a market there are two commodities, one that A makes over to B and one that B makes over to A. As Walras (1952) argued, 'any exchange of two things one for the other consists in a double sale and a double purchase' (p. 44; our translation). So there are two prices, that of commodity a (in units of b) and that of commodity b (in units of a).[2]

Can it be considered, then, that there is a labour market (in the neoclassical sense)? For most economists there is such a market. It is currently presented as the place where supply of and demand for labour come together to yield the determination of a quantity of labour and a price, that of the labour commodity, that is, wages. In fact, two commodities are exchanged on this market: labour, sold by workers and bought by firms; and money, sold by firms and bought by workers.

The labour market is indeed, then, the place of a exchange (a relative one, which is an important qualification): workers supply a certain amount of labour (to meet demand from firms) in exchange of a certain quantity of money made over by the firms. So there are two prices: that of the commodity made over by workers (labour); and that of the commodity made over by firms (money). For all that, neoclassical theory fails to explain the origin of money, or the purchasing power of labour and money. The dichotomous vision it adopts in reasoning about the economy leads it to see the economy as separated into two spheres: one where real magnitudes are determined; and one where monetary magnitudes are determined. It fails to associate the physical output and money. It comes to consider money as a commodity and so as endowed with purchasing power for goods even before it is associated with output; that is, before any production occurs.

1.3 Relative Exchanges

Labour and money as wealth formed independently of any production

Neoclassical theory describes a system where wealth, whether produced or not, is already appropriated and distributed among individuals.

> That is, the goods available in this economy are produced in quantities determined by exogenous forces that then distribute them arbitrarily and free of charge among individuals in the economy. Similarly, the only economic problem of an exchange economy is the optimum redistribution of these goods among the various individuals. (Jessua 1982, p. 7; our translation)

In the neoclassical economy, production is no more than a simple process of transformation by moving matter in space. By referring to Lavoisier's law that in the world of physics nothing is ever created and nothing is ever lost, neoclassical theory finally views production as a mere reproduction of what there was before. In that, it denies the creative character of production and describes a simple relative exchange economy, as emphasized by Cencini (2005): 'production was conceived of as a time-consuming process of transformation subjected to the same mechanism governing relative exchange' (p. 114). Eager to meet their needs and wants, individuals will want to consume goods and services whose use procures them some satisfaction. Should their initial endowments not satisfy them, they will exchange certain goods in certain quantities with other 'market participants', depending on their preferences.

The same reasoning applies to the labour market. The operation economic agents engage in on this market is of the nature of an exchange. This is the time to be clear about the nature of this exchange. Workers, in neoclassical theory, have initial endowments[3] that they can exchange on the various markets with other individuals so as to meet their needs and wants. They already have wealth. Before any production occurs, they have goods and are endowed with abilities to provide market services. The labour market appears to be a place where goods formed previously are exchanged. On the one side, labour is supposedly wealth held by workers that they are prepared to supply to firms. On the other side, money supposedly exists too as wealth held by firms, some of which firms are prepared to make over to workers. So the labour–money exchange – both being forms of wealth that pre-exist production and are formed independently of it – allegedly yields the price of labour, that is, wages. The origin and economic existence of these two commodities go unexplained, though.

A relative exchange of labour and money

On the labour market, the actions that occur are simple transfers: labour moves from workers to firms, and money from firms to workers. Both parties engage in what can be defined as a relative exchange since this operation involves two reciprocal transfers: visibly a mass, that is, a stock (material money) is exchanged for a physical and intellectual activity, that is, a flow (human labour). A problem arises: how can firms buy a flow – labour, physical and intellectual activity – that disappears as it is performed?[4] This transfer cannot be made, in which case firms, in consideration of the sum of money they make over to workers, actually obtain nothing. So if firms do buy something, that something is not strictly speaking labour.

If firms cannot buy labour,[5] it might be thought that, with the money they have, they buy not labour but the result of the productive activity, output. That would imply, then, that the physical product belonged to a group of economic agents, the workers in this instance. But workers cannot make over the output to firms in exchange for money since they do not have it (it is firms that hold the physical output). Workers can only acquire the physical output by spending their wages on the product market. So they cannot make it available, to firms, on the labour market. In any event, it seems that in the neoclassical analysis firms hold money that has purchasing power in exchange over goods and services, and so over labour: the payment of workers is therefore of the nature of a purchase.

1.4 Money is Indissociable from its Purchasing Power

Following neoclassical reasoning, the money firms have allows them to buy a quantity of labour. The money they have is endowed with purchasing power, even before any production operation. Why should this money give them 'power to purchase'?

For mainstream theorists, money is inseparable from its purchasing power, self-evidently. Money is a commodity economic agents possess in their initial endowments and that is involved in exchanges. It invariably appears as an asset endowed with buying power over goods. It is useful in that it is involved in exchanges as a commodity and seems to enable agents to finance net purchases.

The transfer observed on the labour market is of 'purchasing power'. In paying workers, firms transfer purchasing power to them that they can exercise on the product market. We still have no answer as to where the purchasing power of money is initially formed. In any event, it does not appear that this purchasing power is created in the payment of wages: the money firms spend in purchasing labour is merely a transfer of purchasing power. Similarly, the money spent by workers on the product market is transferred to firms. The purchasing power firms made over to workers flows back to them. The money spent on the products market comes from the money injected into the labour market. Walras (1952) explained this in his major work:

> for it is with the money they obtained on the first market from their producer services that landowners, workers and capitalist consumers go onto the second to buy products; and it is with the money they obtained on the second market, from their products, that producer entrepreneurs go onto the first to purchase producer services. (p. 193; our translation)

As purchasing power is 'not destroyed in spending, it is not created either, it is merely passed on in payments' (Bailly 1990, p. 110; our translation).

The dichotomous conception of the economy prevents neoclassical economists from properly understanding money's purchasing power. The theory of money emissions, that will be the analytical support to our final section, provides insight into why paying workers is not like making a purchase.

2. THE MAINSTREAM CHALLENGED PARTIALLY BY POST-KEYNESIANS

The objective of the post-Keynesian school is not just to extend Keynes's theory but also to show that neoclassical theory is unable to provide a proper representation of economic reality.

The main assertion about the labour market in post-Keynesian theory is that it does not really exist.

> Ironically the major aspect of the post-Keynesian view of labour markets is that such markets do not really exist. Whereas one may admit that there is a market for peanuts or for bananas, with well-behaved supply and demand curves, the same hypothesis cannot be made in the case of labour. (Lavoie 1992, p. 217)

For Lavoie, the labour market as conceived of by neoclassical economists is meaningless in the world we live in.

> [T]he labour market does not truly exist; the wage rate is not just another ordinary price: it has much influence on the overall economy; workers are not commodities: norms rule over supply and demand forces; the demand for and the supply of labour are not well-behaved. (Ibid.)

2.1 Wages are not Determined on the Labour Market

Arestis (1992) subscribes to Lavoie's post-Keynesian view of the labour market: there is, he argues, no labour market in the real world as the neoclassical economists understood it. For him, wages are not determined by 'market forces' as part of the general equilibrium but are 'the result of a bargaining process between unions and employers' (p. 165). An agreement on nominal wages arises from the balance of power and conflicts of interest between the two parties. Moreover, for Arestis (1992), 'Wage determination is crucially influenced not just by economics but also by a host of other factors, including political, historical, sociological and psychological forces' (p. 94).

If wages are not determined as the result of a relative exchange of labour against money between workers and firms, could they be determined by a bargaining process between workers and firms? It seems that such a process leads to setting individual wage levels. It will be seen later that the formation of wages is not the result of a market process as neoclassical economists conceived of it; nor does it involve any balance of power between workers and firms, but it stems from a quite specific economic operation. We may ask whether it is not rather over the distribution of the aggregate wage that 'bargaining' among unions and employers has its place. And so a market process.

2.2 Labour is Something Different from a Commodity

For Lavoie (1992) the neoclassical analysis is invalidated not just because the labour market, as neoclassical economists conceive of it, does not exist in the world we live in but also because there is a major difference between commodities and labour.

> An essential distinction, emphasized by Eichner,[6] between labour and commodities is that the former cannot be stored. If labour is not used in one period, because of cyclical unemployment, it is lost forever.

Then, following Seccareccia (1991), Lavoie (1992) explains that workers 'bring with them [on the labour market] not only their labour power but also their past history' (p. 218).

It is obvious that workers do not supply just physical and intellectual activity. They make available to their firm their time and their past and present skills. It is certain that their physical and intellectual activity, in so far as it is productive of goods and services, depends on these qualities. However, the problem of the exact definition and the economic measurement of these qualities remains unresolved. The notion of labour Eichner speaks of corresponds, in truth, to these physical and intellectual qualities. Of course, as Eichner observes, these are not tangible qualities; they are not objects workers carry with them and that they are ready to make over to their potential employer. Even so, it is not this notion that must be used in a macroeconomic analysis of the labour market but actual labour, that is, as will be seen, labour as expenditure of energy. So, as will be seen in the final section, it will appear that the idea of physical conservation put forward by Eichner is not what differentiates labour from a commodity; a number of market services are in this position.

Workers have energy, in a sense, that they are ready to implement, to expend for the productive activity in which they will take part if employed. Here we touch upon an important point in our analysis: the energy workers expend in production, that is, in the transformation of matter and the creation of utility forms, exists in economic space only because it is materialized in the goods produced. Labour is a flow that vanishes in the course of the productive activity. It cannot therefore be lost if it is not used since it exists only in respect of goods produced. Obviously the unemployed may see a decline in their skill levels, say. But labour as a flow of energy cannot be 'lost forever' if it is 'not used in one period' as its economic existence only comes about by it being embodied in some useful form.[7]

It can be seen that the post-Keynesian analysis is critical of the neoclassical view of the labour market. However, radical as it is and while offering new avenues for enquiry, this criticism is partial and does not address the fundamental failings of the mainstream theory. Although they claim to dismiss its microeconomic foundations, post-Keynesians do not depart entirely from the neoclassical analysis and retain the view of an aggregated macroeconomy.

> The position endorsed by post-Keynesian economists differs from that supported by mainstream economics to the extent that their 'analysis is in part based on postulates as to group behaviour' (S.C. Dow, 1996, p. 99) rather than on axioms of individual behaviour . . . post-Keynesians consider macroeconomics as being the science investigating group or aggregate behaviour and how this influences individual behaviour. (Cencini 2005, p. 55)

These need to be set aside to understand the labour market in a logical manner. The wage determination operation must be envisaged in monetary terms and in a macroeconomic framework, that is, independently of economic agents' behaviour. This is the subject of the final section.

3. FOR A NEW ANALYSIS OF THE LABOUR MARKET

First, it is important to set the analysis in macroeconomic terms. The microeconomic foundations of neoclassical, new-Keynesian and post-Keynesian theories must be set aside. It is essential to position ourselves from the outset in a monetary framework of production where individual behaviour is not a determinant of economic relations. Like Guitton (1984), we can postulate that the foundations of macroeconomics are macroeconomic.

After trying to replace labour in the economic framework, it will be observed that the operation governing the formation of wages is not of the order of a relative exchange but of an absolute exchange, in the sense that workers exchange with themselves. The purchasing power of money is then explained and the payment of wages takes on its full meaning.

3.1 The Foundations of Macroeconomics are Macroeconomic

As said, for neoclassical and new Keynesian economists, the foundations of macroeconomics are to be sought in individual behaviour. They are microeconomic and there can be no other way about it. For contemporary mainstream economists, macroeconomics has no dimension of its own independently of microeconomics. Guitton (1984) argues otherwise: 'In truth, macroeconomics works with different data . . . one should not speak of the microfoundations of macroeconomics . . . It would be more correct to chance the tautology and say: the foundations of macroeconomics are macroeconomic' (p. 23; our translation). These macroeconomic foundations cannot be discovered by analysing human behaviour. People are governed by economic laws, 'that is, laws that are always valid regardless of people's economic behaviour' (De Gottardi 2000, p. 4; our translation). However, these laws cannot be established by mere deduction. 'Analysis of these laws is based both on the observation of economic reality (induction) and on logic (deduction based on the principle of non-contradiction)' (ibid., p. 6; our translation). To grasp economic reality, simple observation of facts is not enough; some degree of abstraction is required. The theory of money emissions developed by Schmitt provides the tools for constructing a valid macroeconomic theory.

3.2 An Absolute Exchange

The payment of wages is not the transfer of any prior wealth; nor is it a stand-off between two magnitudes determined beforehand. Wages are not the monetary counterpart of labour.

For neoclassical economists, labour is a commodity in that it is exchanged on a market. Even before participating in an exchange on the labour market, workers are able to provide a market service. Labour is considered in its physical aspect. There is no question of denying the existence of the physical existence of labour as energy expenditure by workers. It is its economic existence that we must first define.

From this definition it can be deduced that the payment of workers is in no way the result of a relative exchange between a quantity of labour and a quantity of money, between two forms of wealth formed independently of any production. As a second point it will be seen that workers obtain the output they give rise to directly in money form. Their remuneration is of the nature of an absolute exchange.

This remuneration of wage earners means, and this will be the third and final point, the correspondence between physical goods and money. The purchasing power of money is in this way created by the payment of wage earners.

Labour, a notion to be carefully defined

One cannot speak of labour in economics without connecting it with the primary operation of production. The end-purpose of all production is consumption. Workers aim to convert their labour (their energy) into a product satisfying their needs. It is understood that, in this production operation, they will not create or destroy any matter. They will not therefore convert their energy into a physical form nor add even a tiny particle of matter to the 'starting' matter through their expenditure of energy. Through their action, workers will convert their energy into a utility form. Utility is understood as the forms into which people shape matter, forms that are imagined, and so created by people. This utility form applied to matter procures the output that can provide some degree of satisfaction.

It might be thought that each worker exchanges his or her activity (energy expenditure) against a utility form. This cannot be so since the utility form does not exist before workers expend their energy. It cannot be created either before or independently of each worker's energy expenditure. Otherwise it would mean that the utility form had been produced beforehand. By whom and how? No scientific answer can be given. Labour, which is a flow, is implemented by workers for the production process but is destroyed in that same process. It disappears, leaving the place to a utility form.

As Schmitt (1984) points out, '"Exchange" is not a formless word: it has a precise meaning: to exchange is to *change*' (p. 338; our translation). So, as will be seen below, the formation of wages is not the result of a relative exchange but, to use Schmitt's expression, of an absolute exchange. Such an operation is not a transfer of wealth but a creation of wealth.

Relative exchanges give way to absolute exchanges

Production is characterized by a physical activity of transforming matter – labour – and by the creation of utility forms. Workers thus shape matter into the forms they have imagined.[8]

Workers who are wage earners will not obtain, in payment, the physical output to which they give rise. Physical output is deposited in firms' assets. It is itself converted into a money wage by firms and banks. Wage earners do not therefore receive, by way of payment, money that has been formed outside of the production operation in which they take part. The payment of wages is not the result of a relative exchange between wage earners' labour and a sum of money firms hold with no connection with the production of the workers it is used to pay. 'When wages are paid, workers receive the monetary expression of the output they have created' (Bailly 1990, p. 219; our translation). The formation of wages is the result not of a relative exchange between two commodities of labour and money, but an absolute exchange: workers convert a non-commodity, labour, into a non-commodity, money. As Bailly (2003) puts it, 'the exchange presiding the formation of wages is unipolar' (p. 367). It is not a transfer of wealth but a creation of wealth. Wages are not from some pre-existing money 'fund' that firms hold. So it is not through an exchange with firms that wage earners receive their pay but in a exchange with themselves.

3.3 The Formation of the Purchasing Power of Money

Money is bank money. It takes its source in a promise from banks. But at this stage it is just a dimensionless number. Under no circumstances can it be used as a means of payment. Goods cannot be bought with simple numbers. So it has no economic existence as a simple promise issued by banks.

The theory of money emissions opens up a new analytical pathway. Emanating from the banking system, money is initially just a promise. It therefore has no purchasing power over goods. It is only in the payment of workers that money becomes positive: workers introduce a physical output into the nominal form created by banks. Money creation then attains a positive result. So long as it is not associated with the physical product, as has been said, money is just a numerical form. It has no purchasing power. It is through the payment of wages that goods and money are brought into relation.

> Remuneration of [producer] services does not pass on any prior wealth; it creates nominal wealth in correlation with real production. And this relation designates a very precise force: the purchasing power of money. (Schmitt 1966, p. 263; our translation)

The payment of wages is a crucial operation as it is at this moment that the physical product is fully grasped in the money form. The payment of wages is not the transfer of purchasing power, which pre-exists production, from the hands of firms into those of workers: it ensures the creation of purchasing power. Firms cannot, then, buy labour on a market as purchasing power is created in the payment of wages: the payment of workers is therefore not of the nature of a purchase. Workers do not obtain, by way of payment, money that is the counterpart of a physical output they have contributed to giving rise to. They receive the money form of this output, which is why it can be said that workers' remuneration is an absolute exchange.

4. CONCLUSION

Market analysis is no mean problem in the various economic theories.

Neoclassical theory, built on microeconomic foundations, attempts to analyse the labour market in respect of individual behaviour. In a world where endowments in goods and services already exist, neoclassical economists conceive of production as a simple relative exchange. The labour market is then a place where labour is exchanged for money, both being forms of wealth formed outside of any productive activity. The commodity labour can be purchased by firms as they hold money that is endowed from the outset with purchasing power. The payment of workers is thus of the nature of a purchase.

In the lineage of Keynes's discoveries, post-Keynesian theory, while adopting an endogenous conception of money, cannot free itself completely from the microeconomic foundations that characterize the dominant approach. While opening up avenues for enquiry, it does not provide us with the decisive elements that would enlighten us about the role of the labour market in our economic system.

We have to turn to Schmitt's theory of money emissions and his meticulous examination of money and labour to outline any answers. First, we need to shake off the dominant conception of macroeconomics. The foundations of macroeconomics are macroeconomic and they can be discovered without introducing assumptions about agents' behaviour.

Labour is a flow and exists economically only in respect of the utility form in which it is embodied. It cannot, then, be exchanged on a market. The formation of wages is not a relative exchange but an absolute exchange. Wage earners receive the entire output they gave rise to, in money form (the physical output being deposited in firms). Nor is the payment of wage earners a purchase of labour, since money, as a pure numerical form, only really exists in society in so far as it is attached to the objects formed in production.

The economic operation that is the formation of wages now seems more distinct and the study of a labour market more precise. The meaning of the term 'market', which is vague and undetermined because of its multiple senses, makes it more necessary to try to clarify it. If the usual (neoclassical) definition cannot be maintained for the labour market, a new one must be constructed. This future task, it is hoped, will provide insight into the exact role of a labour market (if there is such a thing) in our economies. There is no denying that there may be, in microeconomics, several labour markets. Even so, if it is asked whether there is *a* labour market in macroeconomic terms, we have our answers. Labour is not a commodity and so cannot be bought and sold on any market. Money, a pure dimensionless number, has no purchasing power until it is associated with physical output. So it cannot be used to purchase labour. These points allow us, in the current state of this research, to doubt the existence of a market in macroeconomic terms. However, one certainty seems to arise. The formation of wages is by no means the result of a market process. Such a process may occur in the distribution of wage units constituting aggregate income. It is at this stage that the balance of power and conflict between workers and firms would prove decisive. However, the formation of wages is an operation that concerns an intangible law about the wage relationship that characterizes our monetary production economies.

NOTES

1. The expression is from Walras.
2. This chapter is not about the indeterminacy of relative prices. For further developments see Cencini (1982).
3. According to Patinkin (1972), individuals are endowed 'every Monday morning . . . with an initial collection of goods which, like the manna of the Children of Israel, "fell from Heaven" the night before' (p. 22).
4. The notion of labour as a flow is explained in section 3.2.
5. Which would suppose labour is not a commodity, a supposition confirmed in section 3.2.
6. Eichner considers the post-Keynesian approach to be anthropogenic. On this see Eichner (1985).
7. The notion of utility form is explained below.
8. Production would require fuller development that cannot be given in this short chapter. For more details see Schmitt (1984) and Cencini (1985).

REFERENCES

Alchian, A.A. and Allen W.R. (1969), *Exchange and Production: Theory in Use*, Belmont, CA: Wadsworth Publishing Company.

Arestis, P. (1992), *The Post-Keynesian Approach to Economics*, Aldershot, UK and Brookfield, US: Edward Elgar.

Bailly, J.L. (1990), *Le revenu, élaboration historique d'un concept*, Thèse de Doctorat ès Sciences Economiques, Université de Bourgogne.

Bailly, J.L. (2003), 'On the macroeconomic foundations of the wage–price relationship', in L.P. Rochon and S. Rossi (eds), *Modern Theories of Money*, Cheltenham, UK and Northampton, MA, USA: Edward Elgar, pp. 360–83.

Begg, D., Fischer, S. and Dornbusch, R. (1996), *Macroéconomie*, 2ème édition, Paris: Ediscience International.

Cencini, A. (1982), 'The logical indeterminacy of relative prices', in M. Baranzini (ed.), *Advances in Economic Theory*, Oxford: Blackwell, pp. 126–46.

Cencini, A. (1985), 'L'analyse de la production', in 'Production et Monnaie', *Cahier de la Revue d'Economie Politique*, directed by Bernard Schmitt, Paris: Sirey, pp. 59–82.

Cencini, A. (2005), *Macroeconomic Foundations of Macroeconomics*, London and New York: Routledge.
De Gottardi, C. (2000), *Offre et demande: Equilibre ou identité?*, Thèse de Doctorat ès Sciences économiques et sociales, Université de Fribourg.
Dow, S.C. (1996), *The Methodology of Macroeconomic Thought*, Cheltenham, UK and Brookfield, US: Edward Elgar.
Eichner, A.S. (1985), 'An anthropogenic approach to labor economics', in *Toward a New Economics: Essays in Post-Keynesian and Institutionalist Theory*, London: Macmillan, and Armonk, NY: M.E. Sharpe, pp. 75–97.
Guitton, H. (1984), 'Préface' à B. Schmitt, *Inflations, chômage et malformations du capital*, Paris: Economica, and Albeuve, Suisse: Castella.
Jessua, C. (1982), *Eléments d'analyse macroéconomique*, Paris: Montchrestien.
Lavoie, M. (1992), *Foundations of Post-Keynesian Economic Analysis*, Aldershot, UK and Brookfield, US: Edward Elgar.
Malinvaud, E. (1991), *Voies de la recherche macroéconomique*, Paris: Odile Jacob.
Mankiw, G. (1994), *Macroeconomics*, 3rd edn, New York: Worth Publishers.
Patinkin, D. (1972), *La monnaie, l'intérêt et les prix*, Paris: Presses Universitaires de France.
Schmitt, B. (1966), *Monnaie, Salaires et Profits*, Paris: Presses Universitaires de France.
Schmitt, B. (1984), *Inflation, chômage et malformations du capital*, Paris: Economica, and Albeuve, Suisse: Castella.
Seccareccia, M. (1991), 'An alternative to labour-market orthodoxy: the post-Keynesian/Institutionalist policy view', *Review of Political Economy*, **3** (1), 43–61.
Walras, L. (1952), *Eléments d'économie politique pure*, Paris: Librairie générale de droit et de jurisprudence.

PART II

Growth, development and exchange rates

8. Exchange rate policy in developing countries: the East Asian experience

Mohamed Aslam

INTRODUCTION

Since the 1970s, currency has became a 'commodity' and is heavily traded in the foreign exchange market. The movement of value of a currency *vis-à-vis* other national currencies is becoming more volatile and it frequently distorts macroeconomic stability, mainly in the case of developing countries. The exchange rate is determined in the international currency market rather than supply and demand in the international goods market. The movement of the exchange rate is substantially affected by non-fundamental factors. The expansion of foreign portfolio capital flow is one of the prime factors causing (wild) movement or creating volatility in the exchange rate. The rapid development and expansion of the international capital markets including derivatives and the integration of capital markets at the regional or international level have produced dramatic exchange rate volatility. It is widely accepted that trading and speculation in currency and derivative markets and international portfolio investments are the main causes of exchange rate volatility.

For many developing countries, the exchange rate is one of the measures for maintaining or increasing export competitiveness. The export sector largely contributes to economic growth, employment and macroeconomic stability. Globalization of the financial market has created a dilemma particularly for the developing countries in safeguarding the state of their macroeconomy. Opening up capital accounts and liberalization of the domestic capital market to external influences has actually exacerbated the current account of balance of payments rather than bringing a real benefit to economic welfare. Most developing countries do not have capabilities to ward off speculation on their national currency. If the countries experience a currency crisis, then a question arises whether it is right to abandon the 'old' exchange rate system and replace it with the new one, or whether it is practical to install capital and exchange control mechanisms. The external economy has become the main factor in influencing internal (domestic) economic stability of the countries. As in the Swan–Salter model (or Australian or dependent model), the internal economy could be maintained by the government through fiscal and monetary policies, but if the internal economic sector is largely influenced by the external economic factor, that is, a negative shock to exports or the financial sector, then the countries' economies will be in distress. To ensure the equilibrium of the internal and the external economy the choice of exchange rate system seems to be crucial. The majority of developing countries are open economies and largely producing primary commodities. They depend on industrial nations for market (economic growth and prosperity) and also they are price takers in the international good markets. Therefore, is a flexible exchange rate or a fixed exchange rate or intermediate exchange rate system better for a country? This chapter explores this question by looking at the experience of East Asian countries.

EXCHANGE RATE: DETERMINANTS AND ISSUES

Most of the exchange rate models[1] are based on the purchasing power parity (PPP) doctrine, with other variables that are believed to influence the movement of the exchange rate such as in monetary models. The rational expectations perspective is also included in the model to examine the movement of the exchange rate. Most of those models or any exchange rate model related to the orthodox school claimed to derive the determinants of the exchange rate; however, most of the models have failed to provide solid justification of which main factors cause the exchange rate to move. Many economists agree that fundamental variables are unable to predict future changes in exchange rates.

Mainstream economics, that is, neoclassical, fail to recognize the reality in the international foreign exchange market (FOREX) and micro-structure of the market in their exchange rate model. They build the exchange rate model to estimate determinants or examine either the short-run or long-run equilibrium rate without incorporating the micro-structure of the FOREX. Some argue that in the short run economic fundamentals do not play a role in determining the exchange rate but in the long run fundamental factors may influence it. This is an econometric approach with many kinds of techniques and data manipulations. The study on exchange rate equilibrium in the long run which relies on PPP aims to predict the level of the exchange rate in the future or in the long run without giving any specific date or period. This study is misleading and does not offer a correct justification that the forecasted level of the exchange rate will be the same in the future. In forecasting exchange rate movements, in either nominal or real terms, variables such as money supply, interest rate (central bank policy), or other factors that apparently affect the rate do not provide solid results or justification (Hopper 1997). According to Stein (1997, p. 2),

> none of the existing empirical studies of which we are aware can satisfactorily explain the nominal and real exchange rate. In long-run exchange rate determination, trade factor is an insignificant influence on the rate appreciation of the major currencies in the world.

Fluctuations in real exchange rates are often treated as temporary deviations from the 'long-run' equilibrium real exchange rate. Although PPP is regarded as a benchmark for the relative values of currencies, it provides a poor measure of equilibrium exchange rates in the presence of numerous fundamental real disturbances to both the current and capital accounts.

Since the collapse of the Bretton Woods system in 1971, the floating exchange rate regime has been widely used in the world economy. This regime was adopted for several reasons. First, there was wide variation in liberalization of the capital account of balance of payments in the world economy. Second, the role of US dollar in the international monetary system and expansion of international financial market had increased dramatically. Third, buying–selling currencies are no longer related to demand and supply in the goods or commodities market. Fourth, there were rapid developments in the international capital market in terms of varieties of capital, money and derivatives instruments. This development was associated with the high expansion of various types of funds such as hedge funds, mutual and trust funds. Firms or agents involved in the sector are mainly investment banks and financial brokers, which have grown quite rapidly in terms of numbers and size of assets. Investment from such firms in the international capital market is short term and it does not carry weight in supporting and stimulating the real economy, with the exception of new equity (company stocks/shares) – initial public offering (IPO) – introduced in the equity primary market.

While many firms and financial institutions use derivatives to cover investment or financial risks, there are also many 'market-maker' agents who invest for short-term gains. The expansion of the international capital market including derivatives and the integration of the capital market at the international or regional level has produced great changes in the exchange rate or value of a national currency *vis-à-vis* foreign currency. Therefore the investment in such markets, that is, foreign portfolio capital, has been regarded as a prime factor in causing a (wild) movement or creating volatility in the exchange rate.

Table 8.1 Global foreign exchange market turnover: daily averages in April, US$ billions

	1992	1995	1998	2001	2004	2007
Spot transactions	394	494	568	387	621	1005
Outright forwards	58	97	128	131	208	362
Foreign exchange swaps	324	546	734	656	944	1714
Estimated gaps reporting	43	53	61	26	107	128
Total	820	1190	1490	1200	1880	3210
Total at April 2007	880	1150	1650	1420	1950	3210

Source: BIS, *Quarterly Bulletin*, various issues.

The movement of the exchange rate is largely influenced by non-fundamental factors, particularly by speculation activity in the international FOREX. As noted in Taylor (1995, p. 30), 'there are speculative forces at work in the foreign exchange market which are not reflected in the usual menu of macroeconomic fundamentals'. The nominal or spot exchange rate is determined in the FOREX rather than by supply and demand (exporters and importers) in the international goods market. The main players in FOREX are commercial banks, investment banks, FOREX brokers, hedge funds, trust funds and any fund that is developed for seeking short-term profits through arbitrage. They are the market makers.

Transactions in the FOREX have grown rapidly. Peters (1987, p. 11) claimed that in the 1980s currency–exchange rate transactions totalled $80 trillion a year, of which $4 trillion was financed trade in goods and services. The balance was used for currency speculation. Peters (1987, p. 11) also stated that 'we do not know from day to day the price of money, whether protection or default will close borders or what really will happen with global financing'. Stanislaw and Yergin (1998) mentioned that traders drove a foreign exchange market that was estimated at $1 trillion a day in 1997. Humpage (1998) stated that daily business in the foreign exchange market is approximately equivalent to $1 billion. The Bank of International Settlements (BIS) reported per day transactions in FOREX at about $1.9 trillion in 2004. Based on Peters's (1987) method of estimation, if 10 percent of the amount is for financing trade in goods and services, that was only $0.19 trillion and the remaining about $1.71 trillion was trading that was not related to exports and imports. The annual total amount of transactions in FOREX could exceed $450 trillion (Table 8.1). In 2007, daily turnover in global foreign exchange was about US$3.2 trillion; that is double that in 2004; hence the amount of annual turnover in FOREX will be double. The huge transactions in the global FOREX have caused extreme volatility. Of course the main beneficiaries of the market are the 'market makers', that is, investment banks, mutual funds, hedge funds, FOREX brokers and other agents associated to FOREX. The FOREX, including derivatives, has become what is called the 'casino society', and this society has expand at very fast rate. The 'animal spirits', the phrase coined by Keynes, have been inherited by society and have expanded largely day by day. Exporters and importers are price takers and losers. This group of real-goods traders is vulnerable to disadvantages or manipulation in the currency market. They have to absorb the differences in exchange rate, created by the market makers, in terms of prices but also including other costs such as shipping and insurance. One of the main factors that enables a huge transaction in FOREX is related to the development of telecommunications and Internet technologies, which on the one hand have reduced the time needed for transactions (deal done: buy and sell) and the cost of transactions, but on the other hand has created great instability in the market.

The huge swing in exchange rates has created a problem for most of the developing countries. The amount of money that has moved in the FOREX and into related financial markets can easily destabilize economies. Furthermore, the development of various types of instruments in international financial markets has complicated macroeconomic management. Conventional macroeconomic policies, fiscal and monetary, seem to have become less capable of maintaining sustainable real economic growth, a stable exchange rate and stable inflation pressure. Given the above scenario, therefore, for developing economies the exchange rate system that is adopted may be the single most important macroeconomic decision that a government will make.

For developing countries, the exchange rate is one of the main economic policies and it acts as a tool for maintaining or increasing export markets and increasing demand on labor. The export sector has largely contributed to economic growth and development as well as maintaining macroeconomic stability. However, the opening up of capital accounts and liberalization of capital markets (or convertibility of capital account) have provoked volatility in the exchange rate whereby it exacerbates or lessens export income, or the current account of balance of payment turns to deficit. In most developing countries, the exchange rate is either pegged to the international currency, that is the US dollar, or pegged to a basket of major trade partners' currencies, or they adopt a managed floating regime. In general, most national currencies of developing countries that have adopted either a floating or flexible regime tend to 'follow' the US dollar; in other words the currency is pegged 'softly' to the US dollar. Therefore the movement of the US dollar *vis-à-vis* a national currency (and also movement *vis-à-vis* the Japanese yen, the euro and the Swiss franc) will put pressure on the value of the national currency.

Most developing countries are facing the dilemma of achieving a set of economic objectives and a choice of exchange rate. The economic objectives are to achieve remarkable and sustainable economic growth, to increase the employment rate and to ensure macroeconomic stability. The flexible exchange rate will not guarantee that the countries will achieve the objectives. Overvalued currency against major trade partners' currencies will harm employment growth, while undervalued currency will increase the national debt burden and import inflation. The experience of the debt crises in 1980s and the currency-cum-financial crises that erupted in Mexico in 1994/95 and in Asia in 1997/98, for instance, has alerted most of the central bankers and government to the need to maintain a stable exchange rate so that the export industries will expand at a sustainable level. Developing countries are too dependent on the external sector for real economic growth and employment generation. The export-oriented strategies that were pursued in the countries need to have and maintain a favorable international price, that is in terms of the dollar, to promote the growth and expansion of the export industries and stimulate economic growth.

THE IMPOSSIBLE TRINITY AND MONETARY REGIME

Which exchange rate system is practical and effective for developing countries? This is very hard question to answer. The adoption of the system of exchange rates will affect the stand of monetary policy. The classic argument, such as that related to Mundell prepositions, is that a floating exchange rate allows independence of monetary policy in which there is a role for the policy in gearing the domestic economy. In the fixed exchange rate regime the independence of monetary policy is lost since the policy's main objective is to maintain the peg by changing the level of the international reserve. These prepositions are known as the theorem of the impossible trinity. In other words, the theorem states that it is impossible to have simultaneously a fixed exchange rate, a national monetary policy, and free capital mobility. Based on the theorem, and as argued by the orthodox economic school, the best choice for a country is to give up the fixed exchange rate (Figure 8.1).

If a country chooses to fix the exchange rate, the country must have enough international reserve to act against any speculation or to prevent any attack on the system. If the country chooses to float, it should be able

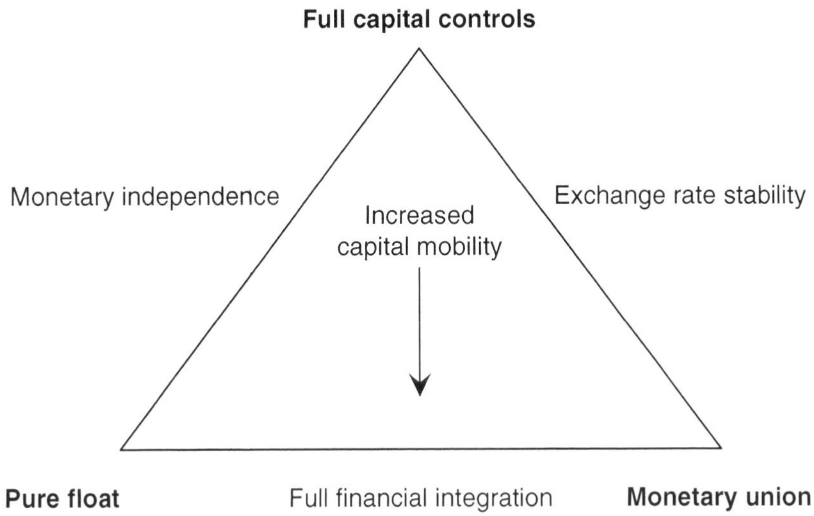

Figure 8.1 The impossible trinity

to deal with the currency swing. If the country joins a monetary union, then it will lose the ability to control its currency. Therefore, and as indicated in Figure 8.1, there is a trade-off between interest rates, exchange rates and capital controls (Stanek 2002). Out of the three variables, a country can only control two of them. If the country fixes the exchange rate and allows capital to flow, it cannot control interest rates. If the country controls interest rates and allows capital flows, then it cannot fix the exchange rate. The last alternative is that the country controls the capital flow but not interest rates or the exchange rate.

Does the above happen in the real world? Some people or groups support the theorem of the impossible trinity and some are against the theorem. Which is correct? There are differences of opinion between economic theorists and policy makers with respect to the exchange rate system and monetary policy independence. Economic theorists who belong to the mainstream school are in favor of a free float, whereas policy makers often prefer systems that permit only a limited range of variability (Klein 1987). Given the economics of international financial markets and problems produced by the market, it is hard to say what a country's ideal exchange rate will be.

In respect of the exchange rate system, since the collapse of the Bretton Woods system four main features have emerged. First, many countries have adopted the flexible exchange rate system and central banks, when needed, intervene in the foreign exchange market to push upward or downward

Table 8.2 International monetary system and currency crises

Regime	Period	Number of currency crises
Gold Standard	1880–1913	22
War periods (WW1 and WW2)	1913–1919	0
	1920–1939	48
Bretton Woods era	1940–1971	45
Post-Bretton Woods era	1972–1998	162
	1999–2002	7

Source: Bordo et al. (2001); Breuer (2004).

the exchange rate level. This shows that the impossible trinity theorem has been indirectly rejected by most developing countries and some of the industrial countries as well. Second, the US dollar is fully convertible and the Federal Reserve remains reluctant to intervene in the FOREX market when the dollar appreciates and has experienced persistent current account deficits. It seems that the US government upholds the theorem. But when the dollar faced a crisis, for example being too expensive as compared to the currencies of members of the G-7 such as Japan and Germany, the US government advised the members of the group to intervene in the FOREX on their behalf. Central banks of industrial countries, namely the Bank of Japan, the Bundesbank and the Bank of England, had to intervene in the FOREX on behalf of the USA either to bring down or increase the value of the dollar *vis-à-vis* the yen or the euro (Deutschmark). There were a few international agreements on the matter, such as the Plaza Accord in 1985, the Louvre Accord in 1987 and the Reversed Plaza Accord in 1996, and in the early 2000s central bank members of the G-7 intervened in the FOREX to change the rate between the US dollar and the euro. Third, international organizations, particularly the International Monetary Fund (IMF) and the World Bank, embedded the theorem in their aid packages or in their aid for structural adjustment lending program. Also, elements of the theorem is included in the Washington Consensus. Fourth, however, four main proposals for the management of international currency exchange rates have emerged. They are monetary unification, fixed rates, freely floating rates and an intermediate regime, which maintains 'reasonable' limits of variability. The proposal was made since trust in the floating regime and the purely fixed exchange rate has decreased.

Since the collapse of the Bretton Woods system, currency crises have happened frequently (Table 8.2). During the Gold Standard, crises occurred about 22 times, while during the Bretton Woods period they did so about 45 times. Post-Bretton Woods there have been 169 currency crises. The growing number of crises has worried governments especially those of developing countries. However, based on IMF exchange rate arrangements, the number of countries adopting the fixed regime declined from 76.4 percent (number of countries 107) in 1980 to 55.6 percent (number of countries 104), while countries that have opted for the flexible regime have increased from 23.6 percent (number of countries 33) to 44.4 percent (number of countries 83), respectively. The figure does not indicate how many countries opt for the intermediate regime. In the year 2000, countries that opted for the intermediate regime were about 62 percent (number of countries 98), hard peg 24 percent (number of countries 45) and float about 42 percent (number of countries 77) (Fischer 2001).

Related to the impossible trinity theorem, another view of the international monetary system, as stated by Fischer (2001), is the bipolar view. The view emerged since the aftermath of the Asian crisis and is related to many countries that have opted for the intermediate regime. Fischer (2001) argues that for countries to liberalize capital flow or implement capital account convertibility, (i) soft exchange rate pegs are not sustainable; but (ii) a wide variety of flexible rate arrangements remains possible; and (iii) it is to be expected that the policy in most countries will not be indifferent to exchange rate movements. To quote, he said:

> if exchange rate arrangements lie along a line connecting hard pegs like currency unions, currency boards, and dollarization on the left, with free floating on the right, the intent of the bipolar view is not to rule out everything but the two corners, but rather to pronounce as unsustainable a segment of that line representing a variety of soft pegging exchange rate arrangements. (Fischer 2001, p. 5)

Based on his statement and on Figure 8.1, the exchange rate and monetary regimes in developing countries are in between the exchange rate and capital control. Most East Asian countries have adopted an intermediate regime of a managed exchange rate with different degrees of capital controls (Hagiwara 2005). The intermediate regime without capital controls offers the combination of exchange rate stability, exchange rate targeting and exchange rate variation. Given capital market integration in East Asia, which is not perfect, and the role of foreign portfolio capital in the integrating process, the regime seems to be unsustainable and vulnerable to speculative attack, as happened in 1997. However, a regime with capital controls, as shown in case of Malaysia, China and Taiwan, permits the government, that is, the monetary authorities, to implement monetary policy and exchange rate policy separately. Figure 8.1 shows that the exchange rate and monetary regime are not separate. This chapter stresses

Table 8.3 Changes in foreign exchange reserves in selected regions, US$ billion

	2000	2001	2002	2003	2004	2005	2006
Japan	347	388	451	653	824	829	875
USA	43	41	39	39	39	38	41
Eurozone	219	208	216	188	181	167	184
UK	34	29	31	29	34	36	39
East Asia	657	725	877	1110	1446	1690	2048
China	*166*	*212*	*286*	*403*	*610*	*819*	*1066*
NIEs	*390*	*411*	*476*	*574*	*675*	*703*	*774*
ASEAN-4	*102*	*102*	*115*	*133*	*162*	*168*	*207*
BRICs (excluding China)	94	114	148	220	299	360	551
Oil-producing countries	85	90	93	116	154	204	na

Note: East Asia: P.R. China, ASEAN-4 (Indonesia, Malaysia, Philippines, Thailand), NIEs (S. Korea, Taiwan, Hong Kong and Singapore); BRICs (Brazil, Russia, India and China).

Source: IMF, *International Financial Statistics*.

that an exchange rate is an economic policy and it must be consistent with macroeconomic policy rather than only being attached to monetary policy. Related to the Asian crisis, it is not clear to what extent the impossibility trinity theorem could explain it. As mentioned, any attempt by a country to achieve all three – fixed exchange rate, capital mobility and monetary independence – will cause a currency crisis. Some economists are suspicious of the validity of the impossibility trinity theorem, especially with regard to the developing countries (Frankel 1999).

One of the main lessons that was learned by countries affected or not by the currency crisis is the need for a large international reserve that not only can stabilize the exchange rate but avoid any possibilities for illiquidity and to ward off speculative attack. Since 1997, countries in East Asia have been piling up international reserves (Table 8.3). East Asia has accumulated about US$2.05 trillion reserve in 2006 compared to US$657 billion in 2000. ASEAN-4 (Indonesia, Malaysia, the Philippines and Thailand) accumulated international reserves of about US$207 billion in 2006, increased more than 100 percent from the year 2000. For newly industrializing economies (NIEs), the reserve increased more than 100 percent, while China piled up reserves of about US$1.1 trillion by 2006.

What has happened in Asian countries is that most of the countries affected by the financial crises experienced a huge inflow of portfolio

Table 8.4 Impossible trinity: different opinions – Asian crisis

	Capital control	High interest	Exchange rate
International Monetary Fund	No	Yes	Yes
Paul Krugman	Yes	No	Yes
Jeffrey Sachs	Yes	Yes	No
Mahathir	Yes	No	No

Sources: Low (2006), Mahathir (2000, pp. 43–8).

capital, appreciation of currency value against the US dollar, inflation of asset prices, current account deficits, large credit to the property market and personal loans (buying stock). The inflow of foreign porfolio capital and the overvalued exchange rate caused an upward pressure inflation. Sterilization by the central banks failed to mop up excess liquidity from the financial system (banking system) since the amount of government bonds and treasury bills were inadequate to clear the market. Open market operations were unsuccessful, as also were non-sterilization activities. It is generally agreed that the downfall of the exchange rates in East Asia in 1997–98 was due to speculative capital flows.[2] In the case of Malaysia, there is no concrete evidence that the fluctuation of the exchange rate in the short term was caused by trade factors, but there is evidence that investment by foreigners in the asset market had an influence on the movement of the exchange rate in the early 1990s (BNM 1994).[3]

Implicitly, the economies were virtually 'locked in' or faced a dilemma to maintain the pegging in the environment of a liberalized capital account, partially or fully. Pre-crises currencies of East Asian countries had made limited changes but in real terms, most of the currencies were overvalued and during the crisis the exchange rate depreciated more than 40 percent. Moreover, the level of international reserves decreased at an alarming rate and governments were unable to prevent speculation in the FOREX and stock market. Also governments were unable to curtail the sudden outflow of portfolio capital, and this subsequently forced them to float their currencies. Conventional macroeconomic policy was unable to reflate the economies successfully. The crisis shows that unorthodox measures should be used to regain market confidence and stimulate the economies. Some economists have weighed in with suggestions. For example, Paul Krugman suggested that countries affected can impose a temporary capital control and go for devaluation, but not high interest rates because it will hurt the real economy or will not help the economy to reflate (Table 8.4). On the other hand, Jeffrey Sachs is against any devaluation but supports a temporary capital control with high interest rate. Among the countries affected were Indonesia, Korea, Thailand and Malaysia, and only Malaysia was not in favor of IMF remedies. The country imposed a temporary capital control of outflow of foreign portfolio capital, fixed the exchanged rate at US$1 = RM3.80 plus with illegalized trading or de-internationalization of the ringgit in offshore markets, reduced interest rates and ran budget deficits. Explicitly, Table 8.4 indicates that the theorem of the impossible trinity is indeed impossible for developing countries to adopt as the theorem proposed.

DEVELOPING COUNTRIES: CHOICE OF EXCHANGE RATE

In general, developing countries produce and export primary commodities and import finished products, including intermediate and investment goods from industrial countries. Trade balances are unfavorable to developing countries since most of them rely on industrial economies for markets. The main reasons are obvious. First, the prices of commodities are set in commodities future markets. Most of the markets, such as petroleum, grains and metal, are located in industrial countries. Since the capital and FOREX markets of developing countries are undeveloped, the industrial nations have a greater advantage in influencing commodity prices. Developing countries do not have any advantage in influencing the movement of their commodities and currency prices. They are the price takers. If there is a wild movement or shock in the exchange rate, developing countries will receive the negative impact substantially and significantly more than industrial countries through the commodities sector. Second, related to the first point, primary commodities producers and exporters face an inelastic demand curve and elastic supply curve. A fall in price will reduce a big size of export income and eventually will reduce real economic growth. Third, the prices of goods (and services) are rigid or staggered in the short run. The nominal wage is also staggered, but staggered more than the price of goods. Therefore in the short run the real wage hardly moves, but since the price is less staggered than the nominal wage at least in one year, many developing countries experience a fall in real wage or decrease in labor's (households') purchasing power. On the other hand, the nominal exchange rate moves stochastically and in an indeterminstic manner; consequently the countries experience instability in the real exchange rate (RER).

The standard formula for calculating RER is $RER = E.(P^f/P^d)$, where E is nominal exchange rate, P^f is foreign price of goods and P^d is domestic price of goods. E is determined in FOREX, in which developing countries have no power to influence it. P^f and P^d are determined in commodity markets in which producers or sellers influence price setting. Since the prices of goods hardly move in the short run, while the movement of exchange rates is very flexible, the changes in RER are associated with changes in the nominal exchange rate. Explicitly, the market maker in FOREX influences the price or export competitiveness of the producers or traders.

If there is a fluctutation in the exchange rate, it has a bigger impact on inflation as well as on trade and financial systems in developing countries than in developed countries. The fluctuation or changes in exchange rate will spill over and pass through to goods prices.[4] Many studies have looked at the pass-through of fluctuation in exchange rates to prices in developing countries. Most agree that changes in exchange rate do cause the domestic price to change. Choudhri and Hakura (2001) examined 71 countries, consisting of both developed and developing countries. They found that there is a strong positive correlation between pass-through and the average inflation rate across countries. Similarly, Devereux and Yetman (2003) find a positive non-linear relationship between pass-through and mean inflation and exchange rate in 122 countries. Ho and McCauley (2003) found that the pass-through from exchange rates to domestic prices is greater in emerging markets than in developed ones, because developing countries (emerging markets) rely largely on the commodity sector. For instance, the proportion of a year's change in the consumer price index (CPI) that can be explained by fluctuations in the exchange rate is 41 percent in Indonesia and 48 percent in Hungary, but only 2 percent in the USA (Ho and McCauley 2003).

As mentioned earlier, financial markets in most developing countries are underdeveloped and the market in general is vulnerable to wild exchange rate fluctuations. Large capital inflows (mainly short-term borrowing and portfolio investment) put upward pressure on real exchange rates and drive a steep increase in asset prices. If investors lose confidence in the markets, portfolio capital can suddenly go into reverse without giving any signal to the economy, and the value of currency exchange against major trade partners' currencies will depreciate. As experienced by many developing countries, the reversal of foreign portfolio investment (FPI) creates trouble particularly in reducing international reserves (foreign exchange reserves), such as experienced in the case of Mexican peso and in the Asian financial crises. The balance of payments and monetary sector were in a distress position, due to the depletion of foreign exchange reserves. To defend the depreciating value of currency *vis-à-vis* international currency (i.e. the US dollar), a significant amount of foreign exchange reserve is needed. However, since developing countries are not in a strong position and incapable of having a large foreign exchange reserve, they need to borrow money. When the currency is threatened or financial crises get under way, there is decreasing international confidence in the economies; therefore investors (or international banks) are unwilling to lend to developing countries and local banks and companies end up laden with debts denominated in foreign currencies, while asset prices fall and the assets become undervalued in terms of foreign currencies. Defaults will follow and economic performance will be in a negative position.

Based on the above argument, what would be the appropriate exchange rate system that should be adopted by the developing countries? In respect of internal–external equilibrium, that is, concerning employment and income distribution, the floating exchange rate is an unreliable choice. Since most developing countries are primary commodities producers and rely on industrial countries for their markets, using the flexible exchange rate and given the micro-structure and RER formula would result in an unstable price of commodities in the international market. As this market is controlled by industrial countries, export income will be unstable.[5] For developing countries, income distribution and creation of employment are determined by the external sector and these factors (income and employment) are crucial for sustaining economic development. In addition, if there is a wild and persistent fluctuation in the exchange rate, it will affect the business sector in decision making and future corporate planning.

Since developing countries are the price takers and the factor determining the exchange rate is non-fundamental, the flexible exchange rate is not a good choice. Flexibility in the exchange rate is good, but if the main determinant of the movement of the exchange rate is news, noise or non-fundamental factors (determined in the international financial market), thereby exacerbating trade performance, then the system should be reconsidered. Based on Keynes's works, indirectly he did not favor the flexible exchange rate. He may have advocated the fixed exchange rate but with some adjustments or flexibility. This was based on the case of India, as he mentioned in *Indian Currency and Finance* (1913). Keynes suggested that India fix the rupee against gold. Keynes's major concern was the use and management of the government (central bank) reserves. The paper currency, the rupee, was backed 100 percent by gold and silver. Since the terms of trade of primary commodities had fallen sharply and affected the economy, Keynes suggested that the reserve be used to extend credit to the agricultural sector. In his opinion, the system would help restore confidence in the economy. The internal price of money is determined by the interest rate but the external price of money is influenced by the exchange rate. Even though Keynes focused less on international economics in his *General Theory*, one of his main contributions is that the Central Bank should play a bigger role in determining an interest rate so as to ensure that the economy will achieve a high employment level. The role of the interest rate will be affected if the external factor is allowed into the market and determines the price of money. And if there is a high interest rate differential it would distort the macroeconomic stability and the exchange rate. In order to avoid any influences from the external economy, it is wise to fix the exchange rate mainly to permit the government to follow its own domestic monetary policies. In other words, the interest rate could do its job without any interference from the external economy. However, the system might not work efficiently without a mechanism of control on capital flows and currency trading. These matters are crucial to developing economies. The monetary authorities in the countries have only one instrument, short-term interest rate, and because the FOREX market is small, the open capital market and cross-border flows are mobile, sterilized interventions will not work.

In selecting an exchange rate regime, developing countries should consider the factors described in Table 8.5. Wrong choice of exchange rate strategy will produce an unfavorable outcome for the economy.

EAST ASIA: EXPORT-LED GROWTH AND EXCHANGE RATE

In general, developing countries including East Asia lack the main sources of economic growth and development, that is, productive capital, manufacturing technology, product brands, entrepreneurship and skilled workers. To improve economic performance and to increase capabilities in resource utilization, countries in the region have diversified the structure of production and trade by promoting development of the manufacturing sector. Industrial policies that comprise trade liberalization, foreign investment liberalization including very liberal ownership, fiscal incentives including pioneer industries status, relaxed labor law or amended labor law to reduce or eliminate labor union formation or demand for wages, building industrial zones (export processing zone or free trade zone areas) are needed to attract foreign direct investment (FDI) for developing and expanding the manufacturing sector. The inflow of FDI has increased the capabilities of the countries in gaining market access to industrial countries via operation of foreign firms. As a result of the policies, a few countries have been proclaimed as in the first tier of newly industrializing economies (NIEs): Korea, Taiwan, Hong Kong and Singapore; and in the second tier are Malaysia, Thailand and Indonesia; and a new East Asian dragon is emerging: China.

The main economic development policy pursued in East Asia is export-led growth (ELG). Obviously, the main ingredient of the ELG policy is

Table 8.5 Developing countries: criteria for exchange rate regime selection

Criteria	Degree of exchange rate flexibility
Size of economy	The larger the economy, the smaller the case for a flexible rate. Example: P.R. China and India
Openness (export economy)	The more open the economy or the higher the degree of export orientation, the more desirable is stable price in foreign currency
Geographic concentration of trade	The larger the proportion of an economy's trade with one large country, the greater is the incentive to peg to the currency of that country. The major trade partner for Latin American and East Asian is the USA; value of countries currencies' tend to follow US dollar
Divergence of domestic inflation from world inflation	The more divergence in a country's inflation rate from that of its main trading partners, the greater is the need for frequent exchange rate adjustments. (But for a country with extremely high inflation, a fixed exchange rate may provide greater policy discipline and credibility to a stabilization program)
Degree of economic or financial development	The greater the degree of economic and financial development, the less good the choice for flexible exchange rate regime, given the experiences of developing countries that were affected by currency or financial crises. May need capital or exchange control
Labor mobility	The greater the degree of labor mobility when wages and prices are downwardly sticky, the less difficult (and costly) is the adjustment to external shocks with a fixed exchange rate
Capital mobility	The higher the degree of capital mobility, the more difficult it is to sustain a pegged but adjustable exchange rate regime and floating may not be a good choice either. Need to install capital and exchange controls

Source: Based on IMF (1997), *World Economic Outlook 1998* with some modifications.

foreign direct investment (FDI). The investment is supposed to increase production of goods mostly for export markets. Demand-led growth (DLG) policies were tested and implemented in the region in the late 1950s; however, the outcome of the policies was very unfavorable. Since the DLG policies failed, the policy of ELG was drafted and implemented in most East Asian countries. The ELG policy increased demand for labor and stimulated real economic growth. South Korea and Taiwan began with DLG and then shifted to ELG in the 1960s and since then both countries have experienced rapid economic development and growth and finally joined the NIEs group. In the case of Malaysia and Singapore, in their early stage of industrial development the policy of DLG was sought. However, the policy failed in generating solid real economic growth. The main reason was that their market was relatively small. Thus the policy of ELG was initiated and implemented. Since then economic growth and development in both countries has expanded rapidly. The size of the market does not guarantee that DLG policy will produce concrete results that stimulate real economic growth and reduce unemployment. This is shown in the case of Thailand and China. The rapid economic growth in China was, on average, 10 percent from 1996 to 2006, accounted for largely by foreign investment; the growth of export of manufactured goods subsequently increased dramatically. Now China is known as the 'Workshop of the World', producing and supplying many electrical and electronic products such as microwave ovens, DVD players, cameras and televisions for world demand. China pursued ELG mainly to eradicate poverty and to reduce unemployment. These two economic problems had been worrying the government since the late 1970s. The governments in the East Asian region realized that the ELG policy was a reliable economic measure in reducing unemployment and eradicating poverty. The success of East Asian economies has been documented in many books and articles; some have even stated that what has happened in the regions is a 'miracle'.

Given factors such as a stable political environment, low cost of labor and strategic location, the ELG policy has managed to persuade foreign firms to invest. The inflow of FDI, particularly from Japan and the USA, has accelerated demand for labor. The capital contributed to the increased marginal product of labor (MPL) compared to the contribution of domestic investment in MPL, which was relatively low. Given the rigidity of nominal wages in the short term, and since the wages are 'controllable costs', foreign firms exploited the low costs of labor to a great extent. The government deliberately allowed foreign firms to depress wages or oppress low-skilled labor. These measures are not against the law. To attract new industries such as electrical and electronics, the government has amended labor laws that do not allow formation of trade unions in the new industries. Also, there is no law on minimum wages. Socially, the actions by the governments and foreign firms are against the will of the people and weakened the rights of labor. Economically, investment by foreign firms has reduced the unemployment rate and this economic statement is taken by the national government as advocating the benefits of FDI.

In export-oriented economies such as in East Asia, while the exports of manufactured goods increased, concurrently imports of mainly intermediate and investment goods accelerated. The imports have fueled or financed the expansion of manufactured goods production and exports.

We do not deny that the ELG has indirectly pushed the expansion of linked or supporting industries to meet demand from foreign firms. Also, local industries in consumer goods have accelerated to meet the increasing demand from the growing number of households. Non-manufactured or non-tradable goods or services industries have also expanded subsequently. Although the policy of ELG has increased economic growth rapidly through acceleratation of export of manufactured goods, the question regarding the net benefit in the long run of such policies has been raised. Are the economies benefiting from the policy or not? It seems that disadvantages of the policy are not a real issue for the government. What the government needs is to achieve high economic growth and low unemployment to impede expansion of social costs such as crime.

To ensure that the policy of ELG produces an outstanding result, governments in East Asia indirectly determine the price of goods in terms of foreign currencies. They redirect the prices from the equilibrium level or distort the determination of prices to increase competitiveness in export markets. Therefore a stable exchange rate or value of national currencies *vis-à-vis* foreign currencies, namely to the US dollar, is needed to preserve price competitiveness. This is vital not only to promote export growth but to ensure the cost of production (labor costs in terms of US dollars), to be competitive as well as to act as an incentive to attract further FDI. In highly globalized economies, price competitiveness is a main factor in increasing and sustaining economic growth (i.e. to maintain employment level and price stability). If the exchange rate or value of the currency is more expensive than that of the trading partner or competing countries, the exchange rate will hurt the production sector in the long run. Relative price in terms of foreign currency is an important element in expanding the production of the tradable sector. With a relative low price, that is, tradable price against non-tradable price, economic resources will be diverted to the tradable sector, thereby absorbing unemployed labor and building up international reserves. The fixed exchange rate is more reliable and capable of accommodating to the situation and ensuring competitiveness and stability of prices. A stable exchange rate will ensure better economic (business) decision making and economic resources will be allocated more efficiently. Eventually, economic welfare will also improve. The exchange rate regime is one of the key policies that enables East Asian countries to 'dominate' in the world commodities market in a short time.

Why do the governments in East Asia stress the importance of having high real economic growth, a low unemployment rate and a significant surplus of trade balance, and a stable exchange rate level? The motive can be explained by using an internal–external demand model, as depicted in Figure 8.2. The internal and external balance (or demand) is related to the

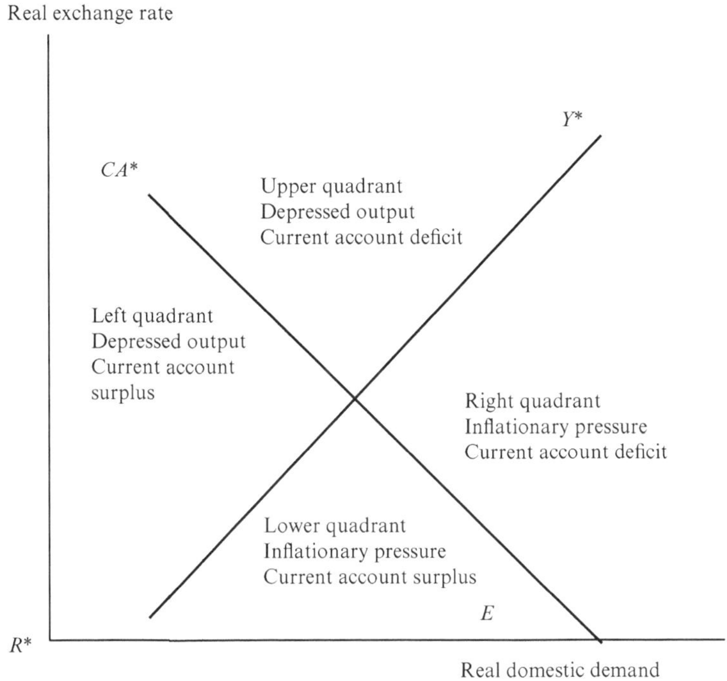

Source: Krugman (1990).

Figure 8.2 Internal and external balance

Swan–Salter analysis. The model is also known as an Australian model or dependent economic model. Internal demand refers to achieving the level of potential output, while external balance is defined as achieving equilibrium in balance of payments, that is, current account equal to capital account ($CA = KA$). The vertical axis indicates the real effective exchange rate, hereafter the real exchange rate, and the horizontal axis indicates the level of real domestic demand (RDD) as measured by the level of real output or real income. Internal demand is shown by the Y^* line, which represents a combination of RER and RDD at which the economy is at full employment. We know that in Keynes's works there is no such thing as full employment. However, in this respect we assume that achieving full employment or pushing the economy towards full employment is a main objective or goal of any economy in the world; the same goes for East Asian countries. Full employment is a desirable objective. The slope is correlated positively between RER and RDD, indicating that as the RER increases, more domestic demand is diverted from domestic goods to imported goods. If an economy moves on the right axis towards RDD, an increase of domestic demand will induce domestic price to increase; also an increase in RDD means that the level of unemployment decreases. From the four quadrants as indicated in Figure 8.2, most developing countries would desire the lower quadrant. The main objective of any developing country is to reduce the unemployment level while maintaining price stability. The economic development policy implemented by most East Asian countries is pro-employment and pro-poverty reduction. Some of the countries have been in the lower quadrant, and some of them have also experienced the right quadrant, such as Malaysia, Thailand and Korea before the currency-cum-financial crisis erupted in July 1997. The government liberalizes trade and FDI in order to achieve low poverty and unemployment rates. Furthermore, the government is spending a huge amount of money in building free trade zone areas and good infrastructure.

East Asian economies are trade dependent. In East Asia trade openness (exports/GDP) are over 70 percent. In the case of Malaysia and Singapore the index is over 100 percent. The real economic growth of China from 1990 to 2006 was on average about 10 percent per year. The unemployment rate on average increased from 2 percent in 1990–93 to 4 percent in 2003–06. The trade balance increased from US$2.3 billion in 1990–93 to US$73.5 billion in 2002–06. The inflation rate on average was about 9.0 percent in 1990–93 and about 3.4 percent in 2002–06. The RER increased marginally from 110 in 1990–1993 to 117 in 2002–06. In other countries, as indicated in Table 8.6, most countries experienced high economic growth prior to 1997. During and in post-financial crisis 1997, most affected countries (Indonesia, Korea, Malaysia and Thailand) experienced on average real economic growth of about 5 percent. The unemployment rate increased marginally in all countries. The trade balance in the countries increased considerably. The surplus in the trade balance is attributed to the undervaluation of the currencies, as indicated by the level of the RER. The Malaysian ringgit and Thai baht were undervalued; however, in the case of the Indonesian rupiah and the Korean won the currencies appreciated in the period of 2002–06. The RER rate shows that the price of goods in foreign currencies (in US dollars) plays a crucial role in maintaining export competitiveness in the world market. ADB (2007), Arndt and Huemer (2004) and Athukorala (2004) found that that the responsiveness of exports to real exchange rate changes tends to be low in East Asia. One explanation is that production network integration in the region expanded at a rapid pace. In other words, trade expansion in the regions is more toward intra-firm trade, and goods in the export basket seem to be less diversified; that is, there is a concentration in electrical and electronics goods.

Table 8.6 East Asia (selected countries). Internal–external demand (ID–ED)

	1990–1993	1994–1997	1998–2001	2002–2006
P.R. China				
GDP real growth rate	10.3	10.8	8.0	10.1
Unemployment rate	2.4	3.0	3.2	4.2
Inflation rate	9.0	10.6	0.5	3.4
Trade balance, $ bil.	2.3	18.7	29.8	73.5
Current account, $ bil.	4.9	13.4	22.6	112.1
RER rate	110.94	123.54	110.30	117.04
Rep. of Korea				
GDP real growth rate	7.7	7.3	3.7	4.8
Unemployment rate	2.6	2.3	5.4	3.6
Inflation rate	7.3	5.0	3.5	3.0
Trade balance, $ bil.	−5.3	−11.4	21.0	18.8
Current account, $ bil.	−3.4	−11.0	21.3	13.3
RER rate	100.93	101.64	129.48	110.22
Malaysia				
GDP real growth rate	9.3	9.1	2.0	5.8
Unemployment rate	4.0	2.8	3.3	3.5
Inflation rate	3.9	3.3	2.7	2.2
Trade balance, $ bil.	2.4	2.3	19.9	28.5
Current account, $ bil.	−2.7	−5.1	10.1	16.3
RER rate	98.23	98.78	118.28	112.45
Thailand				
GDP real growth rate	9.0	5.7	0.2	5.6
Unemployment rate	2.7	1.8	3.9	2.0
Inflation rate	4.8	5.6	2.9	2.9
Trade balance, $ bil.	−5.1	−4.7	12.6	9.8
Current account, $ bil,	−6.7	−9.6	10.6	1.5
RER rate	100.05	101.08	122.32	122.89
Indonesia				
GDP real growth rate	8.1	7.1	−0.9	5.1
Unemployment rate	2.6	5.3	6.5	10.0
Inflation rate	8.4	8.0	25.1	9.0
Trade balance, $ bil.	6.4	7.6	21.7	23.1
Current account, $ bil.	−3.0	−5.5	6.2	5.5
RER rate	101.66	104.05	169.20	120.54

Table 8.6 (continued)

	1990–1993	1994–1997	1998–2001	2002–2006
Singapore				
GDP real growth rate	8.7	9.0	3.4	6.1
Unemployment rate	2.1	2.0	3.3	4.1
Inflation rate	2.9	2.1	0.5	0.6
Trade balance, $ bil.	−1.6	1.4	13.8	32.5
Current account, $ bil.	4.5	14.3	15.8	24.2
RER rate	95.66	87.97	89.31	96.22

Notes: Internal balance: GDP real growth rate, unemployment rate, inflation rate. External balance: trade balance (net exports), current account, RER.

Source: Asian Development Bank, *Key Indicators 2007*, Manila.

EXCHANGE RATE FLEXIBILITY AND THE ROLE OF THE US DOLLAR

By looking at the nominal exchange rate of East Asia countries, the variability of the exchange rate is minimal. As shown in Table 8.7, the yuan (China), the ringgit (Malaysia) and the Singapore dollar fluctuate less than other countries. The rupiah (Indonesia) seemed to be more volatile than the rest of the currencies in the region. Consequently, exports of the country are more responsive to changes in the real exchange rate (RER) than other countries in the region (ADB 2007). Depreciation of currencies' value (or increase in exchange rate) can make a country's exports cheaper and imports more expensive. By depreciating against the US dollar, products in East Asia whose currencies are pegged to the dollar will become more competitive against third-country products. This can boost their exports, curb imports and improve their trade balances with countries other than the USA. If the countries adopt floating exchange rates, their currencies will appreciate and reduce the trade balance.

It should be stressed that, since 2006, no countries in the region are pegged to the US dollar except for Hong Kong. Even though other countries have adopted the flexible exchange rate regime, the value of national currencies 'stick to' the US dollar rather than to the Japanese yen, even though Japan was a major contributor of FDI. Most East Asian currencies are 'softly' pegged to the US dollar. This is in line with McKinnon and Frankel's works, which state that most exchange rates before the Asian crisis followed the US dollar; in other words the exchange rate

Table 8.7 East Asia: exchange rate flexibility (%)

	1995–1996	2000–2002	2003–2005	2006–2007
PR China	0.1	0.0	0.1	0.3
Indonesia	0.4	3.8	1.5	1.6
Rep. Korea	0.8	1.5	1.3	1.2
Malaysia	0.6	0.0	0.0	0.9
Philippines	0.5	1.5	0.8	1.3
Singapore	0.5	0.9	0.8	0.8
Thailand	0.3	1.3	1.0	1.2

Note: Data refer to average absolute monthly percentage changes in exchange rate against the US dollar.

Sources: CEIC Data Company Ltd; International Monetary Fund, *International Financial Statistics* online database; www.cbc.gov.tw; all downloaded 10 September 2007. *Asian Development Outlook 2007 Update.*

Table 8.8 Weights of US dollar and Japanese Yen in nominal values of selected East Asian countries

Currency	Before 1994[a]	Feb 94–May 95[b]	Jun 97–Dec 98[c]	30 Nov 2005[d]
Korean won	0.96	0.97	1.22	0.58
Singapore dollar	0.75	0.82	0.69	0.50
Malaysian ringgit	0.78	0.88	0.77	0.99
Indonesia rupiah	0.95	1.00	0.48	0.67
Thai baht	0.91	092	0.64	0.61
Chinese yuan	–	1.00	0.99	0.92

Notes: [a] Frankel and Wei (1994); data; [b] McKinnon and Schnabl (2002); data 2 February 1994–30 May 1997; [c] McKinnon and Schnabl (2002); data 1 June 1997–31 December 1998; [d] Ogawa and Shimizu (2006); data 30 November 2005.

Sources: McKinnon and Schnabl (2002); Ogawa and Shimizu (2006); Frankel and Wei (1994).

was 'quasi-pegged' to the dollar. Frankel and Wei (1994), based on their econometeric results, showed that the movement of currencies of East Asia *vis-à-vis* to the US dollar, were pegged to the dollar (Table 8.8). McKinnon and Schnabl (2002) used Frankel and Wei's technique in estimating exchange rate volatility in the region. In their analysis, they assumed the Swiss franc as an outside currency. The analysis indicated, for instance in the case of Korea, that changes of the won against the US

Table 8.9 Currency (US$) invoicing in exports and imports in selected East Asia countries

Country	Year	Export	Import	US share in thc country exports
Japan	2003	48.0	68.7	24.8
Korea	2004	84.6	78.3	17.0
Indonesia	2004	93.6	82.5	22.0
Malaysia	2000	90.0	90.0	20.5
Thailand	2003	84.4	76.0	17.0

Sources: Gao (2007) and Kamps (2006).

dollar of the currency basket closed at 100 percent. Ogawa and Shimizu (2006) used the same technique as Frankel and Wei and McKinnon, but the results were slightly changed. The weight of the US dollar in the currency basket dropped in the case of Korea, Indonesia, Thailand and Singapore. For Malaysia and China the weight was closed to 100 percent, even though the ringgit and the yuan floated by June 2005.

McKinnon and Schnabl (2002) believed that East Asian countries that pegged to the US dollar took a reasonable option, but the financial crises that erupted in 1997–98 show that the pegging caused some damage to the economy. However, post-crisis the countries maintain 'the soft pegging' to the US dollar, even though the countries that experienced the financial crisis have changed their regime. As Fukuda and Ohno (2003) mentioned, after early 2000, the East Asian currencies began reverting to *de facto* pegs against the US dollar. The main reason for this was that transactions in current and capital accounts of balance of payments are largely in dollars. The USA is the major trade partner of East Asian countries and total trade between the regions ranges from 20 to 40 percent. Intra-trade in ASEAN is about 23 percent, and intra-trade between ASEAN and China, Korea and Japan is on average about 30 percent. But most imports and exports of East Asian countries were largely bills in US dollars and the amount was more than 80 percent, particularly for Korea, Indonesia, Malaysia and Thailand (Table 8.9). We believe that exports and imports of China would also be more than 80 percent. Trade denominated in the national currency or yen or euro was below 20 percent (Kamps 2006).

CONCLUSION

Of all the aspects of globalization, international financial markets have proven to be the most difficult to manage. Overwhelming expansion of the markets with varieties of financial instruments including FOREX and derivatives have complicated macroeconomic management. Some people, particularly from the finance sector, argue that such financial instruments are needed to facilitate firm and trade financing, but based on data available this is not borne out. The same argument also holds for derivatives, that is, the instruments needed for hedging; however, investments in the sector are hardly for hedging (Solomon 1999, p. 112). Trading in the market is scarcely linked to economic fundamentals. Determinants of the exchange rate are no longer correlated to economic fundamentals, as they were during the Gold Standard and Bretton Woods eras. Nowadays it is the market makers of the (international) financial market who determine the currency value of a country.

In relation to the exchange rate system, in general, developing countries reject the impossible trinity theorem, which provides a package either for a floating or fixed exchange rate. The trinity sounds and looks beautiful in macroeconomic textbooks, but not in the real world. Neoclassical economists claim that the flexible exchange rate is better than the fixed exchange rate, but it is still an open discussion. For developing countries, an exchange rate system is one of the main macroeconomic tools. In general, countries adopt an intermediate regime, which allows the government to intervene or maneuver the exchange rate movement to preserve export competitiveness. Governments often use interest rates or intervene in the FOREX to achieve their implicit target exchange rate. 'Fear of floating' seems to be the reason for the threat of high inflation and financial crisis. Fear of floating only makes sense if a country is piling up a huge debt denominated in foreign currencies. Devaluation of the currency will provide a negative shock to the economy. If a country has fewer international debts denominated in foreign currencies or more debts in national curriences, then the possibility of suffering a balance of payments crisis may be slim. The possibility of losing price competitiveness due to an overvalued currency is also a reason for not letting the exchange rate float freely.

Although the exchange rate and monetary policies are managed separately, the two policies should be coordinated to achieve the best results for the country. If the exchange rate is determined by unproductive factors (external source), the implication for the economy will be undesirable. Relatively closed economies are able to pursue domestic objectives without suffering intolerable pain from currency swings. For the majority of smaller, more open economies, however, the costs of the floating exchange rate are difficult to absorb. Volatile exchange rate swings produce almost unbearable costs to the economies in terms of the impact to the production sector and the cost to the government in terms of managing the impact.

In the case of East Asia, the exchange rate regime is a crucial macroeconomic measure. The regime will determine whether countries in the region are able to promote economic growth from trade channels by changing foreign prices. Although trade with the USA accounted for about 20 percent, the exchange rate of value of currencies of the countries stick to the US dollar rather than to the Japanese yen. Transactions of capital and current accounts of balance of payments are more than approximately 80 percent and yet the East Asian economies remain reluctant to dollarize their economy. The rationale of East Asia holds the exchange rate as a separate economic policy, for the reason mentioned above – mainly to preserve price competitiveness. This is crucial to achieving economic objectives; that is, to achieve high real economic growth and a low unemployment rate. Even though the 'soft pegging' to the US dollar, had a severe negative impact on some of the East Asian countries, that is, the Asian crisis of 1997, most currencies in the region remain *de facto* pegged against the US dollar.

One main lesson that countries in East Asia must learn is that opening capital accounts (capital account convertibility) needs to be monitored (the inflow and outflow of short-term capital) and guided with some element of capital or exchange controls. This is to ensure that movement of the capital will not significantly disrupt producers and exporters in setting prices. While capital inflows may be desirable for the economic growth because the marginal product of capital is larger in developing countries, rapid reversals of this capital can lead to domestic liquidity problems. Most economists agree that countries tend to prosper when they open up to trade. But wide open capital markets have always been controversial.

> One of the stark realities of a rapidly globalizing world is that you can run, but you cannot hide. When a financial crisis hits one country, it can complicate business strategy, operations, and financial results for companies around the world – even those without operations in the crisis country. (Barton and et al., 2003, p. 36)

Since there is no international financial architecture, the emerging markets (developing countries) have to fight against foreign portfolio capital on their own. As experienced by few countries in East Asia, central banks are unable to carry on the complete sterilization of foreign capital inflow on a long-term basis as it is too costly for them. Even though Malaysia has lifted capital controls on outflow of foreign portfolio capital in 2001 and unpegged the ringgit from the US dollar in July 2005, the ringgit remains de-internationalized. Similarly for the yuan, the Chinese government still controls buying and selling of the yuan after it was unpegged in July 2005. When the Thai baht appreciated extraordinarily in December 2006, the central bank of Thailand imposed capital controls to reduce the appreciation. The main reason for those measures is to preserve export competitiveness and to ensure that the role of ELG in promoting a sustainable economic growth will not fail. Frankel (1999) said, 'there is no single currency regime system right for all countries or at all times'.

NOTES

1. Most of the exchange rate models are introduced to analyze the movement of the exchange rate in developed countries. The exchange rate movement of the developed world is wider but fairly stable compared to developing countries, where it is violent and unstable due to international economic pressure. The financial (including capital) market in developed countries is more structured and advanced than in the developing world.
2. Foreign exchange markets in Asian emerging economies are more variable, relative to those of Japan and other industrialized countries. The immediate impact of shocks on volatility in the emerging markets is larger than that in the mature markets. This characteristic makes the currencies in the emerging markets more vulnerable to spectacular external shocks (Wang and Wang 1999).
3. The move to floating exchange rates and the ensuing growth of international financial markets point to the importance of asset markets in determining the nominal exchange rate. In general, studies on market efficiency suggest that the major foreign exchange markets exhibit behavior that is characteristic of other asset markets. Exchange rates react quickly to news; rates are volatile and difficult to forecast (Levich 1985).
4. The usual method employed in looking at the relationship between changes in exchange rate and domestic prices is to estimate how much change in exchange rate is pass-through to import prices of importing countries. Under the PPP assumption, exchange rate pass-through to domestic prices is always immediate and complete. However, in the real world the goods market is imperfect, so exchange rate pass-through to goods prices (import or export prices) is incomplete. Pass-through depends upon the pricing strategy of firms. The pass-through method cannot look at the complete or actual price-setting or behavior of firms or producers in determining their goods prices. Exchange rate or import price is one element of pricing, besides costs of tranportation, storage, taxes (sales, excise or tariffs) and profit margin. The final price that the consumer pays is CPI = domestic price = Pm + mark-up, where the mark-up comprises changes in exchange rate costs of tranportation, storage, taxes (sales, excise or tariffs) and profit margin. Therefore the estimation of pass-through may seem to mislead or be biased.
5. As mentioned, since the FOREX is dominated by players of industrial countries, these countries can manipulate the exchange rate or make the currency value of developing countries cheaper so that they can buy or import commodities more cheaply. This was one of the main reasons why structural adjustment lending (SAL) by the World Bank and IMF were depressing the income of the export sector of receiver countries, since one of the main policies under SAL was exchange rate flexibility. Developing countries have no market power in the FOREX.

REFERENCE

Arndt, S.W. and A. Huemer (2004), 'Trade, production networks and the exchange rate', Lowe Institute of Political Economy, Claremont McKenna College, CA, mimeo.

Asian Development Bank (2007), *Asian Development Outlook 2007*, Manila: ADB.

Athukorala, P. (2004), 'Post-crisis export performance in Thailand', *ASEAN Economic Bulletin*, **21** (1), 19–36.

Barton, Dominic, Roberto Newell and Gregory Wilson (2003), *Dangerous Markets. Managing in Financial Crises*, New York: John Wiley & Sons.

BNM (Bank Negara Malaysia) (1995), *Annual Report 1994*, Kuala Lumpur: BNM.

Bordo, Michael, Barry Eichengreen, Daniela Klingebiel and Mania Soledad Martinez-peria (2001), 'Is the crisis problem growing more severe?', *Economic Policy*, **16** (32), 53–82.

Breuer, Janich Boucher (2004), 'An exegesis on currency and banking crises', *Journal of Economic Surveys*, **18**, 293–320.

Choudhri, E. and D. Hakura (2001), 'Exchange rate pass-through to domestic prices: does the inflationary environment matter', IMF Working Paper no. 01/194.

Devereux, Michael and James Yetman (2003), 'Predetermined prices and the persistent effects of money on output', *Journal of Money, Credit and Banking*, **35**, 729–42.

Fischer, Stanley (2001), 'Exchange rate regimes: is the bipolar view correct?', *Journal of Economic Perspectives*, **15** (2), 3–24.

Frankel, Jeffrey (1999), 'No single currency regime is right for all countries or at all times', Frank Graham Memorial Lecture, Princeton University, 20 April.

Frankel, Jeffrey A. and Shang-Jin Wei (1994), 'Yen bloc or dollar bloc? Exchange rate policies of the East Asian economies', in Takatoshi Ito and Anne O. Krueger (eds), *Macroeconomic Linkage: Savings, Exchange Rates, and Capital Flows*, Chicago, IL: University of Chicago Press, pp. 295–355.

Fukuda, Shin-ichi and Sanae Ohno (2003), 'Exchange rate regimes in East Asia after the crisis: implications from intra-daily data', Discussion Paper, CIRJE-F-247, University of Tokyo, Tokyo, Japan.

Gao, Haihong (2007), 'Current global dollar standard: problems and regional solutions for East Asia', Chinese Academy of Social Sciences, Beijing, mimeo.

Hagiwara, Akiko Terada (2005), 'Foreign exchange reserves, exchange rate regimes, and monetary policy issues in Asia', ERD Working Paper No. 61, Asian Development Bank, Manila.

Ho, Corraine and Robert McCauley (2003), 'Living with flexible exchange rates: issues and recent experience in inflation targeting emerging market economies', BIS Working Paper No. 130, February.

Hopper, Gregory P. (1997), 'What determines the exchange rate: economic factors or market sentiment?', *Business Review*, FRB of Philadelphia, September/November.

Humpage, O. (1998), 'A hitchhiker's guide to understanding exchange rates', *Economic Commentary*, January, 1–4.

Kamps, Annette (2006), 'The euro as invoicing currency in international trade', Working Paper No. 665, European Central Bank, Frankfurt, Germany.

Keynes, J.M. (1913), *Indian Currency and Finance*, London: Macmillan.

Klein, Lawrence R. (1987), 'The choice among alternative exchange-rate regimes', *Journal of Policy Modeling*, **9** (1), 7–18.

Krugman, Paul R. (1990), 'Equilibrium exchange rates', in Willaim H. Branson, Jacob A. Frenkel and Morris Goldstein (eds), *International Policy Coordination and Exchange Rate Fluctuations*, Chicago, IL: University of Chicago Press, pp 159–95.

Levich, R.M. (1985), 'Empirical studies of exchange rates: price behaviour, rate determination and market efficiency', *Handbook of International Economics*, vol. 2, Amsterdam: Elsevier, pp. 979–1040.
Low, Linda (2006), 'A putative East Asian business model', *International Journal of Social Economics*, **33** (7), 512–28.
Mahathir, Mohamad (2000), *The Malaysian Currency Crisis. How and Why It Happened*, Pelanduk Publication, Kuala Lumpur, Malaysia.
McKinnon, Ronald I. and Gunther Schnabl (2002), 'Synchronized business cycles in East Asia: fluctuations in the yen/dollar exchange rate and China's stabilizing role', Department of Economics, Stanford University, CA, mimeo.
Ogawa, Eiji and Junko Shimizu (2006), 'Progress toward a common currency basket system in East Asia', RIETI Discussion Paper Series 07-E-002, 6 November.
Peters, Tom (1987), *Thriving on Chaos: Handbook for a Management Revolution*, Schaumburg, IL: Harper Perennial.
Solomon, Robert (1999), *Money on the Move. The Revolution in International Finance since 1980*, Princeton, New Jersey: Princeton University Press.
Stanek, Mary Beth (2002), 'A review of exchange rate policies and their effect upon nations and fims', *Management Research News*, **25** (4), 19–34.
Stanislaw, J. and D. Yergin (1998), *The Commanding Heights: The Battle between Government and the Marketplace that is Remaking the Modern World*, New York: Simon & Schuster.
Stein, Jerome (1997), *Fundamental Determinants of Exchange rates*, Oxford: Clarendon Press.
Taylor, Mark P. (1995), 'The Economics of exchange rates', *Journal of Economic Literature*, **33** (March), 13–47.
Wang, Peijie and Ping Wang (1999), 'Foreign exchange market volatility in Southeast Asia', *Asia-Pacific Financial Markets*, **6** (3), 215–33.

9. A Keynesian–structuralist growth strategy for Latin America*

Julio Lopez and Fernando J. Cardim de Carvalho[1]

1. INTRODUCTION

The liberal reforms introduced in practically all Latin American countries in the 1980s[2] did not meet the expectations of their proponents and supporters. Of all the macroeconomic gains expected to follow the policies of the period, only one, although very important, the control of inflation, was actually achieved.[3]

Liberal opinion explains the failure to resume economic growth in the region by the inability or unwillingness of governments to really commit to a liberal revolution. Half-hearted reforms, it is argued, could not lead to sustained growth because they were not enough to change the incentive structure of the economy that promoted rent-seeking behavior instead of the entrepreneurial spirit.

The opposite view, to which the authors of this chapter largely subscribe, maintains that it was rather the paralysis of the state generated by the crises of the 1970s and 1980s that deprived the economies of the region of an important lever to resume and sustain growth. In practically all Latin American nations economic performance deteriorated drastically in the liberal era, in comparison with the rates witnessed from 1945 to the 1970s, or even the 1980s;[4] or in contrast with East Asian economies where the state did intervene extensively in economic affairs. If this hypothesis is correct, then, to overcome stagnation it will be necessary to reconstruct the state's capacity to implement pro-growth policies.

Surprisingly, most critics of the liberal view have tended to assume one of two positions. Some believe that all that is needed is to implement expansionary policies that stimulate domestic demand to revive employment and output, 'to restart the engine', so to speak, supposing that the economy will then move on and begin growing. Others, in contrast, seem to believe that there are no alternatives to orthodox macroeconomic short-term policies so that non-liberal critics should focus only on long-term possibilities, policies and instruments, such as the formulation of industrial policies.

Following Keynes's and Kalecki's ideas, but also classical development economists (Prebisch 1949; Furtado 1953; Mandelbaum 1945), we propose in this chapter a different view. We argue, first, that in a modern capitalist economy, a monetary economy, short-term macroeconomic policies should be used to reduce unemployment and to increase the degree of capacity utilization, which will promote the generation of profits to firms and to wake up entrepreneurs' animal spirits. We also maintain that domestic expansionary policies should be coupled with measures to foster exports and import substitution, so as to avoid balance of payments problems. We argue, finally, that long-term policies must complete the package, signaling: (a) investment priorities to ensure that capacities will be created in strategic sectors and branches of the economy; and (b) sustained increases of effective demand in the future, to make businesspeople anticipate that long-term demand will justify increasing capacity. The importance of keeping the trade balance in check, and the significance of expanding the productive capacities, are of special relevance in developing economies. These are also the areas where we have more to learn from the pioneers of development economics – and from structuralist Latin American economists in particular.

To argue the need for active short- and long-term policies, we begin, in section 2, by setting up our theoretical approach with a brief presentation of the relevant Keynes/Kalecki framework connecting aggregate demand and aggregate profits, complemented by a discussion of the need for long-term growth-promoting policies. Section 3 explores the possibility of adopting expansionary short-term policies in Latin America. Section 4 discusses the necessary elements to define a supporting long-term investment strategy. Section 5 concludes the chapter.

2. CYCLICAL RECOVERY AND SUSTAINED GROWTH

For Keynes, as for Kalecki, involuntary idle capacity and unemployment emerge when aggregate demand is insufficient to absorb the full-employment level of output. This sort of situation tends to perpetuate itself, since, everything else remaining the same, if actual – and expected – demand is low, few jobs are offered, so few people will actually be able to buy consumption goods, confirming the initial expectation of low demand. Furthermore, when aggregate demand is low, profits are low[5] and, as Minsky (1982) reminded us, firms may not be able to honor the debts they incurred in the past without selling assets or issuing more debt. Under these circumstances, even if realized or expected demand for some entrepreneurs' output improves, the situation may not get better if firms are enmeshed in debt. The existence of debt liabilities means that for firms even transitory falls in demand may have lasting adverse effects.

In the Keynes/Kalecki approach, therefore, short-term policies to maintain appropriate levels of aggregate demand are essential to bring about high profits and keep firms financially healthy. If a recession has already started, even more vigorous policies may be necessary to increase demand. Supply-side measures leading to cheaper raw materials or to lower interest rates, though probably helpful – and indeed indispensable in the proposal we advance below – may not be enough if firms are not able to sell their cheaper output. Similarly, lower interest rates may help firms to attenuate the impact of the fall in profits on their ability to honor debts, but should hardly induce them to increase their financial exposure by borrowing to increase production if demand remains subdued.

Now, growing profits generated by increasing aggregate demand should improve the lot of firms in a number of ways. First, they provide them with cash flow, making it possible to service their debts. Second, the increase in internally generated funds also allows them to risk increasing output without exposing them to additional financial risks. Third, as Keynes argued a few times, there is no better way of improving expectations than the actual experience of earning profits.[6]

A recovery of aggregate demand has to originate in those of its elements that are autonomous with respect to current income. Private domestic expenditures may not be the most promising candidates in this case. It is true that a significant fraction of consumption nowadays is actually autonomous with respect to current income, being financed by consumer credit, as is the case of higher-value durable consumption goods. However, it is unlikely that even capitalists, let alone workers, will incur debt to spend on consumption goods when their current income (out of which the debt will have to be serviced) is contracting. On the other hand, a debt-financed rise in consumption does not seem to us the most commendable path to recovery in the present Latin American circumstances.

Under these circumstances, the two avenues left to promote recovery are net exports and what Kalecki (1933) called 'domestic exports', the increase of sales to the government. Expanding net exports has one advantage, of course, which is to prevent or to attenuate balance-of-payments' current account problems caused by the increase in imports that usually accompanies an economic recovery. The means to stimulate export expansion and import substitution will be addressed later in this chapter.

The other possibility is the use of fiscal policies. These can push an economy onto the path to recovery. Contrary to the current mainstream view, Keynes and Kalecki recognized that fiscal deficits could revitalize demand and profits. However, and this is a point not frequently appreciated, their preferred option in this context was not fiscal deficits, but increased government spending. Kalecki in fact supported financing government expenditure with taxes on profits, which would contribute to demand expansion combined with a change in income distribution in favor of labor.[7] Keynes, on the other hand, saw the generation of fiscal deficits as a kind of last resort instrument to be adopted when nothing else worked to fight a recession. Keynes believed that public confidence that the government would act, if necessary, to fight a recession should be guarantee enough to motivate entrepreneurs to maintain adequate expectations. Spending policies did not imply generating deficits because of the income multiplier, which would expand income and, thus, tax revenues when government made its expenditures. If a deficit were generated, its final impact on the economy would depend, to some extent, on how it was financed and the public's liquidity preference that would define the terms on which debt securities could be absorbed in private portfolios.[8] Therefore, for countries with significant structural fiscal deficits, the appeal to political fiscal may demand some previous reconstruction of the ability of governments to control their own fiscal situation.

In the case of developing countries, public spending should give emphasis, first, to public investment. As classical development economists long ago made clear, in developing economies the problem is not only to maintain proper levels of aggregate demand, but also to solve short-term bottlenecks that hamper supply, and to expand productive capacity. The infrastructure provided by the state is fundamental in the process of economic growth, and during the neoliberal period public investment has been drastically neglected. Besides, given that Latin America countries also exhibit appalling income concentration indices, with lower-income groups living in very bad conditions, income transferences to the poor need also to be increased if for no other reason than to show that development is a process that benefits the whole society and not only privileged groups.[9]

In addition, this fiscal push should be accompanied by an accommodating monetary policy that would prevent an increase in interest rates that could create more problems for the private sector. Increases in aggregate demand will raise profits, but they should not be inflationary if there is idle capacity and involuntary unemployment.[10]

Expansionary, though very selective, macropolicies should contribute to accelerating short-term growth in Latin American economies beyond the mediocre levels they have reached in the not so recent past.[11] However, they do not by themselves create conditions for a sustained and high rate of growth of output after capacity utilization reaches its limits, however elastic these limits may be in the short term. Therefore government policies should signal investment opportunities to entrepreneurs at the same time as creating conditions to facilitate the realization of investments. Active promotion of exports and import substitution, for instance, can at least in part fulfill this role. Industrial policies to support investments and to stimulate innovation and increasing productivity are another instrument.[12] In any case, these policies are not alternatives to short-term recovery policies, but their complements.

Therefore, if a recovery is to become an increasing trend, to use Kalecki's terms, businesspeople must be induced to invest beyond the mere replacement of depreciated capital, and to channel their investments to sectors and branches that create productive capacity in the key sectors of the economy. Also essential are measures to make feasible the funding of these investments. In the developing economies of Latin America this means mainly making sure that firms will be able to generate the necessary funds internally, but it also requires that new financing channels are open so that firms can invest beyond the limits set by their own funds.

3. GROWTH IN THE SHORT TERM

3.1 Can a Higher Growth Rate be Achieved in Latin America in the Short Term?

There is abundant, if somewhat scattered, evidence of the short-term potential for accelerating growth in Latin American countries. Available information about unemployment rates and capacity utilization shows that there are large reserves of productive resources kept idle in these economies. In addition, most economies in the region respond very quickly when expansive policies are implemented or wider markets are created, showing no lack of entrepreneurial disposition to take advantage of market opportunities. However, most of the time they been prevented from actualizing their potential by the generalized adoption of contractionary macroeconomic policies. Only those countries showing willingness to shake off the constraints imposed on them by Washington Consensus-inspired policy strategies could enjoy their potentialities.

As can be seen from the tables in the Appendix, except for Argentina in recent years, and to a lesser extent Chile and Colombia, growth rates in the region have been poor, unemployment rates have remained high, and real wages have stagnated. Besides, Argentina after the 2001–02 crisis and Brazil since 1994 illustrate both how fast an economy can grow in response to expansionary policies (the former) and how an economy can waste its potential in semi-stagnation (the latter).

Consistent figures on capacity utilization for the whole region are harder to come by, but nevertheless some information can be gathered. Thus, according to Mexico's statistical office surveys, at the end of 2007 manufacturing firms used only around 83 percent of their capacity, and that rate never exceeded 85 percent in the 1996–2007 period. In Brazil, even in 2004, when the highest rate of GDP growth in recent years was recorded, capacity utilization reached only 82.7 percent. In Argentina, the degree of utilization of capacity in the manufacturing industry has remained below 72 percent between 2004 and 2006, in spite of the fast growth achieved by this country.

Available information probably underestimates these economies' growth potential. The discouraging impact that prolonged unemployment exerts on workers, leading many of them to actually withdraw from the labor market (and the labor unemployment statistics), is well known. On the other hand, capacity utilization is not, in fact, a material constraint defined by engineering calculations. The degree of utilization is estimated by businesspeople, who use as benchmark the level of production they reckon as optimal. It is only natural that these estimates themselves are influenced by expectations and by the state of confidence. When demand is brisk and profit expectations are high, businesspeople naturally take a higher level of production as their benchmark.[13] It is not only because in a prosperous environment businesspeople's animal spirits are stimulated, but they are also stimulated to explore, for instance, x-efficiency factors, that is, to increase their operational efficiency. Thus capacity utilization measures themselves show some 'elasticity' with respect to the growth of demand. It has frequently been observed that in fast-growing economies capacity utilization grows less rapidly than GDP, because businesspeople keep updating their estimates of their maximum possible output.[14]

Better use of currently existing capital equipment may allow fast growth to take place. Argentina's recent economic experience illustrates the point. This is shown in Figure 9.1, where we compare the behavior of the index of economic activity and the index of capacity utilization in manufacturing (both indices are set to 100 for the first quarter of 2002).

In Argentina, GDP growth averaged about 9 percent between 2003 and the second quarter of 2006. Even though the productive capacity expanded, probably the fast economic recovery in this country was possible mostly thanks to a greater utilization of the previously idle capital equipment. As shown in Figure 9.1, the capacity utilization index grew

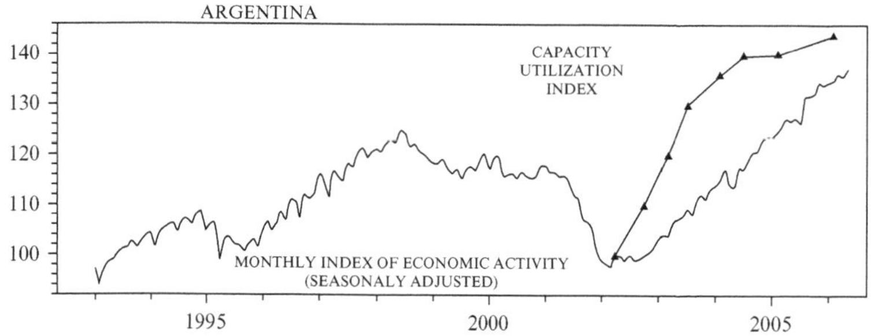

Source: Adapted from Damill (2006).

Figure 9.1 Comparison of economic activity index and capacity utilization index

faster than the economic activity index until 2004, when investment started to grow fast. Most likely it was the recovery that stimulated the investment activity after that date.

3.2 Growth-oriented Short-term Policies

The first two requirements of a short-run economic expansionary strategy should be rather obvious from what we said above. One is an increase in aggregate demand. The second is selective credit expansion. Of course, this entails adopting the notion that the objective of fiscal and monetary policy is safeguarding macroeconomic stability rather than just price stability. There is no reason to expect that, when output is still elastic, increases in effective demand and in the supply of credit are inflationary. If, in addition, measures are taken to make sure that credit will be directed at priority sectors, the impact on prices and on the trade balance should be greatly attenuated.

On this point, we recall again that Keynes (1933) and Kalecki (1944) strongly recommended expansionary fiscal and monetary policies.[15] The European economies in effect successfully carried out expansionary policies in the immediate postwar period. However, one should beware of mechanically transposing the European experiences to other contexts. In particular, European economies were already highly industrialized, and their productive capacity, though partly destroyed in the war, was still ample. Besides, those countries had protected domestic markets, and strictly controlled capital movements; and this was the context assumed by both Keynes and Kalecki. Last, but not least, all the advanced capitalist countries were following expansionary policies at that time, which allowed the mutual enlargement of markets and strengthening of growth stimuli.

Latin American economies are still developing, and this entails peculiarities that make it more difficult to maintain internal and external equilibrium in conditions of fast growth, particularly when the world economy is stagnant. In the first place, a growth revival will rapidly bring about external disequilibrium, which tends to be more acute in our case, because here bottlenecks appear at an early stage of the business upswing. Moreover, lack of reputation of the domestic currency gives rise to capital flight very soon when a trade deficit appears, which means that in our case the room for maneuver is more limited than in developed countries.

Thus a third requirement of economic expansion is that growth of domestic production should be accompanied by strong efforts to improve competitiveness of domestic producers. In the short term, this means management of the exchange rate.

In theory, a large enough currency depreciation would make locally made goods both profitable and competitive. Even production with old and high-cost equipment that today lies idle may become competitive. However, a large depreciation, unless it is accompanied by supportive measures, also creates some risks, particularly in economies that are very open to trade and finance. First, the price hike it may trigger can give rise to adverse expectations about the future stability of prices and the exchange rate. This by itself may lead to capital flight and threaten the balance of payments. Second, depreciation brings about a shift against wages and unleashes inflationary pressures. If money wages fully adjust to prices, a large depreciation of the domestic currency will provoke a wage–price spiral.[16] If they do not fully adjust, real wages and consumption per worker will fall, and obviously a wage fall is something that a progressive government could not accept. Currency depreciation has an additional negative impact on income distribution, because it may give extra profits (but not necessarily higher unit wages) to sectors that were already competitive and highly profitable to begin with. This is particularly the case of exporting sectors based on natural resources.[17] Finally, depreciation increases both the debt ratio of firms and of banks, when they are indebted in foreign currency, and the supply price of imported capital goods. Thus it may weaken the lending capacity of banks, and discourage private investment in fixed capital.

It follows that currency depreciation, adopted in isolation, while it does stimulate exports and import substitution, may harm consumption and investment, even as it worsens income distribution. Some evidence shows that its negative effects on internal demand may be larger than the improvement in trade balance brought about by the depreciation.[18]

Be that as it may, a competitive exchange rate seems indispensable, and in any growth resumption strategy, competitiveness of domestic production must be given a boost (Bresser-Pereira and Nakano 2002). Argentina's recent experience suggests that under certain circumstances the harmful consequences of currency depreciation can be reduced, while its beneficial effects can be fully reaped.

To achieve the gains of currency depreciation even as its negative consequences are minimized, we propose a 'compensated devaluation'.[19] That is, the currency depreciation must come hand in hand with complementary measures. In the first place, the government must ensure that the real purchasing power of workers does not decline, subsidizing them for any loss in their real wage.[20] Second, measures must be taken that compensate firms, at least partially, for the effects of currency depreciation on debt servicing and on the cost of imported inputs. Third, taxes must be levied on extra profits earned by exporting firms that prior to the currency depreciation already fetched high profits to prevent the 'Dutch disease'.[21] In any case, the most important compensation for capitalists and for workers for any harm ensuing from devaluation is output and employment expansion.

Both the currency depreciation and the complementary measures can take many forms. For example, the depreciation may involve a dual or multiple exchange rate system. Alternatively, depreciation could go together with subsidies to domestic production, provided that firms pledge to pass on lower costs to prices and measures are taken to ensure that subsidies are indeed passed on to consumers. A country could get an analogous result with a currency depreciation compensated with a discount in the value added tax for basic consumption goods, or compensated with money transferences to lower-income groups. We cannot go into the details here. We remark, however, that before the adoption of the liberal credo, Latin American nations accumulated a rich and varied experience in this area that is well worth studying.[22]

A fourth requirement of a growth strategy is the ability to regulate capital movements. If it wants to use the exchange rate as an instrument, as we think it should, the government must minimize speculative- or interest-rate-arbitrage-induced currency swings. To reach this objective, the Central Bank should quickly intervene whenever undesired variations of the real exchange rate take place. Also, the monetary authorities should be open to impose controls over capital movements if necessary (Bhaduri and Matzner 1990; Steindl 1990; Bresser-Pereira and Nakano 2002; Frenkel 2006; Sicsú and Ferrari Filho 2006).

Capital controls serve many objectives in the picture we are drawing, the most important of which is to prevent sudden changes in market sentiment, from eroding the influence of the monetary authorities in the stabilization of exchange rates and in keeping interest rates low. Under capital account liberalization, as capital movements in and out of the country are free, exchange rates are much more influenced by conditions in the financial markets than by trade considerations, and interest rates have to be kept higher than adequate to the needs of the economy in order to avoid capital flight.

Capital controls should be considered under three main headings. Financial investments of non-residents should be subjected to entry requirements, as, for instance, those so successfully implemented by Chile in the 1980s and 1990s. Investments abroad by residents, in contrast, should be restricted by exit limitations. Finally, foreign indebtedness of domestic private firms should be controlled and limited to exporting businesses, which enjoy a 'natural' hedge against adverse changes in exchange rates, since their revenues are linked to foreign currencies. These three measures should be enough to provide the government with the necessary control over exchange rates to use them as an instrument of export promotion and import substitution, and room to set domestic interest rates according to growth objectives.

4. LONG-TERM ELEMENTS OF SUSTAINED GROWTH POLICIES

If the government has the will and the power to permanently ensure adequate levels of effective demand, the long-term growth process revolves around three main issues. The first is how to ensure a fast growth of the productive capacity without excessively sacrificing consumption in the short term. The second is how to reach high growth rates of output under conditions of trade balance. The third is how to develop autonomous technological capacities. The three issues are closely interrelated, and in this section we discuss each of them in turn.

Investment plays a central role in the process of growth of productive capacity. A rise in the investment ratio is essential to accelerate the growth rate of output. The pioneers of development economics (Mandelbaum 1945; Prebisch 1951; Furtado 1953; Kalecki 1969) stressed two desirable features of investments appropriate to countries where unemployment is widespread: capital–output ratio should be low, and the life-span of the capital equipment should be extended as far as possible. Under these circumstances, high output growth rates could be achieved even with modest investment rates, or, in other words, without sacrificing too much present consumption.[23]

Is this still a sensible recommendation? We think it is. But we also qualify their proposal. Indeed, extending the life-span of the capital equipment and investing in equipment characterized by low capital intensity may negatively affect the rate of growth of labor productivity. Now, a strategy entailing stagnation, or low growth, of labor productivity will contribute to a rapid absorption of the huge labor surplus, but will soon be exhausted. First of all, once full employment has been reached, the overall rate of growth of output cannot exceed the rate of growth of employment, plus the average rate of growth of labor productivity. If the latter is not high, output growth will be insufficient to achieve a high level of output per head.

On the other hand, there is the foreign trade barrier. Let us assume that output growth shoots up under such a strategy. We know that to keep the trade balance in check, the rate of growth of exports must be accelerated, or the import elasticity of income should come down, or both.[24] Since Latin American economies must grow faster than their trading partners, competitiveness of home production must shoot up. To a certain extent the latter can be improved if the country subsidizes labor costs to bring them closer to their opportunity cost.[25] A competitive exchange rate, as well as ample access to credit, would also help. However, subsidies cannot last for ever, and no country could persistently devalue its currency without generating adverse side effects or inducing retaliation. Therefore a fast-growing country must also make efforts to foster technical progress, to change the export mix in favor of goods for which world demand grows fast, and to sustain increasing levels of labor productivity.

This is why we would rather recommend what we call a strategy to 'walk on both legs' – to use an expression that in the past earned a certain reputation.

First, in those sectors that are somewhat protected from foreign competition (or in which the country has important natural comparative advantages), one should seek to extend the lifetime of their capital equipment, and to use labor-intensive techniques of production, provided of course that these techniques are feasible. This should be accompanied by efforts to diffuse technical progress to these 'protected' sectors so as to upgrade progressively their technical and managerial capacities. However, in those sectors that are more exposed to competition, the adoption of more advanced (and probably more highly capital-intensive) techniques will be required.

Second, Latin American countries should make efforts to change their export and import mixes. This entails a careful selection of investment projects. These should be focused on the one hand towards future possibilities of import substitution, in modern lines of production that currently satisfy their requirements with imports; and on the other hand towards international demand niches, where they can construct new competitive advantages.

Third, they should foster autonomous technical progress. This is especially important and entails two requirements. On the one hand, there are the formal and the informal educational systems. But there are also learning-by-doing effects, and in this regard we recall that there are some particular industries whose workings appear to stimulate technological progress. Technological development is held back when these technology-generating industries are absent, and the country runs the risk of losing the basis for autonomous technological development. Often, it takes time to put these industries in place. This is why it is necessary to start them in the early stages of industrialization.

Accordingly, in our proposal to 'walk on both legs', we suggest that Latin American economies should also channel a share of their new investment towards the promotion of innovations and the development of a *few* very modern industries, even if they are capital- and skill-intensive and thus require considerable capital investment. Why do we emphasize here the word 'few'? Because saving potential is not high in developing countries, even if all resources are fully utilized, and professional and technically skilled labor is scarce. This limits their capacity to establish technologically advanced industries.

5. CONCLUSION

Economic growth has been mediocre in Latin America for about three decades. The poor performance of the region, however, has not been caused by natural disasters or social unrest and civil strife. Beginning in the 1970s, these economies lost strength (except for brief periods such as the oil boom in Mexico in the late 1970s and early 1980s, or the financial-led boom in Argentina during the 1990s) as they suffered a series of strong adverse external shocks, such as the two oil shocks of the 1970s and the interest rate shock generated by the Federal Reserve's twist to monetarism in 1979. After the main countries in the region, Argentina, Brazil and Mexico, went bankrupt in the early 1980s, the protracted process of adjustment that took place was conducted by the IMF under the aegis of liberalism.

In various degrees, the whole region pursued the policies known collectively as the Washington Consensus, dismantling the instruments of intervention of the state in the economy, privatizing companies, deregulating economic activities, removing barriers to the international circulation of goods and capital (but not of labor, as is usually noted). The liberal rhetoric was adopted to advance the idea that unleashing the energies of the private sector should be enough to inaugurate a new era of growth and prosperity unencumbered by the imbalances of the past, manifested by high inflation, balance of payments vulnerabilities and so on.

The historical record is unambiguously unfavorable to these views. In fact, growth has been low not because these countries are unable to reach higher output, but because liberal macroeconomic policies have kept effective output much below potential output. The liberal experiment in Latin America has unwittingly endorsed Keynes's and Kalecki's theory of effective demand by showing that misdirected economic policies can depress aggregate demand, thereby preventing the economy from achieving and sustaining its potential output.

In this chapter we have tried to outline an alternative policy strategy, based on the theory of effective demand and on the classical development theory, which would stimulate growth in the short term, and contribute to high and sustained growth in the longer term. Short-term growth acceleration can be achieved by stimulation of demand through monetary and fiscal policies. We argued, however, that imbalances peculiar to the economies of the region make it necessary to take some additional measures to prevent possible adverse effects of these policies on the profile of income distribution, balance of payments and so on; and make possible high and sustained long-term growth. In our view, more important than the listing of possible instruments, however, are the principles that we are proposing. Namely, that the reconstitution of the partnership between the state and the private sector in the economy is indispensable, and that a successful growth strategy in the region has to contain both short- and long-term sets of policies. Long-term policies will fail in the absence of short-term policies favorable to induce growing output, employment and profits. Short-term policies, on the other hand, may not be sufficient *per se* to induce the type of investment necessary to enlarge productive capacity.

Still, even these considerations may not be enough since, in contrast to Keynes and Kalecki, we are dealing here with developing economies. Although the logic of monetary economies is the same in developed and developing economies, supply constraints are obviously stronger for the latter. Therefore, to sustain growth in the longer term a new set of policies may be necessary, including the use of industrial policy instruments.

NOTES

* This is a condensed and somewhat amended version of the article 'Resuming growth in Latin America: short and long term policies', forthcoming in *The Brazilian Journal of Political Economy*.

1. J. Lopez acknowledges the support received from DGAPA/PAPIIT-Proyecto IN301606. F. Carvalho thanks Brazil's CNPq for financial support.

2. Chile being a precursor since its liberal reforms were introduced by the Pinochet dictatorship in the mid-1970s. Liberal reforms were also introduced in Argentina and Uruguay in the 1970s, but they were discontinued and then later reinstated.
3. It should be noted, however, that the authors are not stating that liberal policies were efficient to control inflation. What is being noted is that inflation control was achieved during the period when liberal policies prevailed.
4. See the tables in the Appendix for details.
5. As Kalecki (1954) showed in his famous profit equation, if we abstract from workers' savings, aggregate profits should be equal to the sum of capitalists' consumption, private investment, public expenditure and net exports. In much less precise terms, Keynes groped around these notions with his widow's cruse metaphor in the *Treatise on Money* (cf. Moggridge (ed.), *CWJMK*, V, p. 125).
6. 'As regards psychology, I maintain that if I am right that a large capital programme would increase the profits of businessmen, this would, after the first blush, have more effect on them than anything else . . . The next means of restoring business confidence is a psychological problem . . . In the long run we do not see how business confidence is likely to be maintained otherwise than by an actual recovery of business profits. This means that if business and employment improve for other reasons, then the effect of this improvement on business confidence may be cumulative; – which is, indeed, a part of the justification for emergency measures of a temporary character. For the effect of judicious emergency measures might be to improve business confidence, after which business confidence might take the place of the emergency measures as providing the necessary stimulus' (*CWJMK*, XX, pp. 361, 443/4).
7. The controversy on this issue between Keynes and Kalecki is summarized in Lopez and Mott (1999).
8. On Keynes's views of the instruments and effects of fiscal policies, see Carvalho (1997). See also Carvalho and Lopez (2007).
9. There are some financial expenditures that are not only wasteful but also have very low impact on aggregate demand, such as public debt service payments. It may also be the case that some other current expenditures may have to be cancelled or postponed. Thus an increase in public investment, which has a significant short-term impact on aggregate demand through the consumption multiplier, should be achieved without necessarily running into fiscal deficits and still have a positive effect on output and employment. Finally, most economies in the region exhibit very low tax revenues/GDP ratios. Raising taxes to finance public investments is still an option for practically all countries in Latin America, except Brazil where the tax revenues/GDP ratio is over 35 percent.
10. In section 3 we debate in some detail the notion of idle capacity.
11. Of course, liberal economists argue that activist states scare away 'investors' (it is never clear which class of 'investors' is being invoked here, since most of the time it seems that the argument relates to financial investors, not really investors in productive facilities). For them a small and balanced government stimulates businesspeople to run risks. Through some obscure economic logic, it is argued that macroeconomic equilibrium would stimulate private investment. In contrast, the argument presented here is based on the idea that investment is a disequilibrium phenomenon since it is induced by an expected disequilibrium between supply and demand large and durable enough to justify building new capacity. Thus the role of macroeconomic policy is precisely to generate the correct type of disequilibrium. Of course, this should not be construed as giving a blank check to government to spend in whatever ways. There are perverse situations to be avoided, such as stimulating further an economy already in full employment. The solution, however, is not the elimination of the government as an economic factor, but defining efficient ways to make good its potentialities.
12. The French postwar experience with indicative planning may be instructive to developing countries.
13. This is Keynes's point in his discussion of the concept of user cost in *The General*

Theory. See Keynes (1964), pp. 69–71. When current profitability of production rises, user costs fall.

14. Thus, paraphrasing Keynes, one could say that capacity utilization, as interest rates, are conventional phenomena, more than psychological phenomena. When the belief is rooted that the economy can grow more and that higher profit expectations are justified, output can be increased without actually facing capacity 'constraints'.
15. Of course, the appropriate policy mix, combining monetary and fiscal instruments, will vary from case to case. A policy mix favoring the growth of private investment, for instance, would prioritize the reduction of interest rates and the implementation of public investment plans. If the expansion of investments is not an immediate concern, expanding government social transference expenditures may be an effective instrument to increase consumption demand. On the general effects of different policy mixes, see, for instance, Kahn (1972) and Tobin (2003), ch. 16.
16. Probably fear of falling back into hyperinflation is one of the reasons why the economic authorities in countries like Brazil or Argentina in the 1990s did not try to correct the trend to currency overvaluation.
17. Soybean producers in Brazil and Argentina are a case in point.
18. Krugman and Taylor (1978), where these problems are formally analysed, is still well worth reading. See also Taylor (1988) and, on the Mexican experience, see for example Lopez (1998) and Loría (2007).
19. We slightly modify an idea originally put forward by two Latin American economists (Schydlowsky 1967; Diamand 1973).
20. The extent of the resulting welfare loss for workers depends on the share of imported goods in the wage basket. In large economies, where wage goods are most locally produced, welfare is not necessarily significantly reduced even if the real value of wages measured in foreign currency falls, since its real value measured in terms of goods may remain largely stable.
21. Of course, it may also help to attenuate fiscal deficits in government expenditure-led recoveries.
22. Raul Prebisch, the founding father of Latin American structuralism, wrote extensively on this subject, particularly while he was at the Argentine Central Bank. See especially Prebisch (1991–93), which collects the pieces he wrote during that period.
23. Note that their emphasis is in contrast with the advice promoted in the present-day literature on industrial strategy, which gives preference to the rapid renewal of capital equipment or to investment in new and technically demanding activities.
24. Thirlwall (1979) expressed this notion, which has come to be known as 'Thirlwall's Law', as follows:

$$y^X = x/\pi$$

where y^X is the rate of growth compatible with external equilibrium, x is the rate of growth of exports, and π is the income elasticity of imports. The same notion had been proposed earlier by Prebisch (1951 [1982]).

25. From the viewpoint of the whole economy, what matters are the factor opportunity costs – that is, how much we lose in production if we take away factor x from where it is least efficient. When a country has idle resources, their opportunity cost is zero. This is why subsidies may be convenient.

REFERENCES

Bhaduri, Amit and Matzner, Egon (1990), 'Relaxing the international constraints on full employment', *Banca Nazionale del Lavoro Quarterly Review*, no. 172, March, 49–61.

Bresser-Pereira, Luiz Carlos and Nakano, Yoshiaki (2002), 'Uma estratégia de desenvolvimento com estabilidade', *Revista de Economia Política*, **22** (3), 146–80.

Carvalho, F. (1997), 'Economic policies for monetary economies', *Revista de Economia Política*, **17** (4), 31–51.

Carvalho, F. and Lopez, J. (2007), 'Are full employment policies obsolete?', *International Journal of Political Economy*, **36** (3), 5–23.

Damill, M. (2006), 'Ahorro, inversión y superávits sectoriales: el escenario posterior a la crisis de 2001–2002', Cedes, Buenos Aires.

Diamand, M. (1973), *Doctrinas económicas, desarrollo e independencia*, Buenos Aires: Editorial Paidos.

Frenkel, R. (2006), 'An alternative to inflation targeting in Latin America: macroeconomic policies focused on employment', *Journal of Post Keynesian Economics*, **28** (4), 573–91.

Furtado, C. (1953), 'La formación del capital y el desarrollo económico', *El Trimestre Económico*, **20** (77), 88–121.

Kahn, R.F. (1972), *Selected Essays on Employment and Growth*, Cambridge: Cambridge University Press.

Kalecki, M. (1933), 'On foreign trade and "domestic" exports', in J. Osiatynsky (ed.), *Collected Works of Michal Kalecki*, Vol. I, Oxford: Oxford University Press, 1990, pp. 165–73.

Kalecki, M. (1944), 'Three ways to full employment', in J. Osiatynsky (ed.), *Collected Works of Michal Kalecki*, Vol. I, Oxford: Oxford University Press, 1990, pp. 357–76.

Kalecki, M. (1954), 'Theory of economic dynamics', in J. Osiatynsky (ed.), *Collected Works of Michal Kalecki*, Vol. II, Oxford: Oxford University Press, 1991, pp. 203–348.

Kalecki, M. (1969), 'Introduction to the theory of growth in a socialist economy', in J. Osiatynsky (ed.), *Collected Works of Michal Kalecki*, Vol. IV, Oxford: Oxford University Press, 1993, pp. 272–388.

Keynes, J.M. (1933), *The Means to Prosperity*, London and New York: MacMillan Harcourt Brace.

Keynes, J.M. (1964), *The General Theory of Employment, Interest and Money*, New York: Harcourt, Brace, Jovanovich, First published 1936.

Krugman, P. and Taylor, L. (1978), 'Contractionary effects of devaluation', *Journal of International Economics*, **8** (3) 445–56.

Lopez, J. (1998), *La macroeconomía de México. El pasado reciente y el futuro posible*, Brazil and Mexico: Editorial Porrua.

Lopez, J. and Mott, T. (1999), 'Kalecki vs. Keynes on the determinants of investment' (with Tracy Mott), *Review of Political Economy*, **11** (3), 291–302.

Loría, E. (2007), *Econometria con aplicaciones*, México: Pearson, Prentice Hall.

Mandelbaum, K. (1945), *The Industrialization of Backward Areas*, Oxford: Basil Blackwell.

Minsky, H. (1982), *Can 'it' Happen Again? Essays on Instability and Finance*, New York: M.E. Sharpe.

Moggridge, D. (ed.) (1930), *The Collected Writings of John Maynard Keynes*, London: Macmillan, vol. 5 (identified as *CWJMK*, V).

Prebisch, R. (1949 [1982]), 'El desarrollo económico de la América Latina y algunos de sus principales problemas', in Adolfo Gurrieri (ed.), *La Obra de Prebisch en la CEPAL*, México: Fondo de Cultura Económica.

Prebisch, R. (1951 [1982]), 'Problems téoricos y práticos del crecimiento económico', in Adolfo Gurrieri (ed.), *La Obra de Prebisch en la CEPAL*, México: Fondo de Cultura Económica.

Prebisch, R. (1991–93), *Obras, 1919–1948*, Buenos Aires: Fundación Raúl Prebisch.

Schydlowsky, D. (1967), 'From import substitution to export promotion for semi-grown-up industries: a policy proposal', *Journal of Development Studies*, **III** (4), 222–35.

Sicsu, J. and Ferrari Filho, F. (eds) (2006), *Cambio e Controle de Capitais. Avaliando a Eficiência des Modelos Economicos*, Rio de Janeiro: Campus Elsevier.

Steindl, J. (1990), 'Relaxing the international constraint on full employment. A comment', *Banca Nazionale del Lavoro Quarterly Review*, March, 63–7.

Taylor, L, (1988), *Varieties of Stabilization Experiences*, Oxford: Clarendon Press.

Thirlwall, A.P. (1979), 'The balance of payments constraint as an explanation of international growth rate differences', *Banca Nazionale del Lavoro Quarterly Review*, **128**, 45–53.

Tobin, J. (2003), *World Finance and Economic Stability. Selected Essays of James Tobin*, Cheltenham, UK and Northampton, MA, USA: Edward Elgar.

APPENDIX LATIN AMERICA, SELECTED COUNTRIES

Table 9A.1 Average annual growth rates of output

Period/ country	Arg.	Brazil	Chile	Col.	Mex.	Peru	Uru.	Ven.
1950–70	3.65	6.11	3.91	4.88	6.56	5.49	1.78	6.91
1970–80	2.55	8.72	2.55	5.51	6.60	3.77	3.02	4.13
1980–90	−1.14	1.57	2.92	3.41	1.81	−1.16	0.39	0.62
1990–96	5.65	2.92	8.47	4.13	2.12	5.09	4.21	2.83
1997	8.11	3.40	6.61	3.43	6.77	6.86	5.05	6.37
1998	3.85	0.00	3.23	0.57	5.03	−0.66	4.54	0.29
1999	−3.39	0.30	−0.76	−4.20	3.76	0.91	−2.85	−5.97
2000	−0.79	4.30	4.49	2.92	6.59	2.95	−1.44	3.69
2001	−4.41	1.30	3.38	2.18	−0.03	0.21	−3.39	3.39
2002	−10.89	2.70	2.18	2.46	0.77	5.02	−11.03	−8.86
2003	8.84	1.10	3.92	4.61	1.39	4.03	2.17	−7.76
2004	9.03	5.70	5.98	4.66	4.16	5.11	11.82	18.29
2005	9.18	2.90	5.71	5.72	2.80	6.74	6.62	10.33
2006	8.47	3.70	3.97	6.80	4.77	7.56	7.00	10.33

Source: ECLAC, with preliminary figures for 2006.

Table 9A.2 Total informal sector (percentage of total urban employed labor force)

Period/ country	Arg.	Brazil[b]	Chile[c]	Col.	Mex.[d]	Peru	Uru.	Ven.[e]
1980[a]	26.4	24.0	36.1	32.0	24.2	...	...	25.7
1985[a]	29.4	30.2	34.2	35.0	29.9	...	...	26.2
1990[a]	32.6	28.6	31.7	31.0	36.0	...	...	26.4
1994	42.7	...	34.6	...	...	...	40.3	45.3
1996	...	46.7	34.3	...	43.6	...	...	...
1997	41.4	...	...	...	...	60.6	42.2	49.4
1998	...	...	34.4	...	44.3	...	...	...
1999	42.2	47.3	...	...	...	63.3	41.5	53.7
2000	43.5	...	32.5	...	42.5	...	42.6	54.6
2001	...	46.2	...	...	...	63.1	...	...
2002	42.5	...	...	...	47.2	...	45.7	56.5

Notes: [a] Obtained from *Revista Mexicana del Trabajo* I, 1st QUARTER, 1993, p. 57. Further description does not apply for these periods. [b] From 1996 to 1998 wage earners in establishments up to five workers. [c] Data obtained from National Socioeconomic Characterization Survey (CASEN). [d] Data from National Survey on Home Income and Expenditure (ENIGH). [e] Total national.

Table 9A.3 Unemployment rates

Year/ country	Arg.	Brazil	Chile	Col.	Mex.	Peru	Urug.	Ven.
1997	N/A	N/A	N/A	N/A	N/A	N/A	N/A	N/A
1998	N/A	N/A	N/A	N/A	N/A	N/A	N/A	N/A
1999	N/A	N/A	N/A	N/A	N/A	N/A	N/A	N/A
2000	15.1	7.1	9.7	17.2	3.4	8.5	13.6	13.9
2001	17.4	6.2	9.9	18.2	3.6	9.3	15.3	13.3
2002	19.7	11.7	9.8	17.6	3.9	9.4	17	15.8
2003	17.3	12.3	9.5	16.7	4.6	9.4	16.9	18
2004	13.6	11.5	10	15.4	5.3	9.4	13.1	15.3
2005	11.6	9.8	9.2	14	4.7	9.6	12.2	12.4
2006	10.4	10.1	7.9	13	4.6	8.5	11.6	9.8

Notes: For Argentina, Mexico and Uruguay rates refer to urban areas. Brazil: six metropolitan areas. Chile and Venezuela: national indices. Colombia: 13 metropolitan areas. Peru: metropolitan Lima.

Source: ECLAC.

Table 9A.4 Real wage index (1990 = 100)

Year/country	Arg.	Brazil	Chile	Col.	Mex.	Peru	Urug.	Ven.
1997	102	106	135.3	121	102	110	109.9	69.7
1998	102	106.1	138.9	121	105	108	111.9	73.5
1999	105	101.4	142.2	126	106	106	113.7	70.1
2000	107	100.3	144.2	131	113	107	112.2	72.9
2001	106	95.4	146.6	131	120	106	N/A	77.9
2002	91.5	93.4	149.5	136	122	111	111.9	69.4
2003	89.8	85.2	150.9	135	124	112	99.9	57.2
2004	98.8	85.8	153.6	138	124	114	87.4	57.3
2005	105	85.5	156.5	139	124	111	87.4	58.8
2006	114	88.5	159.5	143	124	115	91.4	61.8

Notes: For Argentina and Mexico the indices correspond to the manufacturing industry. Brazil: from 2002 onwards, wages for private employed workers affiliated to the social and labor legislation. Chile: general wage index per hour. Colombia: workers in the manufacturing industry. Peru: private sector workers in the Lima metropolitan area. Uruguay: average wage. Venezuela: average income of employed workers in urban areas (after 2000, general wage index).

Source: ECLAC.

Table 9A.5 Export share of total world exports

Period/ country	Arg.	Brazil	Chile	Col.	Mex.	Peru	Uru.	Ven.
1950–59	1.13	1.62	0.46	0.57	0.75	0.29	0.23	1.83
1960–69	0.74	0.86	0.36	0.28	0.58	0.35	0.10	1.41
1970–79	0.47	0.95	0.24	0.20	0.40	0.20	0.05	0.91
1980–89	0.37	1.14	0.21	0.18	1.19	0.14	0.05	0.68
1990–96	0.37	0.94	0.27	0.19	1.39	0.10	0.04	0.41
1997	0.47	0.95	0.32	0.21	1.98	0.12	0.05	0.39
1998	0.48	0.93	0.30	0.20	2.14	0.10	0.05	0.31
1999	0.41	0.84	0.30	0.20	2.39	0.11	0.04	0.35
2000	0.41	0.85	0.30	0.20	2.58	0.11	0.04	0.49
2001	0.43	0.94	0.30	0.20	2.56	0.11	0.03	0.44
2002	0.40	0.93	0.28	0.18	2.48	0.12	0.03	0.38
2003	0.39	0.97	0.29	0.17	2.20	0.12	0.03	0.34
2004	0.38	1.05	0.35	0.18	2.06	0.14	0.03	0.41
2005	0.38	1.13	0.39	0.20	2.05	0.16	0.03	0.53

Source: UNCTAD.

10. Financial development and economic growth through a post-Keynesian lens: Hong Kong case study

Taha Chaiechi

1. INTRODUCTION

Recent years have witnessed an increasing interest in the role of the financial sector in economic development. In the aftermath of the financial crises of 1997–98, it is becoming increasingly clear that a sound understanding of the interaction of financial markets and the real sector is essential for economic growth and long-term prosperity. This clearly calls for further research on this important issue.

The objective of this study is to examine the role of financial market development in producing a virtuous circle of high aggregate demand in Hong Kong. In this study, first, we develop a long-run macroeconomic framework, following Stockhammer and Onaran (2003), which is a dynamic post-Keynesian and open economy model. Second, we account for economic theory by developing structural VAR (vector auto regression) format.

The empirical analysis of this study provides insights into the functioning of the Hong Kong macroeconomy, investigates the dynamic responses of the model to shocks in indicators of financial development and determines whether the effects of such shocks on the long-run relations disappear.

2. THEORETICAL LITERATURE

Development economics emerged as a unique discipline after World War II, However, most of the early literature was concerned with real rather than financial aspects of economic development. Following the regime changes that have occurred in the international financial system after the early 1970s, and given the significance of their impact on the domestic financial structures in developing countries, development finance has emerged as a discipline within the general area of economics – one that attracts significant theoretical and empirical analyses.

Schumpeter (1912) was one of the pioneers in highlighting the importance of the financial sector in promoting economic growth. In particular he argues that economic growth is a product of interactions of financial and real innovations. As Hein and Ochsen (2001) argue, from a Schumpeterian monetary point of view, monetary variables have impacts that extend beyond merely temporary and out-of-equilibrium effects on the real variables of the economic system: production, employment, distribution and growth.

Fisher (1930) outlined the basic functions of credit markets for economic activity, specifically as a way of allocating resources over time, and recognized the importance of risk in the process.

The works of Gurley and Shaw (1967), Shaw (1973) and McKinnon (1973) drew attention to the relationship between real and financial developments in terms of the role of financial intermediation, monetization and capital formation in determining the path and pace of economic development.

Hicks (1969) had similar views, stating that finance plays an essential role in advancement of developed countries. However, Keynes and Keynesians posit that goods-market aggregate demand determines economic growth and labour market outcomes. Thus high and sustainable levels of economic growth require high levels of investment, saving and export performance. Keynes argued for the subjection of financial markets to government intervention and government-controlled aggregate demand. Most Keynesian and post-Keynesian models analysed only the short-term effect and neglect the role of financial markets, particularly in the long run.

Rondo Cameron (1967) argues that financial systems may be both growth inducing and growth induced, but he emphasizes the crucial role of the quality of their services and the efficiency with which they are provided. He subsequently summarizes important features of the financial system, in particular of banks, by which financial intermediation serves as a vehicle for channelling small funds from risk-averse savers to less risk-averse people with entrepreneurial skills, which results in increased availability of funds for the latter. Second, financial intermediation provides motivations to investors. Declining costs of borrowing encourage entrepreneurs to make larger investments.

Joan Robinson (1952) suggested that financial systems develop in response to prospects in the real sector, yet the literature over the last decade has tended to argue that the real sector responds to financial development. The more recent literature examining the causal relationship between finance and growth includes King and Levine (1993a), Tullio Jappelli and Marco Pagano (1989), Jith Jayaratne and Philip Strahan (1996), and Rajan and Zingales (1998).

2.1 What is Financial Sector Development?

The financial sector is all the wholesale, retail, formal and informal institutions in an economy offering financial services to consumers, businesses and other financial institutions. In its broadest definition, the financial sector includes banks, stock exchanges, the capital market, insurers, credit unions, microfinance institutions and money lenders.

Its development requires growth in the volume and sophistication of activities as well as changes in the structure of the market. Generally, as the economy develops, the expectation is that the volume of transactions in the financial sector will increase and there will be less dependence on whether the financial market is bank based or equity based, at least for long-term credit.

According to Levine (1997), by definition, the financial sector can be called 'developed' if the efficiency, stability and competitiveness of the sector improve, and the range of financial services and diversity of financial institution increase. The increase in the amount of money that is intermediated through the financial sector or the capital that is allocated by the private sector is an other sign of development in financial markets.

Modern growth theory identifies the way that financial sector development affects long-run growth through its impact on capital accumulation, and through its impact on the rate of technological progress. Since financial institutions play an essential intermediation role, sector development may result in higher levels of capital accumulation and savings, thus promoting economic growth.

2.2 The Financial Market in Hong Kong

The economic success of Hong Kong over the past two or three decades is undisputed. Hong Kong is one of the leading international financial centres in Asia. In terms of financial infrastructure, it has the most advanced multicurrency payment and settlement system in Asia, which meets international standards.

In terms of the market structure, traditionally there are two major types of financial systems: bank-based and market-based systems. In countries with bank-based systems, long-term finance is largely provided by banks, while in market-based systems bonds and equity finance play a much greater role. The structure of financial markets in Hong Kong is more bank based, because government ownership of banks has been a dominated form. This may have either a positive or adverse impact on development of this market as it gives the politicians power over credit allocations, which may impact adversely on the efficiency in the financial and real sector.

In the 1990s efforts were made to develop the money market, including the improvement in the financial infrastructure (e.g. Central Money Market Unit Service, and the Real Time Gross Settlement System). The establishment of the Hong Kong Monetary Authority in 1994 was another step taken towards the improvement of banking conduct and banking transparency. Lee and Jao (1982, p. 23) argue that the rapid economic growth in Hong Kong is attributable in part to the efficiency of the banking system.

Monetization variables are designed to show the real size of the financial sector in a growing economy, and these ratios are expected to rise over time if the financial sector develops faster than the real sector. This is certainly the case for Hong Kong, in which the movement of monetization variables in general has continued to rise steadily with real income during the last decade.

We have seen that the financial sector of Hong Kong combines state-controlled credit allocation and private sector participation in mobilizing the financial resources, with notable investment in the banking sector. Accordingly, in this study, financial development is proxied by level of broad money circulating through the market and level of private sector capital allocated between financial and real markets.

2.3 Post-Keynesian Macroeconomic Models and Financialization

The post-Keynesian common approach to money is to assume that the quantity of money intermediated in the economy influences final demand, either through the consumption of households or investment of firms or households. This relationship can be direct or indirect. Money and credit might also influence production, since firms need it to purchase inputs or pay wages.

We follow Duménil and Lévy (1993) in presuming that banks accommodate the demand for money for the financing of production, and the corresponding flows and stocks are not modelled.

In a short-term equilibrium, the money stock affects the general level of activity. The sequence of short-term equilibria reflects the influence of the dynamics of money on the macroeconomy. This chapter assumes that long-term equilibrium cannot be defined independently of money, because monetary mechanisms are responsible for the convergence of short-term to long-term equilibrium.

For example, Duménil and Lévy (1993) argue that the issue of money is correlated with the difference between the average of capacity utilization rate and inflation rate. Accordingly, it is neither exogenously determined nor purely accommodative.

The sequence of short-term equilibria reflects the influence of the dynamics of money on the macroeconomy. In the long run, monetary mechanisms are responsible for the convergence of short-term to long-term equilibrium.

3. THE MODEL

A number of conflicts between Keynesian and classical economists are simply due to the fact that within the two frameworks, Keynesian short-term and classical long-term equilibrium are not clearly distinguished. The relationship between these two schools has always remained somewhat ambiguous.

Lavoie and Ramirez-Gaston (1993) and Dutt (1984) argue that a sequence of Keynesian short-term equilibria converges toward a Keynesian long-term equilibrium, in which resources are not fully used. The convergence to a classical equilibrium follows from specific assumptions concerning the dynamics of number of variables, such as capital stock, money stock, prices and so on, called long-term variables. These variables are treated as constant parameters within short-term equilibria, and are slowly modified as the economy transits between two short-term equilibria.

The model presented here, for analysing the dynamic effect of financial development, is a post-Keynesian open economy model. Based on the foregoing discussion, we utilize Stockhammer and Onaran's (2002 and 2005) post-Keynesian open economy model, which is augmented by a demand-driven labour market, a reserve army effect, as befits the Marxian sense, and technological change. The goods market consists of behavioural functions for accumulation, savings and net exports, which is then complemented by a distribution function, a productivity function and an unemployment function. The equations of the model are listed below:

Accumulation
$$g_t^i \equiv \frac{I_t}{K_t} = \alpha_0 + \alpha_1 z_{t-1} + \alpha_2 \pi_{t-1} + \alpha_3 r_t + \alpha_4 gx_{t-1} + \alpha_5 fd \qquad (10.1)$$

Savings $$g_t^s = \beta_1 z_t + \beta_2 \pi_t + \beta_3 fd \quad (10.2)$$

Income distribution $$\pi_t = \gamma_0 + \gamma_1 z_t + \gamma_2 u_t + \gamma_3 gx_t \quad (10.3)$$

Productivity growth $$gx_t = \tau_0 + \tau_1 g_t^i + \tau_2 z_t + \tau_4 fd \quad (10.4)$$

Net export $$nx_t = -\delta_1 z_t + \delta_2 \pi_t \quad (10.5)$$

Unemployment $$u_t = n - e_1 g_t^i - e_2 \Delta z_t - e_3 \pi_t + e_4 u_{t-1} + e_5 gx_t \quad (10.6)$$

Market equilibrium $$g_t^i = g_t^{stotal} = g_t^s - nx \quad (10.7)$$

where
g_t^i : growth of capital stock
g_t^s: domestic savings/capital stock
z: capacity utilization (capital productivity)
π: profit share
nx: net export (normalized by capital stock)
u: unemployment rate
gx: productivity growth
fd: financial development indicator

Equation (10.1) represents the investment decision, which is a function of expected profitability. Expectations are captured by the combination of profit share and capacity utilization rate, which is expected to have a positive effect on investment. As a modern financial system can identify and fund good business opportunities, facilitates the exchange of good and services, and enables trading, hedging and diversification of risk, all of which promote investment, the impact of financial market is captured by the proxies for financial development.

Equation (10.2) models private saving behaviour, such that private domestic savings normalized by the capital stock is a positive function of profit share and capacity utilization, which is a simple Cambridge savings function. Equation (10.2) shows the use of decomposition of the profit rate and linearized saving function. The impact of financial development indicators on savings is ambiguous. According to the theory, financial development raises the proportion of saving and influences the saving rate. Financial markets may ease liquidity constraints on consumers by providing consumer credit that further reduces saving. On the other hand, financial development may increase the rate of return on saving and, thus, boost saving.

According to Kaldor (1960) and Robinson (1965, 1962), income distribution is a determinant of the level of output in the long run. Inclusion of equation (10.3), which defines the income distribution function, provides the model with the ability to achieve equilibrium in short and long term. Equation (10.3) represents the supply side of the model, by making profit share a positive function of the rate of capacity utilization and a negative function of the rate of employment. This is in common with the model in Bhaduri and Marglin (1990).

The model adopts a Kaldorian approach to productivity growth in Equation (10.4), which defines it as a function of accumulation and capacity utilization. Exogenous technical progress is captured by the constant term. The financial development indicator is also included as an exogenous variable in the equation in line with new growth theorists' notion that financial markets can improve the level of productivity in the real sector. The theoretical literature on finance, productivity and growth suggests that financial development can enhance productivity growth in many ways, by raising capital allocation efficiency, and stimulating technological progress by providing financial support to R&D and innovation.

Equation (10.5) incorporates international trade into the model by defining net export as a negative function of capacity utilization and a positive function of the profit share at the level of domestic activity.

The labour market is described by Equation (10.6), which defines the change in the rate of employment as a positive function of growth of capital stock and changes in capacity utilization, which is a variation of Okun's Law. Separating out the impact of competitiveness, it can be assumed that profit share and exports will be positively related.

3.1 Data Sources and the Period of Study

The data were obtained from the various issues of the International Financial Statistics (IFS–IMF), the International Labour Organization (ILO), the World Bank database and the Asian Development Bank (ADB) for the period of 1990 Q1 to 2004 Q4 for Hong Kong.

3.2 Financial Development Indicators

Financial development is usually defined as a process giving rise to improvements in quantity, quality and efficiency of financial intermediary services. In this study we employ two commonly used measures of financial development.

3.2.1 Monetization ratio

The first of these measures is the monetization ratio, MR, which represents the ratio of broad money, M2, to nominal GDP. MR has been used as a standard measure of financial development in numerous studies (World Bank 1989; King and Levine 1993a; Calderon and Liu 2003; Wood 1993; Murinde and Eng 1994; Lyons and Murinde 1994; Berthelemy and Varoudakis 1998; Arestis and Demetriades 1997; and Agung and Ford 1998). The monetization ratio reflects the relative size and depth of the financial market (King and Levine 1993a). An increase in this ratio indicates further expansion in the financial intermediary sector to the rest of the economy. While the monetization ratio does not accurately gauge the effectiveness of the financial sector in ameliorating information asymmetries and diversifying risk, it can be viewed as a general measure of overall financial development.

According to Demetriades and Hussein (1996), this indicator accords well with McKinnon's outside money model where the accumulation of money is necessary before self-financed investment can take place. However, it conflicts somewhat with the debt intermediation approach developed by Gurley and Shaw (1995) and the endogenous growth literature, because a large part of the broad money stock in developing countries is currency held outside banks. As such, an increase in the M2/GDP ratio may reflect an extensive use of currency rather than an increase in bank deposits, and for this reason this measure might be less indicative of the degree of financial intermediation by banking institutions. Financial intermediaries provide liquidity services, which could be relevant for promoting investment and consequently growth. For this reason, Demetriades and Hussein (1996) proposed subtracting the currency outside banks from M2 and taking the ratio of M2 currency to GDP as a proxy for financial development.

3.2.2 Domestic credit

The other measure of financial intermediary development employed in this study is a variable called private credit, which equals the value of credits by financial intermediaries to the private sector divided by GDP. Unlike many of the measures used in the past (King and Levine 1993a, 1993b), this measure excludes credits issued by the central bank and development banks. King and Levine (1993a, 1993b) use a measure of gross claims on the private sector divided by GDP. But this measure includes credits issued by the monetary authority and government agencies, whereas private credit includes only credits issued by deposit money banks and other financial intermediaries. Furthermore, it excludes credit to the public sector and the cross-claims of one group of intermediaries over another.

Private credit is also a broader measure of financial intermediary development than that used by Levine and Zervos (1998) and Levine (1998), since it includes all financial institutions, not only the deposit money banks. This measure of financial development is more than a simple measure of financial sector size.

It is assumed that the credit provided to the private sector generates increased investment and productivity to a much larger extent than do credits to the public sector. It is also argued that loans to the private sector are given under more inflexible conditions and that the improved quality of investment emanating from financial intermediaries' evaluation of project viability is more significant for private sector credits (Mushin and Pentecost 2000).

3.3 Methodology

The main methodological motivation behind this research is to model the dynamic relationship between financial development, accumulation, income distribution and employment in a way that considers simultaneous interaction within a system approach. For this purpose, we adopt structural VAR models (SVAR) based on short-run restrictions, which accommodates the contemporaneous interaction, as well as lagged relationships, which is essential for the purpose of impulse response analysis.

To obtain credible impulse response analysis, Sims (1986) and Bernanke (1986) advocate the use of economic theory to set the required identifying restrictions instead of using an unrestricted VAR model. The structural form of the model can then be conveniently summarized by the impulse response functions and the variance decomposition. The impulse response function describes the in-sample effect of a typical shock to the system and can be used to economically interpret the behaviour of the system. The variance decomposition assesses the importance of different shocks by determining the relative share that each structural shock contributes to the total variance of each variable.

Hence, by imposing enough restrictions based on economic theory, the model is exactly identified and impulse responses may be given a 'structural' interpretation. Short-run restrictions impose some contemporaneous feedback effects among the variables. Impulse responses represent the dynamic adjustment towards the steady state. As the steady state corresponds to the deterministic state of economy, the impulse response function is characterized by the number of periods away from the steady state by which the economy could return to the equilibrium, depending on the structure of the economy.

Consistent with the aim of the chapter, which is to analyse the impact of

Table 10.1 Augmented Dickey–Fuller stationarity test

Variables	Level, no trend	Level with trend	F.D. no trend	F.D. with trend
Investment	−1.417702	−1.886692	−9.612693*	−9.771993*
Savings	−1.463489	−1.628241	−5.947794*	−5.953396*
Income dist.	−0.930750	−2.614681	−3.014243*	−6.496425*
Domestic cr.	−1.510849	−1.918336	−6.830665*	−6.790102*
Monetization	0.388093	−2.269858	−7.856565*	−8.437435*
Interest rate	−2.265138	0.893847	−5.967140*	−5.902427*
Capacity util.	1.188557	−1.923472	−6.667796*	−6.862526*
Productivity	−2.096481	−0.185589	−7.314353*	−8.158344*
Unemployment	−0.690896	−2.804754	−5.172868*	−5.163490*
Net export	−2.064816	−2.050451	−8.161927*	−8.116017*

financial development on key macroeconomic variables, one of the main focuses will be on the responses of these variables to a one-time shock to the financial development indicators.

Pre-analysis In the next section we perform a few tests using EViews to evaluate the characteristics of the time series more deeply and to get the prerequisites to set up our VAR model. Before we build our SVAR, we perform residual tests to make sure that homoscedasticity and normality conditions are not violated.

3.3.1 Data set characteristics

The variables we have included in the SVAR model are the variables from the system of equations, including investment, savings, income distribution, unemployment, productivity growth and net export.

For all six time series equations we have quarterly data for the period ranging from January 1990 to April 2004. The augmented Dickey–Fuller test statistics calculated with EViews in Table 10.1 confirm that all data are integrated at first difference. The conclusion from these tests is that from now on we shall use the first differences of the variable series, which display a stochastic trend.

In the next section we shall perform some tests using EViews to evaluate the characteristics of the time series more deeply and to get the prerequisites to set up our VAR model.

3.3.2 Granger causality

To evaluate whether including certain variables in the VAR makes sense, we first tested to determine the pattern of causality. The results of the

Table 10.2 Pairwise Granger causality test

Pairwise Granger Causality Tests
Sample: 1990:1 2004:1
Lags: 2

Null hypothesis:	Obs.	F-statistic	Probability
INV does not Granger-cause π	55	1.10523	0.33909
π does not Granger-cause INV		4.53360	0.01551
SAV does not Granger-cause π	55	0.64470	0.52913
π does not Granger-cause SAV		0.44934	0.64060
NX does not Granger-cause π	55	2.75055	0.07357
π does not Granger-cause X		0.28059	0.75652
UNEMP does not Granger-cause π	55	0.72258	0.49050
π does not Granger-cause UNEMP		5.91105	0.00496
GX does not Granger-cause π	55	9.19364	0.00040
π does not Granger-cause GX		15.9021	4.5E-06
SAV does not Granger-cause INV	55	1.67780	0.19713
INV does not Granger-cause SAV		3.14275	0.05180
NX does not Granger-cause INV	55	0.16338	0.84972
INV does not Granger-cause NX		0.38190	0.68453
UNEMP does not Granger-cause INV	55	4.80333	0.01236
INV does not Granger-cause UNEMP		1.33859	0.27145
GX does not Granger-cause INV	55	4.24872	0.01976
INV does not Granger-cause GX		0.96154	0.38926
NX does not Granger-cause SAV	55	2.98161	0.05980
SAV does not Granger-cause NX		0.35257	0.70461
UNEMP does not Granger-cause SAV	55	0.27609	0.75990
SAV does not Granger-cause UNEMP		1.79868	0.17606
GX does not Granger-cause SAV	55	1.65194	0.20197
SAV does not Granger-cause GX		0.96682	0.38729
UNEMP does not Granger-cause NX	55	0.96280	0.38879
NX does not Granger-cause UNEMP		0.81791	0.44717
GX does not Granger-cause NX	55	0.24668	0.78233
NX does not Granger-cause GX		2.00657	0.14513
GX does not Granger-cause UNEMP	55	4.67408	0.01377
UNEMP does not Granger-cause GX		2.50347	0.09201

Granger causality test are shown in Table 10.2. Clearly, the overall picture shows that most of the variables are significantly Granger causal for one another at different significance level. Therefore all available variables must be included in the VAR.

Table 10.3 VAR lag order selection criteria

Lag	LogL	LR	FPE	AIC	SC	HQ
0	75.18402	NA	2.96E-09	−2.610718	−2.387666	−2.524943
1	469.7549	684.9155	3.97E-15	−16.14170	−14.58033	−15.54127
2	541.7269	108.6370	1.08E-15	−17.49913	−14.59945*	−16.38405*
3	582.6999	52.56912*	1.02E-15*	−17.68679	−13.44880	−16.05706
4	624.7906	44.47319	1.08E-15	−17.91663*	−12.34033	−15.77225

* Indicates lag order selected by the criterion.

Table 10.4 VAR residual heteroscedasticity joint test

Chi-sq	df	Prob.
515.0737	504	0.3567

3.4 VAR Analysis

3.4.1 Lag order selection

To define the lag order of the VAR (p) model, we look at the following information criteria: final prediction error, Akaike information criterion, the Schwarz information criterion and the Hannan-Quinn information criterion. As shown in Table 10.3, the final prediction error and likelihood ratio suggest 3 lags, the Akaike criterion suggest 4 lags whereas the Schwartz criterion and the Hannan–Quinn criterion suggest 2 lags. The Akaike criterion is known to overstate the number of lags. Therefore we estimate a VAR (3) model.

3.4.2 Heteroscedasticity

White's measure of heteroscedasticity is described as a general test for model misspecification, since the null hypothesis underlying the test assumes that the errors are both homoscedastic and independent of the regressors, and that the linear specification of the model is correct. Failure of any one of these conditions could lead to a significant test statistic. Conversely, a non-significant test statistic implies that none of the three conditions is violated. The result of White test in our model is satisfactory in terms of specification.

3.4.3 LM Tests

Table 10.5 represents the result of autocorrelation LM test, with H_0: no serial correlation as lag order h. The results indicate that autocorrelation is not a major problem.

Table 10.5 Result of autocorrelation LM test

Lags	LM-Stat	Prob
1	0.465410	0.4951
2	2.453624	0.1173
3	0.154241	0.6945
4	4.077702	0.0435

Table 10.6 Orthogonalization: residual covariance (Urzua)

Component	Jarque-Bera	df	Prob.
1	5.727108	2	0.0571
2	5.592340	2	0.0610
3	4.845365	2	0.0887
4	2.604535	2	0.2719
5	2.881957	2	0.2367
6	2.483388	2	0.2889
Joint	118.6964	182	0.9999

3.4.4 VAR residual normality test

Jarque–Bera is a test statistic for testing whether the series is normally distributed. The test statistic measures the departure of errors from a normal distribution as reflected by the skewness and kurtosis of the series. The Jarque–Bera residual normality test compares the third and fourth moments of the residuals to those from normal distribution. The null hypothesis is that residuals are multivariate normal. The results presented in Table 10.6 indicate that the normality condition among residuals is not violated.

3.4.5 Stability condition

The stability condition holds if the roots of the reverse characteristic polynomial of the VAR process lie in or on the complex unit circle. According to Table 10.7, VAR satisfies the stability conditions, which indicates that our VAR is stationary.

Table 10.7 presents the roots of characteristic polynomial, with 13 lag specifications and constant exogenous variable. Fortunately the stability test leads to positive results. EViews uses the MA representation of the VAR process, so that the roots are inside or on the complex unit circle rather than outside. Now that stability is assured, we can proceed to estimation.

Table 10.7 VAR stability test

Root	Modulus
0.964491 − 0.113711i	0.971171
0.964491 + 0.113711i	0.971171
0.868163	0.868163
0.804269 − 0.135622i	0.815624
0.804269 + 0.135622i	0.815624
0.583773 + 0.537016i	0.793206
0.583773 − 0.537016i	0.793206
0.685307 + 0.370700i	0.779144
0.685307 − 0.370700i	0.779144
0.270877 + 0.637533i	0.692692
0.270877 − 0.637533i	0.692692
−0.375449 − 0.495469i	0.621652
−0.375449 + 0.495469i	0.621652
0.341277 − 0.477809i	0.587173
0.341277 + 0.477809i	0.587173
−0.519628 − 0.114809i	0.532160
−0.519628 + 0.114809i	0.532160
−0.255856	0.255856

3.5 SVAR Estimation and Results

In this section we present the SVAR identification and estimation results, and then analyse the impulse response function for the period of 1990:Q1 to 2004:Q4.

In order to be able to plot impulse response functions based on the orthogonal shocks, we must find the structural form errors. The recursiveness approach gives us a lower triangular matrix. This means that the ordering of our six variables plays the crucial role, and they must enter the model based on presumptions of post-Keynesian macroeconomic growth theory. A lower triangular matrix restricts the first variable to be contemporaneously independent of all other variables, whereas the last variable is allowed to be influenced contemporaneously by all other variables.

The ordering given in the problem set and which we used throughout this chapter is the vector:

$$Y_t' = (INV_t, SAV_t, DISTRIBUTION_t, NX_t, PRODUCTIVITY_t, EMP_t)$$

With this ordering, we assume that investment is the variable that can be influenced directly. Employment is put last because we consider that employment is determined endogenously, depending on investment, productivity growth and income distribution. Having defined the ordering, we are able to write the system in VAR representation, which allows us to plot impulse response functions for shocks of structural form, as follows:

$$B_0 y_t = a + bt + B_1 y_{t-1} + B_2 y_{t-2} + \ldots + B_6 y_{t-6} + u_t\, u_t \approx iin(0, 1)$$

Here u_t are the structural shocks that are serially uncorrelated and have an orthonormal variance–covariance matrix. These unobservable structural shocks are related to the observable reduced form residuals by the following relation:

$$e_t = B_0^{-1} u_t$$

where B_0 is the $(k \times k)$ matrix of coefficients (in this study $k = 6$). Multiplication with B_0^{-1} leads to the VAR representation:

$$y_t = \alpha + \beta t + A_1 y_{t-1} + A_2 y_{t-2} + \ldots + A_6 y_{t-6} + B_0^{-1} u_t$$

where $A_i = B_0^{-1} B_i$.

In order to identify shocks, we need to impose $(k\,(k-1)/2) = 15$ restrictions on the B_0 matrix of coefficients. These restrictions can be based on long-run considerations or contemporaneous effects. Following the argument of Faust and Leeper (1997), we do not impose long-run restrictions in order to avoid serious misspecification problems.

The results of SVAR presented in Box 10.1 allow us to conclude that the post-Keynesian model seems to perform well and in line with the theoretical model. The results indicate that a higher level of investment significantly boosts the volume of export, which is in line with out theoretical macroeconomic model [310.89**]. Investment and productivity growth are significantly interrelated, as theory predicts [0.948**].

The interaction of investment and unemployment is positive but not significant; however, it is observed that the higher level of savings creates more job opportunities [22.42640*]. The negative and significant interaction of investment and income distribution [−0.176191*] implies that higher rate of accumulation is accompanied by a higher share of profit, suggesting that the regime of accumulation in Hong Kong is profit led. The negative and significant interaction of productivity and unemployment [−2.8461*] means that higher productivity creates lower unemployment by stimulating employment.

It seems that the interaction between savings and net export is highly significant and negative [−442.3201**]. As consumers tend to save more, consumption reduces and aggregate demand falls, and this in turn diminishes the pace of exports activity.

BOX 10.1 SVAR RESULTS

Model: $Ae = Bu$ where $E[uu'] = I$
Restriction type: short-run pattern matrix

$$\begin{bmatrix} 1 & 0 & 0 & 0 & 0 & 0 \\ \alpha_{21} & 1 & 0 & 0 & 0 & 0 \\ \alpha_{31} & \alpha_{32} & 1 & 0 & 0 & 0 \\ \alpha_{41} & \alpha_{42} & \alpha_{43} & 1 & 0 & 0 \\ \alpha_{51} & \alpha_{52} & \alpha_{53} & \alpha_{54} & 1 & 0 \\ \alpha_{61} & \alpha_{62} & \alpha_{63} & \alpha_{64} & \alpha_{65} & 1 \end{bmatrix} \times \begin{bmatrix} e_{INV} \\ e_{SAV} \\ e_{\pi} \\ e_{PROD} \\ e_{NX} \\ e_{UNEMP} \end{bmatrix}$$

$$= \begin{bmatrix} \beta_{11} & 0 & 0 & 0 & 0 & 0 \\ 0 & \beta_{22} & 0 & 0 & 0 & 0 \\ 0 & 0 & \beta_{33} & 0 & 0 & 0 \\ 0 & 0 & 0 & \beta_{44} & 0 & 0 \\ 0 & 0 & 0 & 0 & \beta_{55} & 0 \\ 0 & 0 & 0 & 0 & 0 & \beta_{66} \end{bmatrix} \times \begin{bmatrix} u_{INV} \\ u_{SAV} \\ u_{\pi} \\ u_{PROD} \\ u_{NX} \\ u_{UNEMP} \end{bmatrix}$$

Estimated A matrix:

$$\begin{bmatrix} 1 & 0 & 0 & 0 & 0 & 0 \\ -0.025351 & 1 & 0 & 0 & 0 & 0 \\ -0.176191^{*} & -0.184468 & 1 & 0 & 0 & 0 \\ 0.948363^{**} & -0.096143 & 3.487676^{**} & 1 & 0 & 0 \\ 310.8936^{**} & -442.3301^{**} & 92.55460 & -6.322162 & 1 & 0 \\ 5.052006 & 22.42640^{*} & -9.213751 & -2.846117^{*} & -0.026916^{*} & 1 \end{bmatrix}$$

Estimated B matrix:

$$\begin{bmatrix} 0.012807^{**} & 0 & 0 & 0 & 0 & 0 \\ 0 & 0.004573^{**} & 0 & 0 & 0 & 0 \\ 0 & 0 & 0.007543^{**} & 0 & 0 & 0 \\ 0 & 0 & 0 & 0.029558^{**} & 0 & 0 \\ 0 & 0 & 0 & 0 & 3.985941^{**} & 0 \\ 0 & 0 & 0 & 0 & 0 & 0.331526^{**} \end{bmatrix}$$

The asterisks show the significance level of the different regressors (*5%, **1%).

3.6 Impulse Response Function

Impulse response functions enable us to analyse reactions of the whole system to shocks (structural or reduced-form shocks). The standard approach to computing impulse responses is to shock the SVAR with a one standard deviation shock from the VAR innovations. The result of impulse response analysis is presented in Figure 10.1. The effect of a financial development variable shock is clearly positive on dynamic investment; however, the effect is negative for savings and productivity growth. The positive impact of this shock on employment continues for at least ten periods.

Figure 10.1 presents the impulse responses (Monte Carlo standard error) for orthogonal shocks to domestic credit. And Figure 10.2 shows the response to orthogonal shocks to the monetization ratio for the period of 20 quarters ahead. These responses are based on Monte Carlo standard errors containing the plus/minus two standard error bands about impulse responses.

We produced a long-run identification of the positive financial development shocks, and examined the responses of different key macroeconomic variables to these shocks. The results lead us to a number of conclusions.

In Figure 10.1 the effect of positive shock to domestic credit on investment is positive up to three periods ahead and then starts to be clearly negative, but tends to vanish in the long run. The response of investment to positive shock to monetization ratio in Figure 10.2 implies the same pattern.

The response of savings to the positive financial development shock is an immediate increase in the short and long run, which does not seem to be exhausted over time. This suggests that financial market improvements are simultaneously linked in the short and long run with the high volume of savings.

The impact of financial development indicators shock in productivity growth is quite satisfying, indicating that financial development impacts growth through the productivity channel, in the short and long run. A positive domestic credit shock causes a subsequent and consistent rise in productivity growth, as well as a positive shock in monetization ratio results in increasing productivity in the short and long run. However, it seems that credit shocks have a much greater impact than money shocks.

From impulse response analysis, it is clear that the development of the financial market in terms of monetization ratio and availability of domestic credit enhance net export strongly and the effect is persistent over the long term and is not exhausted over 20 periods.

It seems that the response of unemployment to positive shock to domestic credit is an immediate decline for at least seven quarters ahead. In the long run, there is some kind of trade-off, but of a smaller magnitude for a few quarters; then the decline in unemployment in the long term prevails.

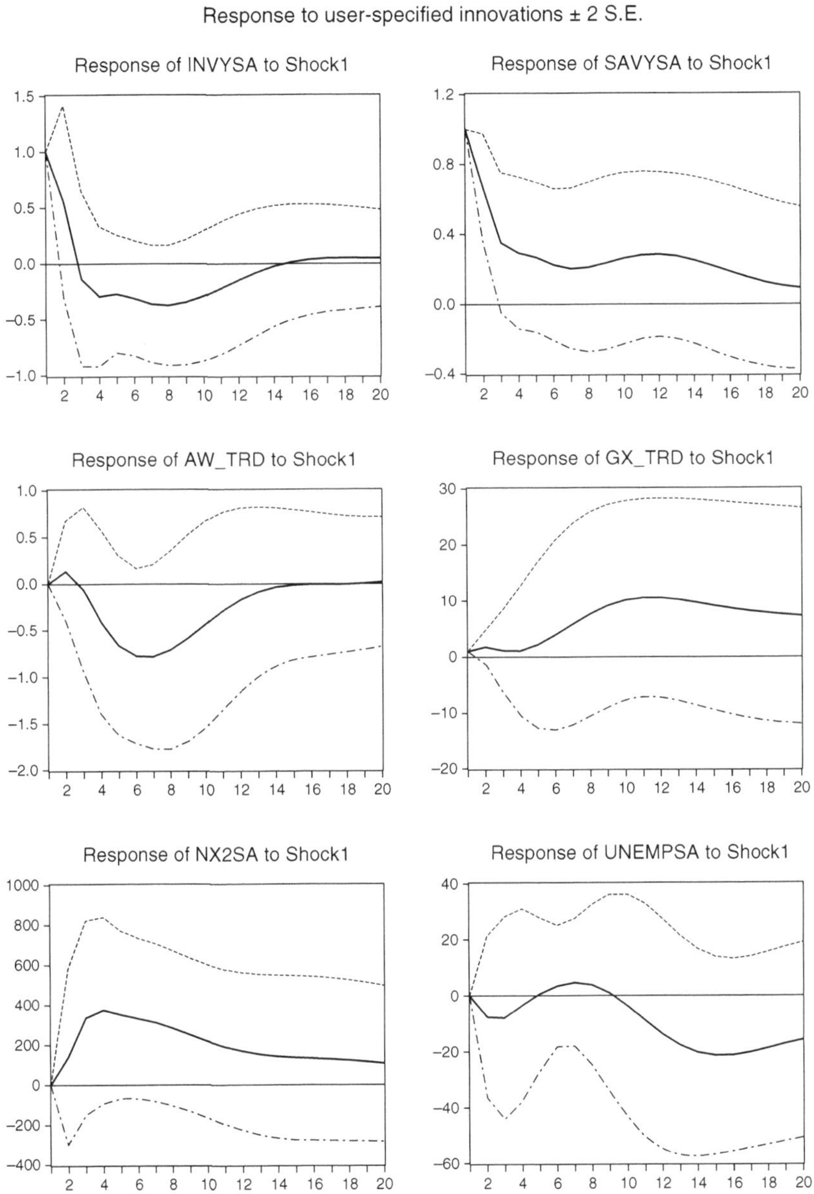

Figure 10.1 Responses to orthogonal shocks to domestic credit

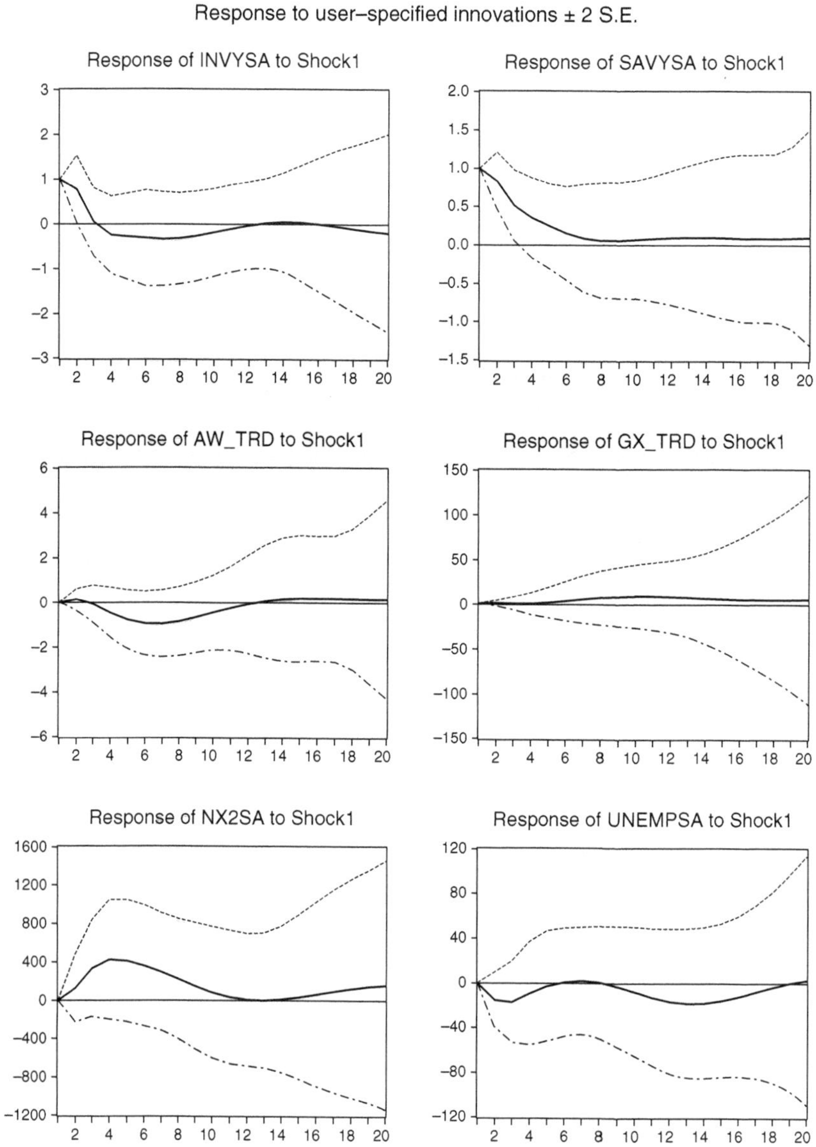

Figure 10.2 Responses to orthogonal shocks to monetization ratio

In terms of improvement in the monetization ratio, unemployment seems to be declining in the short and long run.

4. CONCLUSION

This chapter examines the response of thc Hong Kong economy to the shocks given to financial development indicators. On a pragmatic basis we assumed that financial development indicators will have a beneficial impact on the level of investment, savings and productivity. Using a formal macroeconomic model, with modifications and assumptions built into it, we try to project how the different sectors are likely to grow and react over time due to development in financial markets. Our interest in computing long-run responses and in allowing financial development proxies to interact leads us to apply the structural VAR (SVAR) approach.

The incorporation of the financial sector into the model seems to improve the macroeconomic model. The empirical results from SVAR and the impulse response function suggest that there is short- and long-run and mostly positive relationship between financial development and economic growth indicators in Hong Kong.

Perhaps the most important implication of our findings is that the relationship between financial sector development and economic development and the inclusion of the financial development variables into post-Keynesian models of growth should be revised. I believe that theoretical and methodological grounds could potentially be extended to incorporate some assumptions in this regard. Using the impulse responses approach provides evidence that financial market variables have a real effect on the economy of Hong Kong through investment, savings and productivity channels.

Given the nature of the exercise here, it is worth mentioning that the role of financial markets and variation in financial structure in different economies are particularly important in the process of investigation, since they reveal the challenges that authorities are facing in setting and imposing policies on countries with different degrees of private and public sector participation in their financial markets.

REFERENCES

Agung, F. and J. Ford (1998), 'Financial development, liberalization and economic development in Indonesia, 1966–1996: cointegration and causality', University of Birmingham, Department of Economics Discussion Paper No. 98-12.

Arestis, P. and P. Demetriades (1997), 'Financial development and economic growth: assessing the evidence', *Economic Journal*, **107**, 783–99.
Bernanke, B. (1986), 'Alternative explanations of the money–income correlation', *Carnegie-Rochester Conference Series on Public Policy*, **25**, 49–100.
Berthelemy, J.C. and A. Varoudakis (1998), 'Financial development, financial reforms and growth: a panel data approach', *Review of Economics*, **49** (1), 195–206.
Bhaduri, A. and S. Marglin (1990), 'Unemployment and the real wage: the economic basis for contesting political ideologies', *Cambridge Journal of Economics*, **14**, 375–93.
Calderon, and Liu (2003), 'The direction of causality between financial development and economic growth', *Journal of Development Economics*, **72** (1), 321–34.
Cameron, R. (1967), 'Conclusion', in R. Cameron et al. (eds), *Banking in the Early Stages of Industrialization : A Study in Comparative Economic History*, New York: Oxford University Press, pp. 290–321.
Demetriades, P. and K. Hussein (1996), 'Financial development and economic growth: cointegration and causality tests for 16 countries', *Journal of Development Economics*, **51**, 387–411.
Duménil G. and D. Lévy (1993), *The Economics of the Profit Rate*, Aldershot, UK and Brookfield, US: Edward Elgar.
Dutt, A. (1984), 'Stagnation, income distribution and monopoly power', *Cambridge Journal of Economics*, **8**, 25–40.
Faust, J. and E.M. Leeper (1997), 'When do long-run identifying restrictions give reliable results?', *Journal of Business & Economic Statistics*, **15**, 345–53.
Fisher, I. (1930), *The Theory of Interest: As Determined by the Impatience to Spend Income and Opportunity to Invest it*, New York: Macmillan.
Gurley, J.G. and E.S. Shaw (1967), 'Financial structure and economic development', *Economic Development and Cultural Change*, **15**, 257–68.
Gurley, J.G. and E.S. Shaw (1995), 'Financial aspects of economic development', *American Economic Review*, **45**, 515–38.
Hein, E. and C. Ochsen (2001), 'Regimes of interest rates, income shares, savings and investment: a Kaleckian model and empirical estimations for some advanced OECD-economies', Conference on 'Old and new growth theories: an assessment', 5–7 October, Pisa, Italy.
Hicks, J. (1969), *A Theory of Economic History*, Oxford: Clarendon Press.
Jappelli, T. and M. Pagano (1989), 'Aggregate consumption and capital market imperfections: an international comparison', *American Economic Review*, **79**, 1088–105.
Jayaratne, J. and P.E. Strahan (1996), 'The finance–growth nexus: evidence from bank branch deregulation', *Quarterly Journal of Economics*, **111** (3), 639–70.
Kaldor, N. (1960), 'Introduction', in *Kaldor: Essays on Value and Distribution*, 2nd edn, London: Duckworth, pp. 1–9.
King, R. and R. Levine (1993a), 'Finance and growth: Schumpeter might be right', *Quarterly Journal of Economics*, **108**, 717–38.
King, R.G. and R. Levine (1993b), 'Finance, entrepreneurship, and growth. Theory and evidence', *Journal of Monetary Economics*, **32**, 513–42.
Lavoie, M. and P. Ramirez-Gaston (1993), 'Traverse in a two sector Kaleckian model of growth with target return pricing', University of Ottawa.
Lee, S.-Y. and Y.C. Jao (1982), *Financial Structures and Monetary Policies in Southeast Asia*, New York: St Martin's Press.
Levine, R. (1997), 'Financial development and economic growth: views and agenda', *Journal of Economic Literature*, **35**, 688–726.

Levine, R. (1998), 'The legal environment, banks, and long-run economic growth', *Journal of Money, Credit, and Banking*, **30** (3), 598–613.

Levine, R. and S. Zervos (1998), 'Stock markets, banks and economic growth', *American Economic Review*, **88**, 537–58.

Lyons, S.E. and V. Murinde (1994), 'Cointegration and Granger-causality testing of hypotheses on supply-leading and demand-following', Finance, *Economic Notes*, **23** (2), 308–16.

McKinnon, R. (1973), *Money and Capital in Economic Development*, Washington, DC: Brookings Institution.

Muhsin, K. and E. Pentecost (2000), 'Financial development and economic growth in Turkey: further evidence on causality issue', Centre for International, Financial and Economics Research Department of Economics, Loughborough University, UK.

Murinde, V. and F.S.H. Eng (1994), 'Financial development and economic growth in Singapore: demand-following or supply-leading?', *Applied Financial Economics*, **4** (6), 391–404.

Rajan, R. and L. Zingales (1998), 'Financial dependence and growth', *American Economic Review*, **88** (3), 559–86

Robinson, J. (1952), *The Role of Interest and Other Essays*, London: Macmillan.

Robinson, J. (1962), *Essays in the Theory of Economic Growth*, London: Macmillan.

Robinson, J. (1965), *Collected Economic Papers*, vol. III, Oxford: Basil Blackwell.

Schumpeter, J.A. (1912), *The Theory of Economic Development*, Cambridge, MA: Harvard University Press.

Shaw, E. (1973), *Financial Deepening in Economic Development*, New York: Oxford University Press.

Sims, C. (1986), 'Are forecasting models usable for policy analysis?', *Federal Reserve Bank of Minneapolis Quarterly Review*, 1–16.

Stockhammer, E. and O. Onaran (2002), 'Accumulation, distribution and employment: a structural VAR approach to a post-Keynesian macro model', Working Paper, GEEWP 20, Vienna University and B.A. Research Group: Growth and Employment in Europe: Sustainability and Competitiveness.

Stockhammer, E. and O. Onaran (2003), 'The effect of distribution on accumulation, capacity utilization and employment: testing the wage-led hypothesis for Turkey', in Ric Holt and Steven Pressman (eds), Empirical work in Post Keynesian Economics, London: Routledge.

Stockhammer, E. and O. Onaran (2005), 'Do profits affect investment and employment? An empirical test based on the Bhaduri–Marglin model', Working Paper, GEEWP 44, Vienna University and B.A. Research Group: Growth and Employment in Europe: Sustainability and Competitiveness.

Wood, A. (1993), 'Financial development and economic growth in Barbados: causal evidence', *Savings and Development*, **17** (4), 379–90.

World Bank (1989), *World Development Report*, New York: Oxford University Press for the World Bank.

11. Money and institutions: the long path of the Latin American financial reforms

Eugenia Correa

INTRODUCTION

While the ability to finance development is one of the main issues of Mexican and Latin American economic history, the 1982 debt crisis cast into doubt all capabilities of financing domestic economies and foreign payments. Since those years, the problems of debt and domestic growth have waxed and waned with changes in the international financial markets and financial crises. However, the first emerging world financial crisis in the post-Bretton Woods era renewed structural distrust in local currencies and financial systems in Latin America (LA). Almost 30 years later, we can now identify this crisis as one of many successive episodes of financial market disruptions related to the implosion of credit bubbles. As in other credit crises, the principal origins can be found in the creditors' framework of interests, and to a lesser degree, in bad decisions of borrowers. The approaches that 'blame the victims' within the study of financial crises were criticized even by Stiglitz many years ago. Such conclusions regarding the main forces of the financial crisis, especially in the relatively small world of emerging market financing, do not signify an outright credence in 'dependency theory', as many critics assume. It is merely a recognition that the ruling forces in financial markets reside in developed countries. Since those years, because of changes in domestic financial structures, the theories or presumptions regarding money and credit within developing economies have become insufficient or even wrong.

This chapter proposes that as LA economies have been net capital exporters for long periods of time, the savings shortage in the region is a manifestation of the foreign currency supply deficit in regard to the needs of capital outflows. The second section works with the idea that the foreign currency indebtedness is also linked to monetary and credit processes, in which debt inflows result from credit expansion, which at the same time finances capital exports and, secondarily, the investment process. The third section argues that the processes of overindebtedness and the eruption of financial crises are more acute in developing countries because of their condition as capital exporters. The fourth section presents, in a very synthetic manner, the main lessons from the financial and banking crises as a support for the sixth section, in which some of the most important financial reforms needed in order to promote development financing will be addressed. The fifth section exposes the problem of financial restrictions imposed by the fiscal policies of the Washington Consensus, which have greatly reduced the financing of economies in domestic currency.

Currently, several LA countries are attempting to reconstruct their monetary and credit institutions with the aspiration of financing development. One of the first steps in this direction has been precisely the reduction, the control or the halt of the forces that determine capital outflows.

INSUFFICIENT SAVINGS OR MONETARY ASYMMETRIES

The insufficient domestic savings created in LA countries has been the main explanation to justify public or private foreign debt and foreign direct or portfolio investment. But even a superficial analysis of available data confirms that LA countries have exported savings over broad periods of time (Kregel 1998). As a 'negative net transfer region', LA exports savings in the form of profits, dividends and royalties, and interest payments on debt. Because these profits, dividends and royalties were not invested, saved or consumed in local markets, but rather exported to the financial markets of developed countries, they in fact increased levels of savings, investment and consumption in these countries. In order for these profit outflows to be exported, they must be in foreign currency. As LA economies cannot produce growing and sufficient savings in foreign currency, and the central or commercial local banks cannot create a large volume of liquidity in foreign currency, these capital outflows require new capital inflows, either as new debt, as new direct investment or as new portfolio investment. This circle of foreign currency requirements for the exportation of a part of capital profits, those exported by businesses and local or foreign investors, has been attributed to a lack of savings. However, it is merely a consequence of the huge monetary, commercial and financial asymmetries that have been explained in different forms by the underdevelopment and LA dependency theories (Ocampo 1998).

As such, external loans and the opening of foreign investment are not explained by the internal conditions of the region's countries but rather by the needs created by the exportation of capital and profits. Furthermore, the behaviour of these flows of debt and foreign investment depend on the conditions and economic trends in the developed countries and not on the polices of the region's countries. Therefore, while the necessities of borrowers may be many, it is only the lender or the investor who decides to borrow or invest, how much to borrow or invest and under what conditions of interest and payment. It can therefore be affirmed that since the 1970s, the external debt flows to the largest economies of the region were not created out of the necessity of financing the external deficit or the public deficit of borrower countries. In fact, a large part of new credits that have been offered by transnational banks, and taken by governments and the domestic private sector, were used to pay debt settlements or merely their interest (Correa 1998; Girón 1995).

The process of external indebtedness led to the crisis of 1982, to the Washington led policies of financial opening and to the breakdown of governments' fiscal positions. This process was initiated with the rapid expansion of private credit within the international capital markets during the 1970s. Due to the unwinding of the Bretton Woods agreements during the same decade, a private credit expansion emerged, carried out by large transnational banks, particularly American ones, that within a few years outpaced every financial regulation created during the post-crisis years of the 1930s. These banks attained a privileged financial position in many LA countries and other emerging markets, affording them consistent profits denominated in dollars, the currency in which, until the creation of the euro, profits were denominated throughout the financial world.

It is impossible for LA countries to pay debt and profits on capital while at the same time sustaining capital exportation and the profits of local business if they do not generate growing commercial surpluses. Commercial insertion through the export of primary goods has prevailed even in the most industrial LA countries (with the exception of Brazil). As such, commercial surpluses can only be obtained in periods in which the relative prices of commodities increase, or when countries witness strong contractions in economic growth and imports.

CREDIT AND SAVINGS

Once again, LA external debt provides a good example of the limits of external financing and how foreign capital flows into countries only to later flow out. The rapid growth of debt in the 1970s, mentioned previously, was generated by transnational private banks as an effect of the credit multiplier and the lowering of interest rates. This means that the savings of homes and firms in developed countries were not channeled toward the financing of developing countries. Flows of foreign credit were simply an effect of the bank multiplier; such flows have been able to expand internationally due to the support of the dollar as the international currency (Parguez 2005).

LA countries cannot pay off debt solely through the use of the bank multiplier because they do not create greenbacks, just their own local currencies that do not have an international circulation. The local banks that are not foreign bank subsidiaries cannot directly increase their positions using the bank multiplier in foreign currency, so they have to take on debt, too. In fact, developing countries and LA countries have to pay off debt through exports and created surplus, with the sale of properties, firms, national resources, privatizations or even with the sale of future incomes in financial markets.

Once inserted in global financial markets, the federal government, public enterprises, development banks, commercial banks and large private companies all have to find the way to refinance liabilities, taking on new and bigger debts, which can also be paid by increasing exports, privatizing public companies with a total or partial sale to foreign partners. In this sense, the economic policy recommendations that have been constantly sustained by the IMF are no more than policies directed towards increasing the payment capacity of obligations denominated in foreign currency. But simultaneously they create the conditions in which demand for foreign currency increases, due to the expansion of FDI and portfolio investment. The capacity for payment in foreign currency increases, but soon reaches new limits.

A determinant economic dynamic is therefore produced in the region, whereby the external credits that countries in the region obtain are not based on savings, but funds produced by the transnational banks' credit multiplier, while the same countries must pay their debt, interests and capital gains with commercial surpluses.

Therefore LA countries that have the weakness of not being able to generate massive resources in convertible currencies, due to the fact that their traditional exports have lower prices in international markets and that their production depends in large part on capital inputs, cannot withstand the high costs of the capital inflows (debt, FDI and portfolio allocations).

Even if LA countries create the resources to pay these credits and their interests, the payment has to be made in foreign currency, therefore requiring the creation of surpluses. And even when these surpluses are generated in foreign currencies, the high interest rates and/or the rapid capital flight from the local market sooner or later cause insolvency and currency crises in these economies. As will be shown, the establishment of foreign bank branches has on occasion been able to temporarily halt the outbreak of currency crises. However, their presence exerts strong competitive pressure on domestic banks.

OVERINDEBTEDNESS AND CAPITAL TRANSFERS

In the last 20 years, the financial markets in almost all the world have advanced in different ways towards a conglomerate-based market deregulation. While the successive local and international financial crises have challenged financial authorities' abilities to devise policies to prevent or avoid their most undesirable effects, every effort towards the construction of a new international financial architecture has sought accelerated market deregulation within emerging countries and has promoted market-based regulation among global financial conglomerates. However, the conditions that pushed developing countries to overindebtedness have not been modified. Moreover, this overindebtedness is recurrently presented as part of currency, financial and banking crises. The main examples are the 1994 Mexican crisis, the Southeast Asian crisis of 1997, the Russian crisis of 1998, the Brazilian crisis of 1999 and the Argentinean crisis of 2001.

Although the greater part of the world's population lives in developing countries (85 percent), which represent almost 30 percent of global GDP, their financial markets are relatively marginal, representing between 10 and 15 percent of either worldwide stock market capitalization or domestic credit. Even so, developing countries make annual capital transfers estimated at 4 percent of their GDP, measured as the savings and investment in advanced economies financed with developing countries' savings, according to IMF figures. These transfers limit accumulation in developing countries, especially in LA, presenting tendencies of slow rates of growth, economic stagnation, unemployment, increasing idle capacity and widening poverty.

The interest payments on external debt in LA provide a clear example, averaging US$42 billion per year from 1982 to 2006. During this period, the external debt grew from US$330 to US$880 billion (IMF figures; WEO database). As such, external capital flows, as credit, direct or portfolio investment, have presented a true financial anchor for developing countries.

Overindebtedness is constantly reinforced, as part of locally generated economic surplus is transferred out of domestic economies, generating a savings and investment shortage while diminishing local capital's global profitability, mainly affecting domestic-market-based enterprises with limited international projection. Overindebtedness presents itself, in local or foreign currency, when the costs to finance enterprises, financial institutions, banks and national and local governments increase at a greater rate than income flows. LA has followed this route to eruptions of public, private or bank overindebtedness cycles that have been linked to changes in financing costs and even to the monetary policy of the Federal Reserve.

The new and growing presence of financial global conglomerates in the region's domestic markets contributes to the creation of private management of transfers, carried out through credit policies and exchange rates; but rather than minimizing problems of accumulation, growing capital outflows, unemployment and migration exacerbate the problem.

The existence of the double monetary system and commercial and financial surplus transferrals was not characteristic of the region until the deregulation of interest rates and capital flows created the conditions for a financial crisis. With this change in policy, interest rates became separated from national reference points, and elevated costs of financing were imposed on open domestic economies with high levels of wealth and income concentration. Moreover, in several instances, elevated interest rates may have significantly increased surplus transfers.

LESSONS OF THE BANKING CRISIS

During the last 30 years, the world has recognized the increasing instability of financial and monetary processes, whose explanation can be found in the constant financial deregulation that has moved away from the stable relationship between interests and profits of the postwar period. Yet the loss of accumulated wealth in a large and increasing number of countries and regions hardly compares with the accompanying political and institutional losses, which have translated into a constant deterioration of political support for governments. Likewise, the private sector faces a similar deterioration in its hegemonic capacity to carry out its own political and economic projects. At the same time, increasing right-wing social and political movements are being imposed, leaving the civil society organizations and political parties with diminished legitimacy.

Far from fostering productive capacity and employment, national financial systems (corporations, institutions) now constitute large and complex mechanisms for the concentration of wealth on a global scale. A reduced number of financial conglomerates currently possesses immense economic and political power, transforming national economic spaces into their arena of confrontation.

It is impossible to advance towards proposals for a new monetary and international financial order based on the 'market discipline' of a competitive and expansive financial world, as suggested by the IMF and WB (World Bank), among others. Large conglomerates regulate or deregulate their relationship with the rest of the economy, and have a decisive influence in the transformation of financial structures' regulatory and supervisory entities, determining the juridical and normative framework in which intermediaries operate. Financial conglomerates have assumed a central role in the structural changes of recent years. Recent examples of this phenomenon include: conglomerates' role in the restructuring of foreign debt and the imposition of Washington Consensus policies; their growing expansion in some large developing countries during the late 1990s; their strong position in the new international financial architecture (NIFA) reforms; their role in the changes in financial laws, including the revocation of the McFadden and Glass–Steagall Acts.

Without exhaustively detailing multiple and diverse historical experiences, we can identify several lessons for monetary and financial reorganization in developing countries.

- Financial crises are processes that modify financial and ownership relations, as well as the prices of financial and non-financial assets.
- Financial crises create policy confrontations between different interest groups and change local and international power relationships.
- Financial crises are moments of acute competition and confrontation between conglomerates.
- Debt inflows to developing countries are the consequence of bank-led monetary expansion; meanwhile borrowers must settle the debt via surplus and wealth transfers.
- The resolution of conflicts between lenders and borrowers, and between profits and interests, in short, the resolution of the crisis, establishes the future of development financing, thus explaining the worldwide economic consequences of debt and crisis resolution.
- Monetary and financial opening were not a formula to add resources for local investment, but were rather mechanisms to achieve the export of the local and foreign investors' surpluses.

WASHINGTON CONSENSUS AND FISCAL CONSTRAINTS

The Washington Consensus policies have dismantled the endogenous growth capacity of LA economies, not only because of growing capital transfers and lowered accumulation, but also because of the crumbling of public finances and the bankruptcy of national states (Gnos and Rochon

2004–05). Financial opening and the region's capital outflows, in addition to the diversion of the public's income towards interest payments and the imposition of primary surpluses in public budgets, have restricted accumulation and have undermined profits of domestic companies that depend mainly on the internal market.

The first and most important economic policy recommended by the Washington Consensus since its first years in the 1980s, even before it was formulated by John Williamson, was the reduction of the fiscal deficit. In the second half of the 1990s, with the second-generation reforms, fiscal equilibrium and even higher goals of budget surpluses became demands of adjustment policies (Williamson and Kuczynski 2003).

Diminishing inflation and recuperating payment capacity for external compromises were the primary goals of such policies, signifying a rapid modification of local income distribution and a reduction of business profit and workers' wages. Almost a quarter of a century of these policies has destroyed, although in an uneven manner within the region, not only the sovereign decision-making capacity of nation states over their currency, credit, economy, army and territory, but also their social and political networks that allowed them to construct consensus, legitimacy and governability.

However, in some of the largest economies in the region such as Brazil and Argentina, a minimal reconstruction of legitimacy, consensus and governability is happening, conducted by leaders and social forces attempting to move away from Washington Consensus policies. They recognize that the biggest limit to growth and social and political reconstruction is the ongoing application of IMF policies, although the problematic growth limits imposed by the policies aimed at maintaining fiscal surpluses have yet to be debated (Correa 2002; IMF 2004).

The continental fiscal asymmetry currently determines a growing concentration of income, allowing the USA to maintain a public per capita deficit almost three times bigger than all of Latin America's combined. Therefore the region needs to increase its fiscal position by 3 percent of GDP at least. This would allow gross investment to increase by more than 15 percent and would begin to diminish the asymmetries and the huge concentration of wealth created by over 25 years of Washington Consensus policies.

However, the minimum consensus needed to advance towards overturning the imposed economic and political vision requires cooperative action, arranged and organized by at least a group of the region's nations. All of this seems distant from the dominant ideological and political standards that exist today in the region. The weakness and economic bankruptcy of nation states is not a state exclusive to LA or even to developing countries. This weakness confronts many nation states that are incapable of providing answers to citizens' minimal economic demands and that are constantly pressured to act as lenders of last resort during recurring episodes of financial crisis.

A NEW FINANCIAL STRUCTURE FOR DEVELOPING COUNTRIES

The banking model of originate and distribute that accompanies the securitization of future profits and productive assets of a diverse set of industries, including infrastructure, energy, primary goods and basic public services, has shown its limits in the financial crisis of 2007–08. In Latin America, this model, developed with the widespread presence of global banks and institutional investors, has signified insufficient flows of capital at an elevated cost.

LA countries must reconstruct a financial structure that allows for greater financing of investment, increased employment and wages, and the establishment of profitable conditions for businesses. A new financial structure must permit the reconstruction of the relationship between banks, businesses and governments. In order to provide stable financing, such an institutional reconstruction may require: the strengthening and increased presence of development and public banks; the acceleration of projects related to regional currency and public banking; and the advancement of regional convergence in regard to reaching common goals of employment and social expenditure.

Some of the main ideas for political and economic institutional reconstruction that allow stable financing processes, with emphasis on diminishing the gap between developed and developing countries, could be the following:

- A social dynamic that leads to building new institutions capable of efficiently financing production, especially in economic sectors that play central roles in job creation and consumption growth.
- A new financial structure that rebuilds the relationship between banks, firms and the state, changing the social participation of businesses and banks in economic policy decisions.
- Conglomerates require regulation, which can be efficient if a society can protect social interests against the particular interests of a small group of management that values performance-based options bonds over the interests and/or performance of the firm, and that tend to be distant from the interests of the city, region or country of operation and commitments to job creation, wage growth and so on.

- Monetary circuits are the base of the accumulation process. Money cannot continue to be managed by private conglomerates, which are sufficiently important to require social control over their creation and distribution. This means that in order for monetary expansion to obey the objectives of greater employment and economic growth, deposit banks must be regulated by new social institutions.
- Money creation, domestic or international, must be realized by more democratic institutions, which could reverse losses in employment and production around the world. This could be one of the main results of social changes in the new century.
- The social control of money creation could be the support of local currencies and consolidation of credit expansion.
- A social control over international liquidity, with a money unit independent of local currencies, such as Keynes's Bancor. International credit relationships and local currencies could be regulated with limited settlement capacities, which does not mean dollarization or eurorization.
- Regional currencies and development banks could be created, such as the Banco del Sur project.
- Public cooperation for the institutional regulation of conglomerates.
- The core issue of economic cooperation could become monetary, fiscal and financial cooperation. For example, there could not be a free trade area for the Americas without public foreign debt cancellation, or without convergence in social public expenditure.

ACKNOWLEDGMENTS

The author is grateful to Wesley Marshall and Fernanda Vidal for their translation into English. The usual disclaimers apply.

REFERENCES

Correa, E. (1998), *Crisis y desregulación financiera*, México: Siglo XXI.

Correa, E. (2002), 'La crisis fiscal del Washington Consensus', www.redcelsofurtado.edu.mx.

Girón, A. (1995), *Fin de siglo y deuda externa: Historia sin fin*, México: Cambio XXI–IIEc–UNAM.

Gnos, C. and L.-P. Rochon (2004–05), 'The Washington Consensus and multinational banking in Latin America', *Journal of Post Keynesian Economics*, **27** (2), 315–31.

IMF (2004), 'Rules-Based Fiscal Policy In Emerging Markets' http://www.imf.org/external/np/tr/2004/tr041006.htm, 6 October
Kregel, J. (1998), 'Flujo de capitales, fragilidad e inestabilidad en el desarrollo económico', in A. Girón and E. Correa (eds), *Crisis Financiera: Mercado sin fronteras*, México: El Caballito, pp. 39–65.
Ocampo, J.A. (1998), Globalización y desarrollo, http://www.eclac.cl/prensa/noticias/noticias/2/9272/jaoglobalizacion-2.pdf
Parguez, A. (2005), 'Dinero y crédito en el capitalismo contemporáneo', in E. Correa and A. Girón (eds), *Economía Financiera Contemporánea*, México: Miguel Angel Porrua, pp. 15–54.
Williamson, J. and P.P. Kuczynski (2003), *After Washington Consensus Restarting Growth and Reform in Latin America*, Washington, DC: Institute for International Economics.

12. The effect of interest rates in developing countries: can central bank monetary policy instruments modify economic growth?

Noemi Levy Orlik[1]

INTRODUCTION

Throughout economic history interest rate determinants have been subjected to a wide discussion that has gained importance since globalization now dominates the world economy. The increased capital mobility in new international settings made obvious an important limitation of monetarism: central banks cannot control money supply; nor can monetary aggregates operate as monetary policy instruments.

A new consensus was reached that rests upon the assumptions that money supply is endogenous and the central bank sets the ruling rate of interest, which turns into an important policy instrument. Therefore the discussion shifted to the limitations that central banks have in determining the rate of interest. The major points of disagreement are whether the rate of interest impacts on real variables or modifies the distribution of income; and whether there is, or is not, a price transmission mechanism to interest rates.

In this chapter I argue that the rate of interest is a distributional variable and is the result of social conflicts among the ruling sectors of the society (entrepreneurs, *rentiers* or financiers and workers). Therefore interest rates only modify the distribution of income, with no direct impact on economic growth, unless interest rate movements are extremely severe. Consequently, there is no price transmission mechanism to interest rates.

In developing countries, particularly those with open economies, the central bank reaction function is more complicated since it needs to guarantee the stability of financial capital purchasing power in terms of international reserve currencies. In these conditions, interest rates tend to offset financial capital losses, modifying the distribution of income in favor of capital owners. An important point to bear in mind is that it is a political decision.

The discussion will have two limitations. First, at the theoretical level the debate will be set around the determinants of the monetary rate of interest, set by the central bank, which is independent of the 'natural' or profit rate. This discussion will be based on the argument that central banks accommodate commercial bank reserves to avoid financial instability (see, among others, Aglietta 1996; Rochon 1999; Wray 1998; 2004, 2007b; Blinder 1998; Bindseil 2004). Second, the main theoretical findings will be discussed considering only developing countries whose main characteristics are their technological dependence and economic openness, which increases in periods of financial globalization.

The chapter is divided in four sections. After the introduction, the second section deals with the theoretical debate around the central bank determination of the interest rate and its limitations. The third section will analyze how monetary interest rates are determined in developing countries; and, finally, the main conclusions of the chapter will be presented.

DIFFERENT VIEWS ON INTEREST RATES AND THE CURRENT DISCUSSION OF MONETARY POLICY RULES

The discussion around interest rates has undergone an interesting twist in the last three decades. On the one hand, the mainstream adopted a new view on interest rates, incorporating Keynes's idea that the rate of interest is a monetary variable not determined by investment and savings. Consequently mainstream theories based on the assumption of the real interest rate in nominal terms were displaced (e.g., monetarism, in Friedman 1971; and Rational Expectations as in Lucas and Sargent 1981), and new theories emerged. In the mainstream, the new classical consensus (hereafter NCC), which embodies the Taylor rule, and the post-Keynesian School, in which the notion of endogenous money was deepened, reached a partial consensus that the rate of interest is an exogenous variable (see, among others, Kaldor 1983; Moore 1988; Chick and Dow 2002; Rochon 1999) that affects the distribution of income (Lavoie and Seccareccia 1999; Rochon and Setterfield 2007; Smithin 2004, 2006; Wray 1998, 2004, 2007b), but there were differences in terms of the rules that central banks should follow. In order to disentangle this discussion, this section is divided in two subsections. The first discusses the theoretical background of the monetary interest rates.

The Rate of Interest, Credit and Investment

The first proponents of the view that there is a monetary interest rate, set by the central bank, independent of the profit rate, is found among the classical economists. Adam Smith and François Quesnay argued that central banks can set a monetary rate of interest, independent of profits, which should be as low as possible to deter speculation. In Smith's view, the legal rate should impose upper limits to banks' interest rates and offset extravagant consumption (see Toporowski 2005, pp. 1–13). Quesnay went further and laid down the foundations of a 'fair' rate of interest (followed by Pasinetti), stating that monetary authorities should set the interest rate equal to changes in land productivity. In his view, *rentiers* (capital owners) should be rewarded in proportion to the value added by advances in agriculture (ibid., pp. 17–25).

The divorce between interest and profit rates was reinforced by Keynes, who defined the rate of interest as a monetary variable. It followed his 'Ex-ante theory of interest rate' (1937), where he argues that commercial banks hold a key position in the provision of finance in transitional periods from lower to higher economic activity. It can be inferred that so long as the central bank satisfies all banks' reserve demand at a constant interest rate, credit supply is unlimited (this introduced the concept of creditworthiness; see Rochon 1999). This argument highlights that credits are independent of interest rate movements and are demand determined, highly related to investment finance. Therefore investment is not limited by the provisions of real resources (savings) but by 'the determination of relative spot prices of durables based on the current market rate of interest' (Kregel 1984, p. 147). In these conditions, 'Banks allow their balance sheet to adjust by fully satisfying the additional demand at the prevailing rate of interest' (ibid.). The key point is that central banks should reduce interest rates sufficiently to persuade entrepreneurs to hold additional productive assets or to keep interest rates from rising, thus preventing entrepreneurs from changing the assessment of profitability (ibid., p. 151). In this context, 'Credit provides not an alternative of increased savings, but a necessary preparation for it. It is the parent, not the twin, of increased savings' (Keynes 1939, cited in Kregel, ibid.).

Another important economist of the twentieth century is Hawtrey (for a broad discussion, see Toporowski 2005, pp. 71–4). He emphasized, even before Keynes, the importance of credit, arguing that banks can systematically generate and propagate economic disequilibria and, more importantly, credit can be transformed into income and determine spending, but is unable to induce borrowers to demand credits from banks. Banks can only modify the rate of interest, with the hope of attracting borrowers or discouraging them from doing so.

From the above arguments it can be inferred that money is endogenous, which means that credit demand determines its supply, the rate of interest is set by the central bank, independent of investment and saving, and credit paves the way for investment spending.

There is a second argument put forward by Wicksell (1907) and Keynes himself (1936)[2] that relates directly (in negative terms) interest rates and investment spending, setting aside credit. Both economists argue that there is a monetary interest rate set by the central bank and a 'natural' or a profit rate, and the differential of these two variables is the main investment determinant, differing in terms of causality between the two.

Wicksell claimed that the 'natural' (real) rate determines the monetary rate, which is set by the central bank. Hence the monetary rate adjusts to the natural rate with temporal lags (see Pivetti 1998, p. 42); a cumulative process takes place with partial disequilibria without disturbing the level of income. Lower monetary rates set off bank credit and investment spending (above savings) without inducing financial instability, since it is assumed that it is a self-correcting process. The 'natural' rate of interest is a real variable, determined by capital scarcity and technological innovations, while the monetary rate induces bank credit demand which, at a going rate of rate, is supplied. There is no credit restriction from savings or bank reserves.

It should be noted that in Wicksell's argument prices and returns go up (costs remaining constant) taking place an inflationary process *á la* Fisher; that in a later stage pushes up monetary interest rates, once the central bank acknowledges the higher prices, which lowers investment spending, returning the analysis to the neoclassical view that the 'natural' (real) interest rate sets the pace of economic growth.

Keynes (1936) offers a different explanation. Equilibrium is reached when the marginal efficiency of capital (hereafter MEC) is equal to the (long-term) rate of interest,[3] which is determined by capital owners' liquidity preference and a given money supply. Higher levels of uncertainty increase the liquidity preference and, for a given amount of money supply, the interest rate rises, reducing the MEC and the interest rate differential, which shows a direct (negative) relation between the rate of interest and investment. Wicksell's causation is reversed since the MEC adapts to the rate of interest.

The impact of prices on interest rates is also modified, since prices directly affect costs and, especially, the purchasing power of wages (set in nominal terms) and other productive factor incomes, while interest rate movements directly modify the MEC and the market rate of interest differential. However, Keynes argues that there is an asymmetrical effect when the rates of interest descend, summarized in the absolute liquidity preference concept.[4]

Two important elements can be emphasized from the above discussion. First, the direct relation between credit and investment given a rate interest (Keynes 1937) is replaced by the negative relation between interest rates and investment spending. Smithin (2007, pp. 104–5) argues that if Keynes had stated that 'growth depends on profitability and a cut in real interest rates, while reducing *rentier* income nonetheless increases entrepreneurial profits', his message might have been better understood. Second, Keynes acknowledges that monetary policy on its own cannot reverse the economic cycle; hence he advocates active fiscal policies to outgrow periods of recession.

The first conclusion is highly controversial, especially among post-Keynesian 'horizontalists' and 'circuitists', who argue that the rate of interest is an administrative price that affects the distribution of income without modifying commercial banks' credit (unless interest rates changes are extremely high) and, for income to increase, credit demand needs to rise, facing no limitation from real resources or monetary reserve restrictions. Uncertainty is reflected by changing levels of creditworthiness (Rochon 1999).

Finally, following post-Keynesian 'horizontalism', the monetary cycle analysis put forward by Fisher in his famous paper 'Debt deflation theory of the Great Depression' (1933) and Minsky's (1986) financial instability hypothesis also are rejected (see Rochon 1999), since lower interest rates do not expand credit unless credit is demanded (due to higher profits) that in any case induces higher income. Consequently overindebtedness is not caused by higher interest rates but by lower income.

The Rate of Interest: Monetary Policy Rules

The propositions related to the central bank reaction function can be classified in two main views (see Rochon and Setterfield 2007 and Rochon 2007). On one side is the Taylor (1993) rule that put forward a direct (negative) relation between interest rates and investment. On the other, there are different rules composed by Pasinetti's (1980–81) 'natural' interest rate that Lavoie and Seccareccia (1999) labeled the 'fair' rule; the Smithin rule; and the one related to Kansas City group, all of which are based on endogenous money.

The new classical consensus model and the Taylor rule

The Taylor rule (Taylor 1993), adopted by the new classical consensus model, replaces the LM curve put forward by the neoclassical synthesis (Hicks 1937) and assumes that the monetary rate of interest (i_t) is determined by observed inflation (π_t), the real interest rate (r^*_t) and the gaps between observed and target inflation (π_t^*) and observed (y_t) and potential income (y_t^*). The Taylor rule is expressed as follows:

$$i_t = \pi_t + r_t^* + \alpha_\pi(\pi_t - \pi_t^*) + \alpha_y(y_t - y_t^*), \tag{12.1}$$

where $\alpha_s > 0$

if

$$\pi_t - \pi_t^* = 0 \tag{12.1$'$}$$

and

$$y_t - y_t^* = 0 \tag{12.1$''$}$$

then

$$i_t - \pi_t = r_t^* \tag{12.1$'''$}$$

According to equations (12.1′) and (12.1″), when the observed and 'target' inflation and the observed and 'potential' income are equal, the nominal interest rate less inflation equals the real interest rate (12.1‴).

This Wicksellian analysis reappears in the Taylor rule. The central bank interest rate is set on real terms and is based on a 'natural' rate (whereby investment and savings are equal) that adjusts to inflation and income gaps. These two views have important similarities, including the endogenous money notion and the neoclassical argument that the 'natural' rate sets the monetary rate that halts investment; therefore the monetary interest rate has a direct impact on economic growth. Inflation is considered to be led by demand factors; central banks can impose a 'correct' interest rate (equal to the 'natural' rate) if they follow certain rules (e.g. the Taylor rule); consequently 'adequate' monetary policy can reach a stable full employment level (i.e. free of inflation) if central bank decisions are efficient, transparent and not tainted by political factors.[5]

Active fiscal policy is not acceptable since money is considered to be neutral; therefore it only affects prices (Friedman's arguments are revived). This means that the crowding-out effect reappears since capital is supposed to be scarce; and the level of income and unemployment is linked to the supply conditions of the economy (based on the NAIRU – non-accelerating interest rate of unemployment). Accordingly, higher wages (although near subsistence level) will induce inflation. We can state that Wicksell's theory resurfaces in a modern skin, or, as stated by Lavoie (2004), it is like 'old wine in a new bottle'.

Post-Keynesian monetary policy rule

As was stated, post-Keynesianism offers three alternatives views to the Taylor rule, which put forward different rules for 'parking' the monetary interest rate.

The 'fair or natural' rule The main idea behind this argument is that monetary policy should not modify the distribution of income, and all the production factors, including capital, should be rewarded in proportion to their contribution to the value added. On this basis, Pasinetti (1980–81) put forward the idea of a 'natural' rate, which is 'a rate that causes no deviation from the "labor principle of income distribution"' (ibid., p. 189) and differs from the 'natural – neoclassical' rate of interest.[6] To comply with this condition the 'fair or natural' rate is set on real terms (inflation is deducted – r_r) and it is equal to changes in labor productivity ($\Delta\pi_L$). It is expressed as follows:

$$r_r = \Delta\pi_L \text{ for } r_r / Y \tag{12.2}$$

Interests are a payment that benefits the capital owners and entrepreneurs. The former are rewarded for 'renting' capital, which is a 'pure' remuneration of capital, whatever the form of capital is in use (financial or real capital) and irrespective of the types – credits, bonds, share or firms' own capital (see Pivetti 1991, p. 23) – while the latter are paid for putting capital to work, which is the compensation for the 'risk and trouble' and other 'objective' elements (e.g. illiquidity risk; ibid., p. 25). Therefore the normal rate of profit in each particular sphere (r_o) is the sum of the long-term interest rate (i) (considered to be highly unstable) plus the normal profit of enterprise (np_e) that remains constant and independent of the former. It is formalized as followed:

$$r_o = i + np_e \tag{12.3}$$

The 'fair or natural' rate is based on the assumption that nominal salaries are given (not real salaries as in Ricardian and Marxian analysis) and there is a transmission mechanism from prices to interest rates for the profit share to remain constant, while the labor force share depend on exogenous variables such us institutional and political forces.[7]

The argument is as follows. The central bank sets the nominal interest rate (r_n), competition induces equal rate of returns in all sectors, for which inflation needs to be deduced. Hence the proxy variable for the rate of return is the real interest rate (r_r), and price movements modify the nominal rate of interest. These relations are expressed as follows:

$$r_n = r_r + (1 + r_r)\,\Delta p/p \tag{12.4}$$

$$\Delta p/p = \Delta w/w \tag{12.4a}$$

$\therefore$

$$r_n = r_r + (1 + r_r)\,\Delta w/w \tag{12.4b}$$

The main point to stress is that the monetary rate of interest (the reward of 'pure' capital and 'in operation') is modified by nominal wage adjustment, which contains productivity changes and price inflation, for the distribution of income to remain constant, or the financial capital purchasing power remains unmodified when wage changes.

These arguments have some flaws. First, capital is supposed to add to wealth, as any other production factor (labor force). This argument is quite dubious since existing capital is a reward for previous profits (the 'pure' remuneration portion) that would continue to increase for the 'sake' of ownership. Second, and more importantly in terms of post-Keynesian theory, money is costless and no existing capital is required to expand or increase production; hence past capital (especially in the case of *rentiers* – pure remuneration of capital) is not a precondition for production spending. Finally, for a given level of productivity, there is a relation that goes from wages to prices and interest rates, which means that financial instability is caused by wage movements, a highly critical assumption in developing countries. Pivetti (1991, pp. 58–9) argues that wage rises (above productivity) lead to higher inflation (even though there are unemployed production factors), which increases interest rates and induces external capital inflows, followed by exchange rate appreciation and external current account disequilibria that eventually are 'corrected' through exchange rate devaluations.

The Smithin rule The main role of monetary policy according to Smithin (2004, 2007) is to preserve the value (purchasing power) of financial capital that includes 'past profits and non-spent wages' (2004, p. 27). The argument for the rate of interest being a payment to accommodate credits is left aside (since banks obtain profit from financial margins) but he argues that capital owners are entitled to preserve the purchasing power of non-spent income.

The central bank rate of interest should be equal to the reciprocal of prices; hence the central bank reaction function ought to set the real rate of interest very near to zero, the reason being that in a capitalist system *rentiers* are part of the social system, although credit is not related to interest rates (i.e. it is costless). In Smithin's words: 'First, if capitalism is to persist as a social order the "social contract" must include the financial interest rate as well as non-financial business and labor. Second, "zero" is a too precarious target and gives no leeway for mistakes in the wrong direction' (2004, p. 65).

Three important elements need to be emphasized in Smithin's analysis. First, he departs from the 'fair or natural' rate proposition since he rejects that past profits ('pure' remuneration of capital) should be rewarded with new profits, but for political reasons the capital owner's purchasing power should remain constant; hence, unlike Keynes, he does not propose the euthanasia of rentiers.

Second, Smithin is highly critical of the Taylor rule. He rejects the notion of the 'natural–neoclassical' interest rate, the inflation 'target' and the 'potential' product. These variables are not observable in the sense that they cannot be calculated over statistical estimates. They are 'simple social constructions', especially in the case of the inflationary 'target'. More importantly, they do not necessarily correspond to what is going on in reality. 'Looked at from such a skeptical point of view, arguments to the effect that the natural rate of interest has risen, that the natural rate of output has fallen or that the inflation target should be lower, might *all* be seen as simple excuses to raise the interest rate' (2004, p. 59). Moreover, the 'natural–neoclassical' rate of interest cannot be considered a theoretical concept. From the perspective of the capital distribution theory it is foolish to maintain that the rate of interest is determined by the marginal productivity of labor (Petri, cited in Smithin 2004). The 'temporal preference rate' belongs to a representative agent and it needs to be constant to indicate what should be the natural rate of interest, which is unviable (see Kam 2000 and Smithin 2003, cited in Smithin 2004). Regarding the natural rate, its existence is debatable in a monetary capitalist economy because it is assumed to be determined by a (fictitious) barter in the capital market, where savings are expressed by physical capital that can be sold to investors as capital goods of specific production sectors, which does not correspond to reality.

Finally, Smithin (2007, p. 107) reinforces the argument for setting the monetary interest rate in real terms on the basis of a negative relation between interest rates and inflation. He argues that lower real interest rates will augment non-monetary assets, which will raise credit and therefore increase set off prices and, consequently, set off inflationary pressures.

These relations are debatable, unless the assumptions are made clear. Higher credit and economic growth might increase prices if the economy is near full employment, or inflation can be short term if is assumed that money is non-neutral (higher levels of money would also increase the supply conditions of the economy). Again higher wages certainly affect prices if effective demand is near full capacity, but if the economy faces unutilized production factors, higher demand will increase sales and returns. Therefore, in this argument Smithin accepts the notion of limits to production capacity, put forward by the Taylor rule. Another important element is that in Smithin's analysis the view that money is not a commodity is weakened, since the value of money is related to a basket of commodities to retain its purchasing power (more of that in the next section).

The Kansas City rule The main argument here is that the interest rate is set in nominal terms and should be equal to zero. This proposition is based on the assumption that financial capital is a result of previous profits; hence capital owners are not entitled to new profits (similar to Keynes's *rentiers'* euthanasia argument) and hence monetary policy need not guarantee a constant purchasing power for financial capital.

According to this view the main central bank function (and monetary policy objective) is to stabilize the liquidity of the financial system, for which monetary policy ought to equilibrate government operations to assure adequate reserves in the banking system (Wray 1998, p. 225). The main monetary policy operational instrument, besides open market operations, is the short-term rate of interest unrelated to money demand or supply, since the central bank monopolizes the creation of money while tax payments destroy the creation of money (based on the chartalist view). Second, monetary policy needs to be connected to fiscal policy (it cannot operate independently) because one of the central bank's main functions is to prevent financial distress.[8] Third, governments do not need previous (real) resources to spend (government bond issues and debt have different purposes) since public spending takes place through 'crediting' commercial banks' accounts while tax collection is done through 'debiting' commercial bank agents' accounts, reducing their payment capacity (see Forstater and Mosler 2005; Wray 1998, 2007a). Finally, short-term government sovereign debt and its short-term rate are a close substitute for overnight credit reserve, and a longer rate of interest of sovereign debt depends on future short-term interest rate expectations (Wary 2007a); therefore bank reserves can be modified according to the central bank's objective.

The salient point is that monetary policy depends on the government financial situation (debtor or creditor). A deficit implies that net savings are held by the rest of society (non-government external or domestic agents) and banks holds excess reserves; thereby the rate of interest may approach zero. Alternatively, a government surplus implies that public savings increase, commercial bank reserves go down and, against 'common' belief, the interest rate increases. The government treasury department, through the central bank, can prevent the bond price from rising or falling via selling bonds (in the case of deficit) or buying them (in the case of surplus). This intervention is done through short-term open market operations or via treasury sovereign bonds, whose time span is longer. Alternatively the central bank can pay interest to commercial bank deposits and therefore eliminate debts. In this context, the nominal interest rate can be equal to zero and, the central bank, by modifying the overnight interest rate (price of commercial bank reserves) guarantees the financial system liquidity requirements (injecting or withdrawing liquidity).

Finally, Wray (2007b, pp. 125–6) refutes that there is a transmission mechanism from future inflation to the central bank rate of interest since all the asset value will be equally affected by price movements.[9] His view is that 'the entire analysis of determination of asset prices and rates of return is conducted without reference to prices of any particular group of commodities such as consumption goods' (ibid.) and he states: 'Entrepreneurial profit maximization is directed to equalizing nominal own rates – not towards maintaining a constant purchasing power of asset values in terms of consumption baskets' (ibid.). Additionally, the impact of expected future inflation over the asset price spectrum is small and directly affects production and employment.

Summing up, then there is wide agreement that the rate of interest is determined by the central bank. Second, an important conclusion among the three post-Keynesian views revised here is that the interest rate does not affect investment and the distribution of income is modified. Third, there is disagreement over whether *rentiers* ought to participate in the distribution of income, and if there is or is not a transmission mechanism of prices (future inflation) to the monetary rate of interest.

In this context I support Wray's conclusions that the central bank determination of the interest rate is a political decision, is set on nominal terms, and depends on the class strength of the different social groups. Therefore, to avoid political pressures, the rate of interest should be set at a nominal level equal to zero.

THE DETERMINATION OF THE MONETARY INTEREST RATE IN THE MEXICAN ECONOMY

In this section we attempt to determine which of the above explanations are relevant in the Mexican economy during recent decades. In order to do that, first, we need to spell out the main characteristics of the Mexican financial sector. This will help us to determine whether the specific characteristics of these countries, especially in open and deregulated periods, modify the determination of the central bank rate of interest.

The Main Characteristics of the Mexican Financial Sector

In the 1980s the Mexican financial sector went through different phases of deregulation and globalization, which increased the participation of the non-banking sector in the financial market. In terms of monetary policy, this meant that the central bank dropped monetary aggregates as their main monetary policy instrument (the legal reserve requirement was abolished)[10] and central bank interest rates became the main explicit monetary policy instrument, increasing the importance of net internal credit movements (see Levy and Toporowski 2007).

Second, the exchange market strengthened via increased participation of public bonds in the financial market,[11] becoming the treasury bonds' most important central bank reference rate. At present the Mexican financial system operates in a system of zero average legal reserve requirement[12] and policies that put the financial system in 'long' and 'short' positions.[13] In other words, interest rates on fringe internal credits operate to attain specific short and medium inflation targets. This means that money aggregates accommodate to inflation targets through sliding interest rates for margin reserves (see Martinez et al. 2001). Finally, the financial market globalization (1989) along with NAFTA became the most important adjustment(s) of the financial market structure.

The exchange rate is another important feature of developing countries, and it has been a central variable in Mexican economic history. Its structure has been modified a number of times in the last 30 years. After the 1982 crisis, a flexible exchange rate structure was imposed, replaced in 1989 by a band system, dropped after the 1994 macro-devaluation, with foreign reserves becoming the anchor of monetary policy to stabilize the exchange rate,[14] along with a more flexible exchange rate structure and sterilization policies.[15] This policy was strengthened by granting autonomy to the Mexican central bank in April 1994.

Finally, developing economies (certainly the Mexican economy) turn out to be more dependent as a result of the increased trade and financial globalization induced by the mid-1980s and mid-1990s reforms (Mexico joined the GATT and unilaterally lifted all its commercial barriers and the NAFTA imposition). The Latin American features of unequal terms of trade and, especially, the structural inflation, became worse. Exports' and imports' demand-income elasticity increased, as did their demand-price inelasticity.

In these conditions, Latin American countries, certainly Mexico, pursued monetary policies to control inflation, relying on a stable and overvalued exchange rate to avoid cost-push inflation pressures induced by import goods (the import content of domestic and exports rose drastically, against purchasing power parity predictions). In this situation, wages in real terms turn out to be the accommodative variable to guarantee capital owners' income share stability, which means that the distribution of income became more unequal for the labor force, reducing internal demand.

Therefore developing economies, notably in deregulated and globalizing periods, do not share the same economic structure as industrial countries, and require a stable exchange rate, which distorts prices and may induce financial instability.

The Effect of Interest Rates and Credits on Investment

When the relation between monetary interest rate and investment spending is analyzed, two positions result. On one hand, independent of the dominant causality, the rate of interest has a direct (negative) relation with investment (see, among others, Wicksell 1907; Keynes 1936) and credits (Fisher, Minsky); and, on other hand, credits have a direct (positive) impact on investment (Keynes 1937) independent of monetary interest rate movements.

In terms of the Mexican economy, we find no direct relation between interest rate movements and investment spending during the years of financial and trade deregulation and globalization; see Figure 12.1. The investment coefficient shows steady growth between 1986 and 1994, interrupted by the 1994 exchange rate crisis that reduced drastically the investment coefficient in 1995, which took off after 1996, flattening its growth rate from 2000 onwards. The movements of the rate of interest showed a downward trend in the first period, increasing sharply during the crisis years, with ups and downs from then on. Hence there is no direct negative relation between the two variables, although sharp rises in the interest rate reduce investment spending.

These findings, on one hand, weaken Wicksell's arguments and, in a lesser way, Keynes's (1936) MEC and interest rate equilibrium proposition, since Keynes himself argued that there is a weak connection between these variables (especially in stagnant periods when absolute liquidity preference can take place). However, these results reinforce the post-Keynesian 'horizontalist' and 'circuitist' view that rejects the 'natural–neoclassical' interest rate definition (determined by investment and saving) and, more importantly, Keynes's view that the interest rate is determined

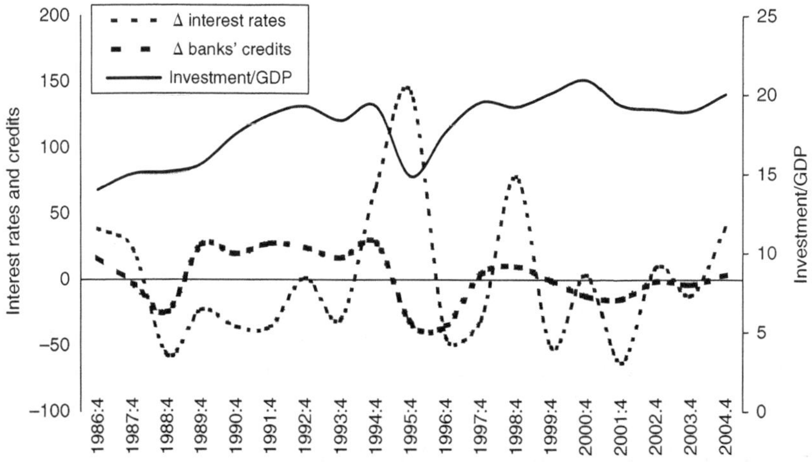

Figure 12.1 Interest rate movements, credit flows and investment coefficient

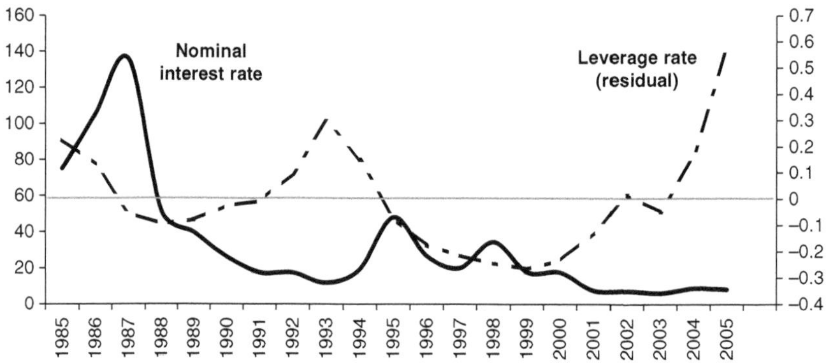

Figure 12.2 Leverage rate residual and the treasury bond rate

by market forces such as money demand (where liquidity preference through uncertainty has the more important role) and money supply.

A second important feature is that the rate of interest is not associated with credit movements that become more evident after the 1994 crisis, on the basis of which it can be claimed that the interest rate is an administrative variable, set by the central bank.

Another important observation that reinforces the disconnection between credits and interest rates is the relation between the leverage coefficient[16] residual[17] and the nominal interest rate; see Figure 12.2. Between 1989 and 1994 the nominal interest rate shows a downward

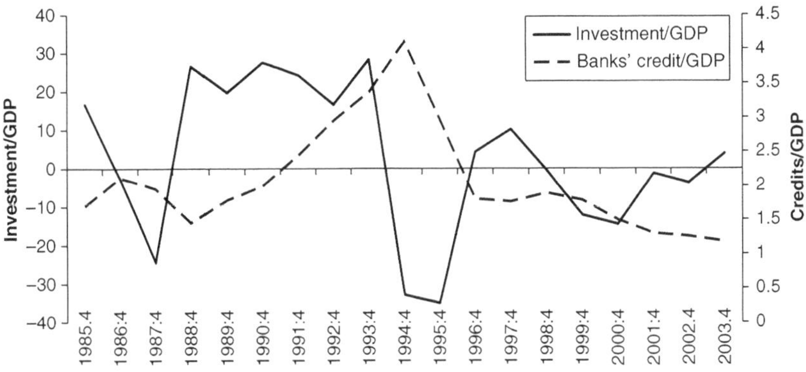

Figure 12.3 Investment and bank credit coefficients

trend, while the leverage coefficient residual goes up. This means that 'cheap' interest rates raise bank liabilities, portraying a Minskian expansive cycle. However, from 1995 the gap between observed and 'normal' leverage goes down and up (especially after 2000) with no relation to the monetary interest rate, which seems to be determined by other factors. Consequently overindebtedness is not related to interest rates, as Fisher and Minsky assumed.

The most striking finding is that credits and investment spending does not show the expected trends; see Figure 12.3. There is a positive relation between these two variables, between 1987 and 1993, from which can be inferred the existence of an expanded monetary cycle. However, after 1995 (the year of economic stagnation) the recovery of the investment coefficient was unconnected to credits, the reason being that multinationals, dominant in the Mexican productive system after NAFTA was enforced (see Levy 2007a), did not demand finance in the domestic system (Levy 2007b). Big enterprises (foreign and domestic multinationals) resort to the international financial system because credit costs are cheaper and, since nearly all of them engage in export activity, the exchange risk is reduced – or at least their competitors are equally affected. The central bank survey of enterprise finance sources reinforces this finding, showing that firms (irrespective of their size) do not demand bank credits in the Mexican financial market, intra-firm finance becoming the most important source.[18] This result is quite atypical for all the revised streams of thought, illustrating the external structural dependence of the Mexican economy.

Finally, another important relation takes place between financial returns in the stock market and the rate of interest; see Figure 12.4. Following Kregel's arguments, whenever financial gains are high, given

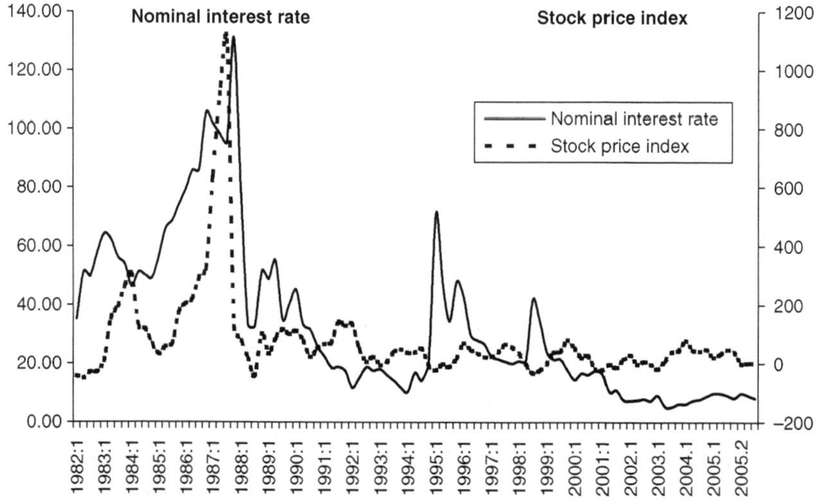

Figure 12.4 Stock price index movement and nominal interest rates

liquidity preference, interest rates should be low, to reinforce entrepreneurs' decisions to increase non-financial assets or at least not to revise their decisions. Another explanation is that whenever financial gains drop, interest rates rise, to compensate capital owners' losses. This has been the dominant situation in Mexico since 1990, when the financial market opened up to the international market, showing an important disconnect between finance and investment.

Second, the use of restrictive monetary policy to burst financial bubbles is not very effective, as stated by Toporowski (2000), even in developing countries such as Mexico, since interest rates increase as a result of exchange rate devaluation. The 1987 bubble was burst due to international financial market events that induced the 1987 Mexican exchange rate devaluation, followed by a higher rate of interest. The same happened in 1994 and, from then onwards, financial inflation has been the result of FDI (achieved by NAFTA) with no drastic exchange rate movement (a mild exchange rate movement took place in 1998 and 2000).

We can summarize this section by stating that there is no strong empirical evidence to claim that a lower monetary rate of interest induces higher investment spending or higher credit volumes, and monetary interest movements do not seem to affect over(under)indebtness. The most important variable that sets off financial crisis is exchange rate movements followed by interest rate hikes.

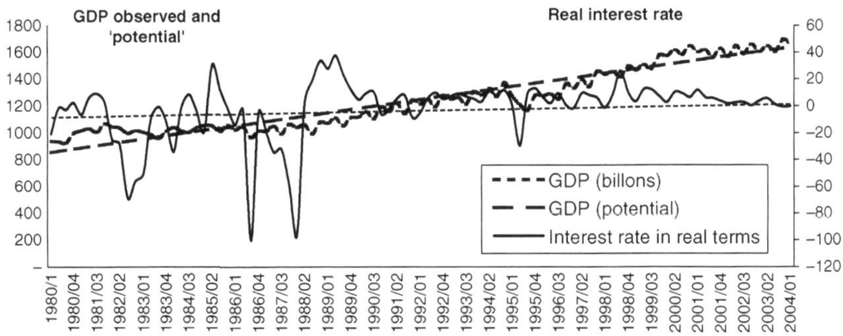

Figure 12.5 Product gap and interest rate movements

The Taylor Rule in the New Classical Consensus Model

To evaluate the Taylor rule in the Mexican economy, we needed to analyze the relation between the rate of interest in real terms (inflation deducted), the income gap and inflation. There is no possibility to establish the 'natural–neoclassical' interest rate level since it is an unobservable variable and cannot be calculated (see Smithin critics). Regarding 'potential' income, although we agree that it is a 'simple social construction', we shall evaluate the effects of monetary interest rate movements on the difference between observed and maximum possible income levels (calculated by an econometric regression). The closest theoretical construction to this argument is the NAIRU, which assumes that when demand (observed GDP) is above potential supply (fitted regression based on GDP observations), the central bank should increase the monetary rate of interest. This relation holds in the Mexican economy.

As observed in Figure 12.5, there is no connection between the difference in the observed and 'calculated' income and the monetary rate of interest movement set in real terms. The reason for this disconnection is that the central bank reaction function considers a third variable, which is the exchange rate.

Regarding the inflation gap, also considered a 'simple social construction', we shall assess the relation in terms of observed inflation, based on the consumer price index, and the 'target' inflation, which is explicitly set by the central bank; see Figure 12.6. Again the monetary rate of interest set by the central bank is not related to the inflationary gap, because the process of inflation is not demand led. The neoclassical relation that lower interest rates induce higher spending and put upward pressure on prices is not valid in terms of the Mexican economy, since inflation is a supply-led process, caused mainly by exchange rate devaluations, due to increased

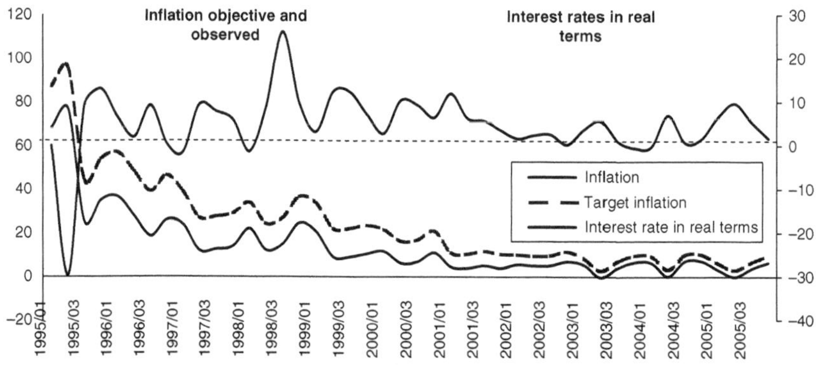

Figure 12.6 Observed and targeted inflation and interest rate movement

technological dependence, expressed through unequal terms of trade and structural inflation.

The Rate of Interest is a Distributional Variable

Finally, we discuss the post-Keynesian rules. It should be recalled that their common feature is that the interest rate is a distributional variable, being three different expressions of what should be the central bank monetary rate of interest.

The 'fair or natural' rule is based on the notion of 'neutral' income distribution, which means that interest rates should be rewarded in relation to what credits add to production (valued added); that is, interest rates should be equal to labor productivity changes. Although it was argued that this view is in conflict with the post-Keynesian basic assumption that money is costless and, in the case of Mexico, investment is not related to bank credits, our finding shows that the central bank rate is not 'neutral'; it favors capital owners.

There are two relations that will be analyzed to verify the non-neutral position of the rate of interest. First, the relation of average manufacturing labor productivity and labor force income in real terms (including wages and other incomes related to wages); see Figure 12.7. It should be noted that that Mexico is characterized as having a big disparity in labor productivity among the different productive sectors, being manufacturing, the sector with the highest labor productivity. This disparity also applies to workers' income. The treasury bonds rate is the lowest rate that capital owners can obtain; hence workers' share will be overestimated and capital participation underestimated.

The first thing to notice is that labor remuneration is below productivity

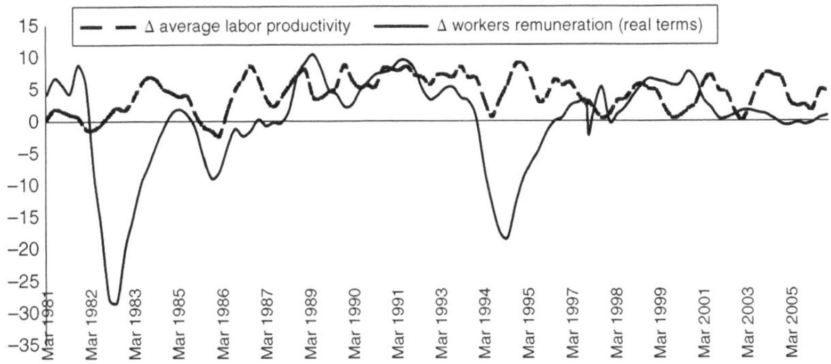

Figure 12.7 Movements in average labor productivity and workers' remuneration (real terms) (moving averages)

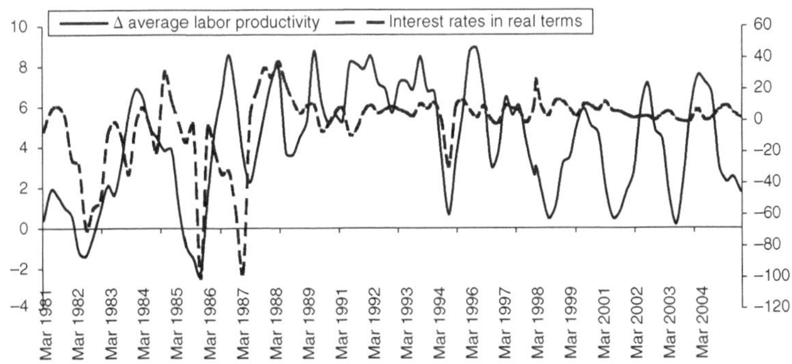

Figure 12.8 Movements of average productivity and interest rates in real terms

movements, which means that workers obtain less value in relation to what they contribute. Apart from a few quarters, throughout the period the movements of labor productivity are above labor income; see Figure 12.7. If we look at the other side of the distribution of income – Figure 12.8 – we see that the situation differs for central bank interest rates in real terms and average labor productivity movements. Monetary interest rate movements on average, are above labor productivity movements, which means that capital owners get more than they 'contribute', although in Mexico investment is unrelated to credits.

As a result of the above finding, it can be stated that the Smithin rule obviously is not followed, since that money rate of interest in real terms is well over zero and, certainly, the same applies to the Kansas City rule. This means that capital owners, even by central bank standards, are rewarded above workers' contribution, for the simple reason that they hold capital.

From the above discussion it can be concluded that monetary policy in Mexico is not neutral, even in terms of the 'fair or natural' rule, which in part explains the low internal demand of the Mexican economy, since the labor force does not benefit from pension funds and non-spent wages are very low. Thus Wray's (2007b) discussion whether interest movements affect, or not, effective demand is clear cut in the Mexican economy. Whenever interest rates increase, effective demand is reduced and capital returns rise, which are either channeled to the Mexican upper class, whose marginal propensity to consume is relatively low (in relation to workers' income) or to foreign capital owners, who have an important share of financial savings. Such returns are not recirculated to the domestic financial market.

The reason for not operating the post-Keynesian rules in developing economies and, particularly in Mexico, is because they do not consider adequately the role of exchange rates in highly technological dependent countries, a topic that is discussed next.

Exchange Rate, Inflation and Interest Rate

During the period of commercial and financial deregulation and globalization, Mexico increased the openness of its economy and it could be argued that the Mexican authorities chose to be one of the more open economies of the Latin American region. The economic structure in the 1980s underwent a process of de-industrializing the most important high-tech sectors, which was replaced in the 1990s by outward-orientated high-tech industry, mainly owned by external capital and, more importantly, highly disconnected from domestic sectors. Consequently, the exchange rate regained an even more important role in containing inflation and guaranteeing financial capital purchasing power in relation to external reserve currency. Exchange rate stability turned out to be a precondition of low inflation and exchange rate depreciation, instead of increasing domestic production, induced an inflationary process due to the high external content of domestic production, including exports.

In Figure 12.9, it can be seen that whenever the exchange rate is devalued, prices go up and the rate of interest rises; while in periods of stable exchange rates, inflation is contained and the rate of interest goes down. The dominant causality runs from exchange rate devaluation to higher prices, which increases the rate of interest without restoring wages' purchasing power, which means that the wage share in income is lowered.

There is an asymmetrical impact of exchange rate movements on the income of the different factors of production. As a result of higher interest

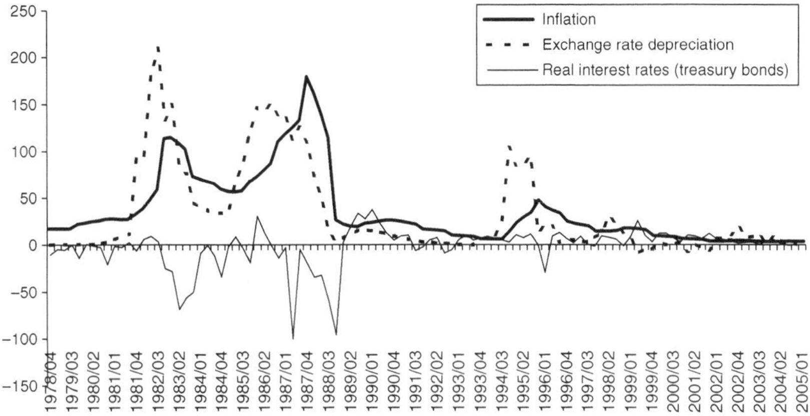

Figure 12.9 Exchange rates and real interest movements and inflation

rates, financial capital losses are neutralized, while wage reductions in real terms are not neutralized.

The next argument that needs to be analyzed is whether there is no other alternative for developing countries than to increase interest rates and reduce wages. Although this discussion is outside the scope of this chapter, a few arguments will be put forward. First, since the rate of interest is a distributional variable, it is politically determined; therefore developing economic policy can decide to reduce external dependence. This would require a less servile attitude towards external capital owners' interests, for which it is necessary to develop domestic industries based on local inputs (raw materials in terms of Mexico, for example, would be the oil industry) and protect local industries, not in terms of reducing import costs (capital and intermediate goods), but developing domestic technology. Additionally, FDI should be forced to increase links with domestic production or limit their operation to a few sectors of the economy (see Chang and Grabel 2004) to be developed by domestic industry. Another important issue for development is to modify the terms of finance. In this context the Regional Bank (created by Brazil and Venezuela) can be of the utmost importance to finance commerce among countries with equal development. Finally, commerce should take place between equal countries.

CONCLUSIONS

The discussions around interest rates have been at the center of theoretical debates and, more importantly, in the setting of economic policy.

From the onset of economic thought it was recognized that the central bank can set monetary interest rates, although it was not grasped that interest rates are distributional variables and can, thus modify the distribution of income. This became clear with the recent post-Keynesian debate, developed in the light of the Taylor rule and other dominant monetary policies.

As a result of this discussion, there is consensus that the rate of interest is a monetary variable set by central banks and there is disagreement on whether it affects or not investment spending and credit availability or if it only modifies the distribution of income.

According to mainstream economists, central bank monetary interest rates can control inflation through limiting demand, and monetary interest rates react to the income and inflation gaps. Keynes and some post-Keynesians put forward a similar idea, differing in terms of the causality between interest rate and the rate of profit, and more importantly in terms of the price transmission mechanism.

The post-Keynesian rules based on the endogenous-horizontalism paradigm and non-neutral money put forward a different vision, whereby it is argued that interest rate movements affect the distribution of income. In light of this view, the Taylor rule and Wicksell's arguments are rejected and, more importantly, Keynes's long-term rate of interest (determined by the money market) and MEC (however interpreted) equality is under doubt, as well as Fisher's and Minsky's monetary cycles explanation. The idea that the monetary rate of interest is independent of investment and economic growth is supported.

The three post-Keynesian rules discussed are based on the idea that interest rates only affect the distribution of income, however, it can be argued that the 'fair or natural' and the Smithin rules still share some characteristics with the dominant view that capital owners contribute to the production process and therefore credits are not costless (capital owners need to be rewarded in relation to their contribution to the value added) or that money is not totally independent of commodities and therefore should have a minimum price. The Kansas City rule is more explicit in terms of the political forces behind the central bank behavior and the idea that money is costless and unrelated to any commodity.

In terms of the empirical analysis, it is clear that in Mexico the relation among the monetary rate of interest, investment and credits does not hold; moreover, the monetary cycles *à la* Fisher and Minsky are not relevant. The Mexican central bank reaction function is non-neutral and favors financial capital (*rentiers* or financiers). The reason is quite simple. The external dependence of the Mexican economy makes the exchange rate a central price of the economy that needs to be overvalued for external capital flows to finance current account disequilibria and, more importantly, finance external inputs for economic growth to take place. An important element is that exchange rate movements affect social sectors asymmetrically. In the case of exchange rate devaluations, wages are lowered while interest rates are increased. The dominant causality goes from exchange rate devaluations, higher prices, reduction of financial capital and salaries' purchasing power, followed by higher monetary interest rates that neutralize the financial capital losses.

We argue that this is not a natural state of affairs. If developing countries reduce their external dependence, they can follow an independent monetary policy, which can set the central bank rate of interest in nominal terms at a zero level. Second, flexible exchange rates do not guarantee an independent monetary policy since in highly open and technologically dependent countries exchange rate devaluations induce inflation and low economic growth. Developing countries' financial capital's purchasing power, in terms of international reserves, is required to finance economic growth.

NOTES

1. This chapter is part of the foundations of the research project 'Estructuras financieras y financiamiento del desarrollo económico'. I am indebted to L.-P. Rochon and the participants of the 'Post-Keynesian Principles of Economic Policies' conference held in Dijon, and to Wesley Marshall for helping with the English language. All errors are solely my responsibility.
2. Keynes's (1936) argument for the monetary rate of interest determination differs. Uncertainty is moved from commercial bank decisions to the determination of money demand, particularly of the liquidity preference motive. The central bank role is diminished and (money) market mechanisms become more important.
3. Another important shortcoming is that Keynes reintroduces the equilibrium position already surpassed in Hawtrey's analysis.
4. The concept of absolute liquidity preference theory became highly confusing and induced a long discussion, missing the point that in economic downturns the only way to induce economic growth is via active fiscal policies.
5. There is an interesting literature on the problems faced by central banks when the first monetary rules were imposed; see, among others, Rogoff (1985), Barro and Gordon (1983) and Piga (2000).
6. Lavoie and Seccareccia (1999, p. 543) distinguish between the 'natural fair' and 'natural neoclassical' interest rates. The former is 'socially justified on equity considerations, and that would be fair to both lender and borrowers . . . [while] the neoclassical conception of an equilibrium rate, as exemplified by the Wicksellian natural rate of interest, and to the rate of interest which (a) financial investor may feel justified to invoke, given the riskiness of their debt instrument'.
7. Kalecki's (1943, 1954) argument is that in stagnant periods real salaries go down more than profit margins for prices not to increase; hence there is an income distribution in favor of (the) capitalist sector, specifically *financiers*.
8. To the lender of last resort central bank function is added continuous central bank surveillance in order to prevent financial crisis.
9. Wray (2007b) argues that changing expectations affect differently the components of

expected returns in monetary terms. 'Increased confidence about the future economic performance will raise *q*s on capital assets (*quasi rents*) while lowering the subjective value assigned to liquid positions . . . In that case, capital assets will be produced . . . and the full range of prices [will] adjust (pp. 124–5).

10. In 1997 the objective of stabilizing monetary aggregates was explicitly dropped.
11. In 1978 Mexican treasury bonds appeared and became negotiable only from 1981.
12. The zero average legal reserve requirement works as follows: debtor balances posted at the close of each day in the current accounts of each credit institution with the Bank of Mexico must be compensated, within 28-day periods, by posting, on other days, creditor balances of at least equal amounts in the same accounts. Non-compliance with the stated requirement makes the delinquent bank subject to a monetary penalty, which is calculated on the basis of the accumulated shortfall and an interest rate equivalent to twice the prevailing 28-day CETES rate (Banco de Mexico, *Annual Report*, 1996).
13. Putting the system in 'short' indirectly modifies the short-term interest rates to fulfill monetary base objectives: 'The Institute establishes or increases the negative target for the consolidated balance of the current accounts it holds for banks. This tends to temporarily raise short-term interest rates, which limits the effect of existing inflationary pressures on prices' (Banco de Mexico, *Annual Report*, 1999, p. 93).
14. In 1980 the share of external reserves on the monetary base amounted to 11.6%, in 1990 the represented 35.2%, in 2000, 52% and in 2005, 71%.
15. External capital flows, not related to productive spending, cancelled previous existing debt, increasing drastically the Mexican public internal debt.
16. This leverage coefficient is defined by bank liabilities to GDP, the former being overestimated since they are the sum of public, commercial and central banks, including intra-bank debts.
17. The residual liability coefficient results from an econometric regression, which is the difference between the observed and fitted observations.
18. See Banco de México, *Resultados de la Encuesta*.

REFERENCES

Aglietta, M. (1996), 'Systemic risk, financial innovations and the financial safety net', in G. Deleplace and E. Nell (eds), *Money in Motion: the Post Keynesian and Circulation Approaches*, New York: The Jerome Levy Economic Institute, pp. 552–79.

Banco de México (various years), *Annual Report*: *Resultados de las encuestas de evaluación coyuntural del mercado crediticio*, www.banxico.ord, Estadísticas, Encuesta del mercado crediticio.

Barro, R.J. and D.B. Gordon (1983), 'Rules, discretion and reputation in a model of monetary policy', *Journal of Monetary Economics*, **12** (1), 101–21.

Bindseil, U. (2004), *Monetary Policy Implementation. Theory, Past, and Present*, Oxford: Oxford University Press.

Blinder, A. (1998), *Central Banking in Theory and Practice*, Cambridge, MA: MIT Press.

Chick, V. and S. Dow (2002), 'Monetary policy with endogenous money and liquidity preference: a non dualistic treatment', *Journal of Post Keynesian Economics*, **22** (4), 587–608.

Chang, H.-J. and I. Grabel (2004), *Reclaiming Development*, New York: Zed Books.

Fisher, I. (1933), 'The debt deflation theory of the Great Depression', *Econometrica*, **1** (4), 337–57, www.jstor.org.

Forstater, M. and W. Mosler (2005), 'The rate of interest is zero', *Journal of Economic Issues*, **39** (2), 535–42.
Friedman, M. (1971), 'Un marco teórico para el análisis monetario', in R.J. Gordon (ed.), *El marco monetario de Milton Friedman. Un debate con sus críticos*, México, 1979, pp. 13–79.
Hicks, J. (1937), 'Mr. Keynes and the "Classics". A suggested interpretation', *Econometrica*, **5** (2), 147–59, www.jstor.org.
Kaldor, N. (1983), 'Keynesian economics after fifty years', in D. Worswick and J. Trevitich (eds), *Keynes and the Modern World. Proceedings of the Keynes Century Conference*, Cambridge: Cambridge University Press, 2nd edn, 1984, pp. 1–27.
Kalecki, M. (1943, 1954), 'Costos y Precios', in *Ensayos Escogidos Dinámica de la economía capitalista*', México: Fondo de Cultura Económica, pp. 57–76.
Keynes, J.M. (1936), *The General Theory of Employment, Interest, and Money*, First Harvest/Harcourt, Inc., 1964.
Keynes, J.M. (1937), 'Alternative theories of the rate of interest', republished in *Collected Writings of John Maynard Keynes*, Vol. XIV, D. Moggridge (ed.), London: Macmillan, 1973, pp. 201–14.
Kregel, J. (1984), 'Constraints on the expansion of output and employment: real or monetary?', *Journal of Post Keynesian Economics*, **VII** (2), pp. 139–52.
Lavoie, M. (2004), 'The new consensus on monetary policy seen from a Post-Keynesian perspective', in M. Lavoie and M. Seccareccia (eds), *Central Banking in the Modern World: Alternative Perspectives*, Cheltenham, UK and Northampton, MA, USA: Edward Elgar, pp. 15–34.
Lavoie, M. and M. Seccareccia (1999), 'Interest rate: fair', in *Encyclopedia of Political Economy*, vol. 1, London: Routledge, pp. 543–5.
Levy, N. (2007a), 'El Comportamiento de la Inversión: Revalorización de Factores Micro y Macroeconómicos en Mercados Globalizados en la Economía Mexicana', in G. Sánchez (ed.), *Microeconomía Heterodoxa*, DGAPA–Facultad de Economía–UNAM, pp. 111–33.
Levy, N. (2007b), 'Imperfecciones del Mercado y hegemonía bancaria: El caso mexicano', in S. Ruesgas and R. Cordera (eds), *El Estado ante la globalización. Políticas macroeconómicas. Migraciones y empleo*, Marcial Pons, España, pp. 147–71.
Levy, N. and J. Toporowski (2007), 'Open market operations in emerging economies: the Mexican experience', in David G. Mayes and Jan Toporowski (eds), *Open Market Operations and Financial Markets*, London: Routledge International Studies in Money and Banking, pp. 157–77.
Lucas, R.E. and T.J. Sargent (1981), 'After Keynesian macroeconomics', in *Rational Expectations and Econometric Practice*, Minneapolis, MN: University of Minnesota Press, pp. 295–319.
Martínez, L., O. Sánchez and A. Werner (2001), 'Consideraciones sobre la Conducción de la Política Monetaria y el Mecanismo de Transmisión en México', Working Paper, Banco de México, www.banxico.org.mx.
Minsky, H. (1986), *Stabilizing an Unstable Economy*, New York: Twentieth Century Fund.
Moore, B. (1988), *Horizontalists and Verticalists: The Macroeconomics of Credit Money*, Cambridge: Cambridge University Press.
Pasinetti, L. (1980–81), 'The rate of interest and the distribution of income in a pure labor economy', *Journal of Post Keynesian Economics*, **3** (2), 170–82.

Piga, G. (2000), 'Dependent and accountable: evidence from the modern theory of central banking', *Journal of Economic Surveys*, **14** (5), 563–95.
Pivetti, M. (1991), *Essays on Money and distribution*, London: Macmillan.
Pivetti, M. (1998), 'Thomas Tooke and the influence of the rate of interest on prices: implications for distribution theory', *Contributions to Political Economy*, **17**, 39–53.
Rochon, L.-P. (1999), 'Horizontalism: setting the record straight', in L.-P. Rochon and M. Vernango (eds), *Credit, Interest Rates and the Open Economy*, Cheltenham UK and Northampton, MA, USA: Edward Elgar, pp. 31–65.
Rochon, L.-P. (2007), 'The state of Post Keynesian interest rate policy: where are we and where are we going?', *Journal of Post Keynesian Economics*, **30** (1), 3–11.
Rochon, L.-P. and M. Setterfield (2007), 'Interest rate, income distribution and monetary policy dominance: Post Keynesian and the "fair rate"', *Journal of Post Keynesian Economics*, **30** (1), 13–42.
Rogoff, K. (1985), 'The optimal degree of commitment to an intermediate monetary target', *Quarterly Journal of Economics*, **100** (4), 1169–89.
Smithin, J. (2004), 'Interest rate procedures and income distribution', in M. Lavoie and M. Seccareccia (eds), *Central Banking in the Modern World. Alternative Perspectives*, Cheltenham UK and Northampton, MA, USA: Edward Elgar, pp. 57–69.
Smithin, J. (2006), 'The theories of interest rates', in P. Arestis and M. Sawyer (eds), *A Handbook of Alternative Monetary Economics*, Cheltenham, UK and Northampton, MA, USA: Edward Elgar, pp. 273–90.
Smithin, J. (2007), 'A real interest rate rule for monetary policy?', *Journal of Post Keynesian Economics*, **30** (1), pp. 101–18.
Taylor, J. (1993), 'Discretion *vs* policy rules in practice', *Carnegie–Rochester Conference Series on Public Policy*, **39**, 195–214.
Toporowski, J. (2000), *The End of Finance: Capital Market Inflation, Financial Derivatives and pension Fund Capitalism*, New York and London: Routledge.
Toporowski, J. (2005), *Theories of Financial Disturbance: an examination of critical theories of finance from Adam Smith to the present day*, Cheltenham UK and Northampton, MA, USA: Edward Elgar.
Wicksell, K. (1907), 'The influence of the rate of interest on prices', *The Economic Journal*, **17** (66), 213–20, www.jstor.org.
Wray, R. (1998), *El papel del dinero hoy: La clave del pleno empleo y la estabilidad de precios*, Mexico: UNAM.
Wray, R. (2004), 'International aspects of current account policy', Working Paper No. 31, Levy Institute, online.
Wray, R. (2007a), 'Entendiendo la Política Económica en un Régimen Cambiario de Libre Flotación', in G. Mántey and N. Levy (eds), *Políticas Macroeconómicas para países en desarrollo*, México: PORRUA, UNAM–DGAPA–ACATLAN, pp. 207–43.
Wray, R. (2007b), 'A Post Keynesian view of central bank independence, policy targets, and the rules versus discretion debate', *Journal of Post Keynesian Economics*, **30** (1), 119–41.

13. International capital flows and Latin America: making sense of disappointing results

Wesley C. Marshall

INTRODUCTION

To a large degree, the history of international relations of economic power can be described and analyzed through the lens of capital flows. While the reception of consistent inflows of capital is a fairly reliable guarantee of a country's increased accumulation of wealth and international presence, consistent outflows of capital equally often condemn countries to poverty and economic irrelevance. As a historical net exporter of capital, Latin America has not escaped this tendency. Apart from few exceptional periods, the region has been unable to retain and utilize its capital to a sufficient degree to achieve local economic development or international economic and political sovereignty. With the ushering in of the neoliberal economic ideology that became dominant in the region during the 1970s and 1980s, this problem was reinterpreted and presented through a simplistic viewpoint that offered an equally simplistic solution. Whereas enormous amounts of accumulated capital exist in developed countries, but investment opportunities are limited, in underdeveloped countries capital is scarce, but opportunities for investment abound. Therefore the financial opening of previously hermetic Latin American countries would offer mutual benefits. Capital from developed countries would have new opportunities for investment, and countries of the region would receive steady inflows of capital. However, now a full three decades since the first neoliberal-inspired policies of financial opening were implemented, this result has clearly not materialized.

This chapter will assert that financial opening and related reforms have failed to produce their explicit objectives because they were never true objectives. Rather, neoliberal-based economic policies have obeyed a single underlying objective – the expansion of American and European multinational corporations (MNCs) – which has systematically undermined the fulfillment of explicit objectives. This argument will be developed in several related sections. First, a brief outline of the historical antecedents of the recent projection of MNCs towards Latin America will be presented. Then the principle tenets of neoliberal policy recommendations will be examined. In later sections, the results of these policies will be analyzed. As the leading determinants of capital in- and outflows, the specific issues of financial opening, foreign direct investment (FDI) and privatizations, FDI and banks, and foreign banks and capital flows will be given special attention in separate parts. These sections, with the exception of the last, will analyze the results of policy recommendations, examining the degree to which both explicit goals and underlying goals have been fulfilled. As will be shown, in all cases, the interests of MNCs have trumped explicit policy goals and have violated the principles of the same neoliberal ideology that was used to justify their presence in the region.

CHANGES IN THE DYNAMICS OF THE GLOBAL ECONOMY

While this chapter deals mainly with events that have occurred between the late 1970s and the present in Latin America,[1] due to the influence that American, and to a lesser degree European, MNCs have exerted on the region during this timeframe, a brief digression into the origins of their recent expansion is necessary.

In the decades prior to the 1970s, economic exchange between Western countries was restricted in various ways. Commercial flows were regulated through tariffs and other such barriers to entry, and international finance was managed by the Bretton Woods system, established in 1944. Under this scheme, capital flows were highly regulated at a systemic and international level, and for decades much of the world witnessed high rates of steady economic growth.

However, towards the end of the 1960s, the USA was confronted by a multitude of economic challenges. Internally, economic and social relations between the economic actors that were able to maintain acceptable rates of profit for decades began to crumble (Wolfson 1986; Bowles et al. 1992; De Bernis 1988). In the international sphere, as the principal administrator of the Bretton Woods system, the USA assumed various sacrifices to its international competitiveness and economic opportunities (Hirst and Thompson 1996). Simultaneously, the growing expenditures of the war in Vietnam and greater competition from other countries, notably Germany and Japan, challenged America's economic dominance (Glyn and Sutcliffe 1999). As a consequence of these and other factors, in 1971

America officially abandoned the Bretton Woods system and the international economic order that it sustained. This rupture not only accelerated and deepened the incipient international monetary disorder, but also coincided with a greater international projection of US-based corporations (Hymer 1972).

THE RISE OF NEOLIBERALISM IN LATIN AMERICA

The transition of the American economy, which from the 1970s onward would increasingly depend on financial activity and the outward expansion of its corporations, would have enormous impacts on the economic evolution of Latin America. As such, the group of economic ideas that has justified and sustained these shifts in economic strategy is of great importance. The set of beliefs that has come to be known as neoliberal ideology proposes that the reduction of the state's role in the economy, as both a regulator and a direct actor, and financial and commercial liberalization, offer the greatest possibilities for an economy to efficiently create and distribute wealth. Put forth by authors such as McKinnon (1973), Dornbusch (1988) and Calvo (1991), such ideas, while not new, have been pivotal in the formulation of economic policy in Latin America.

In the wake of the debt crisis of 1982, neoliberal-inspired economic policies that facilitated the expansion of American capital in Latin America were applied in much of the region. In 1990, John Williamson coined the term the Washington Consensus (WC), referring to the ten principal economic policy recommendations that for years had been actively pursued by the World Bank (WB), the International Monetary Fund (IMF), the Inter-American Development Bank (IADB), creditor banks to the region, and American financial and economic authorities. Upon formulating this consensus, Williamson states that robust economic growth in the region, to be achieved through the application of WC policies, is the surest way to pay off external foreign debt (Williamson 1990). As asserted, the WC has both underlying and explicit goals. The former will be analyzed first.

The goal of opening the region to expansionary American capital was sought, and achieved, in three ways. First, Latin American overindebtedness was used to create opportunities for financial profit and for the expansion of American banks in the region. The requirement of budget surpluses (the first point of the WC), and financial market opening and deregulation were the mechanisms employed to this end. Second, ownership of many of the region's strategic enterprises was transferred from the state to MNCs. Privatization, the strengthening of property rights, and the abolition of entry barriers for FDI, all points of the WC, allowed

MNCs to expand into the region. And third, the WC recommendation of eliminating commercial tariffs created favorable conditions for the local consumption of imported products in the region, allowing for the displacement of domestic producers by principally American ones.

Although the underlying goal of the WC has been fulfilled (as will be further demonstrated), these policies were obviously presented with different objectives. Adhering to the neoliberal vision of how economies worked, and predicting how they would work in the future, the explicit goal of the WC was to accelerate economic growth in the region, which would be achieved in various ways. As mentioned in the introduction, a crucial concept underpinning the coherence of the neoliberal argument was that once the state removed financial regulations, abundant capital from developing countries would steadily flow into the underdeveloped region of Latin America, creating greater levels of savings and investment, lowering interest rates, and therefore stimulating productivity and economic growth (Fischer 1997; Forbes 2004).

At the same time, the removal of state interference in the economy in the form of ownership of companies would also spur sustainable growth. According to the neoliberal vision, the public sector is inherently less capable than the private sector in the administration of businesses. This inferiority is due to the fact that public sector companies are not exposed to market-imposed regulation, such as the threat of a buyout from other private sector firms or the market discipline imposed through lenders and shareholders or stakeholders (Williamson 1990; UNCTAD 1992). With less market discipline and fewer incentives to expand, state-owned companies are intrinsically inefficient, invest less and provide inferior services.

Yet financial and commercial opening would not only allow inefficient state-owned companies to be purchased by private sector firms. A principal argument in favor of commercial opening was that the free entry of national and international businesses, not only those involved in privatizations, would increase the depth and scope of economic activity. Given a greater number of businesses in operation, economic competition would increase, therefore creating greater levels of production, which would in turn deliver greater investment, lower prices, and improved goods and services. The fact that the majority of entering businesses would be successful international firms that employ cutting-edge technology and efficient methods of organization and production would mean that their presence in local economies would bring important spillovers, further strengthening economic conditions in local markets (UNCTAD 1992).

While many publications have fine-tuned arguments for and against the application of neoliberal-inspired policies decades after their implementation, the debate over whether these policies would fulfill their explicit or underlying goals, as they are presented here, has existed since the conception of such policies. As will be shown in the coming sections, with now almost 30 years of hindsight, the interests of MNCs have overwhelmingly prevailed over all other considerations.

CAPITAL FLOWS AND FINANCIAL OPENING

As stated, neoliberal theory has argued that financial opening would increase financial flows to underdeveloped countries, which would lead to lower local interest rates and would foster savings, investment and economic growth. However, the evidence from Latin America clearly demonstrates that financial opening has produced none of these results.

As Figure 13 1 plainly shows, capital has not flown into the region in a steady fashion, therefore preventing the materialization of the predicted secondary effects of lower interest rates and higher levels of saving and investment. Although the point is quite obvious, neoliberal-based policies of financial opening overlooked a key element of any investment, namely, that it seeks returns. As such, when foreign investments are successful for the investor, inflows of capital in the form of foreign investment will later be followed by capital outflows through the remittance of profits. Such periodization of capital inflows/outflows can be seen in Figure 13.1. After the

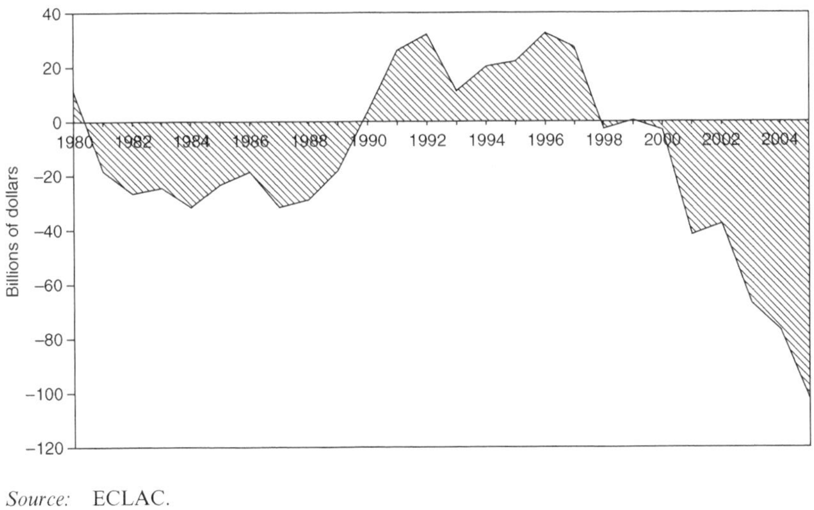

Source: ECLAC.

Figure 13.1 Latin America and the Caribbean: net inflows of capital and net transfer of resources

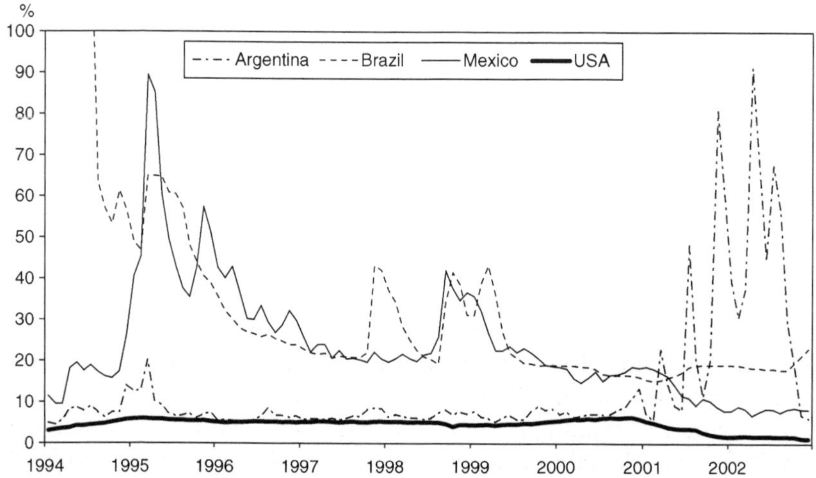

Source: IMF.

Figure 13.2 Money market interest rates

debt crisis of 1982, the servicing of external debt dominated capital flows until the commercial and financial opening of the early 1990s, which once again brought large-scale investments and capital inflows to the region. Between 1991 and 1994, portfolio investments, particularly those directed towards Mexico, represented the greatest share of capital inflows, yet after the country's crisis of 1994–95, FDI became the dominant source of capital entering the region. By 1999, after most state-owned firms of the region had been transferred to the private sector, the remittance of profits on previous investments and the ongoing payment of foreign public debt began to dominate the growing tendency of capital outflows from the region.

Within this general periodization of capital flows to and from the region, Figure 13.2 highlights another important chronology, that of the financial crisis, witnessed in Mexico in 1994–95, and in Argentina in 1995 and in 2001–02. In such moments, capital inflows sharply decline, reflected in equally sharp increases in interest rates. However, of equal note is that even in moments of relative financial calm, Latin American interest rates, particularly those of Brazil, remain well above those of the USA. Taken together, Figures 13.1 and 13.2 debunk the position that financial and commercial opening would create relatively lower interest rates and stable capital inflows to the region.

The results highlighted by Figures 13.1 and 13.2 also underline another key consideration regarding financial opening – that more volatile capital can leave a country with the same ease that it can enter. Financial opening is therefore not only a mechanism for the entry of speculative capital, but for its flight as well. The liberation of capital movements, along with other elements of financial market deregulation applied during the period examined, have opened the door to widespread capital flight, systematically derailing the achievement of the explicit goals of the WC. This outcome can be explained by both logical theory and historical experience.

On the one hand, authors such as Correa (1998) and Díaz-Alejandro (1995) affirm the direct relationship between financial opening and deregulation and Latin American financial crises, moments in which capital flight flourishes. On the other hand, even in moments of financial stability, given the historic fragility of local financial systems and the lack of confidence in them, financial liberation and elevated interest rates pervert incentives for both local saving and investment. Due in large part to this dynamic, despite higher interest rates in the region, savings rates have fallen in virtually all Latin American countries in the last 20 years, a point highlighted by Kucynsky (2003).

The Argentine experience offers a historical testimonial to this type of phenomenon. As Basualdo (2002) highlights, although the years of convertibility in Argentina[2] witnessed a complete financial liberalization, the quantity of capital that entered the country was inferior to the amount that left. The combination of high domestic interest rates and complete financial liberalization gave rise to a monetary circuit in which speculative gains made in the domestic market were not deposited in the highly fragile national banking system, where higher savings could have been channeled towards investment, but rather saved outside of the country. Gaggero (2004, p.4) describes the economic incentives of the era as creating 'an efficient system for the pumping of wealth out of the country that posed insoluble and growing demands for its financing'.

CONTRADICTIONS OF FINANCIAL LIBERALIZATION

In order to understand the disappointing results of financial opening in Latin America and the behavior of capital flows, a descriptive examination of the shortcomings of WC policies is insufficient; the underlying goals of WC initiatives must also be analyzed. As proposed at the beginning of the chapter, by examining how the interests of MNCs have prevailed over the interests of national economies and how MNCs have not adhered to the economic ideology that allowed them to displace local interests greatly supports the argument that the explicit goals of the WC were never meant to be fulfilled. Such contradictions will first be analyzed in the case of financial liberalization.

While proposing that the explicit overall goal of the WC was to foster economic growth in the region, even Williamson recognized a fundamental contradiction between this goal and WC proposals: the payment of foreign debt (Williamson 1990). If the true priority of the WC were for the region's economies to grow, foreign debt would have been pardoned. The servicing of the debt has represented an enormous and irrefutable financial burden for Latin American countries. According to the Economic Commission for Latin America and the Caribbean (ECLAC), considering only the years 1994 through 2006, Mexico, Argentina and Brazil transferred over $900 billion to the servicing of foreign debts. The most recent information from 2004 shows that the remaining external public debt between the three countries is more than $281 billion (ECLAC, information on line). Yet while authors such as Calvo (1991) argue that a renegotiation of the debt on the side of the debtors would generate distortions in the market due to moral hazard, similar arguments did not dissuade the American government from bailing out the creditors involved in the Latin American debt crisis, most notably the bank Continental Illinois.

While the debt's servicing has brought to light important contradictions between the interests of American capital and both the well-being of Latin American economies and the tenets of neoliberal ideology, such conflicts are also present in the application of the economic policies needed to keep up with debt payments. Even though policies of maintaining a fiscal surplus, elevated interest rates and an overvalued currency (all in the context of financial liberalization) have constituted a fundamental impediment to growth for countries of the region, they are largely necessary for a country to attract and retain international portfolio investment. A fiscal surplus is the strongest guarantee that a government can offer in regard to its capacity to continue debt payments. It is also the first point of the WC. At the same time, for financial investments to be profitable, relatively high interest rates must be maintained, and the exchange rate must not be allowed to devalue. However, as underdeveloped countries tend to experience lower gains in productivity and higher rates of inflation than developed countries, a stable exchange rate soon becomes overvalued.

Although maintaining a budget surplus, a stable exchange rate and high interest rates guarantee financial profit for international financial actors, these conditions systematically subvert economic growth. The reduction of public spending minimizes investment in vital sectors of the economy such as infrastructure, education and health. Elevated interest rates divert productive investment towards the financial sector, and an overvalued currency subsidizes imports while forcing down the production and profit margins of national producers. Taken as a whole, the application of the economic model of external financing is to a large degree responsible for Latin America's economic stagnation during the 1980s and 1990s.

At the same time, while restrictive public spending policies are applied in Latin America, such policies are not exercised in the economies of the USA and Europe. These countries' constant fiscal deficits have signified an import stimulus to their economies and corporations, particularly in moments of financial turbulence. After the popping of the NASDAQ bubble in 2000–2001, the American government was free to expand public spending and lower its interest rates in order to avoid a greater short-term economic downturn. This experience stands in stark contrast to the neoliberal-based policy recommendations issued from Washington during Mexico's financial crisis of 1994–95 and those of Argentina during 1995 and 2001–02, when reduced public spending and dramatically higher interest rates were imposed. As such, similar situations do not result in similar recommendations from Washington. When American and European banks are creditors to foreign actors, financial crises require one set of policies, yet when these same banks are creditors to national actors, including other banks, crisis situations call for a completely different set of policies. In situations of financial stability, the economic interests of American financial interests trump considerations of the well-being of Latin American economies. In moments of financial distress, the economic interests of American financial interests also trump economic ideology.

FOREIGN DIRECT INVESTMENT AND PRIVATIZATIONS

The policy of privatizing state-owned companies is another basic tenet of the WC. As mentioned earlier, the neoliberal viewpoint holds that state-owned companies are by nature less efficient than privately owned ones. As such, they are less capable of providing the investment and services that national economies require. By allowing such firms to be privatized, and by permitting the entry of other MNCs not involved in privatizations, neoliberal theory has argued that investment would increase, as would the number of firms operating in the economy, resulting in heightened competition, lower prices, and improved goods and services.

Justified by these arguments, foreign capital has been able to expand strongly in the region. However, despite the significant increase in FDI over the past decades, a large proportion of these investments have taken the form of mergers and acquisitions (M&A). According to figures of the *World Investment Report*, during the period examined these represent more than half of all FDI. However, despite being the authoritative source on the subject, the *World Investment Report* considers intra-firm loans and the reinvestment of earnings as FDI. When taking into account only new FDI, the proportion of M&A greatly increases. Likewise, the vast majority of M&A have focused on state-owned companies in Mexico, Brazil and Argentina. These investments have been heavily concentrated in the telecommunications sector, with the energy sector also receiving significant quantities of FDI (Vidal 2001).

Such results belie the notion that commercial and financial opening would promote the establishment of new businesses in the region. Rather, the strategy of MNCs has been to acquire established companies, and in particular those that operate in strategic areas of the economy where monopolic or oligopolic structures exist, as is the case of financial infrastructure (banks) and physical infrastructure, including highways, ports, telephony and energy.

While the number of businesses in the region has not expanded as predicted by neoliberal policy makers, the entry of MNCs in strategic sectors of the economy has also not produced the expected increases in investment. Because Latin American countries have historically suffered from a lack of physical and financial infrastructure, the argument that privatizations would create greater levels of investment, and therefore greater coverage and deeper penetration in these areas, was fundamental in the justification of privatization policies. However, in the three countries examined, rates of gross capital formation have consistently fallen since the years in which privatizations were carried out. As Vidal points out, rather than creating greater investment, the most consequential outcome of the displacement of public investment by private sources has been a significant increase in profits remitted to the home countries of MNCs (Vidal 2001, 2005), an important element in the increasing drain of the region's capital.

Latin American banking systems have experienced an analogous evolution. Until the 1980s, the Latin American state played a central role in banking through development banks and national and provincially owned commercial banks. However, due to the elimination and/or privatization of many institutions of this type, their market positions have been drastically reduced. At the same time, foreign-owned banks have greatly strengthened their positions in recent decades in the three countries examined. The entry of foreign banks was justified by the notion that multinational banks by definition are endowed with internationally diversified assets and greater access to global financial markets, granting such banks greater stability than their national peers. In addition, as large corporations with superior organizational and technological capabilities, neoliberal theory has argued that foreign banks would operate more efficiently than locally owned banks.

However, upon analyzing the Mexican case, the facts have not borne out such predictions. Just as gross capital formation represents the most relevant benchmark for measuring the compliance of private sector firms with neoliberal policy expectations in regard to the privatization of physical infrastructure, the clearest benchmark for evaluating the privatization and subsequent internationalization of financial infrastructure (banking systems) is the interest rate spread, the most common measure of a bank's operational efficiency. Since 2002, when foreign banks gained full ownership of the country's five largest banks, which account for over 80 percent of the sector's assets, profits earned through the interest rate spread as a proportion to total performing loans have exhibited a constant increase, growing from 18.63 percent in 2002 to 28.26 percent in 2006 (CNBV various years). Yet while these results highlight a clear rupture with the expectations put forth by neoliberal theory, the increased presence of foreign banks has also failed to bestow greater stability on national banking system, a point that will be analyzed next.

CONTRADICTIONS BETWEEN FDI AND PRIVATIZATIONS

In addition to not fulfilling the arguments presented by neoliberal theory, privatizations and the entry of FDI in the region present stark contradictions between the interests of MNCs and national economies and between the interests of MNCs and neoliberal ideology. As stated, the explicit goal of the WC policies to expand investment in infrastructure has not been fulfilled. However, several MNCs have been able to register significant profits from their activities in Latin America. Telefonica and Repsol are emblematic cases. Before their expansion into Latin America, the activities of both companies, which were both previously state owned, were limited to Spanish territories. But with the commercial and financial opening of Latin America, these two corporations have secured positions in monopolistic or oligopolistic sectors of national economies, where substantial profits have elevated them to the status of worldwide leaders in their respective areas (Vidal 2001). The cases of several American and European banks, which will be examined in the following section, offer similar trajectories.

While theoretical arguments in favor of privatizations have been debunked by the large gap between the benefits obtained by national economies and MNCs, the contradictions between neoliberal ideology and the interests of MNCs discredit such arguments even further. Two outstanding examples in this context are the privatizations of Aerolíneas

Argentinas and Compañía Vale do Río Doce. The first case offers a telling violation of the principal tenet of privatization ideology that dictates that states should not control companies, as at the moment of its acquisition of Aerolíneas Argentinas, the company Iberia was itself state owned. Meanwhile, the sale of the highly profitable Brazilian Compañía Vale do Río Doce lacked any ideological argument. The only explanation given for its sale was the urgency of the Brazilian government to raise funds (*Financial Times* 1997).

FDI AND BANKS

The cases of foreign banks operating in Mexico and Argentina offer even more convincing evidence of the contradictions between the well-being of local economies and the interests of MNCs and between their interests and neoliberal ideology. In Argentina's case, foreign banks gained control of over half of the local market in the second half of the 1990s. This rapid rise was due in large part to neoliberal-based policy decisions. Under the terms of convertibility, the Argentine Central Bank lost almost all capacity to act as a lender of last resort. As such, nationally owned banks became particularly vulnerable to financial distress. Conversely, as MNCs, foreign banks would be able to access international credit even in the case of a financial crisis, at which point national corporations would be subject to a rationing of international credit (Damill et al. 2003). Capitalizing on this comparative advantage, foreign banks made the explicit promise to clients that local branches and subsidiaries would be unconditionally supported by their parent companies in the event of any and all financial distress (Clarín 2002a).

However, as the crisis deepened in Argentina throughout 2001, the headquarters of foreign banks operating in the country froze their credit lines and repatriated record quantities of dollars from Argentina, creating a grave lack of funds that greatly contributed to the declaration of 'el corralito' (Página 12, 2002), the partial freeze on deposits that announced the beginning of the banking crisis in the country at the end of the year. In the midst of the crisis, several large foreign banks abandoned the Argentine market or threatened their withdrawal, sharpening the financial contraction and causing several moments of panic in the banking sectors and in the overall population (Clarín 2002b).

Such actions showed not only the absolute priority of short-term financial concerns over any ideological coherence or considerations regarding the well-being of the national economy, but also the degree of control that foreign banks can exercise over international capital flows when they hold a systemic position. This point will be further considered in the next section.

Although the case of Argentina is very different from that of Mexico, many of the same foreign banks that were protagonists in the Argentine crisis currently maintain an oligopolic control over the Mexican banking system. Likewise, their actions have discredited the arguments that accompanied their entry into the country, such as that the presence of foreign banks would elevate the efficiency of the banking system and increase the amount of credit issued. While, as mentioned, interest rate spreads remain very high by international standards, credit as a percentage of GDP has not increased since the internationalization of the banking system, despite sharp increases in consumer credit in recent years. The fact that foreign banks operate in an oligopolic market allows them to maintain interest rate spreads and commissions at levels far exceeding those of their home countries without any accompanying expansion of credit, creating a situation in which Mexican subsidiaries represent the principal centers of wealth accumulation for such banks (Girón 2005).

CAPITAL FLOWS AND FOREIGN BANKS

Although the establishment and behavior of foreign banks present many similarities with other MNCs that have entered the region through privatizations, by virtue of being one of the principal determinants and controllers of international capital flows, banks occupy a unique space both in national economies and in this chapter. During the Argentine crisis, foreign banks demonstrated the real effects of their exceptional economic power. Together with the IMF and exporting firms, foreign banks represented one of the few sources of dollars for the economy. When the government opted for economic measures contrary to the interests of foreign banks and other members of the international financial community, the IMF and foreign banks effectively shut off the flow of dollars into the country, meanwhile draining national dollar reserves through the IMF's insistence on immediate debt payment and the large-scale repatriation of dollars by foreign banks (Marshall 2008). In the midst of the deepest economic collapse in its history, international flows of capital became completely unidirectional and outward, greatly contributing to the depth of the crisis.

The fact that there has not been a similar direct confrontation between foreign banks and Mexico's national government does not negate the determining role that foreign banks play in regard to the country's capital flows. At present, the Mexican banking system does not fulfill its social function of channeling funds to business investment in the country. However, as much as the system's dysfunctionality has limited the national economy in recent years, changing conditions in international financial markets could impose a far more negative panorama for the Mexican economy. With foreign banks dominating the local banking system, national economic stability no longer depends on decisions made by domestic actors. As increased global financial distress affects international banks, their Mexican subsidiaries will likely transfer even more capital out of Mexico to strengthen conglomerates' balance sheets. If the situation further deteriorates, foreign banks may well withdraw from the local market entirely. As shown by the Argentine case, if such changes in the market's structure are made abruptly, significant financial distress could follow. The possibility that foreign banks can import financial crises, particularly when they command a dominant market position, is recognized even by the IMF (IMF 2002).

CONCLUSION

The crisis of the American economy during the 1970s produced a new economic dynamic for the entire region of Latin America. WC policies, presented and implemented under false pretenses, opened the region to capital inflows and created new opportunities for financial profitability for international actors. However, as initial investments mature, one-time capital inflows transform into consistent capital outflows. Debt payments and capital flight further augment the implacable transfer of economic surpluses out of the region, retarding local accumulation of capital, deepening social and economic inequalities within Latin American countries, and widening the gap between these economies and their developed peers. Without substantial changes in the region's economic policies, such as those that have been initiated in several South American countries, such as Argentina, the dominance of foreign capital in local economic structures will guarantee a stagnation of the region's domestic economies, accompanied by a tendency towards greater capital outflows that is already clearly visible.

NOTES

1. This chapter will focus mainly on Mexico, Brazil and Argentina, the three largest economies of Latin America and historical bellwethers of the region's economic tendencies.
2. From 1991 to 2001, Argentina maintained a one to one parity between the Argentine peso and the US dollar, commonly referred to as convertibility.

REFERENCES

Basualdo, Eduardo (2002), 'Las reformas estructurales y el Plan de Convertibilidad durante la década de los noventa. El auge y la crisis de la valorización financiera', Universidad de Buenos Aires.

Bowles, Samuel, Gordon, David M. and Weisskopf, Thomas E. (1992), 'Poderes empresariales e impasse económico: una retrospectiva estructural sobre la economía conservadora, 1979–1987', *Investigacion Económica*, no. 199, January–March, 223–47.

Calvo, Guillermo, with Jacob Frenkel (1991), 'From centrally-planned to market economy: the road from CPE to PCPE', *Staff Papers*, June, 268–99.

CEPAL, Online information, Latin America and the Caribbean Statistics.

Clarín (2002a), 7/24/02, Buenos Aires.

Clarín (2002b), 4/30/02, Buenos Aires.

Comisión Nacional Bancaria y de Valores (CNBV) (various years), *Boletín de banca mulitple.*

Correa, Eugenia (1998), *Crisis y desregulación financiera*, Mexico: UNAM, Instituto de Investigaciones Económicas – Siglo XXI.

Damill, Mario, Salvatore, Nicolás and Simpson, Lucio (2003), 'Diagnóstico y perspectivas del sistema financiero argentino II) El sistema financiero de la Argentina bajo el régimen de convertibilidad y la transición a un nuevo modelo de intermediación', CESPA, Buenos Aires.

De Bernis, Gerard (1988), *El Capitalismo Contemporaneo*, Mexico: Editorial Nuestro Tiempo.

Díaz-Alejandro, Carlos (1995), 'Adios represión financiera ¡que tal, crac financiero!', *Revista CEMLA*, **XIIX** (8), 140–72.

Dornbusch, Rudiger, with Leshie Helmers (1988), *The Open Economy: Tools for Policy Makers in Developing Countries*, Oxford: Oxford University Press.

Financial Times (1997), 'Charge of the heavy brigade: Geoff Dyer explains the implications of Brazil's elephant-sized privatisation programme', 20 August.

Fischer, S. (1997), 'Capital account liberalization and the role of the IMF', paper presented at the IMF Seminar Asia and the IMF, Hong Kong, 19 September.

Forbes, K.J. (2004), 'Capital controls: mud in the wheels of market discipline', NBER Working Paper Series, WP 10284, National Bureau of Economic Research, Cambridge, MA.

Gaggero, Jorge (2004), 'La cuestión fiscal bajo el régimen de convertibilidad (Argentina 1991–2001)', paper presented in *XIX Jornadas de Historia Económica*, Asociación Argentina de Historia Económica, San Martín de los Andes, Argentina.

Girón, Alicia (2005), *México: los bancos que perdimos*, Mexico: IIEc–UNAM.

Glyn, A., and Sutcliffe, B. (1999), 'El nuevo orden capitalista ¿global pero sin liderazgo?', in John Saxe-Fernández (ed.), *Globalización, crítica a un paradigma*, México: Plaza y Janés, pp. 103–30.

Hirst, Paul and Thompson, Graham (1996), *Globalization in Question: The International Economy and the Possibilities of Governance*, London: Polity Press.

Hymer, Stephen (1972), *Empresas Multinacionales: la internacionalizacion del capital*, Buenos Aires: Ediciones periferia.

International Monetary Fund (2002), *Global Financial Stability Report (Market Development and Issues)*, Washington, DC: IMF.

Kucynsky, P.P. (2003), 'Setting the stage', in P.P. Kucynsky and J. Williamson (eds), *After the Washington Consensus: Restarting Growth and Reform in Latin America*, Washington, DC: Institute for International Economics.
Marshall, Wesley (2008), 'Foreign banks and political sovereignty: the case of Argentina', *Review of Political Economy*, **20** (3), 355.
McKinnon, Ronald I. (1973), *Money and Capital in International Development*, Washington, DC: Brookings Institution.
Página 12 (2002), 2/18/2002, Buenos Aires.
UNCTAD (1992), *World Investment Report: TNC as Engines of Growth*, New York and Geneva: United Nations.
UNCTAD (2007), *World Investment Report: Transnational Corporations, Extractive Industries and Development*, New York and Geneva: United Nations.
Vidal, Gregorio (2001), *Privatizaciones, Fusiones y Adquisiciones: Las Grandes Empresas en América Latina*, Mexico: Anthropos.
Vidal, Gregorio (2005), 'Privatizaciones, capital extranjero y concentración económica en América Latina', in *Trayectorias Revista de Ciencias Sociales*, No. 17, Universidad Autónoma de Nuevo León. September – December. Mexico.
Williamson, J. (1990), 'What Washington means by policy reform', in J. Williamson (ed.) (1990), *Latin American Adjustment. How Much Has Happened?*, Washington, DC: Institute for International Economics, p. 8.
Wolfson, Martin H. (1986), Financial Crisis, New York: M.E. Sharpe.

14. Inflation targeting by the 'tyrannical auctioneer': the predominance of a normative approach in monetary policy

Etelberto Ortiz Cruz

1. THE ISSUES

How is it possible that the usual recipe for orthodox monetary policy persists, in spite of its extremely feeble theoretical structure? This chapter argues that the reason rests on its normative base, and not on its theoretical structure. This is evident because its main line of policy intervention does not arise from its price, monetary or macro theory, but from its normative view. The chapter presents an alternative framework to analyze the way in which inflation targeting works in a small open economy.

The new monetary consensus revolves around a model of 'inflation targeting', which is concerned with coordination and the compromise of the Central Bank (CB) to strive for one particular rate of inflation. That orthodox model can be reduced to three equations: the first is a sort of IS curve; the second is a sort of Phillips augmented expectations model; and the third might be something like a Taylor rule.[1] Information and compromise presumably create a more transparent framework, reducing discretion through a reference price: i, the rate of interest. Within this framework the presumption is that monetary policy is neutral and the level of activity in the economy is determined by a host of real factors such as technological change, capital accumulation and so on. Inflation is conceived predominantly as a demand phenomenon and to some extent also as a cost impact. The effect of asset inflation and exchange rate overvaluation plays no role in that model. Disturbances can exist only for market or government failure.

In that model, the level of economic activity is a given and its long-run equilibrium cannot be altered by any government action. Therefore monetary policy implies an agenda that follows straightforwardly from its normative view, namely:

- *Rules are preferable to discretion* This is meant to reduce the enormous power vested in the CB in order to avoid unnecessary impacts on private agents, particularly financial intermediaries.
- *Accountability* is meant to enforce responsible decision making on monetary policy makers.
- *The neutrality of monetary policy* cannot be understood as a real condition, but as a task for policy makers, namely, a call not to induce biased effects through monetary policy that may be harmful to some while privileging others. Real impacts are meant to increase or reduce effective demand and output, without any distributive impacts.
- Monetary policy becomes the leading policy, over and above other policies, particularly trade and fiscal policies. Evidently the main concern is the rate of inflation, while growth, overindebtedness and unemployment turn into secondary targets.

For the orthodox policy agenda the rest of the issues are by and large secondary or conditional. For example, for monetarism mark I the CB exerts control through the quantity of money, while for monetarism mark II it does so through the rate of interest.

Nevertheless, the situation for a small open economy poses a threefold difficulty:

- Recent models place the emphasis on targeting inflation expectations and the rate of interest (Taylor 1993, 2001), but neglects completely the particular characteristics of a small open economy, as is evident in Clarida et al. (2001). They assume that an open economy is isomorphic to a closed economy, and the price equations ignore any incidence of an external price linkage.[2]
- The dynamics of adjustment of interest and exchange rates is complex. It is not reduced to assets and money substitution; it goes all the way into the pricing structure. Therefore nothing is clear about the transition from one state of equilibrium to another. The sole consideration of the welfare properties of two points of partial equilibrium is by and large insufficient to understand the dynamics of adjustment.
- Inflation targeting through (E, i) can turn into contradictory impacts because they can give rise to differing expectations on inflation rates and adjustment paths. The difficulty is not reduced to different time paths for adjustment and equilibrium, as in Ball (2001). The difficulty is that both variables go through different channels of incidence,[3] but necessarily have an impact on real prices and distribution.

But conventional wisdom in monetary theory seems to be at odds with the common practice of day-to-day operation of monetary policy. It reasserts the neutrality of money and monetary policy even if the CB does not fix the necessary amount of money every day.[4] The actual direction of monetary policy appears as a basic price vector (BPV) for the economy, namely the rate of interest, and for an open economy we also have to consider the exchange rate, (E, i).[5] The quantity of money then adjusts consequently under any CB regime. But the structure of prices and distribution cannot remain the same.

The open economy introduces complexity, because it has to give proper consideration to two characteristics:

- The monetary policy price vector must consider that there is a very complex interaction between the rate of interest and the exchange rate; that generally is not considered in 'macro' and 'microfundamental' models.[6] The path of incidence has to be analyzed within the pricing process.
- Those two prices, the interest rate and exchange rate, are crucial for the profitability of investment, distribution of income, and overall for the stability of the system, particularly for the real and financial sectors.

Consequently, the theoretical framework necessary to analyze monetary policy is a pricing structure where it is possible to consider the different impacts of both the interest rate and the exchange rate on a price structure that is not necessarily homogeneous. Pricing in such an economy is always in the world of actual monetary transactions, and is open for adjustment to the vector of basic prices they receive, the exchange rate E, and the rate of interest i. That vector (E, i), even if it is open for the interplay of different markets, has a strong interaction through the capital market, but always on the basis of the price vector the CB is sending to the economy. The role of the CB is to find the right price vector for the economy. In a small open economy that task goes even further, also fixing the minimum wage w, which in turn regulates the wage bargain. Nevertheless, for the time being the incidence of w will not be fully analyzed for the sake of simplicity.[7]

The essential proposition is that actual monetary policy can best be understood in a model that builds the relationship between the real and monetary side through the structure of pricing. The link is built between pricing and the investment decision. This is the form in which concerned agents, firms and banks, decide the amount of investment and prices for a particular BPV, namely: (E, i, w), and then decide a certain demand of credit. Monetary policy then is essential to form the magnitudes of effective demand and the basic framework in which firms decide their price vector. The coherence of the BPV is to be realized at the end of the process if firms are able to pay back their debts and/or recover the capital advanced in production. Within this context the neutrality of money is meaningless.[8] The general macroeconomic framework is conceived as in a circuit model, as in Rochon (1999).

The working of a BPV (*E*, *i*, *w*) may have a strong resemblance to the standard model of the Walrasian auctioneer. Let us recall that the image of the Walrasian auctioneer is a figurative construct about the form in which pricing forms a general equilibrium price vector. A price vector is sent by the auctioneer, and the excess demand and supply equations, one for every commodity in the economy, provide him with a disequilibrium signal. Then the auctioneer kindly adjusts the price vector, observing the sign of those excess demand equations. The adjustment process continues until every agent is in equilibrium because he can sell and buy as much as he wants, given a certain budgetary constraint. It is only then that exchange can take place.

The operation of the BPV sent by the CB takes three forms:

- There is one institution, the CB, that works as a real auctioneer – not through the auction of dollars or debt instruments, but through the basic price vector targeted by monetary policy: (*E*, *i*, *w*).
- The CB has a figuration of equilibrium from a set of balances that it can actually observe, and are of its own concern, namely: the current account deficit, the balance with the banking system, and the balance with the public sector.[9]
- The CB does not receive, and seems not to be interested in, the actual balance of the main economic agents in the economy, that is firms and workers. Therefore the accumulation of unused production capacity, unemployment and debts is ignored.

The last two characteristics led me to name that model the 'Tyrannical Auctioneer' (TA), because he who sets the basic price vector takes no account of the impact of the BPV on economic agents. This is not to be characterized as rigidity. The TA actually adjusts daily, but not necessarily in response to the disequilibrium perceived by firms. Therefore it is possible that the TA considers he is doing his job very well in terms of his own tasks and balances. He might even consider he has been flexible in responding to market signals, as in a floating model, though being unable to observe the difficulties of concerned agents, that is firms, in order to reach those price signals.

The chapter is presented in four sections. The second introduces a model of investment decision and pricing, including the impact of the rate of exchange and the rate of interest, related to the investment decision. The model is an extension of Ortiz (2003, 2004), following the essentials of Eichner (1984) about the need to consider financial costs in pricing behavior, but now including the difficulties introduced by a financial system that provides credit and requires to be funded in two currencies. Our contention is that the actual and more important difficulty for the system to close, that is, for firms to be able to pay back their debts, has been the blindness of the monetary policy model of the TA, ignoring private deficits. The blindness is introduced by the normative view of the TA. The last section advances some preliminary conclusions on monetary policy and institutional reform.

2. INVESTMENT DECISION: PRICING, FINANCE AND MONETARY POLICY

The essential macroeconomic view rests on a simple circuit model, as in Rochon (1999), which can be represented through the scheme presented in Figure.14.1. The solution of the model is advanced on two levels.

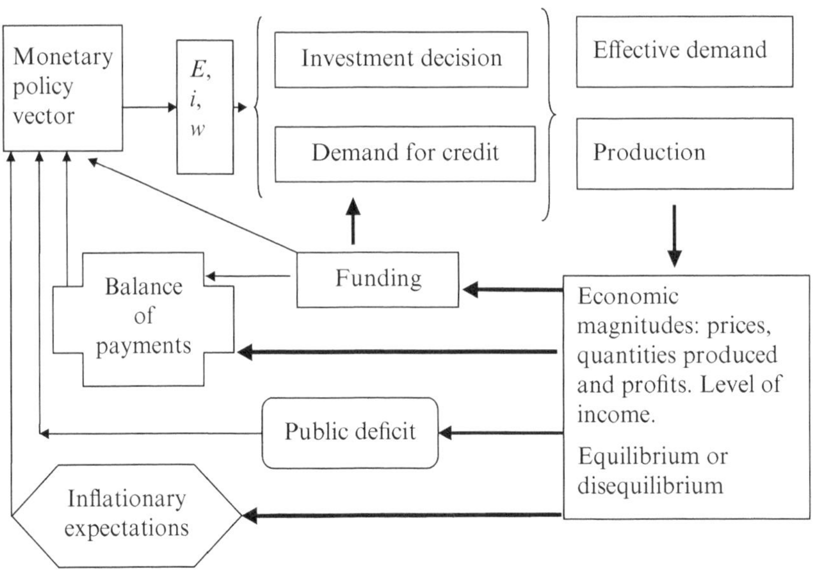

Figure 14.1 Monetary policy in a circuit theory model

- The first considers the whole structure of the model, where the investment decision is the initial step in response to a BPV sent by the TA. It rests on solving the investment–pricing decision as a dual.
- The second reconsiders the adjustment paths open for firms given their price equations. It is shown that the pattern of response to an anti-inflationary policy depends on the conditions of firms, as in Minsky's classification, and on actual monetary policy.

This chapter deals with the first problem and suggests a first approach to some of the issues raised by the second. The investment decision is at the core of the model, from the point of view of macro aggregates, but also for the structure of prices and financial proficiency. But the essentials of the economic policy framework are set by monetary policy.

Assuming a one-period economy, the amount of capital advanced as investment is:

$$I_i = \Sigma\, x_{ij}\, P_j + X^m\, P^m\, E + wL_i, \qquad (14.1)$$

which can also be read as fixed plus variable costs plus financial costs; therefore the amount due to be recovered is: $\Sigma\, x_{ij}\, P_j + X^m\, P^m\, E + wL_i + F_i(i)$, plus a profit, Π, as a residual. $F_i(i)$ represents the financial cost necessary to make the investment.

Therefore the investment decision calls for an optimization of the relationship of the value of the capital advanced, I, and the productive resources bought for production, given the outstanding prices $\{P_i / P_j, E, i, w\}$. The optimization problem considers a given technology, and the basic price vector set by the TA. For the time being we can assume constant returns to scale. The budget restriction is set by the size of the amount of capital available, that is, $I_i = H_i + F_i(i) + F_i(i^*)E$, where H is the capital owned and F the capital obtained through finance from either domestic or external sources.

It is important to realize that in fact we have three analytical problems:

1. The investment decision by firms, which in turn has two associated problems: the investment–pricing and the investment–finance decisions. These problems are approached by considering them as a dual.
2. The balance of the TA, concerning at least three balances within his realm: the banks' balance the external account balance and the public deficit. This aspect will not be dealt with here; see, however, Ortiz (2004).
3. The incidence of monetary policy through the basic price vector on firms and the way that feeds back to inflationary expectations and behavior.

Firms maximize the value of the produce obtained, $P_i\, Q_i$, with the inputs $\{\Sigma\, x_{ij}\, P_j + X^m\, P^m\, E + wL_i\}$ advanced as investment, given the actual restriction of capital available, which is $\{I_i = H_i + F_i(i) + F_i(i^*)E\}$. The amount expected to be recovered: $P'_i\, Q'_i$. Therefore the firm's maximization problem has two parts. The first is the investment–pricing decision:

$$[\Sigma\, x_{ij}\, P_j + X^m\, P^m\, E + wL_i\,]\,(1 + \pi^*_i\,)_i + F_i\,(i)) \geq P'_i\, Q'_i \qquad (14.2)$$

This states that the firm would be willing to invest in the means of production necessary to obtain certain amount of production Q'_i at a price that reflects the expectation P'_i to recover the capital advanced.

The second relates to the investment–finance decision:

$$I_{it} = < [(\Sigma\, x_{ij}\, P_j + X^m\, P^m\, E + wL_i\,]\,(1 + \pi^*_I\,)_{it} + F_i\,(i)_t)\,] \qquad (14.3)$$

This states that surplus obtained should pay for the credit obtained plus the outstanding rate of interest.

The TA expresses his policy targets through the basic price vector. The targets are a particular rate of inflation p and a certain amount of external savings to serve the external debt. Therefore the TA would recognize the result of his policy instrument in any deviation of the actual rate of inflation p to the one targeted ($p - \mathbf{p}$) and through changes in external reserves. In the usual targeting model, E would be compromised to stand for an inflationary expectation as an 'anchor'. Consequently the main adjustment variable at hand is the rate of interest. In the presence of an important external debt, the CB will try to control the external spread, and might be reactive to a loss in external reserves and commercial banks' deficits.

The difficulty is with the capability to assess and react to the likely effects of such policies. Next we shall analyze them in the analytical framework provided by the TA model.

The firm's investment problem has two mutually related processes. One is about pricing, namely, that the amount produced and sold should approach the expected value $P'_i\, Q'_i$, which was at the core of the investment decision. The other relates the investment decision to its form of finance and the expected cash flow, given the price expected. The main proposition is that the investment–pricing–finance conditions form a dual. Therefore it is an approach to inflation from capital theory, which in the post-Keynesian tradition demands a model based on the investment decision.

If the price equation is expressed in unit terms, the investment–finance decision for firm k can be represented as the maximization of the rate of profit after paying for current and financial costs:

$$\Pi^*_k = \phi_i [I_k (P'_k) - [(\Sigma a_{ij} P_j + a^m P^m E + wl_i) (1 + \pi_i)] - f_i (i)_i)] \tag{14.4}$$

where (P'_k) is the gap between forward and spot price of the kth firm. In a way (P'_k) is an implicit function of the outstanding BPV: $(P'_k| (E', i', w'))$. Therefore $I_k (P'_k | (E', i', w'))$ represents the marginal efficiency of capital as an investment function in response to the BPV. (Given the complexity and extension of the optimization problem, it is presented in the Appendix.) The reaction functions obtained for the pricing problem are:

$$\frac{dp_k}{dE} = \frac{I'_{kp(E)} - a^m P^m (1 + \pi_k)}{I'_{kp(p)} - (a_{kj}) (1 + \pi_k)} \geq or \leq 0 \tag{14.5}$$

$$\frac{dp_k}{di} = \frac{I'_{kp(i)} - (1 + f'_k(i))}{I'_{k(p)} - a_{kj}(1 + \pi_k)} \geq or \leq 0 \tag{14.6}$$

$$\frac{dp_k}{dw} = \frac{I'_{kp(w)} - (l_k) (1 + \pi_k)}{I'_{k(p)} - a_{kj}(1 + \pi_k)} \geq or \leq 0 \tag{14.7}$$

There are 16 possible cases, depending on the size and sign of the investment elasticity coefficient. Essentially two general patterns are considered, such that the price gap between spot and forward prices gives rise either to additional investment or to inflationary pressure.

Equation (14.5) shows the alternative reaction patterns of prices to variations in the exchange rate. It will be positive when devaluation induces a price adjustment such that price increments induce an increase in investment higher than the increase in costs of imported inputs. And it will be negative when the induced price increment induces more inflation and a reduction of investment.

Equation (14.6) shows the alternative reaction patterns of prices to variations in the rate of interest. It will be positive when the price impact induces an increase in investment higher than the increase in financial costs and is high enough to absorb the impact on profitability. And it will be negative in two cases: (1) when the increase in financial costs is higher than the investment elasticity coefficient, and (2) when firms look for an increase in profitability through an increase in prices rather than through productivity.

Equation (14.7) shows the alternative reaction patterns of prices to variations in the wage rate. It will be positive when a wage rise allows a higher investment rate, because the rise of productivity is higher than the

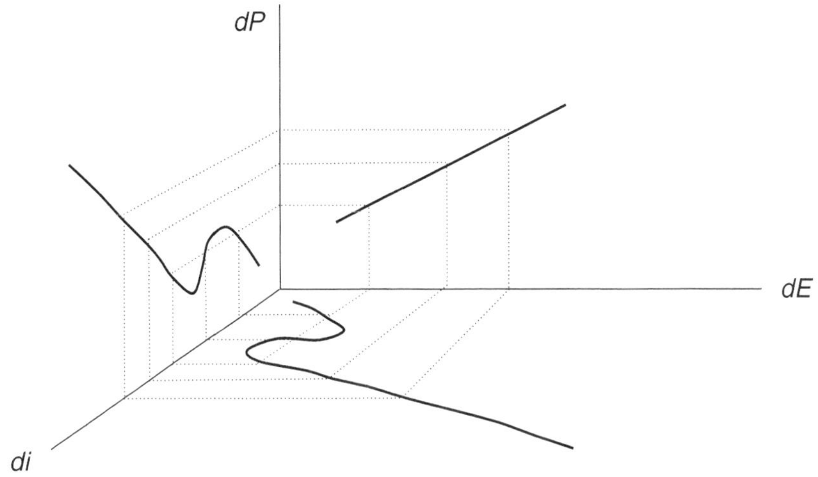

Figure 14.2 *Price reaction functions to* dE *and* di

increase in labor costs. Consequently wage increases would not lead to a distributional inflation race. It will be negative otherwise.

The usual policy trade-off between rates of interest and exchange rates can be analyzed through the following expression:

$$\frac{dE}{di} = \frac{I'_{kp(i)} - (1 + f'_k(i))}{I'_{kp(E)} - a^m p^m (1 + \pi_k)} \geq or \leq 0 \qquad (14.8)$$

The (E, i) relationship shows itself to be very sensitive to the elasticity coefficient of finance and the demands for imported inputs. This is a complex relationship for two reasons. First, when $f'_i(i)$ rises, π diminishes. For inflation targeting to work, it is necessary for the numerator to be positive. For equation (14.8) to show a negative slope it is necessary for the denominator to be negative; that is, the increase in import costs needs to be higher than the increase in domestic prices to induce an increase in investment. This condition can only be fulfilled at all if inflation is at a low level. Therefore the condition for inflation targeting success is that inflation is not seen as too high by firms. Then, how is it that inflation targeting can work when inflation is indeed a problem? Firms should be forced to absorb the increase in financial costs without increasing prices through a reduction in the profit margin. But that would not be a condition leading to higher rates of investment and level of activity. In fact it should lead to a reduction of income and employment that does not necessarily lead to curbing inflation. Figure 14.2 presents the impact on inflation of changes in interest and exchange rates. It

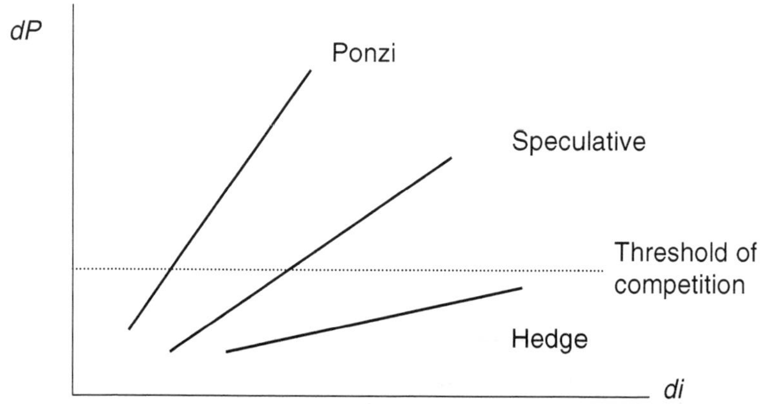

Figure 14.3 *Firms' financial condition and their interest-price reaction*

makes it clear that it can only be effective within a small range of values for (*E*, *i*). After that the impact can turn entirely adverse.

Therefore the elasticity coefficients are likely to be small or even negative. But if both sides are negative, the (*E*, *i*) relationship can show a positive slope, therefore feeding back again for inflation increase. In this case further increases in the cost of finance would render a loss and push firms to look for a nominal adjustment.

The orthodox case reduces to a small fraction of the price reaction function. The analysis from the point of view of prices in fact shows that the policy trade-off is between price (nominal) adjustment and productivity, given the firm's financial conditions.

2.1 Pricing and Firms' Financial Conditions

Given the price model, profitability essentially depends on labor productivity and the wage rate. Net profitability depends on a twofold effect of the rate of interest: the impact on financial costs; and the impact on the level of economic activity. If real (direct) costs are sensitive to the level of activity (either increasing returns or diminishing returns to scale), we should expect a differentiated response to increments of the rate of interest. There are three cases, presented in Figure 14.3, that demand our attention:

First, a small f' coefficient, slightly sensitive to changes in the rate of interest, which can be associated to the notion of a firm in a hedge position. The speculative case, with a medium f', more sensitive to variations in the rate of interest. And the third, with a high f', very sensitive to changes in the rate of interest, which is the case of a Ponzi condition.

Figure 14.3 represents how prone firms would be to look for adjustment in nominal prices, given their financial condition. Overall the impact of a monetary policy increasing the rate of interest depends on the actual composition of firms across the economy. Theory and experience suggest that permanent shocks would tend to move firms from hedge to speculative and from speculative to Ponzi conditions (Kregel 2004). Therefore, for a rise in interest rates to induce a reduction of inflation, two conditions would be necessary:

- The assumption that there is no change in the financial conditions of firms, which amounts to assuming that firms would be ready to cope with the impact on profitability.
- The additional financial cost will not be transferred to prices, because there is another policy instrument that actually stops prices, the threshold of competition, that will be at a lower level, according to the overvaluation of the exchange rate.

The need to adjust nominal prices has to be contrasted with the capabilities of a firm to succeed in terms of a real adjustment in respect of the other firms. This depends not only on competitive conditions but also on the actual structure, which allows to adjust to changes in the BPV. Therefore part of the adjustment is absorbed through real prices and part through nominal adjustment.

Consequently successful reduction of inflation through a rise of interest rates essentially works through the destruction of firms' profitability, therefore with real costs to the level of income and employment. It might be argued that getting rid of Ponzi firms is positive for the economy. But moving all firms to their limit can lead to a condition of systemic financial instability and crisis. That is why the leading question should be: why can a firm not find another path of adjustment except to adjust its price level? I find three reasons:

1. The need to adjust to some other price increments, either wages or input prices. This sort of adjustment may come through inflationary expectations, and has also been analyzed as a cost-push effect.
2. The need to adjust because there are windows of opportunity given by market conditions. This may include effects of demand and profitability, and could be partly demand driven. But it may also imply looking for an increase in the rate of profit. A real adjustment will then be induced.
3. The need to adjust given that its profitability *vis-à-vis* financial conditions is untenable. This is a situation not considered properly

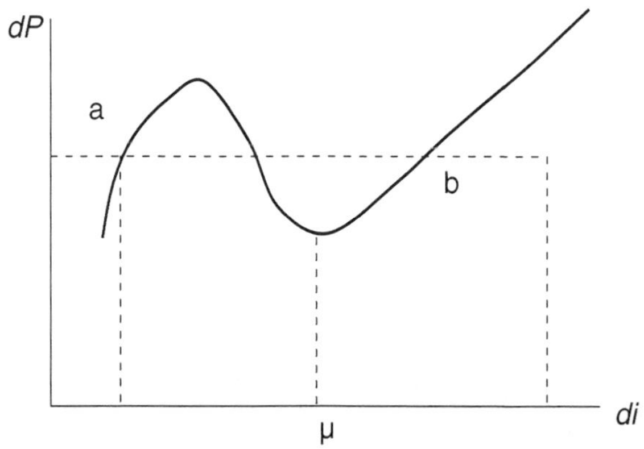

Figure 14.4 *Mapping of {dP di} bifurcation in the face of inflation targeting policies*

in the literature when inflation is induced by restrictive monetary policies.

The notion that an increase in the rate of interest induces a reduction in the level of investment and activity may find support either in neoclassical and new Keynesian literature or in some post-Keynesian views. But the marginal efficiency of capital is the result of the comparison of spot with future prices, with the spot and the expected rate of interest. If the contrast results in contango,[10] it turns into a reduction of the rate of investment, but if and only if firms are unable to increase their future prices. Notionally, then, two paths of reaction appear to a firm: either to reduce its rate of investment, or try to increase its actual prices. That indeed depends on competition and the level of economic activity. But it depends largely on monetary policy: if the CB increases the rate of interest with the intention to reduce inflation, there is but one possibility open for firms working in Ponzi and speculative conditions: to look for a nominal adjustment, even if temporarily.

But competition pushes back prices, reducing the rate of inflation in so far as it also pinches profitability across every firm. This can be coped with for a short while by speculative firms, up to the point where they are driven to the limit to turn into Ponzi conditions.

Once a point like μ in Figure 14.4 is reached, inflationary expectations will bifurcate in the face of a basic price vector set by the monetary authority. This is likely to occur after a point like μ, where further increases in the rate of interest would force firms to look once again for higher nominal prices. Inflation targeting, then, is subject to very stringent conditions about the presumed paths of adjustment open for firms. A policy proceeding otherwise becomes contradictory.

2.2 Inflation Targeting and Information

There is another difficulty introduced by the price signal itself, namely, a higher nominal rate of interest carries the information that the inflationary expectation is higher than the rate already recognized, therefore hitting the expected rate of profit.[11] Firms then might try to pass the impact on to consumers. This is associated with a fall in real wages and effective demand.

But the core of the argument is between the structure of prices and pricing behavior in relationship to the pricing process induced by monetary policy through the BPV on (w, E, i). The very notion of inflation targeting rests on this relationship and not solely on 'inflationary expectations', as if these were to work in a sort of vacuum of pricing structure.

Let us recall that inflation targeting partly works through information. In the usual expectations approach, if: ($i = r + \boldsymbol{p}$), where $\boldsymbol{p}$ the expected rate of inflation, carries and projects the CB inflationary expectation. In a world of rational expectations every concerned agent in the economy knows the likely distribution of values for p at all times. Therefore, for an increase in the nominal rate of interest, no distributional impacts are expected as everybody is able to adjust, including nominal and real wages. If 'rational agents' know in advance the real value of r,[12] and the nominal rate of interest, a rise in the rate of interest informs three conflicting propositions:

- agents will have to face a higher rate of inflation;
- they will have to face an increase in financial costs and a reduction of effective demand; or
- their present capital stock is excessive or is overvalued.

Whichever is the understanding of the message, a rise in interest rates pushes in the direction of trouble signaled by Minsky. The real issue for firms is: how to adjust? In the rational expectations approach the whole process of adjustment is ignored, while the crucial question is: why should an increase in the nominal rate of interest lead to a reduction in the rate of inflation? It is evident that it is not through a reduction of M_h, because such a reduction will occur as another consequence of the reduction of decisions to invest. In fact a reduction in M_h may come about through an increase in liquidity preference as a reaction to the uncertainty introduced by inflation targeting itself.

The case of the open economy is far more complex. Inflation targeting involves two major difficulties. The first is the relationship between the nominal exchange rate and the rate of inflation. This can be analyzed through changes in the real rate of exchange, which reflects the difference in rates of inflation between the domestic economy and the rest of the world. The fact that the CB pegs to a particular exchange rate does not imply that the expected rate of inflation should move on a par with inflation in the rest of the world. In fact it can only tell us that the CB is ready to penalize domestic firms for their attempts to adjust through higher nominal prices.

The market is then informed by two differing and not necessarily converging notions for the inflation path:

- the one implicit in the rate of interest, and
- another, implicit in the exchange rate.

It is evident that they may not necessarily be the same or convergent. The impact on profitability is complex, because it also carries a long-run impact of depressing the growth of productivity. The immediate impact on the capital value of export activities is evident. In spite of the real cost, nevertheless, usually in this case the issue reduces to a bet on how long the CB will be able to maintain that rate.

The impact through the credit channel can be consistent with a reduction in the level of economic activity, but not necessarily with a reduction in nominal prices. That depends on the form of the pricing functions.

Now it is evident that if the CB looks to reduce the rate of inflation through an increment of the rate of interest, it might well obtain the obverse. The sole point of a minimum rate of inflation is consistent with a particular rate of adjustment of the exchange rate at E' and with a maximum for the rate of interest at point μ, where we have: min $\{dE, di, dP\}$. With a fixed rate of exchange, ($dE \rightarrow 0$), an increase of the rate of interest can only move to lower rates of inflation when the economy is to the left of μ, because in that phase the increase in di is associated with an adjustment of speculative and hedge firms, which is feasible with a reduction of dP. Nevertheless, once that point is reached, to the right of μ any further increase in the rate of interest leads to an increase in the rate of inflation. Increments of the rate of interest can only weaken the financial position of otherwise healthy firms, pushing them to look for another kind of adjustment. If the economy were to be in that position, the optimal policy would be a reduction of the rate of interest with a non-overvalued real exchange rate.

3. INFLATION TARGETING THROUGH THE BPV PRODUCES A BIFURCATION BETWEEN FIRMS AND BANKS AND IN 'INFLATIONARY EXPECTATIONS'

Why, then, is it that the rule of increasing the rate of interest to fight inflation is so popular? The reason is that it can seem effective for a short while, because by pegging the exchange rate, imports can restrain domestic prices. However, it is not a higher rate of interest that stops inflation but the fixed exchange rate. Therefore the actual short-run price anchor turns out to be the exchange rate. In this case the higher rate of interest is powerless to stop inflation. This policy has a twofold impact: a drop in productivity across the economy, given the threshold of competition; and a growing gap between inflationary expectations induced by the exchange rate and the interest rate. Consequently, the exchange rate is highly questionable as a consistent anchor on price expectations, not only because a small open economy does not have unlimited access to supplies of external savings. Any CB knows that such a policy opens a gap for a speculative attack on the rate of exchange that unavoidably develops into sudden and violent inflation episodes. This can have very high costs not only in terms of stability, financial conditions, and in the level of income and employment. The sole reason to increase the rate of interest might be to widen the gap between the external and the domestic rates in order to attract external short-term capital flows, just to bridge the growing trade deficit.

If inflationary expectations consistently follow the movement in the rate of inflation, the sole way in which the monetary authority can manage both is if they are the same, let us say at dP_1. Therefore the pair (E, i) might be consistent with a particular inflationary expectation $E(P_i)$ at (E_1, i_1), the one at which the rate of change in dE and di are at a level dP_1. The difficulty arises from the fact that two rates of change for the interest rate might be consistent with dP_1, the first with a decreasing rate of inflation, the second with a growing rate of inflation. This problem stems from the fact that inflation expectations are not stationary at point a or b in Figure 14.4. If a divine inspiration were to direct the TA to set the vector (E_1, i_1) consistent with point μ, at least he could argue that the vector chosen would make inflationary expectation for both prices consistent. Nevertheless, once a BPV prevails, inflation targeting policies force the CB to be compromised to stand for it, which again is contradictory to the essentials of inflation targeting itself.

What is characteristic of a point like μ? From what we have observed it is not a fixed E, but a rate that could have the lower rate of adjustment, given the rate of change in rates of interest. Such a rate can be one that keeps domestic prices aligned with foreign prices, namely, a constant real exchange rate, not a constant nominal exchange rate. A lower rate of adjustment to the exchange rate means looking for a lower rate of inflation than the rest of the world, which would have to be paid for dearly. This indeed can be a step towards 'flexible rules'.

One of the leading ideas in the presentation already advanced is that the CB acts as the 'tyrannical auctioneer' (TA) because it is ready and able to recognize that there are disequilibria associated with its BPV (E, i, w) when there is a growing disequilibrium in the balance of payments and in the financial condition between commercial banks and firms. According to our analysis, the TA should also recognize that there is a disequilibrium induced by monetary policy when there is a growing fiscal deficit with constant public expenditure. The issue then is if a CB, following the usual standard orthodox rule, just as the TA, can have a proper understanding of the actual impact of its policy. The argument is that it cannot because the standard reading of its own balances may not show individual firms and government disequilibria.

The point in dispute is that macroeconomic equilibrium may occur with individual disequilibria. According to Minsky (1986) and Kregel (2004), such disequilibria end up in systemic financial instability. What is the main signal of individual firms' disequilibria? No doubt one is the financial instability syndrome, as Minsky and Kregel argued. But there is another equally important: the fall in productivity associated with the recessive conditions that standard policy rules impose. Therefore another idea for flexible rules might be that the CB should not wait to see growing non-performing assets in the banks to stop the increment of the rate of interest.

Usually a target inflation policy pegs to the rate of exchange and increases the gap between the domestic and the international rates of interest. The result could be that instead of one problem, we would have four additional problems:

- A growing trade deficit
- A growing fiscal deficit
- A growing external saving deficit accompanied by growing non-performing assets in banks' portfolios
- A continuous deterioration of the financial system (Kregel 2004; Ortiz 2004).

But there may be five, not just four, problems, because the issue is if, in the presence of those growing deficits, there is a credible argument for inflationary expectations to be curbed. The line of reasoning already advanced is that there is no reason to accept that inflationary expectations should be reduced. They have been repressed at the cost of financial stability for the whole economy. Whether commercial banks and the CB like it or not, the other path of adjustment opens its way – increasing valueless liabilities for the banking system. From experience we know that the limit comes when the international financial community considers it no longer feasible to accept additional external debt, neither private nor public. This is a point of bifurcation, namely a crisis.

Once the devaluation frees the repressed inflation, overshooting may contribute to accelerating inflation, which generally would be accompanied by further increases of the nominal and real rates of interest. The inflation bubble may go as far that the CB is unable to stand for a credible policy and introduces alternative adjustment dynamics. Inflation targeting under these conditions can work for a very short while only if the real expected rate of interest is almost nil or even negative, in order to consolidate the financial position of leading firms: hedge and speculative firms. In the long run, what turns out to be the actual inflation anchor, no doubt, is the wage rate, regrettably on the back of the labor class. Note that w is also part of the BPV.

But we have also reached another important result. It is no longer possible to say that, *ex ante*, inflation targeting is necessarily consistent under any condition. The reason is that the core issue is the trade-off between inflation versus productivity, and this cannot be solved through increments in the rate of interest. If inflation is a viable way of adjustment for firms, instead of looking for better productive and competitive capabilities, then inflation targeting necessarily leads to financial fragility and not to growing productivity.

The main difficulty in the long run is that inflation targeting actually eliminates the more important source of adjustment for economies facing long-run or structural inflationary pressures, that is, its productivity growth. It kills the possibility for firms to introduce dynamic responses, technological, organizational and financial, to respond to disequilibria. From a dynamic perspective it destroys the virtuous circle of productivity and accumulation that is at the root of a reasonably well-ordered operating capital market.

Which path of adjustment is actually open for firms? Essentially that depends on monetary policy. But in a context of a contracting economy, firms are pushed to increase their level of indebtedness or to push for higher prices. This has been an important means of adjustment induced by financial reforms, and not because firms hide information from the banks. Banks might be interested in preserving firms, even ignoring if they are Ponzi, if for no other reason than because otherwise they might have to face a bigger problem if they go bankrupt. And this may well be the road for systemic instability and financial fragility.

Therefore what we actually find is that inflation targeting formed from a particular price vector (*E*, *i*, *w*), although it is particularly directed to work within the first two adjustment mechanisms, is systematically biased towards a rather poor performance on both paths. What is even more paradoxical is that monetary policy, oriented to work through the price adjustment and the capital reallocation paths, necessarily diminishes or even destroys the third means of adjustment, which is actually more important, and necessarily the means with the greater potential to create a real and strong capital market.

The dominant discourse about rules has led to the independence of CBs, although in no way is it a guarantee that monetary policy can be made neutral or can be run properly in the best interest of society. Globalization and the current policy model turned monetary policy into an extremely important component of everyday decision making. The rule cannot be reduced to 'make monetary policy neutral', because such a thing cannot be done. Therefore, if monetary policy cannot be neutral in any meaningful way, a call for a new institutional device is in order. The TA is extremely powerful to define economic performance, resource allocation and the distribution of income. The imagined neutrality of monetary policy can only contribute to poor policy performance and crisis.

The proposition that the BPV is decided by the CB in fact amounts to saying that it cannot be formed by market forces in any straightforward way. This is not to deny that there are market forces at play. The point at issue is if they can 'form' the market. It is the conviction that market forces by themselves cannot provide a stable operation for those prices contained in the BPV that has led to the actual economic model.

The sole piece of advice in the direction of 'inflation targeting' and 'flexible rules' is that, in order to reduce the impact on productivity and the level of income, it is better to settle for a rate of exchange that fixes the real rate of exchange around unity. This will put the rate of inflation at the level of the rest of the world and reduce the need for a very wide gap for the domestic interest rate. It will also improve the conditions under which the financial system can run, in so far as it will not hurt otherwise healthy firms. In the long run it should help to avoid speculative attacks and sudden devaluations.

It is evident that the critique of the TA is a call for imagination in the design of new institutions. An alternative should be able to respond to the task of an efficient and reasonably good direction for the whole economy. In a democratic society, such a task cannot be granted to a group of 'wise men' on the grounds of 'CBs' independence', while the whole economy is not independent of monetary policy. Therefore the call is not for 'flexible rules', but for a different institutional environment with societal development at its heart.

NOTES

1. For a broad review of the representation of the new consensus models, see Arestis and Sawyer (2006) and Lavoie (2004, 2006). A critical analysis is also in Smithin (2004).
2. This is also true of a number of models, as in the so-called 'new consensus'; see Allsopp and Vines (2000).
3. New voices come from CBs' orthodoxy, calling for a new approach that Weber, et al. (1991) call 'flexible rules' in order to highlight a growing concern with the 'real impacts' of monetary policy.
4. As in Blinder (1998).
5. See Alvarez et al. (2001), Bernanke and Mishkin (1997) and Woodward (2001).
6. The 'new consensus model' for monetary policy would generally include some form of an IS equation, another kind of Taylor rule and a third that would resemble something like a Phillips curve. For an extensive critique of this model see Lavoie (2004, 2006).
7. Wage control through monetary policy is inherited from the period of 'incomes policies' where price and wage control arose as a necessary tool to curb inflation. Wage control policies were introduced to last, and now form an essential part of monetary policy.
8. There is a huge literature on the presumed 'neutrality' or 'super-neutrality' of money, which will be ignored here for space considerations.
9. An important literature exists questioning the relevance of this result, because it gives rise to an equilibrium that might not be related at all to monetary transactions (Hahn 1985).
10. See Davidson (1994, pp. 67–9).
11. If the CB is unable to identify the 'natural' rate of interest, the realized rate of inflation might differ from the targeted rate.
12. And I agree with Smithin (2004) that it is impossible or nonsense.

REFERENCES

Allsopp, C. and Vines, D. (2000), 'The assessment: macroeconomic policy', *Oxford Review of Economic Policy*, **16** (4), 1–32.

Alvarez, F., Lucas, R. and Weber, W. (2001), 'Recent advances in monetary-policy rules', *American Economic Review, Papers and Proceedings*, pp. 219–25.

Arestis, P. and Sawyer, M. (2006), *A Handbook of Alternative Monetary Economics*, Cheltenham, UK and Northampton, MA, USA: Edward Elgar.

Ball, Laurence (2001), 'Policy rules for open economies', in John Taylor (ed.), *Monetary Policy Rules*, Chicago, IL: NBER, pp. 127–56.

Bernanke, R. and Mishkin, F. (1997), 'Inflation targeting: a new framework for monetary policy?', *Journal of Economic Perspectives*, **11** (2), 97–116.

Blinder, Alan (1998), *Central Banking in Theory and Practice*, Cambridge, MA: The MIT Press.

Clarida, R., Galí, J. and Gertler, M. (2001), 'Optimal monetary policy in open versus closed economies: an integrated approach', *American Economic Review, Papers and Proceedings*, pp. 248–52.

Davidson, Paul (1994), *Post Keynesian Macroeconomic Theory*, Aldershot, UK and Brookfield, US: Edward Elgar.

Eichner, Alfred (1984), 'A general model of investment and pricing', in Nell (ed.), *Growth, Profits & Property. Essays in the Revival of Political Economy*, New York: Cambridge University Press, pp. 118–33.

Hahn, Frank (1985), *Money, Growth and Stability*, Oxford: Basil Blackwell.

Kregel, Jan (2004), 'Can we create a stable international financial environment that ensures net resource transfers to developing countries?', *Journal of Post Keynesian Economics*, **vol** (4), 573–90.

Lavoie, Marc (2004), 'The New Consensus on monetary policy Seen from a Post Keynesian perspective', in Marc Lavoie and Mario Seccareccia (eds), *Central Banking in the Modern World*, Cheltenham, UK and Northampton, MA, USA: Edward Elgar, pp. 15–34.

Lavoie, M. (2006), 'Endogenous money: accommodationist', in P. Arestis and M. Sawyer (eds), *A Handbook of Alternative Monetary Economics*, Cheltenham, UK and Northampton, MA, USA: Edward Elgar, pp. 17–34.

Minsky, Hyman (1986), *Stabilizing an Unstable Economy*, Yale University Press.

Ortiz, Etelberto (2003), 'Pricing in a small open monetary economy. A post Keynesian model', *Journal of Post Keynesian Economics*, **26** (2), 341–56.

Ortiz, Etelberto (2004), 'Stability conditions for a small open Economy', in Randall Wray and Mathew Forstater (eds), *Contemporary Post Keynesian Analysis*, Cheltenham, UK and Northampton, MA, USA: Edward Elgar, pp. 121–39.

Rochon, Louis-Philippe (1999), *Credit Money and Production*, Cheltenham, UK and Northampton, MA, USA: Edward Elgar.

Smithin, J. (2004), 'Interest rate operation procedures and income distribution', in M. Lavoie and M. Seccareccia (eds), *Central Banking in the Modern World*, Cheltenham, UK and Northampton, MA, USA: Edward Elgar, pp. 57–69.

Taylor, John (1993), 'Discretion versus policy rules in practice', *Carnegie–Rochester Conference Series on Public Policy*, **39** (0), 195–214.

Taylor, John (2001), 'The role of exchange rate in monetary-policy rules', *American Economic Review, Papers and Proceedings*, pp. 263–7.

Weber, A., Baldwin, R. and Obstfeld, M. (1991), 'Reputation and credibility in the European Monetary System', *Economic Policy*, **6** (12), 57–102.

Woodward, Michael (2001), 'The Taylor rule and optimal monetary policy', *American Economic Review Papers and Proceedings*; pp. 232–7.

APPENDIX

If the price equation is expressed in unit terms, the investment–finance decision can be represented as the maximization of the rate of profit after current and financial costs:

$$\Pi_k{}^* = \phi_k \, [I_k \, (P'_k \,|\, (E', i', w')) - [(\Sigma \, a_{kj} \, P_j + a^m \, P^m \, E + wl_k) \, (1 + \pi_k)] - f_k(i)_t)] \qquad (14.4)$$

where (P'_k) is the gap between forward and spot price of the kth firm. (P'_k) is an implicit function of the expected BPV: $(P'_k \,|\, (E', i', w'))$ Therefore I_k $(P'_k$ $(E', i', w'))$ represents an investment function of the spot to the forward price for a given BPV, that is, $(E', i', w')$of the kth firm, for which first-order conditions are:

$$\frac{d\phi_k}{dp_k} = \phi_k I'_{k(pk)} - \phi_k a_{kj}(1 + \pi_k) = 0$$

$$\frac{d\phi_k}{dE} = \phi_k I'_{kp(E)} - \phi_k a^m p^m (1 + \pi_k) = 0$$

$$\frac{d\phi_k}{dw} = \phi_k I'_{kp(w)} - (\phi_k l_k)(1 + \pi_k) = 0$$

$$\frac{d\phi_k}{di} = \phi_k I'_{kp(i)} - \phi_k (1 + f'_k(i)) = 0$$

where:

- $I'_{k(pk)}$ is the price elasticity of investment to changes between spot to forward prices.

$$I'_{k(pk)} = \frac{d\Pi_k}{\dfrac{dI}{dP_k}\left(\dfrac{dP_k}{dP_j}\left(\dfrac{\partial P_k}{\partial P_j}\right)\right)}$$

  It would be (+) when an increase in the spot price allows an increase in investment, characterized by $I'_{k(pk)} > 0$ and $I''_{k(pk)} < 0$; and it would be (−) when it allows an increase in the inflation rate.

- $I'_{k(p(E))}$ is the price elasticity of investment to increments in the exchange rate.

$$I'_{k(P(E))} = \frac{d\Pi_k}{\frac{dI}{dP_k}\left(\frac{dP_k}{dE}\left(\frac{\partial P_k}{\partial E}\right)\right)}$$

It would be (+) when a devaluation gives rise to an increase in exports and in investment: $I'_{k(p(E))} > 0$ and $I''_{k(p(E))} < 0$. And it would be (−) when it gives rise to an increase in the inflation rate: $I'_{k(p(E))} < 0$ and $I''_{k(p(E))} > 0$

- $I'_{k(p(w))}$ is the price elasticity of investment to changes in the wage rate

$$I'_{k(P(w))} = \frac{d\Pi_k}{\frac{dI}{dP_k}\left(\frac{dP_k}{dw}\left(\frac{\partial P_k}{\partial w}\right)\right)}$$

It would be (+) when a wage rise gives rise to an increase in effective demand and in investment $I'_{k(p(w))} \geq 0$ and $I'_{k(p(w))} < 0$. And it would be (−) when it gives rise to an increase in the inflation rate: $I'_{k(p(w))} < 0$ and $I'_{k(p(w))} < 0$.

- $I'_{k(p(i))}$ is the price elasticity of investment to changes in the rate of interest.

$$I'_{k(P(i))} = \frac{d\Pi_k}{\frac{dI}{dP_k}\left(\frac{dP_k}{di}\left(\frac{\partial P_k}{\partial i}\right)\right)}$$

It would be (+) when an interest rate rise gives rise to an increase in effective demand and in investment, $I'_{k(p(i))} > 0$ and $I'_{k(p(i))} < 0$. And it would be (−) when it gives rise to an increase in the inflation rate: $I'_{k(p(i))} < 0$ and $I'_{k(p(i))} > 0$.

Evidently, according to the different theoretical views, *ex hypothesis* some of these possible outcomes would be expected to be nil or with particular biases (+, −). The elasticity coefficients show a chaotic behavior with turning points. The model in this form shows that it is very general to encompass different theoretical views. Given that each elasticity of investment may have two values (+, −), the evaluation of this function shows that it can have the following patterns, depending on the size and sign of the structural and elasticity coefficients:

(1) $I'_{k(pk)}(+) > a_{kj}(1 + \pi_k) > 0$; the price gap (spot-forward) is enough to be over the increase in profit margin, leading to ΔI and a reduction of p
(2) $I'_{k(pk)}(+) < a_{kj}(1 + \pi_k) < 0$; the price gap (spot-forward) is not enough to cover the increase in profit margin, leading to $-\Delta I \rightarrow$ small Δp
(3) $I'_{k(pk)}(-) < a_{kj}(1 + \pi_k) < 0$; the price gap (spot-forward) is understood as inflationary, even if smaller than the profit margin, leading to $-\Delta I \rightarrow \Delta p$
(4) $I'_{k(pk)}(-) > a_{kj}(1 + \pi_k) < 0$; the price gap (spot-forward) is understood as inflationary, larger than profit margin, leading to $-\Delta I \rightarrow$ accelerated Δp
(5) $I'_{kp(E)}(+) > a^m p^m(1 + \pi_k) > 0$; devaluation (revaluation) leads to an increase (reduction) of the price gap (spot-forward) that produces an increase (reduction) of investment and exports higher (smaller) than the increase in imports, leading to ΔI (reduction) and a reduction (contained increase) or constant p
(6) $I'_{kp(E)}(+) < a^m p^m(1 + \pi_k) < 0$; devaluation (revaluation) leads to an increase (reduction) of the price gap (spot-forward) that produces an increase (reduction) of exports smaller (greater) than the increase in imports, leading to ΔI and a growing pressure of p, with a growing current account deficit.
(7) $I'_{kp(E)}(-) < a^m p^m(1 + \pi_k) < 0$; devaluation leads to a reduction of the price gap (spot-forward) that produces a reduction of investment and exports smaller than the increase in imports due to a smaller income, leading to $-\Delta I$ and a higher pressure to increase Δp.
(8) $I'_{kp(E)}(-) > a^m p^m(1 + \pi_k) < 0$; devaluation leads to a reduction of the price gap (spot-forward) that produces a reduction of investment and exports higher than the increase in imports due to a smaller income, leading to $-\Delta I$ and to a higher rate of inflation Δp.
(9) $I'_{kp(w)}(+) > (l_k)(1 + \pi_k) > 0$; a wage rise induces an increase of effective demand and in investment higher than the increase in labor costs, leading to ΔI and a reduction of p.
(10) $I'_{kp(w)}(+) < (l_k)(1 + \pi_k) < 0$; a wage rise induces an increase of effective demand and in investment smaller than the increase in labor costs, leading to ΔI, but an increase in inflationary tension of p.
(11) $I'_{kp(w)}(-) < (l_k)(1 + \pi_k) < 0$; a wage rise induces a reduction of effective demand and in investment smaller than the increase in labor costs: leading to $-\Delta I$, and an increase in inflationary tension of p.

(12) $I'_{kp(w)}(-) > (l_k)(1 + \pi_k) < 0$; a wage rise induces a reduction of effective demand and an investment higher than the increase in labor costs, leading to $-\Delta I$ and an increase in inflation Δp.

(13) $I'_{kp(i)}(+) > (1 + f'_k(i)) > 0$; an increase of the rate of interest induces an increase of savings, therefore of investment, higher than the increase in financial costs, leading to ΔI and a reduction of p. This is the orthodox case.

(14) $I'_{kp(i)}(+) < (1 + f'_k(i)) < 0$; an increase of the rate of interest induces an increase of savings, therefore of investment, smaller than the increase in financial costs, leading to ΔI and a small pressure on nominal prices p.

(15) $I'_{kp(i)}(-) < (1 + f'_k(i)) < 0$; an increase of the rate of interest induces a reduction of investment, smaller than the increase in financial costs: leading to $-\Delta I$ and a higher pressure on nominal prices Δp. This case is completely ignored by orthodox literature.

(16) $I'_{kp(i)}(-) > (1 + f'_k(i)) < 0$; an increase of the rate of interest induces a reduction of investment, higher than the increase in financial costs, leading to $-\Delta I$ and a higher inflation Δp. This case is completely ignored by orthodox literature.

Therefore the reaction functions for the inflation – pricing problem are:

$$\frac{dp_k}{dE} = \frac{I'_{kp(E)} - a^m P^m (1 + \pi_k)}{I'_{kp(p)} - (a_{kj})(1 + \pi_k)} \geq or \leq 0 \tag{14.5}$$

$$\frac{dp_k}{di} = \frac{I'_{kp(i)} - (1 + f'_k(i))}{I'_{k(p)} - a_{kj}(1 + \pi_k)} \geq or \leq 0, \tag{14.6}$$

$$\frac{dp_k}{dw} = \frac{I'_{kp(w)} - (l_k)(1 + \pi_k)}{I'_{k(p)} - a_{kj}(1 + \pi_k)} \geq or \leq 0 \tag{14.7}$$

The ratio of (14.6) into (14.5) is

$$\frac{dE}{di} = \frac{I'_{kp(i)} - (1 + f'_k(i))}{I'_{kp(E)} - a^m p^m (1 + \pi_k)} \geq or \leq 0 \tag{14.8}$$

Index